Congress Revealed:
Problems and Solutions

by

Dr. Norton H. Moses

Professor Emeritus of History,
Montana State University-Billings,
1500 University Drive,
Billings, Montana 59101

Campus phone: 406-657-2892
Email: nmoses@msubillings.edu

With great appreciation, I dedicate this book to my helpmate and wife of almost thirty years Jeanette J. Bieber. She has always been extremely generous with her time and effort in helping move this project to completion.

The original version of this book was titled Congress versus Democracy: Issues and Solutions and was copyrighted in 2009 and has Copyright Office Registration Number TXu 1-685-747. It was never published. This is an updated and revised version and was completed on the spring of 2012.

Also by Norton H. Moses:
Lynching and Vigilantism in the United States: An Annotated Bibliography.

Table of Contents

Preface

When I was a history professor paying attention to current and past events, I sought stories about Congress and its processes. Some were shocking, such as the fact that a single Senator could use a so-called "hold" to prevent action favored by a majority. I knew the blocking power of filibusters, but I felt a need for data about lesser known procedures. So, over the years I collected information about Congress. Following retirement from my university teaching career, I did more targeted reading and writing about the federal legislative branch. Congress Revealed: Problems and Solutions is the result.

This book addresses anti-majoritarian procedures in Congress, processes that need to be improved, not just changed, to make Congress a truer part of American democracy.[1] I leave it to others to argue the pros and cons of policy decisions, such as whether Medicaid should pay for erectile-dysfunction medication for convicted sex offenders.[2] But if some procedures were reformed for the better, improved policy would be more likely. Restricting earmarks, for example, could eliminate such boondoggles as an Alaska Representative targeting millions of dollars of federal money to a Florida highway interchange that the Florida district Representative did not support but that was favored by some local businessmen who donated $40,000 to the Alaskan.[3] Earmark reform could prevent such past waste as the subsidy for trophy hunting in Africa, and the appropriation for construction of schools in France for Algerian Jews.[4] Our Dalmatian Congress has a spotty record about putting the American people first.

I use the word "Members" to refer to all who hold office in the entire Congress, both Senators and Representatives. And I avoid the words "Congressman" and "Congresswoman," the reason being that the use of those two titles for Representatives leads to the common confusion of referring to "the Congress and the Senate." That error has even infected Presidents, Senators, and others from whom more accuracy is expected. For example, in 1999 Al Gore was quoted in The New Yorker as saying, "I've served eight years in the Congress, eight years in the Senate, and seven years as Vice-President."[5] A national TV news anchor once explained that voters would be electing "more than a third of the Senate and all 435 members of the Congress."[6] During the 2006 election campaign, a Representative said, "If I get elected to the Senate, I'll be the same man I was in the Congress."[7] Campaigning in Iowa in June 2007, Presidential candidate John Edwards referred to Democrats "running for the Congress and the Senate."[8] Those are not isolated mistakes; they occur with disheartening frequency and are perpetuated by unmindful chattermouths on TV.

Of course, the Senate is part of Congress—the Senate and the Congress are not two separate bodies. Article I of the Constitution clearly states that the "Congress of the United States . . . shall consist of a Senate and a House of Representatives." The plaques on the office doors of Members of the House say "Representative," not "Congressman" or "Congresswoman." If people would use the word "Representative," the perpetuation of the error would diminish.

It would also be helpful if the phrase "U.S. House districts" were to replace "Congressional districts."

On another aspect of the word "Member," take this brief multiple-choice test:
> In both the U.S. Senate and the House of Representatives, which of the following is the "ranking member" of a committee?
> (A) The longest-serving majority-party member on the committee,
> (B) The longest-serving minority-party member on the committee,
> (C) The longest-serving member on the committee regardless of whether Democrat or Republican,
> (D) The chairperson of the committee.[9]

You will find the answer in note 9 to this preface and with further information in the chapter on Arcane Rules and Procedures.

This book does not deal with the sort of corruption that can occur under any system, such as Representatives Randy Cunningham, R-CA, and William Jefferson, D-LA, selling themselves and their power to crooked businessmen. Most Members of Congress are honest. They do not cause a person to wonder why two people were buried in the same grave under a tombstone saying "Here lies a Congressman and an honest politician." They did not give rise to the joke that the difference between a church bell and a politician is that a church bell peals from the steeple.

In addition to the honesty of most Members, they are also dedicated and hardworking. One has only to look at some Congressional rules, reports, and laws to see that they resulted from an enormous amount of effort. Of course, staffers deserve some of that credit, but so do the Members. However, the dedication and hard work of our lawmakers may too often relate to their re-election efforts rather than their legislative responsibilities.

If you read enough about Congress from 1789 onward, you find Members exhibiting many of the best and worst human qualities. They have ranged from such paragons as Henry Clay and John Quincy Adams to men who committed murder while they were Members. And according to archives from the Soviet Union, one Representative from New York was even a Soviet agent while serving in the House.[10]

On C-SPAN in 2008 I saw a Senator speaking at a university event in his home state. His topic required vast knowledge, yet he spoke eloquently at great length without notes.[11] That bore witness to the high intelligence of many Members. It's thus a shame that so many of the great minds in Congress submerge their gifts under waves of self-serving and partisanship that smother the needs of the nation and its people.

Congress has so adulterated parts of American democracy that many people consider actions by Congress and its Members' reprehensible even when those actions are within the lawful bounds crafted by Congress itself. Lawmakers can make legal what might otherwise be thought illegal—or at least beyond the pale.   This book addresses some of those problems.

It's gotten to the point that a letter recently read on CNN television said Congress "should stop screwing around and do the job we pay them to do," which brought the response that "if they stopped screwing around, they wouldn't be doing anything."[12]

I hope this book's main audience will be the general populace, so it can help them push for changes that will finally achieve Lincoln's ideal of "government of the people, by the people, and for the people." And many specialists will find this book valuable.

Some might say that a book about Congress should be written by a Beltway insider. Such a claim would help make my point—that many in Congress and inside the Beltway are anti-democratic and out of touch with the American people. America does not deserve a Congress that can only be understood by the elite.

Someone else may cherry pick among the problems I list and say that a particular one is not very important. And in isolation—isolation only—that may be true. But these issues are not isolated. They have worked together to create, not just a dysfunctional Congress, but an institution of calamitous failure.

During the months I worked to create this book, I often told acquaintances that I was writing a book about how bad Congress is. The response was usually a burst of laughter and a comment or question about how many thousands of pages or how many volumes it would be. One friend's reaction was, "Has it ever been good?"

With this book, I hope to convince many Americans that beneficial changes are needed to make Congress more responsive to the nation's needs.

***

I could not have completed this work without help from others. I am immeasurably grateful to my wife Dr. Jeanette Bieber-Moses, always supportive and encouraging. She read drafts of the book, made valuable suggestions, and helped in numerous other ways. She's so nonirritable and nonirritating it's been a pleasure to live with her these many years. I always found pleasant and capable assistance at the library of Montana State University-Billings; its interlibrary loan program was vital and the staff were great. Pat Amundsen and Sandy Haley, the secretaries for the History Department, were uniformly helpful and friendly. My colleague and friend Dr. James Friguglietti gave me several books which he bought specifically to help me with my research , and he was generous with suggestions and information.   Thanks go to Montana Representative Denny Rehberg and Montana Senators Max Baucus and Jon Tester and for responding to my requests for valuable information.   I'm grateful to the Billings, MT, law firm of Crowley Fleck PLLP for the several times I was able to use its law library.   I also appreciate the consideration shown to me as an emeritus professor by the Montana State University-Billings administration in providing me with an office and a computer. The latter was extremely valuable for accessing data banks provided by the University's library.

Norton H. Moses, February 2012.

Notes: Preface

[1]In a recent book, a famous American avers that it's a mistake to think that Americans don't much care about the processes that produce or implement policy; John W. Dean, Broken Government: How Republican Rule Destroyed the Legislative, Executive, and Judicial Branches (New York: Viking, 2007), pp. xv-xvi, 2-17 (part of the "Process Matters" introduction).

[2]Michael Virtanen, Associated Press, "N.Y. Audit Shows Sex Offenders Get Viagra," May 23, 2005, available on the Internet. France does it too; "France outraged by pedophilia case," USA Today, August 21, 2007, p. 6A. In May 2005, Senator Grassley, R-IA, introduced a bill to prohibit federal expenditures for prescribed erectile dysfunction drugs; see Congressional Record, daily edition, May 24, 2005, p. S5851. It met an unheralded death in the Committee on Finance.

[3]Report on TV program "Anderson Cooper 360," June 7, 2007; Michael Crowley, "Kissing Up for Cash," Reader's Digest, February 2008, p. 35.

[4]Representative Jon Fox, R-PA, was unsuccessful with his amendment to prohibit use of development assistance funds given to other countries "to directly support or promote trophy hunting"; see Congressional Record, daily edition, September 3, 1997, pp. H6734-39. For years, hunters were allowed to donate the trophies to charitable organizations and then claim a tax deduction; see Marc Kaufman, "Big-Game Hunting Brings Big Tax Breaks," The Washington Post, April 5, 2005, pp. A1, A6. For the schools in France see below in the Earmarks chapter, and "Inouye Wins Aid for French Jews," The New York Times, December 28, 1987, p. A12.

[5]Joe Klein and Jane Mayer, "The Anxiety of Influence," The New Yorker, November 22, 1999, p. 70.

[6]Tom Brokaw, NBC Nightly News, August 31, 1998.

[7]Representative Harold Ford, on "Hannity and Colmes," Fox News Network, November 1, 2006. See also Dick Morris, Behind the Oval Office, p. 31: "Reach out to all one hundred senators and all four hundred thirty-five congresspeople"; Chris

Matthews, on TV, 26 Oct 98: "All of the United States Congress is up for reelection, all 435 seats"; Senator Trent Lott, on CNBC, 3 Nov 98: ". . . as I've been all over the country looking at Senate races and Congressional races"; Howard Kurtz, on "Reliable Sources" on CNN, 12 Sep 98: "Are we going to have to go through this with all 435 members of Congress?"; Hendrik Hertzberg, "Comment, Dynastic Voyage," The New Yorker, October 29, 2007, p. 33: ". . . three governors, two senators, nine members of Congress, and four Confederate generals."

[8]"Special Report with Brit Hume," Fox News television, June 18, 2007.

[9]The correct answer is B, the longest-serving minority-party member of the committee. When I and a colleague separately posed this multiple-choice question to over 100 college students, not one chose the correct answer.

[10]See "'Crook': A Soviet Agent in Congress," Chapter 7 in Allen Weinstein and Alexander Vassiliev, The Haunted Wood: Soviet Espionage in America—the Stalin Era (New York: Random House, 1999), pp. 140-50; "The Political Graveyard: Politicians Who Got Into Trouble or Disgrace," available on the Internet. That was Democrat Samuel Dickstein; his Congressional service was from March 4, 1923, to his resignation on December 30, 1945.

[11]It reminded me of two stories about speakers who could orate with lengthy detail and virtually no notes. Future British Prime Minister H. H. Asquith, a notorious alcohol consumer, once spoke with great statistical detail for an hour about excessive drinking and was asked afterwards for a copy of his notes. He gave the requester a slip of paper with the words "Too many pubs"; Walter L. Arnstein, Britain Yesterday and Today: 1830 to the Present, 7th edition (Lexington, MA: D. C. Heath and Co., 1996), pp. 221-22. See also James Friguglietti, "'Zeus, Agamemnon, Zeus," The Chronicle of Higher Education, September 27, 1976, p. 19 (microfilm edition).

[12]CNN, "The Situation Room," September 18, 2007. The responder was the program's Jack Cafferty, not host Wolf Blitzer.

I. American National Democracy

EPIGRAPH: Just because you do not take an interest in politics
                 does not mean politics won't take an interest in you.
                 ---Unsourced, but attributed to Pericles.

EPIGRAPH: As soon as any man says of the affairs of the State, "What
                 does it matter to me?" the State may be given up for lost.
                 ---Jean Jacques Rousseau (1712-1778),
                     Contrat Social (1762), Book III, Chapter 15.

"Celeprosy," my word for extreme interest in celebrities, is something that consumes many Americans. Others seem to think that following some sport is the most important thing in their lives. Would that they would give greater attention to the Congress that makes their laws. If they don't pay much attention to politics, they may get the government they deserve.

One way to correct some of what this book exposes as wrong is for the public to become more concerned and put pressure on Senators and Representatives.

In an American history class, a college student asked me "What is democracy?" Concealing my astonishment, I began with this succinct but accurate answer: "Rule by the people." Of course, the practice of government by the people involves greater complexity. As one writer says, "Democracy is commonly used to describe a political system that involves regular elections, opportunities for citizen involvement, and purported limits on government power."[1] I use the word "democracy" to refer to a representative system with minority protection, not a fully participatory process of all citizens voting on every issue or one in which majorities have unfettered sway.

Democracy is a method for reaching goals, a means for achieving desirable ends for the general populace. Without good results, what is democracy's benefit? People may claim that weakened democratic processes, as in Congress, are okay so long as beneficial rule occurs. But strong, small-d democratic procedures are more likely to achieve that goal. . Good results can occasionally flow from bad procedures used by a benevolent dictator, but at any moment the dictator or his successor can decide to impose malignant outcomes. The chances for widespread benefits decrease as undemocratic processes increase. Flawed means often produce flawed ends. In the federal government, the partial hijacking of democracy for the benefit of parties, incumbent politicians, and narrow special interests militates against the realization of good ends. Processes and results both matter—because procedure affects policy. Tony Coelho, a Democrat who resigned in 1989 as an ethics cloud was about to deluge him, reportedly said in happier times that if he had process, he'd win every time over someone who had substance.[2]

Congressional procedures can be confusing to non-specialists. Sometimes such processes are necessary; other times they are designed for concealment. Whatever their purpose, they can leave an observer as bewildered as the person who wonders if God is an atheist.

The Founding Fathers of the United States created a Constitution that has enabled this country to become, ostensibly, "the world's greatest democracy." While someone might think that decisions in the U.S. democracy are made by majorities, that is not always true. The Founders, despite their revulsion against monarchy and parliament, guarded against an excess of democracy. And through extra-Constitutional procedures, Congress has distanced itself even farther from the citizens. Congress is supposedly the agent of the people, but it often seems that Americans are merely the agents of Senators and Representatives. As one writer explained, "Through a combination of rules changes, use of perquisites, and manipulation of congressional districts, the members of Congress have succeeded in diluting the power of the voters to influence the course of government."[3] He could have listed additional causes of that dilution, such as the campaign-donation racket that amounts to bribery. Other causes are exposed in later chapters of this book.

Some Congressional procedures are arrows in partisan quivers. Some others are not so obviously party weapons but are merely anti-democratic. As for the seekers of party advantage, the Republicrats and Democans are about the same in using House and Senate procedures.

There has occasionally been a status-quo smugness among legislators. Long-ago Speaker of the House Joe Cannon opined that "everything is all right out West and around Danville. The country don't need any legislation."[4] That is reminiscent of the 1864 words attributed to British Prime Minister Lord Palmerston: "Oh, there is really nothing to be done. We cannot go on legislating for ever."[5] Of course, both of those leaders, firmly lodged in cocoons of privilege, were wrong. From time to time awareness of reality ascends even to aristocratic levels, and calculations change about what is right or necessary. Or an election may sweep out solons noted for petrified views.

Good changes can occur, witness the term limits placed on House committee chairs in 1995. Trouble is, achieving such changes is hard and rare. Furthermore, the public may occasionally get an eye-opener about Congressional excess and irresponsibility—and may even vote out some of the offenders, as in the Republican victories in 1994, the Democratic Party successes in 2006 and 2008, and Republican gains in 2010—but many voters then settle into the delusion that a few personnel changes have fixed the system and that they can safely turn their attention elsewhere. Yet, just as Thomas Jefferson said that "the tree of liberty must be refreshed from time to time with the blood of patriots and tyrants," so also constant surveillance must be applied to the powerful. Even when the process is tweaked for the better, vigilance should not be relaxed, because those who benefited from the old ways will try to continue them under new guises. Chattermouths on radio and television, bloggers on the Internet, and print media writers need to make—and keep—the people aware. Why else are freedom of speech and of the press included in the First Amendment?

Though some advances have emerged, they have been limited to short, delicate steps. Bold strides are needed. And all too often Congress ballyhoos an alleged improvement that in reality does little.[6] On the landscape of Congressional history only occasional crags of improvement rise above the flat barrenness of Congress's shortcomings as a democratic body. Quite simply, Congress has too many standards that are substandard.

So many times when it appears Congress is cleaning up its act, we don't have long to wait for another dirty shoe to drop off this many-shoed centipede.

Why have so many Members of Congress not supported good changes? Consider these few reasons from a larger list: • short-term thinking, • concentration on issues seen as helping re-election, • obligations to donors, support groups, and parties, • tradition, • partisanship.

Those who assert that the U.S. was not meant to have pure democracy are, of course, correct. A nation with millions of people cannot function with every issue being decided by all its adults. Representative democracy must exist. But the representatives should not arrogate so much power to themselves that the matured will of the populace has little chance of prevailing.

Consider this one example of the many available: A President may be elected with an overwhelming popular and electoral vote majority, so that his or her nominee for an important government position would seem to have the support of that mandate. Indeed, that nominee might be favored by 99 of the 100 Senators. But under current rules one single Senator can put a "hold" on the consideration of that nomination and thus prevent its confirmation. (See the chapter on "Holding" the Senate Hostage.)

Majorities can be dangerous. A civil liberties advocate wisely noted in 1994 that "democracy must be something more than two wolves and a sheep voting on what to have for dinner."[7]   Recognizing that, the U.S. Founders created a Constitution rife with provisions limiting majority power. The federal judiciary would be appointive rather than elective.   The President would not be elected directly by ordinary voters but only by specially chosen electors, who presumably would be privy to higher wisdom and would not be subject to momentary and destructive manias.

The Senate would be protected from spasms of popular feeling. Senators would be elected by state legislatures, not directly by the populace. And only one-third of the total Senate would be elected every two years. Thus, even if every incumbent seeking reelection in a particular year was defeated, a two-thirds majority of Senators, all holdovers, would serve in the new Senate and be ready to maintain continuity—and perhaps maintain the unresponsive and irrelevant measures of the past.

Popular election of Senators, established by the Seventeenth Amendment in 1913, weakened the Founders' idea that the Senate would act as a brake on ill-considered and possibly unwise legislation—weakened because two groups of Senators are mindful of gusts of popular enthusiasm: Those who are looking forward to their next election and those who have just been elected.

The real protection from overheated public pressure is something else that's bad: Both chambers of Congress are such captives of special interests that popular manias seldom have good legislative results. Elections are supposed to allow the people to hold Members accountable—but the huge costs of campaigns mean that accountability is really owed to the big contributors. Thus, we have merely the substitution of one suspect pressure for another. On occasion, however, public influence can overcome Congressional and special-interest resistance—and this book argues for exertions by the people and the media as corrective solutions.

The American people are too often a minority party. Entrenched special interests each represent only a minority of the people but are frequently a majority of the influence.

The vision of the Founders has been turned on its head with the empowerment of blocs of advantage seekers, not least of which is factions among the 535 Members of Congress. A sampling of other such groups includes labor unions, farmers, various businesses, racial and ethnic associations, environmentalists, immigration advocates, and the promoters of certain foreign policies. The Founders believed that competing factions would cancel out each other's worst excesses so that the best <u>national</u> policies would prevail. Instead, we have the logrolling tradeoffs that too often benefit select groups rather than the general populace. Of course, Congress does not fail in every respect; many laws have been helpful.

Yet its failures have been so manifest that we have this well-publicized message: "If pro is the opposite of con, what is the opposite of progress? . . . Congress!!!"[8]

During 2007and 2008, polls showed that President Bush's approval rating was notoriously at about the freezing point of water. Surprisingly—or not?—approval for Congress was even lower. A Gallup poll taken during May 10-13, 2007, showed Congress with an approval level of 29 percent, when that of the President, so maligned by many in Congress, was 33 percent.[9] By mid-August a new Gallup poll showed that approval of Congress had sunk to 18 percent, matching the lowest ever recorded by Gallup.[10] By late September 2007 a Reuters/Zogby poll found that "a paltry 11 percent rated Congress positively."[11] It got so bad by November that even Speaker Nancy Pelosi joined in the disapproval.[12] Polling results vary, and by mid-June 2008, a Wall Street Journal/NBC News poll found approval of Congress at 13 percent, lowest in the nearly two-decade history of that survey. Polls since then have shown results both higher and lower, with Gallup reporting only 11 percent confidence in Congress in mid-2010.[13]

Low ratings continued in 2011 with, among others, a CBS News/New York Times survey in late October showing approval at only nine percent.

Lack of esteem for the legislative branch is unfortunate but not new: Some years ago when incumbent Representative Vic Fazio charged his election opponent with favoring nuclear war, the challenger got "even nastier, calling Mr. Fazio a 'Member of Congress.'"[14]

It has sometimes been argued that when the Founding Fathers created the Constitution they were tending to their own economic well-being and thus established a system which would advance the interests of economic elites. That idea was first prominently argued by Charles Beard in his 1913 book An Economic Interpretation of the Constitution of the United States and has continued to find favor in some quarters. Beard's thesis holds that most of the Founders were well-to-do men whose finances had been harmed under the Articles of Confederation and that the new frame of government was created for the base motive of selfish aggrandizement.

Surely, that is excessive reductionism. It may have been more accurate in sixteenth-century England when Thomas More described government as "a conspiracy of rich men, procuring their own commodities, under the name and title of the common wealth." But it stretches reality to think that the men at the 1787 Constitutional Convention had only one motive. Perhaps they did pursue rich-men's goals to some extent, but they also devised a system that provided many benefits for ordinary people. People do not always have only one purpose when they do something. But did the Founders throw crumbs to the masses merely to get the necessary support for their overriding selfish objective? Because all history is interpretation, that question may never find a definitive answer.

Would the Founders be judged free of selfish economic sin only if their motives worked against their own interests? Would anyone? Consider Adam Smith's idea that people working for their own interests often advance the more general good of society. The men at Philadelphia that summer knew that a mere utopian structure could not succeed. As two recent historians have argued, "No successful constitution of government was contrivable that did not provide for the harnessing of private interests in order to promote the public good." Perhaps the most important refutation of Beard's thesis was in Forrest McDonald's book We the People: The Economic Origins of the Constitution.[15]

At any rate, the Founders' new system deliberately insulated control from the hoi polloi, and that permitted the existence of Constitutional and extra-Constitutional procedures that can be seen as contrary to democracy and the common good. In creating a system in which minorities could rein in runaway majorities, did the Founders contemplate some of the later additions such as filibusters and holds, the Rules Committee, conference committees, the singular power of the Senate Majority Leader, voting rights in the House for people who are not Representatives, gerrymandering, pro forma sessions without Constitutionally required quorums, and legalized bribery through large campaign contributions?

It has often been claimed that some Congressional procedures exist to protect minorities. In a liberal periodical in 2005 there was this statement: "The whole point of the U.S. government is to thwart 'tyranny of the majority.'" Surely, that's too extreme and reductionist, there being additional bedrock first principles. But the author of that assertion goes on to argue against minority-protecting filibusters by writing, "The majority party shouldn't get to be tyrants, but they should get to be legislators."[16] Safeguards for the minority have often prevented that. It is good to note that James Madison, the father of the Constitution, warned that "a government resting on a minority is an aristocracy, not a republic."[17]

Protecting minorities and minority rights is good—to a point. It's just that the minority should not be one Senator or seven Representatives (the number that can control the House Committee on Rules).

Historically the main use of Congressional minority weapons was to hurt the black minority. In the 1930s, '40s, and '50s, when Southerners largely controlled both houses without being in the majority, Congress was failing the American people in some ways. For example, filibusters, by which one Senator or a few could hold the floor to prevent other action, delayed or permanently defeated civil rights legislation such as voting rights for blacks and federal anti-lynching bills. Thus, protection for a minority of the populace (white Southerners) became rule by a minority in the Senate against the clear and long-standing desire of most members of Congress and of the general public. Despite some later beneficial changes, more good change is needed.

The thesis of this book is this: Congress is too self-serving and anti-majoritarian, but corrective solutions are available. Too often Congressional actions put the nation and the people between the chainsaw and the tree, but the people can force changes. The recommendation that Congress become more majoritarian may be criticized as removing long-standing Constitutional protections for minorities. But that denunciation fails because our history shows that the minorities who have often benefited have included the Southern pro-slavery minority, or Southern segregationists, or business interests seeking to maintain advantages over employees, or labor unions wanting to coerce reluctant workers, or political-party fanatics putting partisanship ahead of the national interest, or special interests raiding the federal treasury, or obstructionists pursuing narrow dogmas.

During the first half of the twentieth century the Framers' design for a government that hobbled the majority in the interest of protecting the minority was adulterated to give excessive power to a few obstructionists. Then the pendulum swung too far in the opposite direction, especially in the thirty or so years before the advent of the twenty-first century, so that House leaders could ram through their agendas while trampling their opponents.

Although Congress still has too many anti-majority procedures, in a few ways Congress, especially the House, has moved too far toward dictatorial majority actions that eliminate even the consideration of minority viewpoints, let alone their passage. A striking illustration of that problem is the House's increasing use of "closed" rules for floor consideration of bills. A closed rule is an agreement that a bill considered by the full House, rather than a committee, cannot be amended and can only be passed or rejected as is.[18] With amendments prohibited, much debate is also shut off. It's one thing for a majority to be able to pass bills, but it's much less desirable for a majority to prevent consideration of minority views.

Procedures intended for minority protection, such as filibusters in the Senate, have long been clubs used by the Congressional acolytes of special interests to beat back the general interest. They are also employed by faction fanatics determined to thwart advances sought by larger groups.

Even the threat of a filibuster is often used to block a bill or a nomination. See this book's chapter on "Holding" the Senate Hostage. And such a threat enjoys Senatorial popularity as a weapon for gaining changes to bills. Minority Republicans used it before assuming control in 1995, as did Democrats for the next several years. Another ploy, "hostage taking," involves a threatened or actual filibuster on one measure for the purpose of achieving changes in another.[19]

In 1964 Senator Joseph Clark of Pennsylvania wrote, "It is in the nature of minorities, as Joseph Chamberlain once said, 'to devise some ingenious machinery by which [they] may be saved from the natural consequences of being outnumbered.' . . . It will not do to defend this machinery as a protection against 'the tyranny of the majority,' for it is nothing of the sort. It is a built-in defense for maintaining a status quo no longer tenable in the face of . . . present conditions at home and abroad. And it violates every principle of popular rule on which free governments are based. It is the 'tyranny of the minorities' we suffer from."[20]

The machinery is no longer quite so anti-majoritarian as 50 years ago.[21] But much of it is still well-maintained. Ready for use are components such as Senate "holds," filibusters and threats of them, gerrymandering to keep incumbents in office, changes by conference committees that supposedly are allowed only to reconcile different Senate and House versions of bills, secret additions to long and complex bills, absolute control by the Speaker of the House and the Majority Leader of the Senate over what business reaches the floors of the two chambers, unrelated items in single bills, multiple substantive and procedural votes that make it difficult for voters to know the true stance of a Member, and the legalized bribery that gives rich people the major influence with Members.

If Congress has failed democracy so badly, how did the U.S. become such a powerful and seemingly successful nation? One part of the answer is that the U.S. has had economic and political systems that encouraged individual and business success. Some years ago a college economics professor argued to me that the main, almost sole, reason the U.S. was successful was that it had enormous natural resources. A few years later, however, when the Soviet Union collapsed, the proof emerged that his assertion was false. The Soviets controlled a country of vast natural resources, but their political and economic systems stifled initiative and hard work and led to massive failure. Meanwhile, Japan, a nation with almost no natural resources other than people, became a successful economic powerhouse because it had systems that rewarded individuals and businesses. Sure, the U.S. has benefited from having great resources, but without its motivating economic and political systems, it might have gone the Soviet way. So we might say that the U.S. became great in spite of Congress.

In this book I have included examples of folly, deception, and misguided processes wherever I found them, and have tried not to select issues and examples to benefit one political party over the other. I've directed negative comments at each party when it has stooped to earn them. Some selections expose Republicans to criticism, partly because they controlled Congress for much of the past sixteen years. Others are critical of Democrats. They produced a sufficiency of horrors during their Congressional domination from 1955 to 1995—and if we expected them not to transgress during their resumed control, we were disappointed. Also, there are many problems having both Democratic and Republican ancestry.

No attempt will be made here to make comparative quantifications regarding alleged Democrat and Republican wrongdoing. And any selection I have included may be criticized as atypical. Nevertheless, let's illustrate with two departures from the same norm, one by each party's House leadership.

Prior to the start of the 110th Congress (January 2007), House Rule XX stipulated no maximum time for electronic voting but decreed a usual fifteen minutes. Normally, an electronic floor vote was allowed to consume fifteen minutes and after that no more Representatives could vote. But in 1987, Speaker Jim Wright held open the vote on a budget bill because the Democrats needed one additional vote for its passage. During the extra time, ten or fifteen minutes, Democratic leadership successfully searched for one "nay" voter they could bulldoze into a change, and the bill passed.[22]

Much the same thing, except for a longer voting time, occurred on November 23, 2003, as Republican leaders sought a victory margin for the Medicare prescription drug bill. They achieved it by 220 to 215 but only after a voting period of two hours and fifty-three minutes in the wee hours of the morning, despite the presiding officer's statement at the start that "Members will have fifteen minutes to record their votes." A majority continuously opposed the bill until telephone calls from President Bush and leadership bullying-and-bribery efforts by Speaker Hastert and others produced the momentary majority that allowed the chair to rule the voting period over.[23] Opponents of the bill were so outraged that even the usually supine House Ethics Committee eventually issued a unanimous chastisement of two Republican Members, citing in particular their violation of the inferred House rule against offering an inducement to a Member for the purpose of obtaining a vote.[24]

And despite there being no actual violation of any voting-length requirement, the fifteen-minute maximum, or close to it, had become so standard a part of "regular order" that several people from both parties issued criticisms with words such as "grotesque, arbitrary, and gross abuse of power" about this outrageous action that was "profoundly ugly and beneath the dignity of Congress."[25] Therefore, on the first day of renewed

Democratic control of the House in January 2007, the rules were revised to state, "A record vote by electronic device shall not be held open for the sole purpose of reversing the outcome of such a vote."[26]

Suppose that someone might deem some of this book's criticisms of Congress invalid. The remaining problems are so numerous that Congress is still far from what it should be. And that's true even though Congress has corrected some shortcomings during the last forty years or so.

There's at least one problem that is so inherent in an assembly where votes determine outcomes that its elimination would be impossible without junking the entire concept of democracy. A single Senator can have great leverage and can force modifications on one side or the other when the proponents and opponents of a bill are so evenly matched that one vote can determine the outcome. It happened in 1993: At one point President Clinton's budget survived in the Senate only by the tie-breaking vote of Vice President Gore. Therefore, on a later vote the budget would be defeated if just one Senator, such as Herb Kohl, D-WI, who initially voted for it did not continue to do so. Kohl said his continued support would be contingent on the gas tax increase being reduced to 4.3 cents per gallon. He got his way. As one observer wrote, "Thus, an ambitious plan to reduce dependence on foreign oil, improve the efficiency of energy use and help clean up the environment went down the drain -- and a $49 billion hole was ripped in Clinton's budget. . . . [It] is a striking example of how . . . the United States Senate . . . defies contemporary understanding of democracy."[27]

This book points out several negative things about Congress -- but it's actually aimed at optimism through the hope, even expectation, that when people learn about problems that need fixing they will put on the sort of pressure that will lead to improvement, and that has led to good changes in the past. To that end most chapters end with a section labeled "Corrective Solutions" that suggests what can be done to make But within the solutions there are yet other difficulties. One is that an improvement in one area can increase a problem in another. For instance, when balanced budgets were achieved in the late 1990s, the argument lost force that federal spending needed reduction.

A second difficulty is that many of the correctives require action by Senators and Representatives who have been more inclined to keep providing themselves with advantages than to delete some of those already existing. As one writer explained, "Congress embraces those reforms which advance the interests of its members and rejects most others."[28] Indeed, long service in Congress might disqualify a person from having credibility in denying Congressional flaws and resisting change.

Too often Members of Congress talk high but act low. For example, when Speaker of the House Dennis Hastert, R-IL, booted Joel Hefley, R-CO, from the chairmanship of the Committee on Standards of Official Conduct (the Ethics Committee) in February 2005 as part of an effort to protect Majority Leader Tom DeLay, Hastert alleged that the reason for the removal was that Hefley's tenure limit on the Committee had been reached. That was disputed by Hefley. Even if Hastert was correct, he could have waived the limit, as he did at the same time to allow David Dreier to continue as chair of the Rules Committee. And Hastert also removed two other Republicans who had been critical of DeLay even though they were not bumping against the term limit.[29]

CORRECTIVE SOLUTIONS

The ultimate corrective may be to replace the old warhorses with fresh Members who have not been "broken" to the system.[30] That can be accomplished by refusals to re-elect, or by elimination of gerrymandering (discussed later), or by a Constitutional amendment for term limits. The latter could be proposed by Congress itself, but it may not be reasonable to expect careerists to take career-shortening action. However, Constitutional amendments can be proposed by conventions. That's a difficult process and no such American convention has met since adoption of the Constitution. One could only convene after application by two-thirds of the state legislatures after which Congress would be required to call a convention into being (see Article V of the Constitution).

Refusal to re-elect incumbents may be the easiest corrective. But the people should not elect replacements who are experienced party operatives—because they've already been infected by training in the systems that mirror Congress. Concerned citizens should elect newcomers.

Difficult actions are often necessary. And if there's enough demand from concerned Americans, they can get the job done. They can pay more attention to their government, and not just during a scandal or at election time. It's not enough that we can vote, for what good is voting if we elect people who fail to solve existing problems and even add new ones. And to elect better lawmakers we need more knowledge about policies, positions, and processes. The media has a responsibility in this. It must present more information about government, even at the cost of being repetitious. And here I'm referring to the mainstream media, for how is the average American to get sufficient knowledge from small, niche providers that exist far below average consciousness? It's a shared responsibility between voters who become more aware and media that helps them do that.

Notes: Chapter I. American National Democracy

In the notes throughout this book, a later citation to a source cited in the same chapter but in an earlier note will be given in short form; an immediately following citation to that source in the same note or the next note will be listed as "ibid." A first citation to that same source but in a different chapter will appear in complete form.

[1]James Bovard, Attention Deficit Democracy (New York: Palgrave Macmillan, 2005), p. 10.

[2]John L. Jackley, <u>Hill Rat: Blowing the Lid Off Congress</u> (Washington: Regnery Gateway, 1992), p. 113. Coelho was Al Gore's Presidential campaign manager until he resigned in June 2000. Coelho's comment was similar to one made by Representative John Dingell; <u>National Review</u>, February 27, 1987, p. 24, quoted in Walter J. Oleszek, <u>Congressional Procedures and the Policy Process</u>, 7th edition (Washington: CQ Press, 2007), p. 12. "Those who control the process control the law"; Mark J. Green, <u>Who Runs Congress?</u>, revised edition (New York: Bantam/Grossman, 1975), p. 59. "You can often win procedurally what you could never achieve substantively on the merits"; ibid., p. 257. "Bad process leads to bad policy"; Thomas E. Mann and Norman J. Ornstein, <u>The Broken Branch: How Congress Is Failing America and How to Get It Back on Track</u> (New York: Oxford University Press, 2006) p. 13.

[3]Clifford Barnhart, "Using the Rules for Abuse," in Gordon S. Jones and John A. Marini, eds., <u>The Imperial Congress: Crisis in the Separation of Powers</u> (New York: Pharos Books, 1988), p. 204.

[4]Paul Boller, <u>Congressional Anecdotes</u> (New York: Oxford University Press, 1991), p. 246.

[5]Donald Southgate, <u>The Passing of the Whigs 1832-1886</u> (London: Macmillan, 1962), p. 299, from P. Colson, ed., <u>Lord Goschen and His Friends</u> (London and New York: Hutchinson, 1946), p. 58.

[6]For example, the earmarks reform of 2007, trumpeted by Members as a great advance, was so loaded with evasive techniques as to be virtually worthless. Publicizing earmarks before a vote on them was required only if "technically feasible." Also, instead of the Senate parliamentarian certifying that a bill meets earmarks disclosure, the Senate Majority Leader was given that power. It was hardly likely that he would rule against one of the majority's own bills. "Earmarks As Usual," <u>The Wall Street Journal</u>, August 1, 2007, p. A14. See also the Earmarks chapter in this book.

[7]James Bovard, <u>Lost Rights: The Destruction of American Liberty</u> (New York: St. Martin's Press, 1994), p. 333.

[8]Written in men's restroom, U.S. House of Representatives, obtained from America Online, March 27, 2005.

[9]Gallup News Service, May 15, 2007, available on the Internet.

[10]Paul Leavitt, "Americans take a dim view of Congress," <u>USA Today</u>, August 22, 2007, p. 9A.

[11]Zogby International, "Bush, Congress at record low ratings," on the Internet.

[12]"Pelosi says she disapproves of Congress," USA Today, November 2, 2007, p. 4A; "Washington Whispers -- Out Loud," U.S. News & World Report., November 12, 2007, p. 18.

[13]For the mid-June 2008 poll see "Congress, Unloved and Supported," The Wall Street Journal, June 17, 2008, p. A2. For the 11 percent in 2010 see "Notable & Quotable," The Wall Street Journal, July 23, 2010, p. A17; and Lydia Saad, "Congress Ranks Last in Confidence in Institutions, July 22, 2010, available on the Internet.

[14]Paul A. Gigot, "Potomac Watch: Despite Bush, GOP May Bag Prince of Perks," The Wall Street Journal, October 23, 1992, p. A12.

[15]The quotation is from Stanley and Eric McKitrick, The Age of Federalism: The Early American Republic, 1788-1800 (New York: Oxford University Press, 1993), p. 97. Publishing data for McDonald's book: Chicago: University of Chicago Press, 1958.

[16]Jonathan Cohn, "Kill Phil," The New Republic, April 25, 2005, p. 6.

[17]Irving Brant, James Madison: The Nationalist, 1780-1787 (Indianapolis: Bobbs-Merrill, 1948), p. 416.

[18]There's more about this in the chapter on the Committee on Rules. For the increasing recent use of closed rules see Mann and Ornstein, The Broken Branch, pp. 8, 172; and Michael E. Hammond and Peter M. Weyrich, "Legislative Lords: Gag Rules and Permanent Staff," in Gordon S. Jones and John A. Marini, eds., The Imperial Congress: Crisis in the Separation of Powers (New York: Pharos Books, 1988), pp. 226-27.

[19]For recent details see Barbara Sinclair, "The New World of U.S. Senators," in Lawrence C. Dodd and Bruce I. Oppenheimer, eds., Congress Reconsidered, 8th edition (Washington: CQ Press, 2005), pp. 7-9.

[20]Joseph S. Clark, Congress: The Sapless Branch (Westport, CT: Greenwood Press, 1964), p. 148.

[21]A few of the beneficial changes are secret-ballot elections of committee chairs and abandonment of strict seniority in choosing chairs, the requirement of a public record of all roll-call votes in committees, and the ending of proxy voting in most cases. However, at the start of the 111th Congress (2009-2011), the Democratic majority, by eliminating the recent six-consecutive-years limit, permitted seniority in the selection of committee chairs. But the new Republican majority in the 112th Congress re-imposed a six-year term limit for the chairs (Rule X).

[22]Mann and Ornstein, Broken Branch , pp. 74-75; Elizabeth Wehr, "Republicans Cry 'Foul' Over Floor Tactics: Wright Finds a Vote to Pass Reconciliation Bill," Congressional Quarterly Weekly Report, October 31, 1987, pp. 2653-55. For minimum

time periods for electronic voting in the 110th Congress, see House Rule XX, clause 2(a), clause 8(c), and clause 9, and Rule XVIII, clause 6(b)(3), clause 6(f) and (g). For earlier rules on this topic see House Rule XV, clause 5(a), and Rule XXIII, clause 2(a) and (c), 105th Congress. Care must be exercised in citing House rules because a topic may be covered in a certain numbered rule of a particular Congress but be dealt with in a different rule of a different Congress.

[23]For a brief history of this, see Mann and Ornstein, Broken Branch, pp. 1-5.

[24]Mann and Ornstein, Broken Branch, p. 4: "The allegations of bribery were taken up by the bipartisan House Ethics Committee in March 2004. At the end of September, the committee unanimously admonished Majority Leader Tom DeLay and Michigan Rep. Candice Miller for violating House rules. Their report said 'Majority Leader DeLay offered to endorse Representative Smith's son in exchange for Representative Smith's vote in favor of the Medicare bill . . . it is improper for a Member to offer or link support for the personal interests of another Member as part of a quid pro quo to achieve a legislative goal.' The Ethics Committee reached the same conclusion about Candice Miller, who made statements to Smith on the floor that Smith 'fairly interpreted . . . as a threat of retaliation against him for voting in opposition to the bill.'[10]" ("10. Report of the Committee on Standards of Official Conduct, September 30, 2004, p. iii.")

Actually, there was and is no House rule that specifically prohibits offering an inducement to obtain a vote. If there were, the "logrolling" that is a regular part of the legislative process would be impermissible. In the above case "the Investigative Subcommittee determined that only Clause 1 of House Rule 23 would be applicable to this matter. . . . [It provides that a Member] 'shall conduct himself at all times in a manner that shall reflect creditably on the House.'"; "Investigation of Certain Allegations Related to Voting on the Medicare Prescription Drug, Improvement, and Modernization Act of 2003," Report of the Committee on Standards of Official Conduct, September 30, 2004, pp. 53-54.

For logrolling as "longstanding and accepted" if used "within the official government process" to "achieve policy goals" or to "serve the interests of constituents" rather than to advance or hinder another Member's personal interests see ibid., pp. 59-60. The Investigative Subcommittee intended its report to be advice "that the linking of official actions with political considerations in the manner described in this Report is impermissible and violates House rules"; ibid., pp. 61-62.

See also House Rule XXIII, clause 16, 110th Congress (a new rule): "A Member . . . may not condition the inclusion of language to provide funding for a congressional earmark . . . on any vote cast by another Member."

"Logrolling" seems to have originated about 2000 years ago when the Roman philosopher and statesman Seneca the Younger said, "You roll my log, and I will roll yours"; John Bartlett, Familiar Quotations, 16th edition (Boston: Little, Brown and Company, 1992), p. 103, #10.

[25]See Mann and Ornstein, Broken Branch, pp. 1-6, 8-9 for a more detailed history of this episode. The quotations are on p. 3. Ibid., p. 175: "Other bills have been accorded the same treatment, most recently the Central American Free Trade Agreement and the

oil refinery bill brought up in the House in the aftermath of Hurricane Katrina. The latter bill, crafted behind closed doors and filled with provisions to waive or obliterate environmental regulations, took nearly an hour to pass (for what was supposed to be a five-minute vote)."

[26]Oleszek, Congressional Procedures, 7th edition, p. 176.

[27]David Broder, "One-Man Senate," The Washington Post, August 3, 1993, p. A17.

[28]Morris P. Fiorina, Congress: Keystone of the Washington Establishment, 2d edition (New Haven: Yale University Press, 1989), p. 76.

[29]Mann and Ornstein, Broken Branch, pp. 189-90; Norman J. Ornstein, "The Warning Signs about Hastert's Leadership Were There," Roll Call, October 5, 2006, available on the Internet. See House Rule X, clause 5(a)(3)(B) and (C), 110th Congress. For an earlier variation see House Rule X, clause 6(a)(2), 105th Congress.

[30]Seeking the 1996 Republican nomination for President, Lamar Alexander often said he'd been in Washington "long enough to be vaccinated but not infected." Many Members, even if they start with intentions of doing good, become "Congressionalized" by years of service on Capitol Hill. Then, instead of doing good, they do well. Some do wealth.

II. The Incumbency Problem

EPIGRAPH: A politician thinks of the next election;
a statesman, of the next generation.
>---James Freeman Clark, quoted in Ralph L. Woods,
editor, A Treasury of the Familiar (New York:
Macmillan, 1943), p. 688.

EPIGRAPH: The primary problem with attracting people to service
is not that salaries are too low, but that the advantages of
incumbency are too high.
>---Representative Thomas J. Ridge, R-PA;
Congressional Record, permanent edition,
February 7, 1989, p. 1716.

There are many quotations about how the number-one priority of politicians is to get re-elected. Here are only three. "The primary and overriding duty and responsibility of each member of the House of Representatives and the Senate is to get re-elected."[1] "Once someone gets elected to Congress, his primary concern is finding ways to stay there."[2] "Most members are using the whole government mainly to win votes."[3]

That priority certainly has long applied to Members of Congress, doubtless to the detriment of the public good. Beneficial policy must often take a back seat to Members' job security. In 1999, meeting with Speaker Dennis Hastert and Senate Majority Leader Trent Lott, Representative Tom Coburn, R-OK, pressed the two to abide by recently voted budget caps. Senator Lott's shocking but all-too-normative response was, "Well, I've got an election coming up in 2000. After that we can have good government."[4] Americans need shelter from that norm.

Back in the 1970s, Representative James A. Burke, D-MA, as reported by Al Hunt in The Wall Street Journal, "explained how he stayed in Congress by voting for every spending bill and against every tax hike and debt-ceiling increase. When a naïve young reporter suggested that this was a prescription for chaos, Jimmy Burke puffed on his cigar, smiled and said, 'You think this place is on the level?'" And another Member once said, "It's easy [to get re-elected]. Vote liberal. Press release conservative."[5]

A surprise abandonment in April 2009 illustrates the treachery that can flow from that number-one priority. Longtime Pennsylvania Republican Senator Arlen Specter announced he was switching to the Democratic Party. When Senator Jim Jeffords jumped in 2001 from Republican to being an independent who would caucus with the Democrats, an angry Specter said, "That kind of instability is not good for governance of the country and the Senate," and he proposed a rule to limit such apostasy. In 2009, however, Specter spoke of no longer being comfortable with Republican philosophy, yet his well-known independent voting led some observers to say he'll not be likely to toe the Democratic line; and, indeed, his first vote after crossing the aisle was against the Democratic federal budget. In his defection speech, he made a longer explanation, referring to several GOP moderates who recently failed to win re-election, and to the new poll indicating he would probably not win the Republican primary in 2010. The clincher that re-election was his main concern is found in his own words: "I am not prepared to have my 29-year record in the United States Senate decided by the Pennsylvania Republican primary electorate."[6] Of course, it was not his already established 29-year record that would be decided—it was his future as an octogenarian seat-warmer in the Senate.

If our Representatives and Senators devote their main efforts to re-election, it must be true that they are shirking their legislative, constituent-service, and oversight responsibilities. And if Members cast votes to please large campaign contributors, such action often opposes what would benefit the nation. If, for example, Congress continued, as it did, for years to shear the taxpayers by providing a huge subsidy to the producers of wool and mohair long after the U.S. military no longer needed to encourage such production, the reason might be found by noting that the House Agriculture Committee was long dominated by Members from Texas, the number-one state in sheep and goats, and that they were no doubt tending to the interests of wool and mohair producers.[7]

The Founding Fathers expected that Members would serve for only a few years and would then return to their private vocations. That would keep Congress fresh with new views and Members who were close to the people. Service in Congress was even, as one book explained, "an honor to be spread among the good citizens of the district. Abraham Lincoln, for example, was denied renomination . . . he had already had his turn."[8]

Elections and personal decisions made the Founders' expectation a reality until about the middle of the twentieth century. From 1790 through 1898 the average turnover of Representatives from one Congress to the next was 45.6 percent.[9] The extreme was 76 percent in 1842. During 1900 through 1922 average turnover was 26.6 percent. For 1924 through 1966 the average was 19.5 percent. The downward trend continued in 1968 through 1988, when the average was 14.2 percent.[10] The average from 1990 through 2008 was 13.54 percent of the House, but that number was larger because of the aberrant years 1992 and 1994 (turnovers of 25.3 percent and 19.54 respectively).[11] The 2010 general elections again increased the average of 1990-2010 (to 14.31) because of a 22 percent turnover as 96 new members were elected. Despite famous pro-Democratic election results in 2006 and 2008, House turnover was only 12.18 in the former year and 11.7 in the latter.

As turnover decreased, length of service increased. During the entire nineteenth century, in each separate Congress the number of Representatives with twelve or more years of consecutive membership averaged 7.8, with the later years skewing the figure upward.[12] Once House membership stabilized at 435 in 1912, there began to be a higher percentage of long-serving Members.[13]   History shows this pattern: A low percentage of extreme tenures prior to 1903 and high percentage thereafter.[14]

Several factors worked toward that change. Some areas of the nation, such as the South, became increasingly dominated by one party, thus expanding the ability of incumbents to win general elections. The District of Columbia gathered greater amenities within its borders, so that Members became more willing to stay there. Its theaters, restaurants, and other places of diversion compensated for its swampy location and difficult climate. The advent of air conditioning also helped.

Then came the more institutionalized and change-resistant seniority system, sometimes called the "senility system."[15] It was not part of the formal rules of either chamber, but was "an unwritten custom, sometimes violated in practice, that length of service in the House and Senate determines eligibility for appointment to committees, and that the majority senior member of a committee succeeds automatically to a vacancy in the chairmanship."[16] By creating greater predictability for advancing to power positions such as committee chairmanships in both chambers, seniority allowed career calculations of greater certainty. As one scholar explained, "The great advantage of the seniority system is that it decentralizes power in the House of Representatives by creating multiple centers of policy influence and increasing the number of good Congressional jobs. This adds to the incentives of the Congressional career."[17]   It also discouraged Members from leaving office for personal or financial reasons and later returning, because they would lose seniority and be back at the bottom of the escalator to chairmanships and other leadership positions. The seniority system also made it clear to voters and power brokers back home that they could not afford to lose the leverage that a long-serving Member possessed; thus there was incentive to avoid putting an old warhorse out to pasture.

During 1909-1911, a House revolt stripped some powers from the Speaker. There are doubtless several reasons why that happened, but, as one book explains, it "can be interpreted as an attempt by the rank and file to reduce the uncertainty surrounding a congressional career. By breaking the arbitrary power of the party leadership and substituting an automatic leadership selection system, individual congressmen could plan a congressional career in a manner not previously possible."[18]

A few words about the advent of the seniority system: In the House, it was strengthened in about 1910 in connection with the reduction of the Speaker's power. Before then, the Speaker of the House possessed unfettered authority to appoint committee members and chairs. But in March 1910 House insurgents were successful in changing the rules to provide election of the Rules Committee by the entire House and to increase its membership from five to ten. The House also provided that the power to appoint other committees and chairs would reside in the Ways and Means Committee, not in the

Speaker.[19]   Democrats then had majority control of the House, and they selected Oscar W. Underwood as Ways and Means chair, thus making him the supreme authority for other committee assignments. He usually made appointments by seniority, explaining "that any other course would lead to turmoil."[20] His decisions needed pro forma approval by the full Ways and Means Committee and by the Democratic Caucus, and that was generally forthcoming. Further, the Democratic Caucus permitted the Republicans to select the minority members of committees.[21]

Members supported the use of seniority because it created reliability about advancement to power positions. But the system was not etched in the rules of the House. Instead the rule about chairmen stated, "At the commencement of each Congress, the House shall elect as chairman of each standing committee one of the members thereof." Those elections did occur, but they were a mere rubber stamping of decisions already made, decisions which were themselves mere concurrence with time-worn, often geriatric, tenure.[22]

The seniority system in the Senate came about more by tradition than in the House. And it did not place such a dead hand on Senatorial ambitions as on those of some Representatives. When it became thoroughly ensconced in the House, a Member might serve on a committee for, say, thirty years and still be outranked for its chairmanship by a Member with longer tenure on that committee.[23] But in the Senate, a solon of short tenure might achieve a committee assignment or chairmanship due to (1) simultaneous membership on several committees, which was not so usual in the House,[24]   (2) advancement to an important Senatorial position because of greater externally derived power due to national exposure, (3) the possibility that he or she might advance to the Presidency,[25] and (4) the smaller number of colleagues, vis-à-vis the House, competing for the influential positions. Moreover, in the Senate, but not in the House, certain types of governmental service, such as having been a governor or a U.S. Representative, counted toward tenure, thus giving some freshmen Senators a leg up on the tenure ladder.[26]

Once seniority was in place, Members of both chambers became more wedded to maintaining their incumbency. They needed re-election to keep advancing toward a better committee or toward a chairmanship. Or, if they had already achieved the god-like status of chairman, they certainly wanted no fall to oblivion. Thus, re-election became a greater priority than before. And with the efforts to achieve re-election came bad results for the common weal. One author wisely pointed out that "unconstrained pursuit of personal goals by members results in the failure of Congress to meet collective responsibilities."[27]

By the late 1980s and early 1990s, portions of the politically aware public were seeing Congressional careerism as a problem. Some of the factors causing that were the following:

• Publicity about the House Bank scandal. This burst upon the public with the release of a General Accounting Office report in September 1991 showing that several hundred

Members had overdrawn their accounts at the House Bank without penalty. Established as a convenience for Representatives, the Bank accepted salary-check deposits and allowed withdrawals from Members' balances. Overdraft amounts came from the common pool of money. Apologists, perhaps seeking to tar the Republicans, asserted that the GOP had "politicized" the GAO report and were seeking partisan advantage in demanding a probe by the Ethics Committee. It was true that no laws had been broken, and that no one lost any money—except the taxpayers, because several hundred thousand dollars per year were expended on salaries for Bank employees and other overhead expenses for that out-of-control, flawed operation.

But violations of law need not occur for something to be a scandal. A scandal can simply be discreditable action, which this surely was. The maladministration of the Bank by House employees was disreputable, as was the inability of Members to simply pay enough attention to maintain proper accounts. The Members who deliberately used the overdrafts for the equivalent of interest-free loans may not have been typical, but Members who merely made mistakes at least exemplified incompetence. And the whole thing showed the Bank's employees as willing to turn a blind eye to the transgressions of powerful people who perversely refused to abide by their own rules. After the names of the overdrafters became public, several Congressional careers soon ended. Much of the public concluded that people who could not properly run a little financial convenience store and who could not even keep track of their own accounts should no longer be entrusted with running the government. A number of retirements and election defeats followed. However, some Members with big war chests and the power of incumbency stayed on; Ron Coleman, D-TX, revealed as having bounced 673 checks, spent $650,000 on his campaign and was re-elected.[28]

Jack Russ, the House Sergeant-At-Arms and overlord of the House bank, apparently made an effort to provide cover for Members—and perhaps save his own job. In October, 1991, the aforementioned Ron Coleman got a letter from Russ including this:
> "Our records show that four of your checks for a combined total of
> $285 were held by the bank for brief periods, usually one to three
> days, until they were covered by a deposit at the end of the month.
> Further, our records show you were *not* notified of the overdrafts
> because they were isolated instances in an account that otherwise
> maintained healthy balances. We regret any inconvenience this may
> have caused you."[29]

That was simply an assemblage of lies. In the previous year a bank employee had told Coleman that his $5,765 in overdrafts at that time could not be covered even if his next monthly paycheck went toward them in its entirety.[30]

● Publicity about the House Post Office scandal. In 1991 the Capitol Police investigated several employees of the postal facility run for the convenience of Representatives. When the Democrats who controlled the House killed that inquiry, the U.S. Postal Service launched its own and issued a report of its findings. Speaker of the House Tom Foley, apparently wanting to shield wrong-doing Members and employees, suppressed the report (and was sustained by a party-line House vote) until 1992, when public interest was whetted by media reports of embezzlement, drug sales, and money laundering. Then Foley initiated a new investigation by the House Administration Committee. Its Democratic majority issued a report that the topic was closed. The Republican minority dissented and listed several unresolved issues. Little came of that until the House Postmaster, Robert Rota, pleaded guilty in July 1993 to criminal charges of embezzlement. By then the public was in full cry against Congressional corruption. Rota implicated Ways and Means Committee chairman Dan Rostenkowski, D-IL, and others. Aside from the sale of cocaine at the H.P.O., the heart of the scandal was that a Representative could get thousands of stamps there, charge them to his office account as needed for official business, and later exchange them for cash and use the money for whatever. "Rosty" did that, which was one reason he was defeated in the 1994 general election. He was later convicted on various charges, including the stamp swindle; served just over a year in prison; and received one of President Clinton's notorious pardons in December 2000. Several smaller fish also went to prison, one being former Representative Joe Kolter, D-PA. Not being such bigwigs as Rostenkowski, they got no Clinton pardons.[31]

- Publicity about the government's runaway spending.

- Publicity about Congressional pay raises. See that section of this book.

- Publicity about the numerous perks enjoyed by Members. See that section of this book.

- Publicity about gerrymandering. See later in this book.

- Publicity about federal deficits and the huge national debt. Concern was so great that in late 1990 leaders from Congress and the Bush 41 administration met at Andrews Air Force Base to craft ways to solve the crisis. Removal of the confab from the usual governmental haunts emphasized the topic's distraction-free importance.

- Publicity about the effort of one Congressional grandee, Senator Robert Byrd, D-WV, to disproportionately benefit his state with federal jobs and dollars.[32]

- A drumbeat of media reports emphasizing negatives about Congress. For example, the cover of the April 16, 1990, issue of Business Week featured an illustration of broken machinery inside the Capitol dome along with "Congress: It Doesn't Work. Let's Fix It." And the August 1992 issue of Money magazine headlined this story: "What Congress Really Costs You: $2.8 Billion a Year" and the subhead stated, "The problems run much deeper than the scandals and perks you have read about. Indeed, no matter how extravagant and inefficient you now believe Congress is with your money, the reality is worse." A cutline in that story said, "The taxpayers' tab for running the 102nd Congress will approach $5.2 million per legislator this year." There was even a 1995 book titled Congress as Public Enemy.[33]

- Newt Gingrich succeeded in his effort to "broaden the public hatred of Congress."[34]

- Publicity about numerous problems in the U.S.: crumbling bridges and highways, inadequate health care, deteriorating school buildings, and education that fails to educate, to list only a few.

- Many Americans, seeing the high Congressional salaries, the numerous perks Members lavished on themselves, and the plethora of unaddressed national problems, concluded that too many Members sought re-election mainly to continue their access to excess.

Concerned people addressed the careerism problem by pushing for term limits, an idea of lengthy pedigree but no doubt considered by Members as hitting below the Beltway. It was part of the Virginia Plan considered by the Constitutional Convention in 1787.[35] Several states applied it to their governors in the late 1700s.[36] By about 1990, many appalled Americans concluded that Congressional failure to eliminate huge deficits, that Members' greed for pay raises and other benefits, and that long House and Senate careers required corrective action. Representative Jamie Whitten, D-MS, began House membership on just before the Pearl Harbor attack and would hold office until January 1995. Still-serving Representative John Dingell, D-MI, has been in the House for 56 years. Senator Strom Thurmond, D-SC, was first elected in 1954 and would serve until January 2003. Robert Byrd, D-WV, became a Senator in January 1959 and served until his death in June 2010. Daniel Inouye, D-HI, Senator since January 1963, is still in office (November 2011). Ted Kennedy served as a Senator from November 1962 to August 2009.[37] With publicity about such long tenures, term limits became popular outside of the governing class.

Political operatives and elected careerists who saw partisan or financial benefit in long service fired heavy cannonades against this power-reducing proposal. They used such falsely alluring arguments as that term limits already existed in the form of elections, deliberately ignoring that incumbents had achieved such electoral advantages that there were often no reasonable prospects of terminating their tenures. They speciously claimed it was antidemocratic to deny voters the right to elect whomever they wanted for as long as they wanted, again casting aside clear evidence that legislators had so bastardized the electoral system that it was what was antidemocratic.

They contended that term limits would also limit the expertise, experience, and institutional memory that existed in Congress and that supposedly prevented bad government. But, wait!, didn't we already have bad government? Hadn't the experienced lawmakers given us high taxes, a huge debt, and a failure to address numerous problems? Hadn't institutional memory been used for institutional protection and much maintenance of the status quo? Hadn't the expertise of the old warhorses in Congress not been used sufficiently for the public good? Wasn't the reverence for "expertise" wildly overdone? Isn't expertise often used for terrible purposes, as in court cases where experts testify in direct contradiction of each other and sometimes support tort frauds? Doesn't our revered jury system, even for complex cases, rest on ordinary people who are not experts and are not career jurors?[38] A 1986 book said, "Sure, the conventional wisdom says a person has to have a lifetime of experience to handle a national office, but the conventional wisdom should take a look around and ask itself exactly how well these lifers are doing."[39]

Another contention finding some support was that term limits "would damage the political clout of small states like Oklahoma and increase voter apathy."[40] It's difficult to see how either of those arguments is valid. If the small-state argument rests on the idea that Members from such areas have longer tenures and, thus, achieve higher and more powerful positions in Congress, how do the sophists who argue against term limits explain the existence of long-serving Members from highly populated places such as California, Texas, and Michigan, to name just a few? Consider the following current (as of November 2011) Representatives, with month and year that service began in parentheses:

John Dingell, D-MI, (December 1955)
John Conyers, D-MI, (January 1965)
Charles Rangel, D-NY, (January 1971)
George Miller, D-CA, (January 1975)
Henry Waxman, D-CA, (January 1975)
Jerry Lewis, R-CA, (January 1979)

Texas currently has no Members of extremely long tenure, partly because of the change from Democratic to Republican domination in that state; but by the late 1900s its Representatives included the following men of long service:

Bill Archer, who served January 1971 to January 2001 (30 years)
Jack Brooks, January 1953-January 1995 (42 years)
Kika de la Garza, January 1965-January 1997 (32 years)
Henry Gonzalez, November 1961-January 1999 (38 years)
Jake Pickle, December 1963-January 1995 (32 years).

Those examples should be sufficient to show that it's not just low-population states that have Members of long tenure.

It may be a matter of opinion as to what population number is the dividing line between small and large states. If Massachusetts, with 6,547,629 people (2010 Census), thus ranking 14th among all U.S. states, is not a small state, how do term-limit opponents argue that lightly populated states are more likely to have Members of long service when Ted Kennedy continuously occupied a Senate seat from 1962 to 2009? Well, they can say that some large states have long-serving Members.

Far from causing voter apathy, term limits might cause greater interest and turnout—because when a Member can no longer serve, the result of the next election will not be a foregone conclusion.

Despite resistance, term limits were enacted for many state and local offices. And, in the early 1990s, twenty-two states put term limits on their Members of Congress. Proposals for a term-limits Constitutional amendment generated wide public support but disdain from many federal solons. Nine-term Representative, Pat Williams, D-MT, with an all-too-typical "We are your betters" attitude, dismissively explained, "Sometimes the American people are simply wrong."[41]

Congressional lifers no doubt worried that their careers could be truncated by term limits. One indication is that they passed a campaign-reform bill including a requirement that pro-term-limit organizations provide the Federal Election Commission lists of all donors of more than $50. What possible decent motive lay behind that? None? Maybe it was included so that proponents of term limits could be identified and intimidated. Here's a clue: "In Washington state, several business leaders suddenly resigned from the board of a pro-term-limit group after being called by aides to House Speaker Tom Foley."[42]

In March 1995, as was to be expected from the entrenched self-servers, the House of Representatives killed several proposed term-limit amendments to the Constitution.[43] And just weeks later the Supreme Court ruled 5-4 against the limits already imposed on federal legislators by states.[44]

Those actions doomed the limits for U.S. Representatives and Senators, though some advocates still clamored against the "dying of the light."[45]

Some of what was worrisome in the early 1990s attracts little current attention due to the other, more important, problems existing now. Further, as people become accustomed to the existence of something, their sense that it's wrong is dulled. They may be desensitized into inertness

With their world made safe from "artificial" restraints, Congressional incumbents could proceed with additional ways to enhance their electoral advantages—fattening the pork they could brag about bringing home, increasing the campaign contributions they could get from influence seekers, and avoiding long work weeks in Washington while engaging in "constituent service" back home. Meanwhile, they successfully dealt with a few national problems, but ignored too many others.

And although most Members of the House opposed any restriction on their time in office, they have apparently come to believe that term limits are good if applied to themselves in a more modest way. They have imposed a maximum of three terms (six years) on the duration of an individual's committee chairmanship. Responding to voter discontent with the entrenched power of Congressional veterans, the Republicans did that first, in January 1995, when they had a House majority for the first time in forty years. The new House Democratic majority continued it in January 2007. One may wonder if the reason many Democrats believed this encroachment acceptable was largely because several of their incoming chairmen were so old that they might retire or die before reaching the three-term limit. Mentioning just three, at the start of the 110th Congress in 2007, one was 80 (John Dingell), another 77 (John Conyers), and a third 76 (Charles Rangel). All three still held their chairmanships two years later as the 111th Congress began in 2009.

Before long, House Democrats changed their minds about limited tenure for chairmen and repealed that limitation at the start of the 111th Congress in 2009. Republican control of the 112th Congress restored the six-year rule.

The Senate, not opening itself to any charge of inconsistency, has no such limit on its committee chairmen.

From January 1995 to January 2003 the House's Rule I limited a Member's service as Speaker to four consecutive Congresses (eight years). [46]

Standpatters' arguments against term limits got stronger after some recent elections shifted party control of Congress and proved to some people that term limits are not needed. Yet the reversals caused by the 1994 and 2006 elections were due to special circumstances that cannot be expected to occur every time a mass injection of new blood would be beneficial. An exceptional confluence of issues that benefited Republicans occurred in 1994.[47]   And, as we well know, the 2006 election shifted control to the Democrats, largely because of dissatisfaction with the war in Iraq and with the corruption of several newly infamous members of the GOP. Even though majority power switched from Democrats to Republicans in 1995 and vice versa in 2007 and the House changed from Democratic to Republican majority in January 2011, many of the most senior denizens of Capitol Hill were not booted out by those reversals.

And an unusually large number of Members did not seek re-election in 1992 because that was the last time they could convert unused campaign funds to personal use upon retirement (see the chapter on Thief-in-the-Night Pay Raises). Their retirements produced many open races where there was no incumbency advantage.

The edge enjoyed by incumbents over opponents in elections was illustrated by the re-election in a runoff race in December 2006 of William Jefferson, D-LA, despite the FBI's discovery of $90,000 of possible bribe money in the freezer of his Louisiana home. He said he was innocent of any wrongdoing, and late-night TV jokester Jay Leno said Jefferson was just trying to protect the money from global warming.[48]   Apparently, his Louisiana voters in 2006 were convinced that his incumbency trumped his possible criminality, but he finally lost in another runoff in 2008. We know that Louisiana has long had a reputation for tolerating crooks in high office. Someone thought the tolerance was so strong that he put out a bumper sticker during Edwin Edwards' 1991 gubernatorial campaign saying "Vote For the Crook. It's important." As an observer of Congress wrote, "Bad government isn't just the work of a deceitful few. It also requires great multitudes willing to be deceived."[49]

Among the reasons why incumbents win most Congressional elections are the following:

● They usually have greater name recognition than challengers. The recent trend allowing early voting for people other than those who will be absent on the usual election day benefits incumbents by truncating the campaign time for challengers to get their names and messages in front of voters.

- Challengers find if difficult to persuade voters to abandon someone they've previously voted for and elected.

- Incumbents usually have an enormous advantage in campaign funds already secured—and in the ability to raise more. Seniority in Congress results in long relationships with important donors and increased opportunities for finding additional contributors.[50]

- An incumbent, typically, has been massaging constituents for months and even years, and thereby gaining support before the challenger breaks into view.

- One way that incumbents stroke potential voters is through constituent service, i.e., solving problems or fulfilling desires. If a constituent is entangled in the federal bureaucracy or merely wants something from the federal government, such as information or a flag that's been flown over the Capitol for five seconds, the Senator or Representative can help. Challengers can't.

A cynical view of constituent service is in the lyrics of the song "Summertime Blues": "I called my Congressman and he said quote, 'I'd like to help you son, but you're too young to vote.'"[51]

- Incumbents tout their records of engorging their states or districts with federal money, often with the explicit promise of more to come. There are often news reports of increased money just before an election.

- People already in Congress have several advantages in getting favorable publicity. They can use their franking privilege (mailing without paying postage) to launch self-promoting information toward voters under the guise of informing them about government. The media is often complicit in publicizing the federal programs and money the incumbents secure for their constituencies. Incumbents can hold hearings which are widely reported by the media and which often excite voters. They can go on "fact-finding missions" to exotic locales and expect significant news coverage (but that can be a two-edged sword that can cut their reputations if seen or reported as mainly a taxpayer-financed pleasure junket). They can often call upon the President or noteworthy fellow Members to attend fundraisers and thus draw bigger crowds. They can often get such newsy "rainmakers" to come to the incumbent's state or district for supportive speeches.

- Incumbents may get party leaders, in and out of Congress, to commit funds to their campaigns—because those leaders do not want to risk losing allies in Congress.

- The districts of incumbent Representatives have often been gerrymandered to their electoral benefit. See the Gerrymanders chapter in this book.

- Incumbent Senators are somewhat insulated from electoral challenges from incumbent Representatives because the latter must abandon their House seats if they seek elevation to the Senate. They are not allowed to run for both chambers simultaneously.

• Incumbents advise voters that their experience and knowledge of the Congressional system should not be lost by electing a beginner.

• Incumbents in leadership positions in House or Senate or who serve as committee or subcommittee chairs tell voters not to give up their clout in favor of challengers who will not achieve such powerful roles for several years.

• Members' staffers, paid with the public's taxes, are sometimes assigned to duties in re-election campaigns. Thus, voters help pay for a result many of them may oppose. Such use of aides can be a gray area: When does the work of a staffer engaged in legislative and constituent service also advance the Member's bid for another term in office? The more careful Members avoid any blatant abuse of this sort. See more about this in the next chapter.

Even in 1776, John Adams could see that lawmakers might use their powers to gain electoral advantage: "A single assembly is apt to grow ambitious, and after a time will not hesitate to vote itself perpetual."[52] And one may well ask, Why did he think such self-serving would not occur with a bicameral congress, when our history shows that it did?

CORRECTIVE SOLUTIONS

Three proposals stand out. One, of course, is term limits, but that has virtually no chance of realization because courts have ruled that state efforts to achieve it for federal lawmakers are unconstitutional and because Members of Congress are hardly likely to propose a Constitutional amendment for career-ending caps. They won't choose to lose. A slim chance rests with the possibility of an amendment through the convention process mentioned at the end of the preceding chapter.

Another improvement would be some way to end the partisan gerrymandering that makes so many House elections non-competitive. That path is difficult and strewn with roadblocks. One obstacle is laws and resultant court decisions that mandate House districts guaranteeing minority representation. Yet some states have made the effort. See the chapter on gerrymandering later in this book.

Thirdly, public financing of campaigns might level the playing field between incumbents and challengers. (See some details in Corrective Solutions section of the chapter on Failure to Devote Enough Time to Legislation.)

Term limits or the abandonment of gerrymandering could make possible the election of new, and perhaps more responsive, Members. Given the difficulties of achieving those reforms, however, the most immediate chance for beneficial changes may lie with publicity and public pressure—and with disgusted voters.

II-A. Problems Related to Careerism

Several chapters in this book touch on problems caused by desires for a Congressional career rather than a limited period of public service. One not dealt with elsewhere is the way careerism sometimes changes Members' voting behavior. The emphasis here on that issue will relate to the House, where it is more potent than in the Senate.

There's a three-level hierarchy of committees in both chambers of Congress.   In the House, so-called "exclusive" committees are highest, followed by "major" panels, and then "minor."[53]

Ambitious Members, meaning virtually all Members, want to be on the most powerful, the "exclusive" committees. They know that party leaders control committee assignments, total number of lawmakers on each panel, and the ratios of Democrats and Republicans on each. They know that they must somehow win the favor of the leaders in order to rise to a higher level. They do so by voting as leaders want.

Leaders want loyal followers. Therefore, leaders look at Members' voting records to determine who should be advanced from minor to major to exclusive committees. If there are not enough loyalists to fill the available party seats on a particular panel, leaders can reduce its membership. If there are more loyalists than slots, committee size or majority party ratio can be expanded.

Knowing all that, Members who covet seats on the most powerful boards sometimes tailor their voting to the wishes of those in control. They thereby signal to the leadership their readiness to be reliable acolytes on the committees where the most important policies are set. They thus sometimes vote differently from what they would do if not consumed by a striving for personal advancement.

That creates a bias that frequently works against majoritarian democracy. When the leadership is more liberal or more conservative than the average Member in the party, as is often the case, this selection process disproportionately loads committees with lawmakers who also do not reflect average party sentiment. The result, of course, is laws that are more liberal or conservative than majority sentiment in the party – and the nation.

CORRECTIVE SOLUTION

The ability of the leaders to skew voting behavior through the reward system of preferred committee assignments could be eliminated with a return to strict seniority – and its attendant problems of putting debilitated or out-of-step elders in powerful slots. Or that ability could be reduced by rules changes that prevent leaders from fiddling with committee sizes or ratios.[54] Or it could be eliminated by a sort of lottery for committee memberships for new Members or by rotation of committee assignments among Members.

Notes: Chapter II. The Incumbency Problem

[1]Said by Representative Adam Clayton Powell; reported in Joseph S. Clark, Congress: The Sapless Branch (Westport, CT: Greenwood Pres s, 1964), p. 32.

[2]Bill Thomas, Club Fed: Power, Money, Sex, and Violence on Capitol Hill (New York: Charles Scribner's Sons, 1994), p. 138; see also p. 97.

[3]George F. Will, Restoration: Congress, Term Limits and the Recovery of Deliberative Democracy (New York: The Free Press, 1992), p. 95. See also Morris P. Fiorina, Congress: Keystone of the Washington Establishment, 2d edition (New Haven: Yale University Press, 1989), pp. 37, 39.
Former Representative Frank E. Smith made this disheartening observation: "All members of Congress have a primary interest in being reelected. Some members have no other interest"; quoted in Mark J. Green, Who Runs Congress, revised edition (New York: Bantam/Grossman, 1975), p. 262. "Rep. Bob Gergland, a two-termer from Minnesota, stated that he devoted most of his first two years in office to getting reelected"; ibid., p. 272.

[4]Tom A. Coburn and John Hart, Breach of Trust: How Washington Turns Outsiders into Insiders (Nashville: WND Books, 2003), pp. xviii-xix.

[5]For the Burke item, Albert R. Hunt, "The Balanced Budget Hoax," The Wall Street Journal, February 10, 1994, p. A17. For the "Press release conservative quotation, "Real House Reform," The Wall Street Journal, September 30, 1993, p. A18.

[6]Various television news reports, April 28 and 29, 2009. See also Jonathan Weisman and Greg Hitt, "Senator Defects to Democrats," The Wall Street Journal, April 29, 2009, pp. A1, A2. Peter Nicholas, "Specter condemned Jim Jeffords' party switch in 2001, Los Angeles Times, April 28, 2009, on the Internet.

[7]Will, Restoration, pp. 19-24, citing Jonathan Rauch, "The Golden Fleece," National Journal, May 18, 1991, pp. 1168-71.

[8]Fiorina, Congress: Keystone, 2d edition, p. 8.

[9]Computed from Will, Restoration, p. 73.

[10]Ibid., p. 73.

[11]In 1992, 110 Representatives retired, died, resigned, or were defeated, a turnover of nearly 25.3 percent; "Election-Year Turnover," Congressional Quarterly Almanac . . . 1992 (Washington: Congressional Quarterly, 1993), p. 24-A. The 65 retirements in 1992 include Members who ran for other offices and those who left largely because 1992 was the last year some Representatives (but not Senators) could convert unused campaign

funds to personal use upon retirement. The defeats of 43 incumbents, 19 in primaries and 24 in the general election, flowed partly from the House Bank scandal; the reason 65 retirements and 43 defeats do not total 110 is because two additional Representatives died in mid-September 1992.

In 1990 the turnover was 10.34 percent of the House.

In 1992 the turnover was nearly 25.3 percent.

In 1994 the turnover was 19.54 percent.

In 1996 the turnover was 16.6 percent.

In 1998 the turnover was 9.19 percent.

In 2000 the turnover was 9.42 percent.

In 2002 the turnover was 12.64 percent.

In 2004 the turnover was 8.5 percent.

In 2006 the turnover was 12.18 percent.

In 2008 the turnover was 11.7 percent.

In 2010 the turnover was 22 percent.

In 1994, the Democrats lost fifty-two House seats, while every incumbent Republican was re-elected; Robert V. Remini, <u>The House: The History of the House of Representatives</u> (New York: Collins, a division of HarperCollins; Smithsonian Books, 2006), p. 482. See note 47 below for the 1994 reasons.

[12]Will, <u>Restoration</u>, pp. 78-79.

[13]The only change in total membership after 1912 was a temporary increase to 437 in 1959 because of the admission of Alaska and Hawaii as states.

[14]In 1811-1813 there were 15 Members with 12 or more years of consecutive membership in a House of 186 members, <u>so the percentage was 8.0</u>. The number of Members with long tenure did not equal or exceed 15 until 1887-1889, when there were 18 such Members in a House of 332, <u>so the percentage was 5.4</u>; the next increase came in 1889-1891, when there were 23 such members in a House of 332, <u>so the percentage was 6.9</u>; another increase occurred in 1903-1905, when there were 35 such members in a House of 391, <u>so the percentage was 8.9</u>; the next increase was during 1909-1911 with 77 such members in a House of 391, <u>so the percentage was 19.6</u>; 1927-1929 brought the next increase with 107 such members, the first time the figure was 100 or more, in a House of 435, <u>so the percentage was 24.6</u>; since 1945-1947 the number of such members has never dropped below 100 and has recently been over 200. I calculated the preceding percentages from the table in Will, <u>Restoration</u>, pp. 78-80, showing number of Representatives with 12 or more years in the House at the end of each Congress, and from membership numbers in the House from the beginning through 2005, on p. 41 of <u>Biographical Directory of the United States Congress 1774-2005</u> (Washington: USGPO, 2005).

[15]Chapter Eleven in Drew Pearson and Jack Anderson, <u>The Case Against Congress</u> (New York: Simon and Schuster, 1968), is titled "The Senility System."

[16]Clark, <u>Congress: The Sapless Branch</u>, p. 178.

[17]Nelson Polsby, quoted in David J. Vogler, The Politics of Congress (Boston: Allyn and Bacon, 1974), p. 171.

[18]Fiorina, Congress: Keystone, 2d ed., p. 8; Will, Restoration, p. 91.

[19]Remini, The House, pp. 72-75, 277-78. See also Nelson W. Polsby, Miriam Gallaher, and Barry Spencer Runquist, "The Growth of the Seniority System in the U.S. House of Representatives," in Nelson W. Polsby, editor, Congressional Behavior (New York: Random House, 1971), pp. 172-202.

[20]Remini, The House, p. 278.

[21]Ibid., p. 278.

[22]Warren Weaver, Jr., Both Your Houses: The Truth About Congress (New York: Praeger Publishers, 1972), p. 67.

[23]See Vogler, Politics of Congress, p. 172, for a relevant quotation.

[24]See Clark, Congress: The Sapless Branch, p. 180.

[25]Vogler, Politics of Congress, p. 173.

[26]Clark, Congress: The Sapless Branch, p. 179; C-SPAN. org, Capitol Questions.

[27]Fiorina, Congress: Keystone, 2d ed., p. xiv.

[28]Thomas, Club Fed, p. 40; Will, Restoration, pp. 15-16; Remini, The House, pp. 479-80.

[29]John L. Jackley, Hill Rat: Blowing the Lid Off Congress (Washington: Regnery Gateway, 1992), p. 290.

[30]Ibid.

[31]Congressional Post Office Scandal, Wikipedia; Joseph P. Kolter, Wikipedia; USDOJ: Office of the Pardon Attorney, Pardons Granted by President Clinton; all on the Internet.

[32]See Will, Restoration, pp. 29-31.

[33]John R. Hibbing and Elizabeth Theiss-Morse, Congress as Public Enemy: Public Attitudes toward American Political Institutions (New York: Cambridge University Press, 1995).

[34]Thomas E. Mann and Norman J. Ornstein, The Broken Branch: How Congress Is Failing America and How to Get It Back on Track (New York: Oxford University Press, 2006), p. 65.

[35]Will, Restoration, p. 4.

[36]Garry Wills, "Undemocratic Vistas," The New York Review of Books, Vol. 39, No. 19 (November 19, 1992), pp. 28-29, in a review of George F. Will's Restoration.

[37]The New York Times reported on November 9, 1962 (page 16), that Kennedy began receiving salary as a Senator on November 7, 1962. U.S. Congress, Biographical Directory of the United States Congress 1774-1989 (Washington: United States Government Printing Office, 1989), pp. 432, note 20, says Kennedy was "elected November 6, 1962 . . . but was unable to be sworn in as Congress was not in session"; however, ibid., p. 432, shows Kennedy as a Senator in the 87th Congress, which ended its sessions on October 13, 1962, but did not technically terminate until January 3, 1963. The Biographical Directory of the United States Congress 1774-2005 (Washington: USGPO, 2005), p. 423, note 20, says that Kennedy's service as a Senator began on November 7, 1962.   Kennedy was not sworn in as a Senator until January 9, 1963; The New York Times, January 10, 1963, p. 4. Thus, the question arises of whether a person becomes a Senator when his or her salary begins or when sworn in. It's the former. It has long been U.S. law that "salaries of Senators elected during a session to succeed appointees shall commence on the day they qualify"; Title 2, U.S. Code, Section 36, 2000 edition. That law applied to Kennedy because although Congress had adjourned sine die before his election, that session of Congress did not technically end until January 3, 1963, and he was elected to succeed an appointee.

[38]Thomas, Club Fed, p. 117.

[39]Susan Trausch, It Came from the Swamp: Your Federal Government at Work (Boston: Houghton Mifflin, 1986), p. 211. Experts are often not expert; for example, several were fooled in an experiment to see if people could distinguish real, high-priced art from paintings done by four-year-old children. "The Real Deal" on ABC-TV program "20/20," August 5, 2005.

[40]Coburn and Hart, Breach of Trust, p. 9.

[41]Kenneth J. Cooper, "House Defeats Four Versions of Term Limits," The Washington Post, March 30, 1995, p. A7, continuation of article from p. A1.

[42]"Politicians Panic," The Wall Street Journal, June 2, 1992, p. A14.

[43]Kenneth J. Cooper, "House Rejects Measures To Require Term Limits," The Washington Post, March 30, 1995, pp. A1, A7.

[44]U.S. Term Limits, Inc., et al. versus Thornton et al., 514 U.S. 779 (1995).

[45]"Do Not Go Gentle Into That Good Night," a poem by Dylan Thomas, includes the words "Rage, rage against the dying of the light."

[46]James V. Saturno, "The Speaker of the House: House Officer, Party Leader, and Representative," CRS Report for Congress, updated January 29, 2007, p. CRS-2, is in error in saying the limit still exists. For its repeal at the start of the 108th Congress, see H. Res. 5, section 2(b), January 7, 2003; Congressional Record, daily edition, January 7, 2003, pp. H7, H12; during the debate on the new rules package there was no mention about why the limit was being rescinded (see pp. H7-H20).

[47]Contract With America. Various scandals—such as allegations about Clinton's extramarital sex, corruption at the House Bank and Post Office, and Travelgate. Ban on assault weapons; see Mann and Ornstein, Broken Branch, p. 93. Clinton's botched health-care plan and its defeat; see Mann and Ornstein, pp. 93-94. Clinton's "Don't ask, don't tell" policy for military homosexuals; Remini, The House, p. 481.

[48]Jay Leno, on "The Tonight Show."

[49]Thomas, Club Fed, p. 10.

[50]Brenarlo, "Out of State Money: How Out of State Interests Are Buying Local Elections," January 15, 2007, on the Internet, republished from the Dakota Beacon newspaper.

[51]"Summertime Blues," a 1958 song, was written by Eddie Cochran and Jerry Capehart and has been recorded by Cochran and numerous other singers.

[52]Quoted in Richard N. Rosenfeld, "What Democracy? The case for abolishing the United States Senate," Harper's Magazine, May 2004, p. 38.

[53]For committees as exclusive, major, and minor, see Mark Crain, "The House Dynasty: A Public Choice Analysis," in Gordon S. Jones and John A. Marini, eds., The Imperial Congress: Crisis in the Separation of Powers (New York: Pharos Books, 1988), pp. 188, 191-93. There are only three exclusive committees: Appropriations, Rules, and Ways and Means.

[54]For the relation between committee assignments and voting behavior, I have relied on ibid., pp. 183-203.

III. Serving and Self-Serving—Members' Perks as Access to Excess

EPIGRAPH: I've had a tough time learning how to act like a congressman.
Today I accidentally spent some of my own money.
---Joseph Patrick Kennedy, II, son of Robert and Ethel,
(quoted in <u>Newsweek</u>, February 9, 1987, p. 21).

Some Members are serving in Congress—others are just self-serving.

Senators and Representatives have lavished such substantial perquisites (benefits above regular salary) on themselves that it seems like they have set themselves up as not only the ruling class but as part of the privileged class. That gives them more incentives for Congressional careerism, and it also puts them too far apart from the common people. It's surely more difficult for them to empathize with the challenges faced by ordinary Americans when they inhabit a cocoon of insulating advantages that gives them much of the outlook of the rich.

True, many Members are still somewhat attuned to the commoners because they must care about, or appear to care about, the needs of ordinary folks if they want to be re-elected. And some of the perks are justifiable as helping Members do their jobs.

But what is allegedly justifiable has been increased beyond necessity.   There are two categories of perks. Some are Constitutionally mandated. For example, Members are immune from arrest, except for "treason, felony, and breach of the peace . . . during their attendance at the session of their respective house, and in going to and returning from the same" (see below for this now being largely inapplicable in <u>all</u> criminal cases); also, they may not be held accountable for anything they say in either chamber.

The second category consists of extra-Constitutional benefits Members have awarded themselves. Again, some may be justifiable, and I leave it to you the reader to judge which are and which are not. Here is at least a partial list:

● Reserved parking spaces on Capitol Hill. One book says, "Of all the perquisites available to members and their staffs, none is more precious than parking."[1]

• Special, and free, parking areas at Reagan National Airport and at Dulles International Airport. Someone apparently believed this could be a negative issue if it was too obvious to the public; so in 1994 the signs saying "Reserved Parking, Supreme Court Justices, Members of Congress, Diplomatic Corps" were changed to read "Restricted Parking Authorized Users Only."[2]

• Free parking for Members and some staffers at various airports around the country. See, for example, "Many get airport parking for free," by Lee Davidson, <u>Deseret Morning News</u> (Salt Lake City), 12-28-05, on the Internet.

• Freedom from the consequences of minor lawbreaking in the Capitol's environs. This is a murky area because of Members' Constitutional immunity from arrest except for "treason, felony, and breach of the peace." Yet, in 1908 the Supreme Court ruled (in <u>Williamson v. United States</u>) that Members are not immune from arrest. The Court said, "As all crimes are offenses against the peace, the phrase 'breach of the peace' would seem to extend to all indictable offenses . . . [including] those which are only constructive breaches of the peace of the government, inasmuch as they violate its good order."   And in July 1976 the Justice Department ruled that Members "were no longer immune from arrest by any police force" and that the previous policy of releasing them had been "based on a misinterpretation of the congressional immunity clause in the Constitution."[3] Nevertheless, the general practice of the Capitol Police is that Members shall not be arrested; but if one is collared by an "overzealous" officer, an "unarrest" may quickly follow, the officer may find himself punished, and any police report of the incident may disappear or be falsified.[4]

• Avoidance of D.C. parking fines. One report exposed that 2,912 tickets were issued by D.C. police in 1998 to cars owned by Members, and not one was paid.[5]   The reason is that a D.C. ordinance permits Members of Congress to park most anywhere and at any time if on "official business."   It used to be that the House sergeant-at-arms would deal with D.C. officials to quash Representatives' parking tickets, but in 1991 Speaker Tom Foley ordered that Members would have to make their own arguments that their illegal parking related to official business.[6]

• Freedom from arrest for minor infractions often extends to Members' staffs, as did the former ticket-fixing.[7]

• Lavish pensions. See that chapter of this book.

• <u>Congressional Record</u> editing to make their speeches look better. See the chapter on Falsified Records later in this book.

• Ability to lard the <u>Congressional Record</u> with recognitions or praise of people in a Member's state or district.[8] Such insertions are often presumed to generate votes. Why else would a busy solon go to the time (and taxpayers' expense) of memorializing the 50th wedding anniversary of strangers, the accomplishment of some sports team, or something like the 25th anniversary of the Northeast Council of Senior Citizens, Inc., in Pennsylvania?[9]

• Generous office allowances, both on Capitol Hill and back home, that were often overspent.[10] It wasn't until June 1976 that the House prohibited Members from cashing in for personal use their unused office stationery and travel allowances.[11]

• Representatives, but not Senators, can use their office expense allowances to pay for leasing vehicles in their districts, and to buy gas and insurance for them. The justification, and it can be a good one, is that such leases can save taxpayers' money because if Members drove their own cars in their districts, they would be reimbursed at the IRS mileage rate per mile that's in force in a particular year. But at least three problems plague this program. One is that the vehicles are supposed to be used for official activities unrelated to personal or political business, but there's no checking to make sure that rule is followed. Who believes there is no political component when a Representative drives around his or her district to talk to people? Second, Members could often lease more cheaply from the General Services Administration, but many don't, sometimes because of misunderstanding or ignorance of that alternative. Third, and most troubling, is that many Representatives lease very expensive, low miles-per-gallon vehicles rather than cheaper ones with better gas mileage. A report in 2006 told of SUVs, Cadillacs, Lincolns, and foreign luxury cars being charged to the taxpayers, and that the total costs were well over one million dollars in 2005. Some Members leased two vehicles, and a few leased three.[12]

• Huge staffs to do much of the work.[13] Due to the demands on Members' time, especially the time needed to feed the ravenous campaign-money monster, staffers often do things in the names of lawmakers and often without the solons' knowledge. For instance, they help craft complicated bills, and is there anyone so naïve as to think that a Member sponsoring such a bill is familiar with its every detail? Staff may issue press releases not seen by the Member: "When a press aide calls with 'a statement from the congressman,' we don't tell the readers of the morning paper that the press aide read a statement that the congressman probably never saw and didn't know he made because the aide wrote it."[14] Or a Member may include in a speech favorable comment about something, but a staffer may say the lawmaker cannot comment on it afterwards because "He hasn't been briefed on this yet."[15] Staffers even decide to place so-called "holds," requests that block Senate action, on bills or nominations.[16] One observer offered this insight: "Basically, the staff has emerged as the fourth branch of government."[17]

In recent years there have been a bit over 30,000 people working for Congress. That figure, however, includes several thousand who labor for Congressional agencies such as the Congressional Research Service or who simply keep Capitol Hill running. Subtracting their number leaves somewhat over 11,000 on the personal staffs of the 535 Members, and about 2,200 on committee staffs.[18]

As if there are not enough personal staffers for Members, they can and sometimes do use committee employees for work properly done by personal staffs.[19]

And, of course staffers are improperly used for all sorts of tasks associated with the personal lives of Members: Fetching and paying for coffee, picking up dry cleaning, chauffeuring, walking dogs, etc.[20] Still, Members are not quite so pampered as nineteenth-century British dukes.

As reported by a man who was a "detail" for a year, Members "found a subterranean way to expand their staffs." A "detail" is a person detailed (i.e., assigned) by a federal agency to work on the staff of a Member or of a Congressional committee. Staffs are also augmented by hundreds of "fellows," people paid by private or government entities to serve on staffs. Details and fellows gain insights that increase public understanding of Congress—but they often act as lobbyists for their organizations, improve its ability to deal with Congress, and enable Members to have more people working for them. Congress has been reluctant to provide much information about the extent of the two programs,[21] yet entering "Congressional fellows" (without quotation marks) on Yahoo's Internet search engine in May 2009 generated almost three million hits.

• Campaign use of staffers whose salaries are paid by the taxpayers. House ethics rules place Swiss-cheese limits on this practice but with loopholes so large that evasion is easy. During a campaign lawmakers can send aides to their districts for the ostensible purpose of constituent service, a representational effort for which almost any activity qualifies -- although the rules put "nonofficial, personal, or campaign activities" out of bounds. Taxpayers get to pay for the staffers' round-trip plane fares. After allegedly spending days on official constituent service, staffers can use their free time for campaigning. They can even take vacation time while in the district and use it for re-election work. Gray areas allow Representatives to claim ethical behavior, as when Representative John Conyers, D-MI, sent his aides to hand out "thousands of press releases at district shopping centers and churches" during a campaign and called it "official representational duty." During one election cycle, Conyers spent only one percent of the average spent by other Representatives on salaries of campaign workers. Could it be that he didn't need many such workers because he used so many staffers for re-election work?[22]

That staffers are close to a "fourth branch of government" can be seen in further examples of their power to enact law.
    "In 1997, Jason Alderman, a staffer for the late Rep. Sidney Yates (D-Ill.) had an altercation with a policeman after being stopped for walking his dog without a leash in Meridian Hill Park in Washington, D.C. Alderman later got language added to a House appropriation bill ordering the National Park Service to build a dog run at the park 'as expeditiously as possible.' Rep. Yates was unaware of the earmark until it appeared in a column by the late journalist . . . Jack Anderson."[23]

Here's another: Having failed to pass appropriations for fiscal year 1989 (starting on October 1, 1988) in a timely fashion, Congress sent a continuing resolution (CR) of 1,194 pages to President Reagan to fund government operations. Buried in the verbiage were "cryptic word changes . . . that will allow 20% increases in House and Senate staff salaries. That was only discovered months later, but what was not discovered was how the changes occurred. Speculation identified the culprit as a "daring staffer." One way the salary-hike provision long escaped notice was that it was not listed in the conference report "that is supposed to disclose the meaning and mechanics of all provisions in the budget bill." That was a violation. As result of this trickery—thievery?—top Congressional staffers at that time would have salaries of $86,815, almost as much as four-star generals, the head of NASA, and under secretaries of executive departments.[24]

See further instances in the chapter on Failure to Devote Enough Time to Legislation (a provision for staff to view income-tax returns) and in the chapter on Retaliation (another enactment by a Yates staffer).

Some of these problems with staffers may be as insidious as the medical type of "staph infection."

● Free travel. This consists of three types: (1) A generous amount of money for taxpayer-funded roundtrips back home to schmooze with the voters. See "Travel Allowances" later in this book. (2) Trips paid for from the Member's campaign fund. (3) Taxpayer-funded "fact-finding" trips to foreign countries or U.S. territories, which often involves questionable motives and activities. The former practice of trips paid for by corporations, lobbyists, and wealthy individuals, was prohibited starting in 2007.

A momentary flap occurred in early 2007 with the news that new Speaker of the House Nancy Pelosi, D-CA, would use a large military jet for frequent trips to her San Francisco district. Her apologists argued that Speaker Dennis Hastert had also used a military plane, so why shouldn't she. They usually did not mention that his plane was much smaller, and therefore less costly, than the one Pelosi wanted. According to some reports, the Pelosi plane could seat 42 people, thus providing transportation for supporters and relatives, and would cost from $15,000 to $22,000 an hour to fly. Whether at the lower or higher cost per hour, just one of Pelosi's numerous trips from D.C. to San Francisco and back costs close to her yearly Congressional salary—and one Member estimated the yearly tab at $15 million.[25]

In this book, I argue in numerous places that the media should publicize Members' excesses fairly constantly, not just once in a while; so it's disheartening that stories about Pelosi's plane flared up only to flare out, leaving people who care about wasteful spending wondering if her continuing travels home were lavish or reasonable.

Travel for "fact finding" can be legitimate. We surely want the people who make our laws to base their actions on facts. The old question "Is this trip necessary?" should control Members' actions. The trouble is that it's the Senators and Representatives, with their record of self-serving perks, who make the decision. And who's to say when a trip with an ostensible legislative purpose crosses the line into luxury vacation at taxpayer expense? Well, sometimes it's rather obvious.

Senator Larry Pressler, R-SD, once embarked on a ten-day jaunt to study whether U.S. consulates in European mini-nations should be closed. "When it became clear that he was doing no such thing, Pressler came up with a new reason for his excursion, namely to 'expand his sensitivity to northern Italy.'"[26] Famous humorist Will Rogers looked askance at that sort of thing: "The taxpayers are sending congressmen on expensive trips abroad. It might be worth it except they keep coming back."

Even if a Member pays for a trip abroad for a private purpose such as shopping or vacation "the State Department customarily provides escort and stenographic service, car and chauffeur, baggage transportation, preregistration in hotels, ice and food in the room, plus liquor if requested," and "any sort of overseas purchase except liquor may be sent home duty-free in the capacious diplomatic pouch."[27]

• The franking privilege, which allows Members to send mail without paid postage, the name coming from the Late Latin francus for "free." Franking is free for Members but costly for taxpayers. Congress reimburses the United States Postal Service for the costs, which are tens of millions of dollars every year. The privilege is considered by many to be a good thing because it encourages Members to keep in touch with constituents and inform them about governmental issues.

But because franking has often been abused for electioneering purposes there have been public outcries against it from time to time with resultant proposals for its elimination or restriction. There are now several limitations: One is that Representatives are forbidden from sending mass, franked mailings within 90 days of a primary or general election in which they are running for re-election. The rules are somewhat different for Senators.[28] A mass mailing is defined as 500 or more pieces. Franked mailings of 500 or more must have prior approval of the Franking Commission (formally the House Commission on Congressional Mailing Standards). A Senate committee has franking responsibilities for that chamber.   But some ethically challenged Members skirt the rules by sending out 499 pieces on one topic to one set of zip codes and 499 pieces on another subject to a different set of zip codes. There are even the terms "499 letters" and "499 mail." [29] The electioneering motivation, usually unadmitted, for franked mailings is reflected in the fact that expenditures on franked mail typically double in an election year.[30]

The calendars I used to receive from a now former Representative, of course had nothing to do with informing me about governmental issues—they were just government-funded advertisements for that Member. I finally returned one of his calendars with a note asking him to stop wasting taxpayers' money.

One author wrote that "the frank is the No. 1 weapon in the re-election arsenal."[31] That's not true now, but the frank was formerly quite important. A Texas Representative was quoted as telling an aide this: "We are going to mail, mail, mail and then mail some more. You're going to mail until you run out of ideas. Then you're going to talk to the rest of the staff and mail until they run out of ideas. After that you're going to come to me and mail until *I* run out of ideas. And when that happens, we're going to staple my picture to pages of the goddamn Yellow Book and mail them out, too."[32]

A grotesque abuse occurred in 1989 that revealed some of the rot in Congressional procedures and Members. By large majorities, both houses passed a reform that outlawed franked mass mailings and transferred the saved money to assistance for cocaine-addicted mothers and babies. Because each chamber's bill was somewhat different, a conference committee would make them identical. Sometimes conference committees don't meet until weeks have passed, but this one convened immediately and proceeded to scuttle majority desire. The ban on franked mass mail disappeared as did the proposals that franked mail display a notice that it was paid for with tax money and that Representatives join Senators in admitting how much mail they franked. Also deep-sixed was the reform that would have required Congress to stop spending more on franked mail than had been appropriated.[33] Despite that perversion of the will of House and Senate majorities, the conference report was accepted by roll-over-and-play-dead Members.[34]

The need to eliminate mass mailing using the frank had become apparent because of publicity about just how massive it was. For example, in 1986 Representatives mailed some 800 million franked missives—"12,000 items went out for every incoming letter."[35] The problem continued. In just two days in 1992, Representatives dispatched 58 million franked items.[36] In fiscal year 2006, 89.4% of House mail expenses were for mass mail. At about 27%, the Senate was more circumspect.[37] Due to "reforms that instituted individual Member allowances and public disclosure of individual Member costs" mass mailing by Members is no longer so massive as it was during the 1980s and '90s. In fiscal year 1988 Congress spent $113.4 million on mail; but the cost was down to $34.3 million in FY2006.[38]

Some Congressional mail is not even informative. What good does it do for an American to send a letter with details about a specific issue to a Member of Congress and get a boilerplate reply like this?: "Thank you for contacting my office. I appreciate you taking the time to bring your concerns and suggestions to my attention. The best information I receive comes directly from constituents in . . . [state listed]. Should you have any further questions, concerns, or problems in dealing with any aspect of the federal government, please feel free to call me. My toll free number is . . ."

● Exemptions from some laws that the public must obey, though that's no longer so extreme as formerly. See that chapter of this book.

● Expensive custom-made office furnishings. As one book reported, "The House and the Senate provide members with elaborate furniture made by dozens of congressional cabinetmakers and upholsterers. In the House, the specially made furniture is available to the leadership, officers, and committee chairmen—roughly two hundred members. In the Senate any member can order it. When they leave office—often to become lobbyists— the members can buy some of the furniture at ridiculously low prices. Often, members order wet bars, refrigerators, and custom cabinets and bookcases installed as well."[39] Tom Foley, D-WA, obtained a stereo cabinet, specially made to his specs and said to cost $12,000.[40] Many times, very similar mass-produced products or in-stock furnishings could be purchased far below the cost of the "bespoke" items. The records of the House's chief administrative officer from the mid-1990s revealed these excesses: "A member ordered furniture that cost $17,610 and would have cost $627 from stock. Another member ordered furniture that cost $14,875 and would have cost $626 from a manufacturer. Draperies that would have cost $1,902 from the House inventory cost $12,107. Carpet that should have cost $3,222 was instead made for $9,338. Upholstery available for $248 cost $3,120.35[41] The indulgers and their toadies say that the respect due to the "people's house" demands high quality; but are many of the above excesses anything other than mere self-gratification?

● Very limited ability to buy some of their office furnishings when they leave office. Though this was formerly a privilege that spawned abuses, it is now so hedged with restrictions that it's hardly a worthwhile perk.[42]

● "Hideaways" in the Capitol for the elite of the elite. Tom Foley, Speaker from 1989 to 1995, even created a two-story suite that included a bedroom, full bath, and kitchen.[43] Presumably, it still exists.

● Assistance from agencies in the executive branch. For example, "the U.S. Census Bureau in 1996 contacted all the offices of all the members of Congress and offered them free data to help them 'target your mailing, locate the most advantageous area to hold your town meetings, or profile your congressional district to assess your constituents' needs,'"[44]

● Formerly reduced taxi fares in D.C., but those, admittedly, sometimes helped all riders. The D.C. government, beholden to Congress, maintained a system of zone fares in the capital. Riders who traveled within just one zone paid only the basic initial fare rather than being charged according to a meter that increased the charge even when the cab was waiting at a red light or in a traffic jam. Thus, a Member could taxi to and from a favorite restaurant or bar more cheaply.[45] If you look at a map of the zones, you will see that the zone including the Capitol had its eastern boundary very close to the Capitol but had the opposite boundary very far to the west. Could it have been arranged that way because few Members would go east to a largely residential African-American area but many would go west to the White House, shops, hotels, K-Street lobbyists, and restaurants, so many of which were within that one zone, thus saving the rider the cost of paying a higher fare that would be incurred by traveling in more than one zone?[46]

As of this writing, however, the zone system, so subject to fraud and confusion, has been replaced by the taxi meters common in other large U.S. cities. In 2006 Senator Carl Levin, D-MI, longtime zone critic, added a metering provision to a bill that passed Congress. It required meters in D.C. taxis a year after enactment, unless the mayor decided otherwise. The mayor opted for meters, which prompted a one-day strike by pro-zone cabbies on Halloween 2007.[47]

● Free "taxi-service," even to destinations as distant as Dulles International Airport, in the cars of the Capitol Police, sometimes with sirens blaring and lights flashing.[48]

• Such free rides for Members' friends.[49]

• Free security checking of Members' homes by officers of the Capitol Police. These checks are often done when the Member has left his family at home while away from D.C., and they may involve police trips to the Virginia-Maryland countryside or even Baltimore.[50]

• Capitol Police protection on demand, especially after a threat.[51]

• Use of the Congressional Research Service of the Library of Congress. Of course, that is a necessity for bill drafting, investigations, and constituent service. Still, it's a perk. Will only the naïve imagine that Members use it strictly for official business?

• In addition to cushy offices on Capitol Hill, Members also benefit from reduced-rate use of gymnasiums (recent yearly fee: $240 for Representatives, $480 for Senators). There's even a tennis court inside the Hart Senate Office Building. New ethics rules in 2007 stipulate that no lobbyists, not even those who are former Members, may use House and Senate exercise facilities.[52] The restaurants, dry-cleaning vendors, barber and beauty shops in the Capitol complex now charge rates similar to those found in the general market.[53]

• Quiescent ethics committees that are reluctant to call Members to account. The House's committee has been referred to as "often moribund" and "a subject of frequent and widespread Hill derision."[54] The critically acclaimed, most-recent history of the House reports that the Ethics Committee often soft-pedaled problems due to "the operation of the buddy system or because of the reluctance of individual members to criticize colleagues" and that the Committee "usually wanted a formal, sworn statement of complaint from a member of Congress before investigating any misconduct."[55] Of course, Members usually preferred a problem that might continue on low-heat to one that might boil into public view.

The Mark Foley scandal that helped destroy the Republican majority in the 2006 elections is a recent case. It's now well accepted that warning flags were aflutter long before the story went public and shattered the leadership's complacency in late September 2006. Representative Foley was a Republican from Florida and was well known to be homosexual although he never publicly admitted it. That alone would not have sunk him. After all, the public homosexuality of Representatives Gerry Studds, D-MA, Barney Frank, D-MA, and Jim Kolbe, R-AZ, did not end their House careers, even though one of Studds's sexual unions was with a seventeen-year-old Congressional page.[56] But Foley's errors, which involved sexually explicit emails to underage Congressional pages and which never apparently resulted in physical sexual contact with pages, were exploited by Democrats and the news media as both hypocrisy and child endangerment. He represented the political party that trumpeted its stance in favor of "family values." Furthering the hypocrisy were Foley's co-founding of the Congressional Missing and Exploited Children's Caucus in 1997, his description of pedophiles as "America's most depraved," and his work on the Adam Walsh Child Protection and Safety Act.[57]   Even all that might not have caused terminal damage to many Republicans without the appearance of a cover-up by House leaders.

Speaker Dennis Hastert, R-IL, tried at first for a leadership meeting to coordinate responses to the Foley problem. That appeared too problematical to some of his lieutenants, who knew it would look bad and run afoul of the Ethics Committee investigation that was imminent. Amid a flurry of reports that Hastert, or at least senior members of his staff, had received Foley warnings, some occurring as early as 2002 or 2003, and another claim that the House officer in charge of pages had been advised in 2001 about "creepy" e-mails from Foley to a former page, it increasingly appeared that the House leadership was willing to be inert in the face of an important problem -- at least as long as it involved a Republican rather than a Democrat.[58]

When the House Ethics Committee finally issued its Foley report in December 2006, it, surprise of all surprises, found no evidence of a cover-up, no violation of House rules, and no need for disciplinary action.[59]

• Stand-by medical help is available for Members who pay extra ($503 in 2009).[60] There's a yearly appropriation of legislative-branch money for the Office of the Attending Physician. Additionally, an ambulance waits at the Capitol in case a Member needs emergency transportation. Its use, however, was once denied for one the plebeians who toil for the patricians when a staffer suffered a heart attack on October 10, 1991, and had to wait several minutes for a public ambulance while the one for Members only maintained its lonely vigil nearby. The staffer died.[61]

• Regarding health care for Members there's much misinformation. For correct facts see the report cited in the footnote for this item: "Members of Congress and retired Members are entitled to participate in the Federal Employees Health Benefits Program (FEHBP) under the same rules as other federal employees."[62]

• Members, but not their dependents, "are authorized to receive medical and emergency dental care in military treatment facilities. There is no charge for outpatient care if provided in the National Capital Region."[63]

• Life insurance for current and retired Members is not an abusive perk, because they are only "entitled to participate in the Federal Employees' Group Life Insurance Program (FEGLI) under the same rules and receive the same benefits as other federal employees."[64]

• A special income-tax itemized deduction of $3,000 per year for D.C. housing.[65]

• Representatives, but not Senators, are allowed personal use of frequent flier benefits that accrue from travel paid by taxpayers.[66] When this issue attracted attention in 1995, Speaker Newt Gingrich said his wife and children had flown on his frequent-flier miles and that the practice should continue for a "family friendly" Congress.[67]

• Senators, but not Representatives, are exempt from the law that requires a reduction in Members' pay for each day they are absent without the cause being their own sickness or that of a family member. And because Representatives never have the law enforced against them, all Members get both their absences and their full salaries. When they can ignore their obligation to tend to the people's business and incur no financial penalty, and when they can violate the law with impunity, those are more perks of office. See more about this in the chapter on Part-Time Congress on Full-Time Salary and in the chapter on Violations.

• Members have radio and TV studios, one for each chamber, in the basement of the Capitol. Columnist Jack Anderson reported that a press aide called the Senate's facility "the mother of all perks." Members use the studios to record messages to their constituents. Local radio and TV stations often broadcast the material. Like the franking privilege, this is justified as a beneficial way to educate people about government activities, but it may be most attractive to Members for advertising themselves during re-election campaigns. Yet, they cannot use the studios within sixty days of a contested election. So, one wonders if they simply record their messages before the 60-day restriction begins. They pay nominal fees for their productions, but the taxpayers are stiffed for the equipment and the salaries of workers. The cumulative cost has mounted to tens of millions of dollars.[68]

• Both House and Senate employ professionals to take group photos of Members and constituents together. When a potential voter who's infected with the stardust of "celeprosy" gets such a self-validating souvenir, it's a powerful incentive to vote for the lawmaker who made it possible.[69]

• Formerly, but no longer, Members had the right to free burial in the Congressional Cemetery at 1801 E Street SE.[70] Nevertheless, that graveyard, where 92 Members are buried, cost the taxpayers as recently as 1998, when Congress appropriated $1 million as an endowment to be joined with private funds for maintenance of the cemetery.[71]

• Cigarettes sold in the Capitol have been cheaper than in other parts of D.C. because they've been exempt from federal and D.C. taxes. That halfway ended when a ban on sale of tobacco products in areas controlled by the Senate went into effect on January 1, 2008.[72]

• Members can nominate someone for the Nobel Peace Prize.[73]

• Last, but far from least, Members enjoy methods for using campaign and PAC funds for personal expenses. For example, campaign funds can be spent to pay a Member's legal fees, even those incurred to respond to a House or Senate ethics investigation. The Federal Election Commission said that's permissible.[74] For other examples see the chapters on Leadership PACs and Thief-in-the-Night Pay Raises.

CORRECTIVE SOLUTIONS

Public outrage—or Members' calculation that electoral advantage can be gained from publicized change—seems to work here.

But what if we ask the very people who benefit to abolish the benefit? Will Members be responsive? Foxes guarding hen houses don't make many anti-fox changes. As long as the people who benefit from the rules won't change the bad rules, or only make cosmetic changes, the only corrective is to change the people.

Notes: Chapter III. Serving and Self-Serving—Members' Perks as Access to
                      Excess

[1]Ronald Kessler, Inside Congress: The Shocking Scandals, Corruption, and Abuse of Power Behind the Scenes on Capitol Hill (New York: Pocket Books, 1997), p. 10.

[2]"Old Signs Towed Away; Special Privilege Remains," The New York Times, May 20, 1994, p. A16.

[3]Kessler, Inside Congress, pp. 21, 26, 191.

[4]Ibid., pp. 15-21.

[5]Internet search, 1-26-07, under the topic "Congressional immunity from arrest," subtopic "pedantic geriatrics."

[6]David E. Rosenbaum, "Speaker Orders End to Congressional Ticket-Fixing," The New York Times, October 9, 1991, p. A14.

[7]Kessler, Inside Congress, pp. 14, 16, 20, 26.

[8]Milton Gwirtzman, "Congress's Daily Advertisement for Itself," The Wall Street Journal, October 8, 1992, p. A14.

[9]For the latter see Congressional Record, daily edition, September 5, 1997, p. E1677.

[10]Kessler, Inside Congress, pp. 154-55.

[11]Robert V. Remini, The House: The History of the House of Representatives (New York: Collins, a division of HarperCollins; Smithsonian Books, 2006), p. 448, citing Congressional Quarterly Almanac . . . 1976 (Washington: Congressional Quarterly, 1977), p. 26.

[12]"Lawmakers run up $1 million in car leases paid by public," Knight Ridder News, Billings Gazette, March 12, 2006, p. 3A.

[13]See Kessler, Inside Congress, p. 80.

[14]Susan Trausch, It Came From the Swamp: Your Federal Government at Work (Boston: Houghton Mifflin, 1986), p. 107.

[15]Trausch, It Came From the Swamp, p. 107.

[16]Barbara Sinclair, "The New World of U.S. Senators," in Lawrence C. Dodd and Bruce I. Oppenheimer, eds., Congress Reconsidered, 8th edition (Washington: CQ Press, 2005), p. 12. For more on holds, see below in the chapter "Holding" the Senate Hostage.

[17]David Brock, "A Regal Battle to Reign," part of cover story on "The Imperial Congress," Insight, August 10, 1987, p. 12, quoting George Carver.

[18]Winslow T. Wheeler, The Wastrels of Defense: How Congress Sabotages U.S. Security (Annapolis: Naval Institute Press, 2004), p. 144. See ibid., pp. 158-59, for "Cutting Staff Augments Partisanship."

[19]Ibid., p. 167.   House Rule X, clause 9, 110th Congress, deals with committee staff and says staff "may not be assigned a duty other than one pertaining to committee business" except for "staff designated by a committee as 'associate' or 'shared' staff"; on this see also Rule XXIII, clause 8(b). Senate rules apparently do not deal with such issues.

[20]Wheeler, Wastrels of Defense, pp. 170-72.

[21]Ibid., pp. 150-53. The quoted phrase is on p. 150.

[22]"Loopholes allow lawmakers to use aides in campaigns," Billings Gazette, July 18, 1993, p. 5A; the story came from Knight-Ridder News Service. With more campaign money and public exposure, Senators are more careful than Representatives about avoiding the questionable practice; ibid.
  In 1980 most of Senator Javits' personal staff and some committee staff volunteered to go to New York City to try to verify enough signatures for him to run as the candidate of a different party after losing in the Republican primary; Wheeler, Wastrels of Defense, p. 174. See also ibid., pp. 177-78, 243.

[23]Tom Finnigan, All About Pork: The Abuse of Earmarks and the Needed Reforms (Washington: Citizens Against Government Waste, Policy Briefing Series, May 3, 2006), p. 8.

[24]"Congre$$ional Staff Whodunit," The Wall Street Journal, February 19, 1988: p. 18.

[25]Estimate made by Representative Dan Burton, R-IN, of money "spent for one person to fly back and forth to California"; Congressional Record, daily edition, February 8, 2007, p. 1376. See also ibid., February 7, 2007, p. H1312; ibid., pp. H1350. H1370,

H1372; various television programs and Carl Hulse, "Speaker's Plane Becomes a Point of Criticism," The New York Times, February 9, 2007, p. A16; Susan Ferrechio, "House Republicans Blast Pelosi Over Request for Larger Airplane," CQ Weekly, February 12, 2007, p. 492. The latter source says, "Guidelines provided by the Pentagon say Pelosi could be accompanied by family members, provided they pay the government coach fare."

[26]Michael Hirschorn, "Mr. Stupid Goes To Washington," Spy, February 1989, p. 86.

[27]Warren Weaver, Jr., Both Your Houses: The Truth About Congress (New York: Praeger Publishers, 1972), p. 223.

[28]Matthew Eric Glassman, "Franking Privilege: Historical Development and Options for Change," CRS Report for Congress, December 5, 2007, p. CRS-20. See this source, passim, for other restrictions.

[29]For "499 letters" and "499 mail" see various entries on the Internet, including Double-Tongued Dictionary; and David Postman, "Taxpayers fund election season mail," posted on November 3, 2006. For the reform leading to this dodge, see Glassman, "Franking Privilege," pp. CRS-6 & 7.

[30]Remini, The House, p. 502.

[31]Gordon S. Jones, "Where Petty Tyrants Rule," The Wall Street Journal, May 26, 1992, p. A14.

[32]John L. Jackley, Hill Rat: Blowing the Lid Off Congress (Washington: Regnery Gateway, 1992), p. 47.

[33]"Frank Babies," The Wall Street Journal, September 27, 1989, p. A22.

[34]Chuck Alston and Janet Hook, "House Does an About-Face To Save Its Newsletters," Congressional Quarterly Weekly Report, September 30, 1989, p. 2531.

[35]"Home Team Shutout," The Wall Street Journal, September 6, 1988, p. 30.

[36]"Politicians Panic," The Wall Street Journal, June 2, 1992, p. A14.

[37]Glassman, "Franking Privilege," p. CRS-16.

[38]Ibid., p. CRS-14. For reforms from 1986 onward see ibid., pp. CRS-7 through CRS-9.

[39]Kessler, Inside Congress, pp. 165-66.

[40]Ibid., p. 166.

[41]Ibid., p. 168.

[42]For the former alleged abuses see ibid., pp. 167-68. Current practice is mentioned in information I obtained through Representative Dennis Rehberg: memorandum to Rehberg from Matthew E. Glassman, "Congressional Perquisites: Answers to Specific Questions," Congressional Research Service, February 12, 2008. See also Mildred Amer, "Selected Privileges and Courtesies Extended to Departing and Former Senators," CRS Report for Congress, updated August 29, 2006, pp. CRS-2 and CRS-3; Mildred Amer, "Selected Privileges and Courtesies Extended to Departing and Former Members of the House of Representatives," CRS Report for Congress, updated August 29, 2006, pp. CRS-2 and CRS-3.

At times in the past, some of the furniture was simply taken away as "the result of some sticky finger work by senators and their aides" when "there were no rules prohibiting taking furniture"; Paul Bedard, "Washington Whispers: Wanted: Pilfered Senate Stuff," U.S. News & World Report, October 13-20, 2008, p. 16.

[43]Kessler, Inside Congress, p. 166.

[44]James Bovard, Attention Deficit Democracy (New York: Palgrave Macmillan, 2005), p. 184.

[45]Weaver, Both Your Houses, p. 223.

[46]You can look at the zone map on the Internet by accessing Official Tourism Site of Washington, DC—Getting Around.

[47]See Public Law 109-356, Section 105; "At Last, the Meter Starts Running," U.S. News & World Report, October 29, 2007, p. 18; Sue Anne Pressley Montes, "Report Adds to Debate Over Putting Meters in D.C. Cabs," The Washington Post, July 28, 2007, p. B1; Sarah Karush, "DC Taxi Drivers Hold One-Day Strike," Associated Press, October 31, 2007, available on the Internet.

[48]Kessler, Inside Congress, pp. 193-95, 207.

[49]Ibid., p. 195.

[50]Ibid., pp. 195-96, 206.

[51]Ibid., p. 196.

[52]Jack Maskell, Memorandum: "Lobbying and Ethics Rules Changes in the 110th Congress," Congressional Research Service, September 24, 2007, p. CRS-13, under "Other."

[53]Information I obtained through Representative Dennis Rehberg: memorandum to Rehberg from Matthew E. Glassman, "Congressional Perquisites: Answers to Specific Questions," Congressional Research Service, February 12, 2008.

[54]Gail Sheehy and Judy Bachrach, "Don't Ask . . . Don't E-Mail," Vanity Fair, January 2007, p. 154.

[55]Remini, The House, p. 448.

[56]Philip Terzian, "A New Page in an Old Book," The Weekly Standard, October 16, 2006, p. 10; "Sexually Explicit Communications Rock Congress," The Wall Street Journal, October 7, 2006, p. A5.

[57]Sheehy and Bachrach, Vanity Fair, January 2007, p. 151.

[58]David Rogers, "House Aide's Resignation Adds To Focus on Timing of Warnings," The Wall Street Journal, October 5, 2006, p. A4; "Foley's e-mails were at issue in 2001," AP story in Billings Gazette, October 11, 2006, p. 3A; Devlin Barrett, Associated Press Writer, "Aide: Hastert's office told about Foley 3 years ago," The Montana Standard, October 5, 2006, p. B8; Christopher Hitchens, "Foley Loaded," The Wall Street Journal, October 16, 2006, p. A14.

[59]"The Foley Report," The Wall Street Journal, December 11, 2006, p. A18.

[60]Information I obtained through Representative Dennis Rehberg: memorandum to Rehberg from Matthew E. Glassman, "Congressional Perquisites: Answers to Specific Questions," Congressional Research Service, February 12, 2008.

[61]Jackley, Hill Rat, p. 4.

[62]Barbara English, "Health Benefits for Members of Congress," CRS Report for Congress, updated September 25, 2007. The quotation is on p. [CRS-1].

[63]Ibid., p. CRS-5.

[64]Information I obtained through Representative Dennis Rehberg: memorandum to Rehberg from Matthew E. Glassman, "Congressional Perquisites: Answers to Specific Questions," Congressional Research Service, February 12, 2008.

[65]Ralph Nader, Stop the Salary Grab, "The Facts About Congressional Pay," 1988, and several more current sources found on the Internet under Congressional Perks.

[66]Several sources on the Internet under Congressional Perks.

[67]Richard Sammon, "GOP Counts a 'Contract' Win As Compliance Bill Clears," Congressional Quarterly Weekly Report, January 21, 1995, p. 197.

[68]Jack Anderson and Michael Binstein, "Hill Studios Called 'Mother of All Perks', The Washington Post, June 11, 1992, p. C11. See also Joseph S. Clark, Congress: The Sapless Branch (Westport, CT: Greenwood Press, 1964), p. 77, and Eric Felten, The Ruling Class: Inside the Imperial Congress, abridged edition (Washington: U.S. Congress Assessment Project, Heritage Foundation, 1993), p. 26.

[69] Clifford Barnhart, "Using the Rules for Abuse," in Gordon S. Jones and John A. Marini, eds., The Imperial Congress: Crisis in the Separation of Powers (New York: Pharos Books, 1988), p. 215.

[70]Kessler, Inside Congress, p. 72.

[71]Jeffrey L. Katz, "CBO, Consultants and Cemetery Enliven Subcommittee Debate Over House Budget Increase," CQ Weekly, June 13, 1998, p. 1603; Carroll J. Doherty, "Senate Manages To Avoid Controversy on Spending Bill For Legislative Branch," ibid., July 25, 1998, p. 2003; Rebecca Adams, "Legislative Branch Bill Completed," ibid., September 19, 1998, p. 2481.

[72]Susan Davis, "Senate Not Blowing Smoke," The Wall Street Journal, November 13, 2007, p. A10.

[73]Robert Wexler with David Fisher, Fire-Breathing Liberal (New York: Thomas Dunne Books, an imprint of St. Martin's Press, 2008), p. 142.

[74]Parade magazine (Sunday newspaper insert), October 5, 2008, p. 6.

IV. Ethics

EPIGRAPH: There comes a time when every man must learn to rise
above principle.
---Representative Dan Flood, quoted in Mark J. Green,
Who Runs Congress?, revised edition (New York:
Bantam/Grossman, 1975), p. 252.

Representative Patricia Schroeder, D-CO, used this joke: "Please don't tell my mother I am a politician. She thinks I am a prostitute."[1]   Low esteem is reinforced by the ethical nudity of some Members.

You can find lists of oxymorons, those phrases that contain two contradictory words, as in "jumbo shrimp" and "pretty ugly." One that is often included is "Congressional ethics," and it's not just cynics who get a chuckle from that. The ethics problems of Congress became so notorious that many members of the 110th Congress, which began in January 2007, were on record as pledging beneficial reform.

With the ethical lapses of some Members, Congress may merely mirror the larger society, where there's too much white-collar crime, boundary-pushing, and excusing of illegalities. And, of course, there's violent crime as well. Despite all those transgressive activities, the U.S. has one of the world's more well-ordered, law-abiding societies. But Americans who tread the straight and narrow often resent the actions and the frequent lack of adequate punishment of those who don't.

Situational ethics are often decried but may sometimes be appropriate. For instance, our laws provide punishments for killing another human being—except in such cases as justifiable homicide, or an execution carried out by the government, or a murder committed by someone legally insane, or lethal action during a military campaign. The trouble with situational ethics is that some individuals may think they can decide which situations fall under the strictures of the law. And it does not help when students are taught, as a University of Washington professor proclaimed on television, that "You have to find your own ethical boundaries."[2] That's what criminals do.

But isn't Congress supposed to lead us to a better world? Its Members' lapses should not be excused as norms. Congress must set a higher standard.

It allegedly has mechanisms to define its higher guidance, to prevent ethical transgressions, and to punish those Members whom the prohibitions did not prohibit. Each chamber has an ethics committee. In the House it was the Committee on Standards of Official Conduct until renamed the Committee on Ethics at the start of the 112th Congress (January 2011), in the Senate the Select Committee on Ethics. Trouble is, all too often those bodies give merely the appearance of self-policing while actually ignoring or soft-pedaling possible wrongdoing. That reluctance to act flows largely from at least three factors: (1) Members' exaggerated respect for each other, at least on the surface, and (2) protection of Congress's reputation from proof, even from charges, that it may be affected or infected by bad Members, and (3) unwillingness to encourage quick resort to investigations that could become precedents for prying into the activities of Members not then under any cloud of suspicion.

The 1980s and '90s saw numerous instances of sexual harassment and extramarital affairs by a few Senators, but as one book says, "Senators regularly instructed the nation on moral values. Their own lives operated by a different standard. If pressed about rumors of sexual harassment, male senators responded that every senator was responsible to the voters. It was not up to the members to enforce rules for proper behavior. There was, it is true, an Ethics Committee, but it was a toothless body."[3] That's not entirely fair. Although the two ethics committees are reluctant to act, they will do so when behavior becomes too outrageous—or too public. For example, Robert Packwood, D-OR, embroiled in sexual molestation and other charges, resigned from the Senate in September 1995 following the unanimous expulsion recommendation by the Ethics Committee.

In 1978 Congress passed the Ethics in Government Act requiring disclosure of Members' personal finances to assure the public that Members did not have conflicts of interest between their own money and their actions as keepers of the public trust. That law only partially accomplishes its purpose. It does not require reporting of the value of Members' residences, and it allows nonspecific reporting and such broad ranges of value for Members' assets that concerned citizens get only a vague, and often misleading, idea of their lawmakers' financial interests. Take, for example, Max Baucus, who was a U.S. Representative from January 1975 to December 1978 and has been a U.S. Senator since December 1978 and comes from a wealthy family. His financial disclosure for the year 2005 listed assets worth in total from $30,000 to $284,000. Can it really be true that after decades of highly paid government service and an affluent background, his assets were that minimal? His disclosure for 2010 shows a net worth of $160,000! Can it really be true that his total assets are worth <u>less than his yearly salary</u>? Perhaps the partial explanation is that Members are not required to list the value of their primary residence nor any assets in a "qualified blind trust." However, information about the home and whether the Member has such a trust is not readily available. Thus, the Baucus example shows that the financial reporting system is grossly flawed. It's a preposterous system that allows a Senator who is probably a millionaire to show a net worth that's less than his yearly pay.   There should be greater specificity, narrower ranges, and no major assets exempt from reporting.[4]

Stock and bond trading based on inside information is illegal for Americans—except for Members of Congress. See below in the chapter on Congressional Exemptions. Not only can Members use knowledge of pending legislative actions for their own enrichment, they can provide such information to their big contributors. For example, Representative Ron Coleman, D-TX, had the "powerful Kastrin family of El Paso" as important financial backers, and his former press secretary reported that "he regularly provided them with detailed inside accounts of Appropriations Committee projects that could affect their business interests."[5]

For most of its existence Congress was willing to tolerate many conflicts of interest and outright influence peddling by Members. Only an occasional indiscretion merited punishment, usually after other Members became fearful of being singed by a firestorm of negative publicity enveloping a colleague. Neither chamber had an ethics committee until 1964, when the Senate established its Select Committee on Standards and Conduct, renamed the Select Committee on Ethics in 1977. Despite the opposition of Speaker John McCormack, in 1966 the House established the Select Committee on Standards and Conduct, later renamed and commonly referred to as the Ethics Committee.[6]

As explained later by Richard Bolling, D-MO, then one of the most prominent Members of the House, McCormack was honest, but
> "the issue simply did not appear relevant to him in a political and a general moral sense. McCormack represented a different age in American urban politics. The old-time member was a product of ethnically saturated politics; special favors, special influence, and the use of one's political power to forward one's personal affairs were all part of a politician's survival-and-advancement kit . . . Such members took a rather casual attitude toward . . . conflicts of interest, collecting and spending of campaign funds, and the use of public funds for semiprivate or private purposes. It wasn't that any of these men were necessarily personally dishonest, but they were not their brother's keeper, either."[7]

In that last clause, Bolling apparently forgot his report that the Speaker was hostile to John F. Kennedy for a while because Kennedy had refused to sign a petition to President Truman asking a pardon for McCormack's "brother" and former Representative James Michael Curley, a convicted and imprisoned felon.[8]

Of course, different ethical standards have often existed in different times. As Stanford law professor Herbert L. Packer wrote, "We can have as much or as little crime as we please, depending on what we choose to count as criminal."[9] Many readers will agree that we have raised our concepts of ethical behavior for Members of Congress since McCormack's time.

Even after the House decided in 1966 to have a permanent apparatus to hold Members to new concepts of integrity, its ethics panel took no action against any Representative until 1972, showing reluctance to venture into an arena where the public might discern additional perpetrators.[10]

The same traditions and rules that require civility among and between Members worked against bringing accusations of ethics transgressions. A recent book refers to the "unwritten truce that had kept any lawmaker from bringing ethics cases to the committee against any other lawmaker."[11] It also reported that in the 109th Congress, Democrats on the House ethics panel boycotted it for months so it could not organize or do anything.[12] That same book refers to "an unwillingness to meet their Constitutional responsibility to police the conduct of members of Congress with a strong and independent ethics process."[13]

There's a type of bribery that seldom gets publicity. It's the common practice of leaders of legislative bodies providing a member with some provision in a bill in exchange for his or her vote on something else. In 2005, for instance, the Republican leadership used earmarks in a transportation bill to "buy" votes for the Central American Free Trade Agreement.[14] The long-used phrase for such exchanges is "logrolling." Its defenders might prefer the term "legitimate compromise." Such reciprocity can hardly be eliminated from the legislative process, and, indeed, it is often legitimate, especially when those on opposite sides of some issue mutually abandon some of their extreme demands. It's less valid, however, when unrelated benefits are bargained and exchanged.

Senator Joseph Clark, D-PA, explained, "The point is that Congress is suspicious of the ethics and standards of members of the executive branch and often seems careless of its own."[15]

It was once possible for Members to fatten their family income by employing their spouses or other near relatives in their Washington, district, or state offices. But that was prohibited by the federal anti-nepotism law of 1967.[16] A House rule instituted in January 2001 dictates that a Representative "may not retain his spouse in a paid position" and that "an employee of the House may not accept compensation for work for a committee on which his spouse serves as a member."[17] The House rule expanded upon the federal law. But it relates to employees in Capitol and district offices and in House committees, not to campaign employment. The Senate has apparently felt no need to supplement federal law with a rule of its own.

Those nepotism restrictions are just fine but leave other areas of personnel abuse untouched. So far, nothing prevents spouses and other near relatives of Members from being paid as campaign workers. In July 2007 the House passed a bill to prevent Congressional spouses from receiving pay for campaign work and to provide for disclosure of campaign payments to other family members.[18] By mid-2008, however, the bill had not passed the Senate, where the black hole of self-interest exerted such pull that chances of its escape were minimal.[19] In these days of the virtually permanent campaign, relatives have an almost unending opportunity for family enrichment from campaign funds. A liberal group called Citizens for Responsibility and Ethics in Washington (CREW) reported in June 2007 that 72 U.S. Representatives paid almost $3.5 million of campaign money to relatives during the election cycles of 2001-2006. Adding payments to a Member's own company and to relatives' businesses and employers pushed the amount up to $5.1 million. In the most extreme case, Zoe Lofgren, D-CA, directed

$285,481 to one of her husband's companies and $62,705 to another. Bob Filner, D-CA, paid his wife's firm $249,004. Gary Miller, R-CA, paid his own company $124,725. Buck McKeon, R-CA, paid his wife $263,168. What was it about California that caused ten of the top twenty payers to represent that state?

In some eyebrow-raising instances, campaigns paid Members' school children. Chris Cannon, R-UT, paid six of his eight kids. Although House rules prohibit Members from employing relatives in their Congressional offices, the campaign loophole permits the same sort of enrichment.[20]

No doubt many relatives worked hard for the money. Who knows, however, if some had no-show jobs or did very little. Whatever the work actually done, the practice is such a questionable way for Members to increase family income that some reformers want restrictions on it.

And many Members' spouses work as lobbyists. What lobbying firm would not have a Member's spouse on its payroll because of concerns about undue influence? Undue influence is exactly what they seek. Of fifty-eight Senate spouses with earned income in 2005, four were registered lobbyists. Others served on corporate boards, as self-employed consultants, in law firms, and in other capacities that might touch on Congress.[21] An occasional Representative's spouse splashes into the news. The lead sentence of a Wall Street Journal article says this: "The wife of Nevada Gov. Jim Gibbons was hired as a consultant to a defense contractor at the same time that her husband, who was then a member of Congress, helped the company get funding for a no-bid federal contract."[22]

Furthermore, nothing prevents former staffers from becoming lobbyists. Nothing prevents former lobbyists from becoming staffers. Nothing prevents relatives of staffers from being lobbyists or from otherwise using their family ties to influence legislation.

And former lawmakers hardly feel constrained by the federal law that requires Senators to wait two years after their terms have ended before lobbying Congress, and that applies a one-year wait to Representatives. Perhaps they don't even feel the need for a wink and a nudge as they skirt that law, because it's legal for them to become paid members of lobbying firms immediately. Many do that. Defeat for re-election does not mean that their gravy train stops running. In fact, their incomes may increase enormously from their new "K-Street" employment. And who's to say that they are violating that law if they discuss legislation with a Member over dinner or during a golf outing? As Matt Kelley wrote in USA Today, "The cozy relationships between lawmakers and lobbyists that embarrassed Congress and cost some lawmakers re-election haven't stopped the revolving door between Capitol Hill and the lobbying industry that seeks to influence legislation."[23] Also, it's legal for former Members to immediately "lobby executive branch officials and direct a firm's congressional lobbying efforts."[24]

Ask yourself what sort of cozy relationship exists when a lawmaker's former Congressional aide becomes a highly paid lobbyist and is also a paid campaign official for that same solon.[25] Could there be any improper influence or quid pro quo? Senator Robert Bennett, R-UT, in another we-think-you're-gullible statement, alleged that "the idea of the revolving door is vastly overrated."[26] And, of course, the door revolves in two directions, with many former lobbyists vaulting onto the Congressional payroll as staffers for Members and committees. A person does not have to come from a lobbying firm to have been a lobbyist, the latter term being defined simply as "a person who tries to influence legislation or administrative decisions on behalf of a special interest."[27] Thus, top corporate executives often lobby—and some of them depart from the private sector to become Congressional staffers.[28]

There's another set of lobbyists in Washington: Members of Congress. As a lobbyist, explained, "The dirty little secret is that the biggest lobby in town is members of Congress lobbying us."[29]   Knowing they can't successfully battle an opponent at re-election time without piles of "warbucks," they lobby for campaign contributions. Mark Green, an experienced and acute observer, explained that "the 'money primary' weeds out good candidates and good incumbents. Potential candidates know they have to succeed not in one but two elections: the first, in which contributors 'vote' with their dollars, comes long before constituents have their say. And if you don't win round one financially, you might as well not bother with round two."[30] Senators, Representatives, and staffers spend so much time beseeching people for money that it's small wonder they don't devote enough time to their legislative duties. In Washington, when not actually legislating, they are likely making money calls on the phone or attending a fund raiser.

Many Members hate the money chase. They see it as a debasing time thief. Former Senator and Vice President Hubert Humphrey said, "Campaigning financing is a curse. It's the most disgusting, demeaning, disenchanting, debilitating experience of a politician's life. It's stinky, it's lousy. I just can't tell you how much I hate it."[31]

Another aspect of Members' unceasing fundathon is the damage done to the concept of independent, impartial voting on legislation. Because a "wrong" decision may eliminate some potential contributions, lawmakers will sometimes shy away from a controversial vote.[32] Members "are human calculators who can weigh how much money every vote will cost or gain them."[33] Another analysis, arguably too extreme, stated that "Constitutional checks and balances no longer have meaning; the only checks that count are the ones you can cash."[34]

Almost gone—we think—are the days when Senators and Representatives were bribed with bundles of cash.[35] But the recent venal activities of such as the imprisoned Randy Cunningham were close to the bad old ways. However, there is a sufficiency of other methods for bribing Members. See the bribery chapters later in this book.

The longtime practice of Members accepting free meals from lobbyists and rich people finally raised enough ethical questions that a 2007 law restricted the practice (see last "bullet" item below). The unreformed attitude was so rotten that a lobbyist said, "It's not unusual for a member to call up and say, 'I'm planning to go to the Capital Grille for dinner. Do you want to come by for a drink and pick up the check?'"[36]

How ethical is it for Congress to require that most executive branch units must return to the Treasury money not spent at the end of each fiscal year, yet not apply that rule to itself? Any unspent money appropriated to Congress gushes into discretionary accounts. The House has such a slush fund jointly controlled exclusively by the Speaker and the chair of the Appropriations Committee. There's virtually no oversight of what they do with the money. In 1991, Speaker Tom Foley's chief-of-staff, his wife Heather (!!), used $314,000 to create in the Capitol a so-called policy office, complete with kitchen and bathrooms, for Democrats. There wasn't unused space available, so the beneficial agency providing the public with copies of bills was booted out and relocated to a "distant annex building."[37]

Democrats took control of both houses of Congress in January 2007 with much braying about ethics reforms. And to the uninitiated they've seemed to live up to the hype. There was somewhat more early publicity about earmarks. Members had to certify that neither they nor their families had a financial interest in any earmark they proposed. Lobbyists who enhance their influence by bundling small campaign contributions into a single donation had to disclose any six-month amount of $15,000 or more. Senators had to pay charter prices for rides on private jets; Representatives could not take such trips. Ex-Senators had to wait two years, up from the previous one year, before directly lobbying anyone in the Senate. Gifts from lobbyists were prohibited. One might ask if banning a gift such as a lunch is an admission that Members can be bought with a free meal, but, no, it's more like trying to address public concern.

One of the ethics rules adopted by the House in January 2007 exhibited ineptitude. It barred Members from using "personal funds, official funds, or campaign funds for a flight on a non-governmental airplane that is not licensed by the Federal Aviation Administration to operate for compensation or hire." It did not occur to the rule makers that they had just barred Members from flying their own planes. After some House aviators complained, common sense reappeared in a rule change.[38]

In a typical effort to exaggerate and put the best face on a flawed product, Congress called its ethics-reform bill the "Honest Leadership and Open Government Act of 2007." Although it does include some mincing little forward steps, it's hardly the sort of progress people expected when hearing Democrats' promises about "draining the swamp" and ending the Republicans' "culture of corruption."

• The requirement for early publicity about earmarks will only occur if "technically feasible." The Senate's Majority Leader, rather than the Senate parliamentarian (as in an early version), gets the power to rule that bills coming to the floor have or have not met disclosure requirements. Members can still insert earmarks from which they will receive a financial windfall. The provision barring earmark trading for Members' votes did not make it into the final bill. As The Wall Street Journal reported, "The bill includes a sham earmark reform provision that falls well short of what Democrats campaigned for last year, and short of what each house passed earlier this year before the watered-down version came out of nowhere."[39] The elimination of stronger provisions flowed partly from the desire "to retain some flexibility to help move spending bills forward."[40] But because earmarks are so important to Members' re-election efforts, you can be sure that such flexibility was not the only reason.

The House, however, modified its rules at the start of the 110th Congress to supposedly prohibit earmark trading by Representatives.[41]

• Will voters defeat an incumbent because they learn that a lobbyist bundled some small campaign contributions. You know that the answer is almost always "No." The real reform would be publicly financed campaigns.

• No one other than lobbyists will have to report any bundling of small campaign contributions into more influential largesse.

• The two-year deferral for ex-Senators to directly lobby those still serving allows all sorts of indirect lobbying. The law does not change the existing requirement that Representatives have to wait one year. Much better would be an absolute prohibition for two years on a former Member, whether from the House or the Senate, being an employee or volunteer in a lobbying firm. An earlier Senate version of the bill included a two-year ban on all lobbying by former Members.

• The ban on free meals from lobbyists is largely a fake reform because that freebie is OK as long as it's labeled "campaign event."[42]

CORRECTIVE SOLUTIONS

Here again public outrage fueled by large doses of publicity works best. With the members of ethics committees in both chambers being reluctant to act against colleagues in all but the most extreme cases, and with law enforcement officials sometimes facing separation of powers constraints, popular pressure looks like the final resort. Such pressure could also work toward term limits and public financing of campaigns.

On March 11, 2008, the House created an outside ethics panel called Office of Congressional Ethics. Its birth was attended by partisan conflict about whether such a body was necessary or desirable. Opponents, largely Republicans, argued that the House should police itself and that the new entity just added an unneeded layer of bureaucracy.

The new panel has six members, none of whom can be current Representatives, federal employees, or lobbyists. They are chosen jointly by the Speaker and Minority Leader. Agreement came in late July on who the six would be. The most well-known was Porter Goss, former Member and CIA Director. As of this writing (October 2011), the OCE has made a few referrals to the House.[43]

With the limited publicity surrounding this creation, it may be questionable whether it's just window dressing to give a false appearance of House action. Even if it's intended that the OCE do real work, the panel may find its job difficult because of the feeling of many Representatives against any outside infringement on the rights of the House and its Members.[44]

As mentioned earlier in this chapter, the financial reporting system for Members' assets is deficient. There should be greater specificity, narrower ranges, and no major assets exempt from reporting.

Notes: Chapter IV. Ethics

[1]Walter L. Updegrave, "What Congress Really Costs You: $2.8 Billion a Year," Money, August 1992, p. 129. In a similar vein, Mary Norton, Representative from New Jersey, 1925-1951, said "I am no lady, I'm a Member of Congress"; Office of History and Preservation, Office of the Clerk, U.S. House of Representatives, Women in Congress, 1917-2006 (Washington: U.S. Government Printing Office, 2006), p. 61

[2]"Dateline NBC," April 16, 2004. It was a business teacher, and she was dealing with the business lessons of the TV program "The Apprentice."

[3]Lewis L. Gould, The Most Exclusive Club: A History of the Modern United States Senate (New York: Basic Books, 2005), p. 298.

[4]Financial disclosure reports and news stories about them are available on the Internet. For the Ethics in Government Act of 1978, see Public Law 95-521, 92 Stat. 1824; but see also its amendments, listed in Title 2, U.S. Code, Sections 701 to 709, 2006 edition.
    A bill to require that financial disclosures reveal the value of all personal residences and mortgage information about them was introduced in the House in 2009 (see Congressional Record, daily edition, April 27, 2009, p. H4839), but it did not pass. It seems Members did want to go beyond even that.

[5]John L. Jackley, Hill Rat: Blowing the Lid Off Congress (Washington: Regnery Gateway, 1992), p. 261.

[6]Congressional Record, permanent edition, October 19, 1966, pp. 27713-30 and D593; Robert V. Remini, The House: The History of the House of Representatives (New York: Collins, a division of HarperCollins; Smithsonian Books, 2006), p. 425. The Internet encyclopedia Wikipedia, a useful source that often must be relied upon with care, says the Committee's history goes back to January 30, 1798, when it dealt with an accusation against Representative Thomas Lyon; but it appears to me that that statement is either an outright error or is meant in the generic sense of an ethics action by the House, rather than by a permanent House committee.

[7]Richard Bolling, Power in the House (New York: E. P. Dutton & Co., 1968), pp. 246-47.

[8]Bolling, Power in the House, p. 205.

[9]In The Limits of the Criminal Sanction, quoted in Time, June 30, 1975, cover story, "The Crime Wave," p. 18.

[10]That first action, other than two "preliminary investigations" [Mark J. Green, Who Runs Congress?, revised edition (New York: Bantam/Grossman, 1975), p. 196], was an investigation of John Dowdy, D-TX, and a recommendation that he be barred from House voting and from committee activities. Due to a negative response from the Rules Committee, the matter never reached the floor of the House. Remini, The House, p. 425.
Before Dowdy was eventually convicted of several felonies (December 1971), his trial was interrupted several times due to his ill health. One delay flowed from a finding by the Bethesda Naval Hospital that he was "unable to consult rationally with counsel in his own defense"; so he "repaired to Congress, presumably a less taxing environment, where he resumed his seat and presided over a D.C. Education subcommittee hearing"; Green, Who Runs Congress?, revised edition, p. 183.

[11]Thomas E. Mann and Norman J. Ornstein, The Broken Branch: How Congress Is Failing America and How to Get It Back on Track (New York: Oxford University Press, 2006), p. 189.

[12]Ibid., p. 191. They did that because chairman "Doc" Hastings (R-WA) "announced that he was going to employ his own personal staffer to help lead the committee staff—violating the long-standing procedure that all staff on the committee were bipartisan"; ibid.

[13]Ibid., p. 215.

[14]Ibid., p. 178.

[15]Joseph S. Clark, Congress: The Sapless Branch (Westport, CT: Greenwood Press, 1964), p. 207.

[16]Title 5, U.S. Code, Section 3110, 2000 edition.

[17]That was done by the 107th Congress. See House Rule XXIII, clause 8(c)(1) and (2), 110th Congress. The rule lists an exception for spouses "whose pertinent employment predates the One Hundred Seventh Congress."

[18]It was H.R. 2630; see Congressional Record, daily edition, July 23, 2007, pp. H8230-34.

[19]See "Senate Kin and the Campaign Kitty," The New York Times, February 29, 2008, p. A22. Citizens for Responsibility and Ethics in Washington (CREW) reported that during 2001-2006 Senator Barbara Boxer, D-CA, paid $320,409.17 to her son Douglas from campaign donations; during that same time, campaign accounts of Senator Mike Enzi, R-WY, paid his daughter-in-law $306,718.18; Shailagh Murray, "Senators Diverting Campaign Funds to Kin; Loophole in Ethics Rules Is One That the Senate Did Not Close Last Year," The Washington Post, February 24, 2008, p. A4.

[20]Matt Kelley, "Lawmakers used campaign funds to pay relatives," USA Today, June 18, 2007, p. 6A. Earlier reports by the Sunlight Foundation exposed similar activities during the 2006 election cycle; see "Find out if Congress is a Family Business" and "Is Congress A Family Business, Round Two," available on the Internet.

[21]"Senate Considers Spouses' Unique Ability to Lobby," on the Internet.

[22]John R. Wilke, "Nevada Company's Capitol Ties," The Wall Street Journal, March 30, 2007, p. A4.

[23]"Ex-lawmakers find work with lobbyists," USA Today, February 22, 2007, p. 1A.

[24]Matt Kelley, "Lobbying restrictions are ineffectual, critics say," USA Today, February 22, 2007, p. 7A.

[25]Ronald Kessler, Inside Congress: The Shocking Scandals, Corruption, and Abuse of Power Behind the Scenes on Capitol Hill (New York: Pocket Books, 1997), p. 105. Former high-level staffers are prohibited for one year from lobbying anyone in the chamber of their erstwhile employment; see Title 18 U.S. Code, Section 207, 2000 edition.

[26]Matt Kelley, "Lobbying restrictions . . .," February 22, 2007, p. 7A.

[27]Random House Webster's College Dictionary, 1991.

[28]On Fox News "Special Report," January 17, 2007, Brit Hume listed several top Congressional staffers who are former high executives of corporations.

[29]Massimo Calabresi, "When the Democrats Take Back K Street," Time, December 4, 2006, p. 49.

[30]Mark Green, Selling Out: How Big Corporate Money Buys Elections, Rams Through Legislation, and Betrays Our Democracy (New York: ReganBooks, a HarperCollins imprint, 2002), p. 16.

[31]Mark J. Green, Who Runs Congress?, revised edition (New York: Bantam/ Grossman, 1975), p. 4.

[32]Mark Green, Selling Out, p. 15.

[33]Ibid., p. 14.

[34]Jackley, Hill Rat, p. 20.

[35]Kessler, Inside Congress, Chapter 8, "Follow the Money," pp. 98-126.

[36]Holly Bailey and Eleanor Clift, "Reform, Washington Style," Newsweek, February 13, 2006, p. 40.

[37]"Congress's Slush Funds," The Wall Street Journal, May 19, 1992, p. A14.

[38]For the flawed Rule XXIII, new clause 15, see Congressional Record, daily edition, January 4, 2007, p. H20. For a complaint see ibid., February 7, 2007, p. H1312. See also ibid., May 2, 2007, pp. H4411-12; Susan Ferrechio, "House Changes Its Operating Rules to Make Travel on Private Planes Easier for Members," CQ Weekly, May 7, 2007, p. 1365.

[39]"Bush and Earmarks," The Wall Street Journal, August 15, 2007, p. A12.

[40]David Rogers, "Congress Approves Lobbying Overhaul," The Wall Street Journal, August 3, 2007, p. A4.

[41]House Rule XXIII, clause 16, 110th Congress.

[42]"Earmarks As Usual," The Wall Street Journal, August 1, 2007, p. A14.

[43]For further information, enter Office of Congressional Ethics on an Internet search site.

[44]On this new entity see Congressional Record, daily edition, March 11, 2008, pp. H1515-36. For the newly appointed members see ibid., July 24, 2008, pp. H7134-35, D945. See also Sarah Lueck, "Willing to Buck Traditions, Pelosi Rules the House, The Wall Street Journal, May 8, 2008, p. A4.

V. Leadership PACs: Skirting the Law and Aiding Incumbents

EPIGRAPH: Leadership PACs are little more than political slush funds
that allow Members of Congress to essentially ignore a
variety of campaign finance laws.
---Meredith McGehee.[1]

A leadership political action committee (PAC) is a legal entity established, usually, by a Member of Congress. Informally, they are less frequently called member PACs and personal PACs.[2] Relevant laws and regulations permit their use to directly aid candidates for office who are not the persons establishing or controlling them.

More generally, the first PAC was probably the one created by the CIO labor organization in 1943. The War Disputes Act (Smith-Connally Act) of 1943 added political contributions by unions to the existing ban on corporate donations, so the CIO created the Congress of Industrial Organizations Political Action Committee (CIO-PAC) to dodge that prohibition. Business associations began their PACs in the 1960s.[3]

The first leadership PAC created by a Member of Congress seems to have been that of Senator Steve Symms, R-ID, the Conservative Victory Fund, organized "Pre-75."[4]

Other early leadership PACs were organized in 1978 by Henry Waxman. He used at least one, the Friends of Congressman Henry A. Waxman, to direct money to fellow-members of the Commerce Committee in the House.[5]

Leadership PACs multiplied thereafter, and by 2006 there were somewhere north of 240 such organizations created by U.S. Senators and Representatives.[6] There are now even larger numbers. Some Members have more than one.

Before leadership PACs mushroomed to their present number, high-profile Members monopolized them. Donors mostly limited their largesse to lawmakers with power flowing from high positions in Congress or from ideological stardom.[7]

However, well before PACs emerged as formal entities, some Members of Congress donated money to other Members who needed more funds for their campaigns. An important example helps explain how Lyndon Johnson built his power in the House of Representatives, leading ultimately, of course, to his occupancy of that other House. Just prior to the 1940 elections, and with dim Democratic prospects for continued control of the lower chamber, Johnson led an effort to hit on Texas oil men for Congressional campaign funds. His initiative produced an increase of eight House seats for the Democrats—and increased power for himself due to gratitude flowing his way.[8]

"Leadership PAC" is a term only recently, and still barely, known to federal laws or regulations.[9]

A leadership PAC may legally accept much larger contributions from donors than the creating Member's own campaign committee may receive. Each such PAC may not directly support the election of the person who organized or controls it but may do so for another candidate. There is a limit $5,000 per election on disbursements to a candidate, and a leadership PAC may not transfer more than $15,000 a year to the national party.

In 1988, when about forty-seven Members had leadership PACs, an article reported that "Members of Congress gave each other more than $5 million in campaign funds during the 1985-86 election cycle." That was up from $3.43 million in 1983-84.[10]

It was formerly difficult to find information about the receipts and disbursements of leadership PACs because the Federal Election Commission did not categorize that type of PAC separately from the thousands of other PACs. Now, however, there's Internet information from the FEC about hundreds of L-PACs.[11]

Originally, the Member creating a Leadership PAC used it to advance the re-election of fellow-party politicians. Such action may have been altruistic or partisan, but there were also selfish motives. One: Those organizations provided their creators a way to "buy" support for Congressional leadership quests or committee chairmanships.

Second: Leadership PACs give the Members who win power a club to use in legislative processes: They can call on the gratitude generated by their help in electing someone, or they can threaten not to provide that help in the next election. When the ethics accusation detailed below in the chapter on Earmarks was lodged against John Murtha, D-PA, in 2007, he garnered support from almost all Democrats, many of whom had received money from the PAC he created in 2006. As one author says, "Just as a new crop of reform-minded Democrats looked like it was headed for Congress, Murtha added a new weapon to his arsenal of influence."[12]

Third: Members sometimes treat Leadership PAC money as slush funds for indirect campaign expenses, a higher life style, and payments to relatives.[13] All too typically, when Senator Harry Reid spends tens of thousands of dollars from his Leadership PAC at various hotels in Las Vegas and Georgetown, his spokesman excuses it as including "donor prospecting . . . donor maintenance," accommodations for staffers, and stays for guests. Other Members have used similar claims for purchases of flowers, jewelry, shaving kits, funerals, and personal meals. One retiring members even spent $30,000 of his PAC money for going-away parties, for himself.[14] Even Members who were not running for re-election have started "last-minute" Leadership PACs to rake in more loot than obtained from their usual fundraising. Were such efforts motivated by a desire to build up funds that could be donated to fellow-partisan office seekers or to create a more opulent post-retirement lifestyle?[15] As described in the chapter on Thief-in-the-Night Pay Raises, effective January 8, 1980, Congress prohibited new Members from taking unused campaign funds for personal use. That's proof that most Members see such conversions as wrong, but Leadership PACs open that supposedly closed door.

Allied to the issues just described, a huge ethical lapse that's attracting little publicity is Congress's failure to prevent Members from converting their PAC money to personal use when they retire. But how much difference is there between taking unused campaign money and taking unused PAC money? Many political action committees act as assistant campaign organizations.

Furthermore, leadership PACs permit Members to engage in the hocus pocus of indirectly converting their unused campaign funds to personal use. But trust innovators to find a way to dodge the amendment to the election campaign law that went into effect on January 8, 1980. A Member can legally transfer leftover campaign money to PACs, even his or her own leadership PAC. Then the laundered campaign funds can be used to pay some of the Member's living expenses. Or, the laundered money can pay a relative for real or imagined work.   Finally, when the lawmaker retires, the former campaign funds can go toward any personal use.[16]

And a Leadership PAC does not automatically go out of existence merely because a Member retires.

Here are several other problems associated with leadership PACs: (1) minimal regulation, (2) avoidance of some donation limits, (3) diversion of money that could go to political parties, (4) deterrence of qualified challengers to incumbents, (5) "fragmentation of Congress" and weakened party unity (although there are countervailing influences such as the Speaker's powers), (6) distortion of "channels of accountability between a PAC and its donors," i.e., lack of donor control on who ultimately gets the money, (7) greater "inequality of access" to Members, (8) ability of PACs to set up tax-exempt entities, (9) a less effective, legitimate, and accountable Congress, (10) worse political inequality, (11) control of some leadership PACs by lobbyists and lawyers outside of Congress, (12) Members sometimes create state leadership PACs which are outside of the few rules applied at the federal level.[17]

There's also a potential downside for the politician who accepts money from a Member's leadership PAC: If the Senator or Representative whose PAC donated the money is later tainted by ethics charges or criminal indictment, the recipient of the money may be battered in the next election campaign by his opponent's charges of being too cozy with the donor. That happened in the 2008 campaign to several Senators who had earlier accepted money from the Leadership PAC of newly indicted Senator Ted Stevens, R-AK.[18]

A Representative reported on the floor of the House in mid-2007 as follows:
- "Searchlight Leadership Fund PAC, in the other body, in the 2006 cycle raised $2,346,000; spent $300,000 of that money to support other candidates in that party, which is an appropriate use of that money. But $2 million of it was spent for God knows what."
  - "Another PAC, Hill PAC raised $2,900,000."
  - "Keeping America's Promises, $7,750,000 raised in the 2006 election cycle."
  - "VOL-PAC, $8 million raised in the 2006 election cycle."
- "There is nothing, Mr. Speaker, in the rules that says that money cannot be converted to personal use when these Members, some of whom have recently, [sic] retired or are going to retire."[19] As noteworthy as the dog that did not bark in the night, there was absolutely no response to this information from any other Representative during the remainder of the debate nor during the rest of the legislative day.

Not satisfied with those insider benefits, the Republican Congressional leadership in 2006 considered creating another. Their change would have allowed the leadership PACs to donate unlimited amounts, rather than current maximums, to national party committees. Those groups could then spend the money to directly support the re-election efforts of the donors. Such action would have completely destroyed the existing limits on campaign finance. The leadership PACs would still have been banned from direct campaign contributions to their creators, but the money laundered through the national party committees could have been used for such direct support.[20]

That unconscionable trick would have given another advantage to incumbents—they would have had the PAC money for their campaigns, and their challengers would not. Adding that underhanded maneuver to a pending lobbying reform bill, as some proposed, "would be the ultimate in congressional chutzpah."[21]

Leadership PACs are a way for Members of Congress to skirt the limits imposed on contributions to federal campaigns. Under current law an individual may give a maximum of $2,300 per primary, runoff, and general election to a federal candidate.[22] But a person may donate an additional $5,000 per year to a candidate's leadership PAC.[23] Thus, by donating to a leadership PAC an individual can channel an extra $10,000 during a two-year election cycle to a Representative, or an extra $30,000 during a six-year cycle to a Senator. Of course, that money is not supposed to be used by the recipient to directly fund his or her own re-election. But the Member can use a leadership PAC indirectly to support re-election by having it pay for travel, polling, and other tangential expenses.[24] Additionally, a leadership PAC is allowed to give $5,000 per election cycle to a candidate's campaign committee.[25]

With such rules, what's to prevent a Member from receiving $5,000 as a donation to his or her campaign committee from each of multiple leadership PACs run by other Members? Answer: nothing. And, surely, Members who want such contributions from their fellows send grants to everyone from whom they desire reciprocity. There must be many Senators and Representatives in that Mutual Backscratching Society. Individuals and the media can learn of these donations, if they want to expend time and effort, because federal law requires PACs, along with committees of candidates and parties, to disclose their incomes and expenditures.[26]

Another problem with these lightly regulated PACs is their use for virtual bribery. Members who have them may sometimes want little in return from the recipients of their money. Other times, of course, the creation of an obligation is intended. What is the aforementioned effort to garner support for election to a leadership post if it's not a bribe? And when a Presidential candidate who's a Member of Congress directs money from his or her leadership PAC to local or state people to bring them onto the campaign organization, how close is that to a bribe? And when such a candidate sends money to a super delegate's campaign for Congress or other elective office, is that a bribe?

For instance, Senator Barack Obama's leadership PAC called "Hopefund" stopped collecting contributions in January 2007 when he announced his candidacy,[27] but unlike Senator Clinton's PAC, unlike Senator McCain's PAC, unlike Mitt Romney's PAC, and unlike most of the PACs of second-tier candidates for President in 2007-2008, Obama's Hopefund continued to give money to innumerable people who might support his bid for the White House. As one source says, "Obama showered lawmakers from Iowa and New Hampshire with contributions while other presidential hopefuls turned their focus to raising money for their presidential campaign accounts."[28] Another source: "Obama then used those PAC contributions [to Hopefund]—including thousands from defense contractors, law firms, and the securities and insurance industries—to build support for his presidential run by making donations to Democratic Party organizations and candidates around the country."[29] And from another source:

> "Obama's Hopefund Inc. distributed more than $180,000 in donations
> to political groups and candidates in the early presidential voting states
> of Iowa, New Hampshire and South Carolina and more than $150,000 to
> federal candidates in other states with primary dates through mid-February.
> The donations accounted for nearly three-quarters of the money the PAC
> has given out since this summer."
>
> An Obama campaign spokesman last week said that 'there is no
> connection' between the PAC donations and the presidential campaign."[30]

In addition to giving incumbents an additional advantage over challengers,[31] Leadership PACs are also advantageous to Members who have given up their incumbency through defeat or retirement. Former Representative Mike Oxley's leadership PAC spent over $20,000 for a Colorado ski trip. A leadership PAC can seemingly go on as long as it has money. It can raise money after its creator is no longer in Congress. Even its creator's death doesn't end it. Representative Paul Gillmor died in September 2007 but his L-PAC spent thousands on food, drinks, and golf during the 2008 election cycle. It should come as no surprise that Congress has not responded to a request from the Federal Election Commission that personal-use spending by such PACs be prohibited.[32]

New entities called Super PACs began in 2010 after the Supreme Court's decision in the Citizens United case that found a First Amendment right for ostensibly independent organizations, as well as unions and corporations, to use political speech for or against candidates for office. Super PAC money is not limited by campaign finance laws, but such organizations may not coordinate their actions directly with any politician's campaign--supposedly. That restriction is easily evaded, and it's not just outsiders like TV "funnyman" Stephen Colbert who have Super PACs.

President Obama has a set of them. OK, neither Obama nor his current aides runs them; Bill Burton and Sean Sweeney do. Burton was Deputy White House Press Secretary, January 2009-February 2011. Sweeney was chief of staff for Rahm Emanuel when Emanuel worked for Obama in the White House. So draw your own conclusion about linkage to Obama's re-election campaign. Mitt Romney has the Restore Our Future Super PAC. OK, Romney does not run it. Charles Spies and Carl Forti are two of the principals in it. Spies and Forti were major officials in Romney's 2008 campaign for the Presidency. Again, draw your own linkage conclusion. And plenty of Super PACs seem to be working more or less hand-in-glove with the campaigns of Senators and Representatives. There does not have to be actual linkage because common ideology and available information allow a campaign and a Super PAC to walk side by side toward the same goal.[33]

CORRECTIVE SOLUTIONS

Suggestions for reform have included: • ban leadership PACs, • prohibit Members from contributing money to other Members, • place more limits on the permissible uses of money by leadership PACs and Members' campaign committees, • "Encourage Members to Establish Special-Interest Committees within Their Party's Campaign Committee," • allow party campaign committees to contribute larger amounts to candidates. As you might expect, there are problems to be overcome with some of those suggestions. Because the Supreme Court ruled in 1976 that spending money in campaigns is protected under the Constitution's freedom of speech, a law banning leadership PACs would probably not survive. But one argument is that the House could simply change its rules to prohibit its Members from having leadership PACs. Another is that one [or both] of the parties in the House could do the same regarding its Representatives.[34] The Senate could do something similar.

Public financing of campaigns, including a ban on candidates accepting or spending non-public money, would close one avenue on which special interests drive their efforts to gain advantages that may not be in the public interest. See more on this topic in the chapter on Failure to Devote Enough Time to Legislation.

Failing any of the above reforms, there's still the open avenue of the print and broadcast media publicizing the rot in leadership PACs and doing it over and over until the public might bestir itself to defeat Senators and Representatives with leadership PACs.

Notes: Chapter V, Leadership PACs: Skirting the Law, Aiding Incumbents.

[1]The Campaign Legal Center, "July 25, 2008 – Leadership PAC Ban Legislation: Statement of Meredith McGehee," on the Internet.

[2] On political committees more generally see Federal Election Commission rules, 11 Code of Federal Regulations, Parts 100-106, 108-13, and 116. A leadership PAC is a type of "multicandidate political committee," "unaffiliated committee," or "nonconnected" PAC, meaning ostensibly not connected to a candidate's campaign or campaign committee; for "multicandidate political committee" see Title 2, U.S. Code, section 433, 2000 edition, and ibid., section 441a.(2) and (4). For years, neither the Federal Election Campaign Act nor the Federal Election Commission placed leadership PACs in a separate subcategory within the broader category of nonconnected PACs. Only recently has "leadership PAC" received an official definition; it's in the Honest Leadership and Open Government Act of 2007 [Public Law 110-81, section 204 (121 Stat. 735, at p. 746)], which is an amendment to the Federal Election Campaign Act of 1971 (2 U.S.C. 434) as section 304(i)(8)(B).

For "member PACs" see Ross K. Baker, <u>The New Fat Cats: Members of Congress as Political Benefactors</u>, A Twentieth Century Fund Paper (New York: Priority Press Publications, 1989), p. 15. For "personal PACs" see The Campaign Legal Center: Campaign Finance Guide: Federal Campaign Finance Laws: Leadership PACs, on the Internet.

[3]Baker, <u>The New Fat Cats</u>, pp. 8; Eleanor Mason, "How PAC's Strategy Worked Out: Its Record in Congress," from the Internet, reproduction from <u>New International</u>, Vol. 11, No. 9, December 1945, pp. 285-88; CIO: Political Action Committee, 1943-1965, from the Internet; Political action committee, Congresspedia, last modified September 2, 2008, on the Internet.

[4]"Unofficial List of Leadership PACs," revision of 5/8/08, Prepared by the Public Records Office, Federal Election Commission (paper copy sent to me in December 2008 by Matthew Rowley, Public Information Specialist). That list continues with the leadership PACs of Thomas O'Neill (Pre-75), Bob Livingston (1976), Ronald Reagan (1977), Tom Daschle (1977), Dan Quayle (1978), Henry Waxman (1978), Bill Thomas (1979, Jesse Helms (1979), Don Nickles (1979), John Tower (1979), etc.

Other sources list some early PACs not on the above list. One is Bob Dole's Campaign America with same name and start-year as Dan Quayle's PAC listed above (source: Big Money PACs, on the Internet). Susan Irby, a spokeswoman for then-Senator Trent Lott said, "Senator Lott has had a leadership PAC since he was first elected whip in the House in the early 1980s"(source: Leslie Wayne, "Congress Shuns Spotlight on Leadership PACs," <u>The New York Times on the Web</u>, March 13, 1997.

One book has a chart based on Federal Election Commission data and showing that eight "Member PACs" existed by 1978; Clyde Wilcox, "Member to Member Giving," in <u>Money, Elections, and Democracy: Reforming Congressional Campaign Finance</u>, edited by Margaret Latus Nugent and John R. Johannes (Boulder, CO: Westview Press, 1990), p. 170. See ibid., p. 171, for a chart showing that those PACs raked in about $400,000.

[5]Baker, The New Fat Cats, pp. 29-32, 49. That source also details how Waxman leap-frogged over a more senior colleague and in part "bought" himself the chairmanship of a Commerce Committee subcommittee by giving money to members of the full committee. See also "Unofficial List of Leadership PACs," revision of 5/8/08, Prepared by the Public Records Office, Federal Election Commission.

[6]"Leadership PACs Are The New Political Slush Funds in D.C.," September 27, 2006, placed on the Internet by the Campaign Legal Center and, separately by CREW (Citizens for Responsibility and Ethics in Washington).

[7]Wilcox, "Member to Member Giving," pp. 171, 180-81.

[8]Baker, The New Fat Cats, pp. 15-19. Baker's sources for the Johnson information are pages 606-36, 659, and 663 in Robert A. Caro, The Years of Lyndon Johnson: The Path to Power (New York: Knopf, 1982).

[9]One reference was in the bill called Lobbying Transparency Act of 2007, section 5(d)(6)(C); see Congressional Record, daily edition, January 4, 2007, pp. S42-48; ibid., January 23, 2007, p. S991; ibid., May 24, 2007, p. H5757. The House passed that bill on May 24, 2007, but on the same day it was melded into the bill called the Honest Leadership and Open Government Act of 2007 (see Congressional Record, daily edition, May 24, 2007, and ibid., July 31, 2007, p. H9209). That last-mentioned bill became Public Law 110-81, 121 Stat. 735. Its section 203(a) uses "leadership PAC" (pp. 743 and 744), and section 204 uses that term (pp. 745 and 746). The term is also used in Federal Election Commission, Notice of Proposed Rulemaking (NRPM) 2007-20; new 2 U.S. Code, section 434(i)(8)(B); 2 U.S. Code, new section 439a(c)(4); 68 Federal Register, pp. 67013-17; and 72 Federal Register at 59954-55.]

[10]"Congressmen Help Each Other Out," Insight, October 24, 1988, p. 30.

[11]See Leadership PACs and Sponsors, Federal Election Commission, undated but refers to the 2010 election cycle.

[12]Stephen Spruiell, "From Abscam On: The career and m.o. of Rep. John P. Murtha," National Review, June 25, 2007, pp. 24, 26; the quotation is on p. 26.

[13]Campaign Legal Center, et al., letter to Representatives, July 25, 2006, on the Internet under Reform Groups Urge Members to Support Bans on the Use of Leadership PACs.

[14]Brody Mullins, "Loose Change: Lawmakers Tap PAC Money to Pay Wide Array of Bills," Wall Street Journal, November 2, 2006, pp. A1, A8.

[15]See Ibid.

[16]Dick Morris and Eileen McGann, "Thompson PAC Coddles Son," New York Post, July 23, 2007; obtained by me from the Internet.

[17]The sources for the numbered items on this list are as follows: Number 1: See Federal Register, Vol. 68, No. 230, December 1, 2003, pp. 67013-18, "Federal Election Commission . . . Supplementary Information" [proposals, comments, and final rule "to address the relationship between authorized committees and . . . 'leadership PACs,'"]; Federal Register, Vol. 72, No. 214, November 6, 2007; 11 Code of Federal Regulations, revised as of January 1, 2008, section 100.5, "Political committee (2 U.S.C. 431 (4), (5), (6)); Federal Election Campaign Act of 1971 and its amendments [see 2 U.S. Code, 441a].   Number 2: Anne H. Bedlington, "Loopholes and Abuses," in Money, Elections, and Democracy, edited by Nugent and Johannes, pp. 70, 75; Wilcox, "Member to Member Giving," in ibid., p. 182.   Number 3: Larry J. Sabato, "PACs and Parties," in ibid., pp. 197-98.   Number 4: L. Sandy Maisel, "The Incumbency Advantage," in ibid., pp. 128-30.   Number 5: Margaret Latus Nugent and John R. Johannes, introduction to "Part II: Problematic Consequences," in ibid., p. 118.   Number 6: Bedlington, in ibid., p. 71; Wilcox, in ibid., pp. 181-82; Sabato, in ibid., p. 197.   Number 7: Bedlington, in ibid., pp. 71-72.   Number 8: Bedlington, in ibid., pp. 82, 83, 93.   Number 9: Nugent and Johannes, in ibid., p. 118; Wilcox, in ibid., p. 183.   Number 10: Nugent and Johannes, in ibid., p. 118.   Number 11: Wilcox, in ibid., p. 183.   Number 12: Trevor Potter, "Where Are We Now? The Current State of Campaign Finance Law," in Campaign Finance Reform: A Sourcebook, edited by Anthony Corrado, et al. (Washington: Brookings Institution Press, 1997), p. 7.

[18]Joel Millman, "Stevens Conviction Weighs On GOP: Democrats Launch Attacks on Senators Who Received Money From Alaskan's PAC," The Wall Street Journal, November 1, 2008, p. A5.

[19]Representative Phil Gingrey, R-GA; Congressional Record, daily edition, July 31, 2007, p. H9207. The four PACs referred to by Gingrey were in order of their lising controlled by Harry Reid, Hillary Clinton, John Kerry, and Bill Frist.

[20] Campaign Legal Center, et al., letter to Representatives, July 28, 2006, on the Internet under Reform Groups Send Letter to Hill on Leadership PAC Proposal.

[21]"Congressional Chutzpah," The Washington Post, July 28, 2006, p. A24.

[22]Additional and larger amounts may be given to party committees.

[23]Such PACs are limited to receipt of $5,000 per year from each individual, other PAC, or party committee; Kathy Gill, "What Is A Leadership PAC?" March 30, 2008, About.com on the Internet.

[24]Ibid.

[25]Ibid.

[26]"Campaign finance in the United States," Wikipedia, modified on September 23, 2008. See Title 2, U.S. Code, Section 434, 2000 edition.

[27]John Solomon, "Obama PAC Is Active In Key Election States," The Washington Post, November 26, 2007, p. A6; John Solomon, "Obama Campaign Worker Discussed PAC Donations," The Washington Post, November 30, 2007, p. A8.

[28]"Wasn't Obama Against Outside PAC's Influence?" posted on August 21, 2008, on the Internet, quoting a report in The Hill, from about a year earlier. See also Kathy Gill, "The Candidates: Obama Current King Of Leadership PACs," March 29, 2008, About.com on the Internet; Alex Knott, "Obama's PAC Targets Early Primary States for Local Giving," CQ Today Online News, November 16, 2007, on the Internet (Yahoo) (this is listed on another Internet site as from CQ Politics, November 16, 2007.)

[29]Scott Helman, "PACs and lobbyists aided Obama's rise," The Boston Globe, August 9, 2007, on the Internet.

[30]Solomon, "Obama Campaign Worker Discussed PAC Donations." If, as Obama campaign officials admitted, "Obama's presidential campaign helped recommend several of the donations his political action committee made in recent months to politicians in key primary states as the campaign was working to secure endorsements," that was a violation of federal law if the donations exceeded $5,000; ibid. See also Jerome Armstrong, "Obama mocks the FEC regulations with his PAC," November 26, 2007, on the Internet.

[31]Baker, The New Fat Cats, pp. 51-54.

[32]Brody Mullins and Brad Haynes, "Some PACs Keep on Running After Politicians Quit," The Wall Street Journal, May 6, 2009, p. A6.

[33]"All the speech money can buy," The Week, December 16, 2001, p. 13, and numerous sources on the Internet, such as Dan Eggen and T. W. Farnam, "New 'Super Pacs' bringing in millions," The Washington Post, September 28, 2010, and Lawrence Lessig, "The Great Promise of Super-PACs," December 20, 2011.

[34]Wilcox, "Member to Member Giving," pp. 183-84; Baker, The New Fat Cats, pp. 64-68 (the quoted bullet item is from p. 65). The Supreme Court decision was in Buckley v. Valeo, 424 U.S. 1 (1976).

VI. Delegates Are Not from States But Are Quasi-Members of the House

EPIGRAPH: When quacks with pills political would dope us.
                        ---Bert Leston Taylor, "Canopus."[1]

Memo to all Americans who care about the integrity of the U.S. Constitution and the power of their U.S. Representative: Both will be debased if the ploy being attempted by some officials in and out of Congress is successful.

Already, the U.S. House of Representatives has diluted the power of its 435 Members by adding as quasi-members the salaried Delegates from American Samoa, the District of Columbia, Guam, the Northern Mariana Islands (only since 2008), the U.S. Virgin Islands, and Puerto Rico (whose delegate is technically a Resident Commissioner). They are not Representatives, but they can vote in House committees and can even introduce bills, which is troubling as a violation of the U.S. Constitution. The Constitution stipulates that "the House . . . shall be composed of members chosen . . . by the people of the several States" (emphasis added). It further requires that Representatives shall be elected by voters in states.

The House does not now allow Delegates to vote on the floor of the House, only in committees, including the Committee of the Whole House. During 1993-1995, the years of the 103d Congress, the Democrats controlling the House permitted the then-five non-Representatives to vote when the House was in Committee of the Whole, and their votes would only be counted when those votes would not determine the success or failure of any overall vote.[3] Because the five votes could not affect the outcome, what was the point? Posturing for voters and the media? Perhaps the new Republican majority in the 104th Congress saw the inanity of this, because it rescinded Committee-of-the-Whole voting by Delegates.

With the Democrats back in control, the 110th Congress again enacted the 1993-1995 rule, granting Delegates "the same powers and privileges as Members" in any Committee of the Whole.[4] But the inane provision was once again included that Delegates' votes would only be counted when meaningless—because "whenever a recorded vote on any question has been decided by a margin within which the votes cast by the Delegates and the Resident Commissioner have been decisive, the Committee of the Whole shall rise and the Speaker shall put such question de novo without intervening motion."[5]   In other words, the House, not its Committee of the Whole, would determine whether the question would pass or fail without the votes of the non-member Delegates. Republican control of the 111th Congress once again resulted in Delegates no longer voting and presiding in the Committee of the Whole.

It surely waters down the committee vote of a true Representative when a person who is not a Representative votes in a committee. Consider this: A bill that is under consideration in a committee might fail to advance because of a nine-for-and-nine-against tie if only Representatives voted, but a Delegate who increases the membership of the committee might vote for the bill, thus providing the necessary majority for committee passage. In such cases the Delegate from, say, American Samoa, where there are only about 66,000 people living on 77 square miles of Pacific Ocean islands, and where the residents do not pay U.S. income taxes, would have as much controlling influence as any of the Constitutionally legitimate Representatives, each of whom represents about 710,767 people (following the 2010 census).

Another problem is that House Delegates (the Senate has no Delegates) can be members of, and can vote in, conference committees, the extremely important groups that eliminate differences in House and Senate versions of bills that are mainly the same. Final legislation must be passed in identical form by both houses. Therefore, whenever a bill is passed by one chamber but has some variations from the same-subject bill crafted by the other, an ad hoc conference committee is appointed to harmonize the two versions. Conference committees often make critical changes in bills, and the final product of a conference may be voted on in each chamber without all Members being fully aware of the changes; thus, members of conference committees have extraordinary authority. And a Constitutionally impermissible Delegate who is part of a conference committee has, at least temporarily, more power than a true Representative who is not one of the conferees.

To this author, it is clearly unconstitutional that non-Representatives are allowed to be members of the House and to vote in units of the House. Case law dealing with the possibly relevant Constitutional provisions seems to support the position that while the District of Columbia may not have a Representative it can have a Delegate.[6] Permission for the latter has been enacted into law and into the rules of the House.[7]

In early 2007 a move was afoot to increase the membership of the House from 435 to 437 by allotting an additional Member to Utah and by morphing the District of Columbia Delegate into a true, full-voting Representative. The latter change should be seen as unconstitutional because, as noted above, the Constitution states that the House is composed of members from states. D.C. is not a state.

The people who incubated this malignant mutation linked an ostensibly plausible argument about Utah to a corruption masquerading as fairness about D.C. The former is that Utah barely missed getting a fourth Representative after the 2000 Census because thousands of Utah Mormon missionaries to other states and foreign lands were not counted as Utah residents. The D.C. case is that it's a civil rights issue, that people there pay taxes, serve in wars to extend democracy, and vote in Presidential elections, so their interests should be reflected by a full-fledged member of the House.[8] The two claims have been joined for the purpose of obtaining passage through bipartisan support because Utah reliably votes Republican while D.C. is Democratic with equal certainty.[9]

The D.C. advocates argue that a 1949 Supreme Court decision (National Mutual Insurance Co. v. Tidewater) is a precedent for their effort to skirt a Constitutional requirement. In that case, the Court allowed federal lawsuits between District of Columbia citizens and state citizens despite the Constitution's statement that U.S. "judicial power shall extend to all cases . . . between citizens of different States" (emphasis added).[10] Setting aside questions of whether the 1949 case about alleged individual rights should control the current issue about collective representation, a strong argument exists that one unconstitutional action should not result in more unconstitutional action.

The D.C./Utah bill passed the House in 2007 but died in the Senate.[11] It was, however, resurrected in the 111th Congress, where it was passed in the Senate but not in the House because of a Senate provision against most gun-control laws for localities.[12]

If Congress ever creates the grotesquerie of a full Representative for an area that is not a state, would the Members who voted for that be violating the oath they took upon assuming office that they would "support and defend the Constitution"? This is just one of several toxic examples of Members who sacrifice the Constitution on the altar of politics.

And in the 112th Congress in January 2011the D.C. Delegate, Eleanor Holmes Norton, introduced a new bill to provide D.C. with a Representative, this time without the Utah provision[13]—because the linkage with an extra Member for Utah has been obviated by the results of the 2010 Census, which gave Utah an additional Member anyway. That removal probably means that the bill will not fare as well as in 2009-2010 because fewer Republican Members will favor it.

And, if the District supporters prevail with the Representative proposal, then what's next—an unconstitutional contrivance to give D.C. two Senators?

CORRECTIVE SOLUTIONS

If the scofflaws who want to violate the Constitution by giving D.C. a full-fledged Member of the House without doing it by Constitutional amendment, succeed in their fraudulent effort, then surely the courts would look favorably on citizen lawsuits to overturn that action. And because every Senator and Representative who votes in favor of that trickery will have violated his/her oath to "support and defend the Constitution of the United States against all enemies, foreign and domestic," and to "bear true faith and allegiance to the same," a grassroots uprising to boot them out of office should occur.

Any attempt at Congressional action to expel such Members would be useless because the fraud would have passed each house by majority vote, and expulsion requires a two-thirds vote.

Notes: Chapter VI. Delegates Are Not from States But Are Quasi-Members
              of the House

[1]Bert Leston Taylor, "Canopus," in Charles Henry Woolbert and Andrew Thomas Weaver, Better Speech, A Textbook of Speech Training for Secondary Schools, revised and enlarged edition (New York: Harcourt, Brace and Co., 1933), p. 231, reprinted from Motley Measures.

[2]But clothes made in the Northern Mariana Islands, on Saipan for instance, qualify for the label "Made in the U.S.A"; ABC-TV, "20/20," March 13, 1998. For further information enter "Northern Mariana Islands" + " Made in the U.S.A." on the Internet. On June 7, 1984, President Reagan issued Proclamation 5207, "Application of Certain Laws of the United States to Citizens of the Northern Mariana Islands"; it dealt with many provisions of many laws.

[3]"House Grants Voting Privileges. . . . . . To Delegates From D.C., Territories," CQ Almanac . . . 1992 (Washington: Congressional Quarterly, 1993), pp. 14-15. For the history of these "statutory representatives" see Abraham Holtzman, "Empire and Representation: The U.S. Congress," Legislative Studies Quarterly, May 1986, pp. 249-73.

[4]House Rule, III, clause 3(a), 110th Congress.

[5]House Rule XVIII, clause 6(h), 110th Congress.

[6]See Kenneth R. Thomas, "The Constitutionality of Awarding the Delegate for the District of Columbia A Vote in the House of Representatives or the Committee of the Whole," CRS Report for Congress, January 24, 2007.

[7]See Title 2, U.S. Code, Section 25a, 2000 edition, for D.C.; Title 48, U.S. Code, Sections 891, 893, & 894, 2000 edition, for Puerto Rico; Title 48, U.S. Code, Sections 1711 & 1715, 2000 edition, for Guam and the Virgin Islands; and Title 48, U.S. Code, Sections 1731 & 1735, 2000 edition, for American Samoa; and House Rule III, clause 3(a) and (b), 110th Congress.

[8]"Big Love," The New Republic, December 25, 2006, p. 7. For arguments pro and con on the issue see "D.C. Voting Representation," Congressional Digest: A Pro & Con Monthly, May 2007.

[9]"D.C. Con," The Wall Street Journal, March 23, 2007, p. A10. This editorial explains that the 2010 Census will probably result in Utah getting an additional

Representative anyway and that some state in the upper Midwest or the Northeast that usually elects Democrats will thereby lose a seat in the House. Thus, increasing House membership to 437 through the Utah-D.C. proposal is a "partisan matter" because it would produce a "net gain for Democrats."

[10]Matthew J. Franck, "Hammering to Fit," September 18, 2006, in National Review Online, from the Internet.

[11]"Senate rejects bill to give D.C. a voting seat in House," USA Today, September 19, 2007, p. 5A; Michael Teitelbaum, "Bill to Give District of Columbia a Vote In the House Falls Short in the Senate," CQ Weekly, September 24, 2007, p. 2773.

[12]See in "District of Columbia voting rights" the section titled "Proposal during administration of Barack Obama," Wikipedia, no date, but April 2010 or later. See also Mary Beth Sheridan and Hamil R. Harris, "D.C. Voting Measure Clears The Senate," The Washington Post, February 27, 2009, on the Internet; Alan K. Ota, "House May Try To Move D.C. Voting Rights Bill," CQ Weekly, April 19, 2010, p. 968; Edward Epstein, "Opposition Kills Bill to Allow D.C. House Seat," CQ Weekly, April 26, 2010.

[13]For the bill's introduction, see Congressional Record, daily edition, January 12, 2011, p. H201.

VII. Insufficient Oversight of the Executive Branch and of Government Sponsored Enterprises

EPIGRAPH: For now we see through a glass darkly.
                ---The Bible, I Corinthians, Chapter XIII, Verse 12.

"Oversight" can mean careful supervision. But it can also mean "omission or error."[1] Through inaction, Congress too often embraces the latter. It overlooks and thus does not fully meet its duty to exercise due diligence in oversight of the executive branch of the federal government. That duty flows partly from the Constitution's provisions, in Article I, that Congress has the power to provide for the "general welfare of the United States" and "to make all laws which shall be necessary and proper for carrying into execution the foregoing powers, and all other powers vested by this Constitution in the government of the United States, or in any department or officer thereof." The Constitutional provisions have been reinforced by the rules of each house of Congress and by laws – such as the Legislative Reorganization Acts of 1946 and 1970, the Congressional Budget Act of 1993, and the Reports Consolidation Act of 2000.

Congress performs oversight by such actions as investigations by committees, appropriations hearings, and authorization hearings to determine if new programs should be created or if existing ones should continue. Those activities are part of our famous and vital system of checks and balances that supports the separation of powers, which is "an indispensable guarantee of liberty."[2]

Congress cannot fulfill its oversight duty—or its legislative duty—if blinded to the actions of executive departments and officers of the government. That blinding can occur in at least two ways: (1) if the executive branch willfully or inadvertently does not supply adequate information, and (2) if, through laziness, inattention, or ideology, Congress does not look at certain federal actions.

When the extreme credit and financial crisis erupted in mid-to-late 2008, we became all too aware of Congress not seeing and acting on problems—and not heeding warnings. Here, we cannot delve into much of the polluted history of this debacle. That's fodder for a separate book. But a few points deserve mention. The Community Reinvestment Act of 1977 required mortgage lenders to make more loans to low-income people.[3] Then the two government-sponsored enterprises (GSEs) named Fannie Mae and Freddie Mac bought and sold huge numbers of those mortgages. Brokers, appraisers, and ordinary lenders such as banks vultured into what became known as the subprime market. Former lending practices that would have prevented predatory loans were abandoned. Partly because of the ideology of expanding home ownership, partly because of Congressional lack of interest in potential problems, and partly because of lobbying by GSEs and other big players in the mortgage morass, reforms did not occur.

Fannie and Freddie ran lobbying operations costing millions of dollars annually.[4] They tied CEO compensation to the volume of their loans so that executives had a personal stake in creating more borrowers. They ran foundations through which they lavished millions of dollars on favored recipients. They inundated some Members of Congress with donations in the apparent expectation that their other excesses would not be abated.[5] The other big-money vultures feeding off millions of poor Americans did much the same, even giving preferential loans at reduced rates to key lawmakers. In the face of all that, Congress slept.

Policy affected process because some Members of Congress invested themselves so heavily in the policy of pressuring lenders to provide mortgages to low-income borrowers that they did not want it sullied by a process of Congressional oversight that would expose problems in the policy.

The few Cassandras who had predicted disaster and suggested reforms were ignored or dismissed as unbalanced zealots, racists, or obstructionists who should be sued. Thus, oversight attempts foundered. One Representative's questioning of the Fannie Mae CEO, who happened to be African-American, caused another Member to say the questioning amounted to a "lynching."[6]

Some local and state officials had greater understanding. When Georgia's governor, with prescient foresight of a future crash, induced the legislature to pass a strong law in 2002 to impose potential liability on firms involved in unfair home loans in Georgia, he and the legislators were engulfed by threats from a wave of lobbyists, including some working for Fannie Mae and Freddie Mac. Caving into that pressure, the legislature wrecked the law in 2003.[7]

Many subprime mortgages metastasized into destructive cancers that shoved the U.S. and world economies into emergency reconstructive surgery. That led Congress to pass the Troubled Asset Relief Program (TARP), itself so flawed that perhaps it should have been called the Troubled Congressional Oversight Program (T-COP). Congress's first step toward TARP was a short bill that failed to pass, resulting in a 777.68 point loss in the Dow Jones Industrial Average on September 29, 2008. After that, Congress's cobbled together a bill of over 400 pages loaded with goodies for favored groups, which President Bush signed, and which gave Treasury Secretary Henry Paulson an initial $350 billion to do with more or less as he wished, and another $350 billion he could request from

Congress later. It soon became apparent that Paulson was not using the initial $350 billion to buy troubled assets like mortgages from the big financial institutions, which many people understood to be the original intention. That idea ran into such practical problems that Paulson switched to helping the banks through infusions of money by purchasing preferred stock from them. The next detour from original intentions came when the banks didn't use the money to make more credit available to strapped businesses and consumers. Sometimes they just sat on the money. Sometimes they used it to buy other banks.

With Congress having turned over much of America's money and future to one man not hedged in by adequate caveats and restrictions, TARP became probably the biggest failure of Congressional oversight in U.S. history. It was as if Congress said, "No conditions. No transparency. No problem." And consequences? It was soon seen that they were a huge problem. As one columnist wrote, "Perhaps it has made Secretary Hank Paulson the fourth branch of government."[8]

The TARP bill that passed in early October as the Emergency Economic Stabilization Act of 2008 (P.L. 110-343) gave a mild nod to oversight.[9] But those provisions were so minimal and their implementation and effect so after-the-fact that the initial expenditure of billions of dollars by Secretary Paulson was inadequately controlled.

Yet even as the aware part of the public began to see the magnitude of the Congressional failure, the majority of voters failed in their oversight of Congress by blindly re-electing many of the Representatives and Senators who had contributed to the original and ongoing messes. And because only about one-third of the Senate is up for election each two years, voters did not even have the opportunity to boot out some problem Senators.

Yet, oversight creates a conflict because of separation of powers. Congress cannot be allowed to supervise—interfere—too closely in the executive branch if that separation is to continue.

Considering separation of powers—and Member's preoccupation with other concerns such as re-election—is there a reasonable way for Congress to exercise enough oversight to prevent abominations such as the Department of Defense reputedly spending nearly a million dollars in 2007 to ship thirty-eight-cents-worth of washers from South Carolina to Texas? There are numerous true stories of DOD paying more than necessary, yet on first impression this seems so outlandish that one wonders if it really happened. It turns out that it did. Twin sisters in South Carolina apparently engaged in a massive fraud that the Pentagon did not discover for years. One sister eventually committed suicide and the other pleaded guilty to overcharges of just over twenty million dollars.[10]

That tension between proper degrees of Congressional oversight and separation of powers will always exist. Strong Presidents and docile Congresses cause movement toward executive domination, while the balance is reversed under weak Presidents.

Another separation of powers issue exists between the legislative and judicial branches. Federal courts will not interfere with the internal workings of Congress.[11] But the reverse does not apply: Congress and its Members are free to influence the courts. For instance, in 2007 Representatives Barney Frank, D-MA, and John Conyers, D-MI, filed with the Supreme Court an amicus brief in favor of permitting lawsuits against companies that have merely done business with another company that has committed wrongful acts. The brief argued that those House committee chairs had standing in the case because of their desire to make possible more lawsuits against corporations.[12]

Many government observers believe that the Republican majority in recent years caused Congress to abandon too much of its necessary—and required—oversight function. As a recent book says, Republicans serving during the tenure of the second President George Bush, "including the leaders of Congress, . . . [saw] themselves as field lieutenants in the president's army far more than they . . . [did] as members of a separate and independent branch of government."[13]   That same book informs us that "the arrival of unified Republican government in 2001 transformed the aggressive and active GOP-led Congress of the Clinton years into a deferential and supine body."[14]

During the part of the Clinton Presidency when there were Republican majorities in Congress, the GOP leadership conducted numerous investigations, issued hundreds of subpoenas, collected tens of thousands of documents, and spent millions of tax dollars in efforts to ferret out imagined Clinton wrongdoing. But with the entrance of George W. Bush into the Oval Office, Republican efforts at executive oversight virtually ceased. That there was nothing needing investigation is as unbelievable as Jonah swallowing the whale.

One major recent failing was the lack of oversight of the new Department of Homeland Security. Because of it being an agglomeration of twenty-two agencies, many with quite different needs and goals, and because of its vital protective responsibilities and potential encroachments on Americans' liberties, oversight was more needed than usual. But the Congressional response was feeble. There was no Senate committee on homeland security until the start of the 109th Congress in January 2005, when the Committee on Governmental Affairs became the Committee on Homeland Security and Governmental Affairs; but even then, several aspects of homeland security were left under the authority of other committees. The House created the Select Committee on Homeland Security in June 2002 and made it a standing committee in January 2005. But the House did not endow it with proper authority, thus leading DHS functionaries to give it short shrift. Meanwhile, scores of other Congressional committees, often pursuing turf-building missions, intruded with demands for testimony and documents from DHS officials. This diffuse, uncoordinated, and unplanned approach wasted both Congressional and DHS resources without compensating accomplishments.

Those failures flowed largely from the reluctance of the Republicans who controlled Congress to be critics of their Republican President's actions and policies. However, another partial cause was the bent of the Bush administration toward secrecy and extension of executive power.

The effort to achieve homeland security led, as was predicted, to another oversight failure. Although the Patriot Act has some good provisions, others have shown its potential for mischief. The FBI was granted authority to issue "national security letters," directed to banks and phone companies for access to individual's records, supposedly in furtherance of a terrorism investigation and without time-consuming subpoenas. But a Justice Department review established that many records were perused when there was no connection to terrorism, only to FBI curiosity. This appears to have been another in a long train of instances in which Congress has acquiesced in FBI requests for more money, power, and personnel despite Bureau scandals. From illegal wiretapping during the civil rights era, through several other scandals, to failure to heed warnings before 9-11 (and even the promotions of agents who refused to take appropriate action), to this recent misstep, Congress has generally abetted the Bureau rather than provided needed controls.[15]

To the extent that Congressional oversight did exist in the last few years, it unfortunately may have included a large dose of making sure that federal agencies spent money on projects and programs earmarked for favored lobbyists and well-positioned Members.

An issue that relates to oversight is the possibility of Presidential refusal to spend some money appropriated by Congress, which often happened from World War II onward.[16] President Franklin Roosevelt "once observed that a Congressional authorization is in the nature of a New Year's resolution, it may or it may not be carried out."[17] President Nixon, having failed to get Congressional authorization for him to choose which appropriations to ignore, carried the practice to new heights and simply engaged in unilateral "impoundment." That was seen by many in Congress as an unconstitutional encroachment on a legislative prerogative.[18] Therefore, Congress passed the Congressional Budget and Impoundment Control Act of 1974 restricting the President's ability to refuse to spend appropriated funds.[19] Nixon's impoundments even became a subject of his impeachment investigation.[20]

Next came the attempted line-item veto, an effort to give the President a more extreme power than impoundment. In appropriation bills passed by Congress, such a veto would let the President prevent some expenditures by killing specific provisions without vetoing the entire bill. That idea is anathema to some Members.

Congressional objections to Presidential impoundment or a line-item veto may be clothed in pious blather about "oversight" or "the imperial Presidency" or co-equal branches of government, but underneath that seemingly sensible raiment is the scabrous disease of incumbent protection. Members usually desire no interference with spendthrift favors that generate campaign contributions and voter gratitude.

Nevertheless, the Republican-majority Congress gave line-item-veto power to President Clinton in March 1996. Why, you might ask, did Republicans bestow such authority on a Democrat? It appears that Congressional majorities experienced a momentary need to do the ostensibly right thing. Senator Dan Coats, R-IN, explained that it was because "there has been an extraordinary abuse of the power of spending."[21] Many Members who were disgusted with huge federal deficits thought this was a way to curb them. As one observer saw it, "Jubilant supporters of the measure anticipate that the new power will wipe out the congressional practice of inserting wasteful pork barrel spending items into otherwise vital bills."[22] And the line-item veto had even been part of the "Contract with America" that Republicans had advanced in 1994 and that was widely credited with helping them win majorities in the House and Senate for the first time in forty years. But in June 1998 the Supreme Court invalidated the line-item veto as unconstitutional.[23]

Spending-restraint forces tried again with the "legislative" line-item veto. That idea, also called enhanced rescission, passed by the House in 2006, would provide that the President could make a "rescission" of a specific spending provision; and if Congress did not override that action within fourteen legislative days, the annulment would stand. The proposal died in the Senate because Majority Leader Bill Frist, R-TN, refused to bring it to the floor.[24] Present practice is that Congress must approve any rescission, but it never does.[25]

From the Congressional viewpoint, the evil twin of the line-item veto is Presidential "signing statements." Although used as early as Andrew Jackson's Presidency,[26] they have multiplied in recent years. When signing a bill containing provisions he deems problematical, the President attaches a statement that some parts of the measure may not be constitutional or legal. This is tantamount to a Presidential refusal to enforce or abide by those parts. In effect, it's a line-item veto.

Bush came to shove when the President included signing statements affecting over 800 items in bills he had signed by early 2007. That's an unprecedented number of such reservations. And perhaps that's one explanation for Bush not having vetoed even one bill during his first five-plus years in office. His first veto came on July 19, 2006. Why should the President veto a bill when he can, in effect, veto the part of it he does not like?

Although Barack Obama campaigned with a promise not to use signing statements, he has continued the practice. An example is his December 31, 2011, reaction to the National Defense Authorization Act for fiscal year 2012.[27]

This raises a Constitutional issue because if the President has signed a bill but has effectively vetoed items in it through a signing statement, Congress is deprived of its Constitutionally granted power to override the President's veto. Furthermore, some people argue that in using a signing statement to kill part of a bill the President is violating the Constitution's requirement that "he shall take care that the laws be faithfully executed." Conversely, it can be argued that any section of a bill killed by a signing statement is not a law. And the Constitutional provision that the President must swear an oath to "preserve, protect and defend the Constitution" is seen by some as validating signing statements that address Presidentially perceived problems in bills. A legal challenge should occur so the Supreme Court can rule on which interpretation is correct.

While George W. Bush was President, the Republican majorities in both houses of Congress were strangely silent about this possible violation of the Constitution and of the legislative branch's ability to enact law. Well, maybe it wasn't so strange considering their general abrogation of oversight.

Champions of Congress as a coequal—or even supreme—branch of government usually want no encroachments on its powers. But many such advocates only pose as purists and are willing adulterators when it suits their larger purposes.

Case in point: So-called free trade. The Constitution (Art. I, Sec. 8) gives Congress the power "to regulate commerce with foreign nations, and among the several States." Yet, the globalizers have strip-mined and clear-cut that authority so that little of it remains, and Congress can now only say "yes" or "no" to the international commerce-regulating it has abandoned to the executive branch. It's done that by granting the President "fast-track" power on trade agreements, treaties such as NAFTA, and U.S. participation in the World Trade Organization (WTO).

There are at least two types of globalizers. One consists of internationalists, one-worlders who see all humanity as occupying a single "lifeboat" that needs everyone working together and who view merely national interests as inimical to the common good. The other is composed of corporate titans, flacks, and apologists who want multi-national businesses to be freed from parochial restraints.

The first group believes it's on the side of the angels. The propaganda of the second group alleges that a free flow of capital, jobs, and people will benefit everyone economically by generating higher demand for goods, greater employment, and better lives.

The first bolsters its case with history's almost unrelieved record of degradation and death due to clashes instead of cooperation. The second emphasizes, inter alia, the negatives of such anti-competitive devices as tariffs.

Both groups largely ignore—in their pronouncements, at least—the greedy side of human nature. Both largely conceal that there will be much trampling of innocent people on the path toward achievement of their goals. Internationalists preen on their own humaneness, but their victims range from unaided genocide sufferers to countries subjected to coalitions of smaller nations, as when the United Nations made Libya the chair of its Commission on Human Rights, a group also including such paragons as Saudi Arabia and Zimbabwe. On the other hand, the exploited victims of multi-national corporatism are individuals but are collectively vast.

Collusion by the two groups can have consequences that would be laughably perverse were it not for their human roadkill. Examples follow.

When Congress allowed U.S. participation in NAFTA in 1993, many Members, ignorant of its details, were taking the infamous "leap in the dark." Little did they know that the

U.S. was surrendering some of its sovereignty. Little did they know they were abetting foreign corporations in raids on U.S. citizens. Little did they know that they were helping free-trade ideology trump rationality. But one observer offered this insight: "If malfeasance won't get you, ignorance will."[28]

They surely knew that Americans would lose jobs to cheap labor in Mexico, but not that U.S. court decisions could be set aside by a predatory foreign corporation, as almost happened in the following case. Jerry O'Keefe, a Mississippi funeral-home owner, won a punitive-damages judgment of $400 million dollars against Canada's Loewen Group in 1995 for using illegal tactics to try to drive him out of business. At the time, that was the largest one-plaintiff jury judgment in U.S. history. Loewen, giving up its right to appeal that decision, agreed to pay the plaintiff $175 million. But in 1998 Loewen sued the federal government for $725 million, claiming that its rights under NAFTA had been violated in Mississippi because some of its assets had been expropriated and its future profits had been reduced. That was a violation of NAFTA's Chapter 11. Because NAFTA stipulates that a foreign corporation does not have to sue a country in that country's own courts, Loewen sued in an international trade court of three people, one of whom was chosen by Loewen. Luckily, in the proceedings before that tribunal, the final result was that in June 2003 the court dismissed Loewen's claims against the U.S.[29] Still, the abrogation of some sovereign rights under multi-national trade agreements, shows Congress willingly abandoning oversight.

When Congress allowed the U.S. to join the WTO in late 1994, many approving Members were doubtless blind to the details of what they were approving. Did they know that WTO kangaroo courts can set aside national or regional decisions on the grounds that they damage a corporation's rights? When the European Union designated that a small percentage of its banana imports would come from some former colonies in the Caribbean, the Clinton administration, at the behest of the money-contributing head of Chiquita Bananas' United Brands, Inc., filed a complaint with the WTO. As the U.S. has no banana export trade itself, that action did not relate to U.S. interests but to those of Chiquita monopolists. The WTO ruled the EU action illegal.[30]

The newly acquired Democratic-Party control of both chambers in 2007, swung the pendulum back toward proper oversight by Congress. But there was the danger that it would swing too far. The possibility was that the new, anti-Bush majorities would seek partisan advantage by weakening the President under the guise of restoring Constitutional balance and of doing what the American people want.

After the 2006 election, one prominent House Democrat, Representative Henry Waxman, chairman of the House Oversight and Government Reform Committee, put forth a list topics that should already have been investigated. Some items on the list: Manipulation of Iraq Intelligence, Treatment of Detainees, Leak of a Covert CIA Agent's Status, Award of Halliburton Contracts, White House Responsibility for the Katrina Response, Secret NSA Wiretaps, Vice President's Energy Task Force, Withholding of Medicare Cost Estimates, Politicization of the Federal Science-Based Agencies, Contract Abuses at the Department of Homeland Security, and Influence of Lobbyists at EPA. To pursue all the possibilities of executive branch nonfeasance, misfeasance, malfeasance, maladministration, and ineptitude, the staff of that committee burgeoned.

Far from Waxman's panel having exclusivity, numerous additional House and Senate committees leaped into expansive oversight and investigation.

Bush critics spent months sniffing on the trail of the leaker of a "covert" CIA agent's name and status. Yet why was there so little Congressional baying of the hounds to find the person who leaked the existence of the telephone and financial transactions surveillances conducted by the Bush administration? Surely, the exposure of national-security programs, so that the enemy could take evasive action, was of more moment than the outing of one CIA agent, who may not by then have been covert at all. The executive branch pursued the leaker/s/ of the SWIFT banking surveillance program, but the quiescence of anti-Bush people about that disclosure is surprising.

As briefly seen above in the chapter on Ethics, Senators will have to pay charter prices for rides on private jets; Representatives will be prohibited from such trips. But while Members placed those restrictions on themselves, they did nothing about the ability of fat cats to influence executive branch officials through free plane rides. Those bureaucrats "are routinely accepting trips from companies and trade associations with a stake in their agencies' decisions, according to a <u>USA Today</u> review of public records."[31] Surely, that's an oversight failure.

Congress has contributed to its oversight failure by passing many laws that are so general as deliberately to toss the power of making detailed provisions to the executive branch. Its an abdication of responsibility in order to avoid accountability. If voters run afoul of a federal regulation that amounts to law but is not in a law passed by Congress, they supposedly won't hold their Representative or Senators responsible for their problem. Bureaucrats will get the blame.

But Members and their lobbyist pals, even while posing as not responsible, actually can have great input to the creation of regulations. They can participate in a "regulation negotiation." In a reg neg, concerned parties participate with the bureaucrats in crafting a regulation. Lobbyists are admitted to the process in exchange for a commitment against mounting a legal challenge to the new ordinance. Negotiators for special interests may have two goals in a reg neg: (1) Rules friendly to their interests, and (2) Entanglements for their competitors.

It's bad enough that the big contributors of campaign money have too much influence in Congress, but their advantage is magnified when Congress abandons its proper role and allows the combination of special interests and executive branch officials to legislate via rule making. That process goes back at least as far as the Interstate Commerce Act of 1887, followed by the Federal Trade Commission Act of 1914. It became much more common under the New Deal in the 1930s and has continued.

Congress, usually so guarding of its place in the separation of powers, has found benefits for its Members in this delegation of some legislative power to the executive branch. As mentioned above, bureaucrats can be blamed for the costs and hassles of regulations. Of course, some regulations create extreme costs and hassles, as "when Lockheed was building its first stealth fighter, OSHA required engineers and workers to use 65 different kinds of protective masks."[32]

Additionally, Members can curry favor with voters by helping them overcome bureaucratic problems. With every expansion of federal agencies and regulations there are more pitfalls and more chances that potential voters can be helped by their Members of Congress. It's called constituent service and is seen by Members as one of their most important activities.

The enlargement of Members' staffs has been largely devoted to constituent service, which has become enormously important in helping incumbents achieve re-election. Staffers who work on constituent service are virtually campaign workers paid by taxpayers.[33]

Congress does have the power to eliminate regulations crafted by federal agencies. To do so, however, requires passage of a joint resolution by both chambers and avoidance or override of a presidential veto.[34]

CORRECTIVE SOLUTIONS

Aside from abrogation of a duty being wrong, one practical lesson for the future is that a partisan majority in Congress does its same-party President a disservice that can have bad electoral consequences if it abandons oversight—because the harm greater than the exposure of a few missteps is that the President may be tempted into more serious improprieties if he sees no restraints. And just as "murder will out," so too eventually will most executive journeys outside the law or into murky ethical waters.

Therefore, Congress must keep watch on every President, regardless of party, to prevent the corruption that power often begets.

But it's not just corruption where a corrective is needed. It's also needed when a President violates the Constitutional requirement that "he shall take care that the laws be faithfully executed" (Article II, Section 3). Congress has an array of weapons it can use against Presidential laxity.
- It can withhold money from programs a President favors. That could take the form of reducing an appropriation or of appropriating no funds at all.
- It can delay or refuse confirmation of Presidential appointees.
- It can take away Presidential power given by Congress rather than the Constitution. Case in point: Fast-track trade agreements.
- It can delay or refuse ratifications of treaties.
- It can hold highly publicized hearings about alleged Presidential dereliction of

duty.

- It can remove the power of the President to make appointments of the "inferior officers" of the U.S. and vest that power in the courts or department heads (see the Constitution, Article II, Section 2.)
- Lastly, and to be used only rarely and with great caution, Congress can impeach, try, and convict a President who manifestly fails in a Constitutionally mandated duty. Of course, there must not be an impeachment for an isolated instance or two; that ultimate sanction must be reserved for use against a long pattern of refusal to enforce laws or a continuing refusal on a supremely important issue.

Use of those weapons should be aimed at the publicly stated target of making a President faithfully execute specified laws. And Congress should avoid any such action that would involve mere partisanship. Oversight for party advantage is illegitimate and will offend many independent voters. But getting Members to avoid partisanship may be as difficult as avoiding burns while embracing a ball of fire.

A corrective is also needed, however, for some actions by Senators and Representatives, as when they use oversight with the following sort of destructive foolishness and misjudgment. In late June 2008 Senator Charles Schumer, D-NY, from his perches on the Banking, Housing, and Urban Affairs Committee, and on the Joint Economic Committee, sent a letter to the Office of Thrift Supervision (OTS) and to the Federal Deposit Insurance Corporation (FDIC) about the California bank called IndyMac. He wrote of his concern "that IndyMac's financial deterioration poses significant risks to both taxpayers and borrowers" and that the bank "could face a failure if prescriptive measures are not taken quickly" and that the bank "appears close to collapse." So far so good. But then, in an act of blind unreason, he released the letter to the press. What followed was totally predictable—except, apparently, to Senator Schumer. Within the next eleven days depositors yanked 1.3 billion dollars from the bank, and it failed. Estimates of the failure's cost to the FDIC: $4 billion to $8 billion.

Schumer claimed that his letter did not cause the run on the bank. And IndyMac might have failed anyway—but later than it did. Nevertheless, the OTS blamed Schumer's release of the letter as the immediate cause. Notice that the OTS allegation was not that the letter was sent to regulators but that it was released to the media. Going public with the letter was virtually a directive to depositors to remove their money.[35] "Run for the hills before a financial tsunami engulfs you."

The remaining issue is, why did Schumer go public with his letter? There may not be enough psychoanalysts in the U.S. to produce a correct answer.

Senate Majority Leader Harry Reid, perversely heedless of the lesson taught by Schumer's blunder, ambushed investors on October 1, 2008, with his announcement that a Member of Congress referred in the Democratic caucus to "a major insurance company—one with a name that everyone knows that's on the verge of going bankrupt." In a market already under pressure for other reasons, Reid's throwing-fuel-on-the-fire comment contributed to a meltdown of insurance share prices the following day.[36] Then a Reid spokesman tried some damage control by saying "Reid is not personally aware of any particular company being on the verge of bankruptcy . . . Rather, his comments were meant to refer to the conditions in the financial sector generally. He regrets any confusion his comments may have caused."[37]   As if the clear meaning of Reid's words was really something else, and as if "any confusion" was in the minds of other people.

So, what corrective applies? Senators and Representatives enjoy immunity for what they say in performing their official duties, but there are legal precedents holding that what they say in newsletters and press releases is not part of their legislative activities and is thus not protected.[38] So, there may be two remedies: People damaged by non-protected utterances can sue, and voters can refuse to re-elect a Member who engages in destructive actions whether shielded or not.

And another corrective might be that Congress should provide for significant criminal penalties for anyone who engages in the sort of backdating that was recently common with stock options and that occurred when the Office of Thrift Supervision allowed an injection of additional capital into IndyBank to be listed as occurring earlier in 2008 than it did, thus causing the bank to be classed as "well capitalized" rather than a lower rating.[39]

Notes: Chapter VII. Insufficient Oversight of the Executive Branch and of
              Government Sponsored Enterprises

[1]Random House Webster's College Dictionary (New York: Random House, 1991).

[2]David B. Rivkin, Jr., and Lee A. Casey, "Constitutional Warp," The Wall Street Journal, January 31, 2007, p. A13.

[3]That law was actually Title VIII of the Housing and Community Development Act of 1977 (Public Law 95-128, 91 Stat. 1111).

[4]For example, an Associated Press story of October 20, 2008, begins thusly: "Freddie Mac secretly paid a Republican consulting firm $2 million to kill legislation that would have regulated and trimmed the mortgage finance giant and its sister company, Fannie Mae, three years before the government took control to prevent their collapse." Enter "Freddie Mac" + "stealth campaign" on an Internet search engine to find this on numerous sites.

[5]For some of the favored recipients, and for some Members feeding off the two mortgage giants, see "Fannie Mae's Political Immunity," The Wall Street Journal, July 29, 2008, p. A16. The Fannie and Freddie foundations gave away $21 million and $25 million respectively in 2007; ibid. When Senator Jim DeMint offered an amendment to a bailout bill in July 2008 to outlaw political contributions and lobbying by Fan and Fred, Majority Leader Harry Reid, D-NV, would not allow it to be voted on; ibid.

For Fannie and Freddie more generally, see Gretchen Morgenson and Joshua Rosner, <u>Reckless Endangerment: How Outsized Ambition, Greed, and Corruption Led to Economic Armageddon</u> (New York: Times Books, Henry Holt and Company, 2011).

[6]William McGurn, "Shouting 'Fannie!' in a Crowded Congress," <u>The Wall Street Journal</u>, October 14, 2008, p. A19. The Representative was Richard H. Baker, R-LA.

[7]Michael Hirsh, "The Predators' Ball," <u>Newsweek</u>, August 18/August 25, 2008, pp. 32-33.

[8]George F. Will, "TARP and ADD," <u>Newsweek,</u> December 1, 2008, p. 64.

[9]See Public Law 110-343 (October 3, 2008), Sec. 104, Financial Stability Oversight Board); Sec. 116, Oversights and Audits (conducted by the Comptroller General of the United States, a Presidential appointee); Sec. 121, Special Inspector General for the Troubled Asset Relief Program (a Presidential appointee); and Sec. 125, Congressional Oversight Panel.
Senate confirmation of President Bush's appointment of Neil M. Barofsky as the Special Inspector General was delayed by one Senator's secret hold (thought by some to have come from Senator Jim Bunning, R-KY). However, Barofsky was confirmed on December 8 after the hold was lifted a few days earlier.

[10]Renae Merle, "Defense Contractor Was Paid $1 Million to Ship 2 Washers." <u>The Washington Post</u>, August 17, 2007, p. D02, on the Internet; Matthew Zimmerman, "Convicted War Profiteer Still Lives High Life," ABC News, June 19, 2008, The Blotter from Brian Ross, on the Internet.

[11]See <u>Gregg v. Barrett</u>, 771 F.2d 539 (1985) at 542: "Our analysis precludes this Court from reviewing congressional practices and procedures when they primarily and directly affect the way Congress does its legislative business"; and ibid., at 549: Our deference and esteem for the institution as a whole <u>and for the constitutional command that the institution be allowed to manage its own affairs</u> precludes us from even attempting a diagnosis of the problem" [emphasis added].

[12]"Barney Frank's Muse," <u>The Wall Street Journal</u>, August 10, 2007, p. A10. This source pointed out that the brief was written by a law firm that has lobbied for the National Association of Securities and Commercial Law Attorneys since 1998. Some of the lawyers involved in this effort to pick more deep pockets are lobbyists for the new American Association for Justice, the let's-improve our-image euphemism for the former Association of Trial Lawyers of America.

[13]Thomas E. Mann and Norman J. Ornstein, <u>The Broken Branch: How Congress Is Failing America and How to Get It Back on Track</u> (New York: Oxford University Press, 2006), p. 155.

[14]Mann and Ornstein, <u>Broken Branch</u>, p. 215.

[15]Dan K. Thomasson, "It's time for Congress to start doing its duty of overseeing FBI," Las Vegas Sun, March 15, 2007, p. 5; Romesh Ratnesar and Timothy J. Burger, "The FBI: Does It Want to Be Fixed?" Time, December 30, 2002, p. 40; Amanda Ripley and Maggie Sieger, "The Special Agent," Time, December 30, 2002, pp. 34-40, part of cover story "Persons of the Year: The Whistleblowers."

[16]David J. Vogler, The Politics of Congress (Boston: Allyn and Bacon, 1974), p. 234. "Line-Item Victory," The Wall Street Journal, June 24, 2006, p. A10, says impoundment was a Presidential power "going back to the republic's early days" and that Congress "stole" that power in the 1970s.

[17]Richard Bolling, Power in the House (New York: E. P. Dutton & Co., 1968), p. 232.

[18]Remini, The House, p. 432.

[19]Ibid., pp. 465, 467. Title X of that 1974 law can be cited as the Impoundment Control Act of 1974.

[20]Remini, The House, p. 438.

[21]Congressional Record, permanent edition, March 27, 1996, p. 6566.

[22]Andrew Taylor, "Congress Hands President A Budgetary Scalpel, Congressional Quarterly Weekly Report, March 30, 1996, p. 864.

[23]See Clinton v. City of New York, 524 U.S. 417 (1998).

[24]Steven T. Dennis, "A Promise for a Line-Item Veto," CQ Weekly, January 22, 2007, p. 252.

[25]"Line-Item Victory," The Wall Street Journal, June 24, 2006, p. A10.

[26]Edward Whelan, "Shut Up, They Explained," The Weekly Standard, August 7, 2006, p. 12; Morton Kondracke, "Bush sets record for ignoring laws mandated by Congress," Billings Gazette, August 13, 2006, p. 12C.

[27]See Aaron Dykes, "Obama's Signing Statement on NDAA," January 1, 2012, on the Internet.

[28]Jim Hightower, If the Gods Had Meant Us to Vote They Would Have Given Us Candidates, revised edition (New York: Perennial, a HarperCollins imprint, 2001), p. 355.

[29]Hightower, If the Gods, pp. 355-60; "The Loewen Group, Inc. and Raymond L. Loewen v. United States of America," on the Internet; Jonathan Harr, "The Burial," The

New Yorker, November 1, 1999, pp. 70, 72-76, 78- 81, 83-95. See also John Sedgwick, "The Next Great Art Destination," Worth, June 2002, pp. 88-92, 94, for O'Keefe's philanthropy.

[30]Hightower, If the Gods, pp. 347-53.

[31]Ken Dilanian, "Trips paid by firms officials regulate: Agencies see no ethical conflict," USA Today, August 23, 2007, p. 1A.

[32]The quotation comes from Arthur Herman, "The Silver Lining to Defense Budget Cuts," The Wall Street Journal, January 18, 2012, p. A15.

[33]The preceding five paragraphs are largely based on Eric Felten, The Ruling Class: Inside the Imperial Congress, abridged edition (Washington: U.S. Congress Assessment Project, Heritage Foundation, 1993), pp. 35-43, 61-64, 68-71, 79-81, 93-94. See also Morris P. Fiorina, Congress: Keystone of the Washington Establishment, 2d edition (New Haven: Yale University Press, 1989), "Constituency service" in the index.

Find a critic satisfied by a change and you can find another regretting it. Thus, if Congress puts details into laws rather than allowing executive branch bureaucrats to write regulations, it will be criticized for "micromanaging." See Philip K. Howard, "Let's 'Restructure' Washington While We're at It," The Wall Street Journal, December 19, 2008, p. A17, which lambastes "the 2001 No Child Left Behind law, a 670-page statute" for not delegating power to the Secretary of Education and instead being "a model of micromanagement."

[34]See the Contract with America Advancement Act of 1996, Public Law 104-121(110 Stat. 847-75), in which Title II (the Small Business Regulatory Enforcement Fairness Act), Subtitle E, Section 251, is "Congressional Review of Agency Rulemaking" and is an amendment as new chapter 8 to Title 5, U.S. Code. This is sometimes referred to as the Congressional Review Act

[35]Louise Story, "Regulators seize IndyMac After a Run on the Bank," The New York Times, July 12, 2008, Sec. C, p. 5, on LexisNexis Academic; Associated Press, "Schumer denies role in IndyMac takeover, Newsday, July 14, 2008, p. A24, on LexisNexis Academic; "The $4 Billion Senator," The Wall Street Journal, July 15, 2008, p. A18; Vikas Bajaj, "Timeline of bank's rebirth and bust: In IndyMac's failure, the blame is disputed," The International Herald Tribune, July 30, 2008, p. 14, on LexisNexis Academic; Dean Foust, "Why Did IndyMac Implode?" Business Week, August 4, 2008, p. 24, on LexisNexis Academic; Ellen Yan, "Schumer draws fire for IndyMac letters," Newsday, August 22, 2008, p. A43, on LexisNexis Academic. The quotations from Schumer's letter are from Bloomberg News, "Senator asks regulators to probe the financial health of IndyMac," Los Angeles Times, June 27, 2008, Part C, p. 2, on LexisNexis Academic, search phrase: IndyMac.

After arguably triggering what was then the second-largest bank failure in U.S. history, Senator Schumer had the effrontery to write an op-ed titled "How to Rescue the Banks"; it's in The Wall Street Journal, October 14, 2008, p. A21. On "triggering" versus "causing," see Jim Lindgren, "Is Schumer to blame for IndyMac's collapse? Not really," The Volokh Conspiracy, on the Internet.

[36]"The Trouble With Harry," <u>The Wall Street Journal</u>, October 4, 2008, p. A14.

[37]"Reid backs off insurance company claim," found on numerous Internet sites by entering that phrase.

[38]Article I, Section 6 of the Constitution says that "for any speech or debate in either House, they [Senators and Representatives] shall not be questioned in any other place." Federal courts have held that even Members' speech outside of either chamber is constitutionally protected if it's made in pursuit of legislative duties but in some instances such as press releases and newsletters is not protected if not essential to legislative activity. Thus, it may be arguable whether the actions of Schumer and Reid were protected. See <u>Hutchinson v. Proxmire</u>, 443 U.S. 111 (1979); and 487 U.S. 1240, certiorari denied (from <u>Sundquist v. Chastain</u>, 266 U.S. App. D.C, 833 F. 2d 311[1987]).

[39]Jessica Holzer, "OTS Let IndyMac Backdate Infusion," <u>The Wall Street Journal</u>, December 23, 2008, p. A4.

VIII. Deficient Oversight of Subordinate Congressional Operations

EPIGRAPH: Eyes have they, but they see not.
                    ---The Bible, Psalms, Number CXV, Verse 6.

Two scandals erupted in the 1990s involving offshoots the House had set up for the convenience of Representatives, a post office and a so-called bank. Those are both dealt with above in the chapter on Incumbency. In each case so little supervision occurred that Members and employees were able to engage in criminal and unethical conduct.

Despite lackadaisical coverage by the three TV networks, problems at the House Bank leaped into public view in late 1991. It was not technically a bank and was not subject to any federal supervisory or regulatory agency such as the Federal Deposit Insurance Corporation. It might be called a financial convenience store. It was so poorly and archaically managed that the books were kept in handwritten ledgers. Members could deposit their paychecks and then draw money from their balances. But the operation was so loose that no regular account statements or notices of overdrafts were sent out, and deposits were often not posted to accounts, sometimes not until several weeks later. Hundreds of Representatives made thousands of overdrafts. Many Members did not do so knowingly but wrote "bad" checks simply because their accounts had not been credited with deposits they had made. Others, however, deliberately took advantage of the laxity to obtain money they had no right to. Eventually, the investigations into the scandal uncovered more wide-ranging transgressions, resulting in convictions of four former Members, a former D.C. delegate, and the former sergeant-at-arms, though the assigned guilt was not always technically related to the check-kiting.

As the post-office scandal entered public consciousness in 1992, the high and mighty Poo-Bahs of the House went beyond lack of supervision into cover-up. The chairman of the House Administration Committee, Rep. Charlie Rose, D-NC, disseminator of a whitewashing report, alleged that "there is no credible evidence to back up allegations of wrongdoing against any individual."[1] How did that committee not see the evidence that eventually led to guilty pleas by several House Post Office employees and that eventually helped send Ways and Means Committee chairman Dan Rostenkowski, D-IL, and Representative Joe Kolter, D-PA, to prison? The three major TV networks were complicit in the effort to establish that nothing wrong occurred: They ran few stories about the scandal.[2] Even after the grist-mill of justice began to grind down the guilty, 237 Representatives voted in March 1994 against a House investigation. Their excuse was that a House inquiry would jeopardize the work of federal prosecutors.[3]

CORRECTIVE SOLUTIONS

The Legislative Branch subcommittees of each chamber's Appropriations Committee should be more diligent about digging into the records every year of all agencies that are part of the legislative branch to see if there are illegalities, inefficiencies, or ethical lapses. A stand-alone report addressing those three topics should be produced annually.

And if Members spent more time paying attention to their legislative responsibilities, and directing their staffs to do the same, they might avoid the sort of embarrassment that arose with the news in May 2008 that Congress sent to the President a "farm" bill that omitted thirty-four pages of provisions passed by Congress. Yet, in that case and to give the benefit of the doubt, the error occurred at the so-called "enrollment" (printing) stage in the legislative process and perhaps outside of the immediate purview of Members and their staffers.[4] Is it expecting too much that a bill worked on by Members for eighteen months would be free of major error? On the other hand, that the bill had several hundred pages might be an excuse.

Notes: Chapter VIII. Deficient Oversight of Subordinate Congressional Operations

[1]"Stand Fast, Rosty," The Wall Street Journal, May 27, 1994, p. A8.

[2]L. Brent Bozell III, "Ten Reasons Ethics News Reeks of Bias," January 9, 1997, available on the Internet.

[3]See list of them in "Stand Fast, Rosty."

[4]Catharine Richert, "Clerical Error Extends Farm Bill Saga," CQ Weekly, May 26, 2008, p. 1417.

IX. Great Power: Senate Majority Leader and Speaker of the House

EPIGRAPH: The highest proof of virtue is to possess boundless
               power without abusing it.
                   ---Thomas Babington, Lord Macaulay,
                       Review of Aiken's Life of Addison (1843).

One potentially harmful Congressional action is that a leader commanding a majority in either chamber sometimes refuses to allow a proposal to come to a vote. It may be a good or a bad idea, but it never gets a fair test. It's questionable whether the Speaker and the Senate Majority Leader have a full commitment to democratic principles when they refuse to allow a vote merely because they oppose the measure—or because their partisanship dictates that they not burden Members of their party with a vote that might be hard to defend when running for re-election.[1]

It can be argued that neither the Senate Majority Leader nor the Speaker of the House can exercise that power or those noted below unless they have majority support in their respective chambers, and that such exercise is therefore not anti-majoritarian nor a perversion of American national democracy.

That claim may be true much of the time. The claim fails, however, when a majority of Senators or Representatives wants to accomplish a particular action but is prevented from it by the Majority Leader or the Speaker. The claimants can further argue that a majority can remove either of those officials to prevent blockage of majority will. But there are at least two situations in which those officials can block a majority and not suffer removal from office. One is that a majority suffering blockage in House or Senate may be composed of some members of both political parties and that most members of the majority party may be supporting their leader. In such case, of course, there would not be enough votes to remove either official. Second is that even if most members of the majority party are at odds with their leader's action, they may not feel the conflict to be of sufficient magnitude to warrant ouster. Without early removal, the Speaker's term continues until the end of the Congress during which he or she was elected.[2]

Senate Majority Leader

A majority of U.S. Senators might want to pass a bill or resolution—or at least give it an up or down vote—but if the leader of the majority party in the Senate does not favor such action, he can prevent it. That power of his is absolute. He has sole authority about what comes to the floor of the Senate. His decision controls whether a proposal will even be voted on in the full Senate.

Of course, there must be some process to establish an orderly way of doing business in the Senate, and the majority party can dictate the procedure. It would not do to have a party caucus and vote prior to every floor action. Therefore, the majority party selects its Majority Leader and places in his hands certain powers such as establishing the agenda for floor action (as opposed to committee activities). He retains those powers so long as he continues as Majority Leader. Were he to get seriously and frequently out of step with his party colleagues, a rebellion by them might produce a leadership change.

The upside of this is efficiency. The downside is Caesarism, putting the fortunes of the entire country at the whim of one person. Of course, the Constitution puts the President in such a position, but the Majority Leader's unilateral power is extra-Constitutional and therefore open to greater questioning. Further, because the public is less informed about the nuances of Congressional activities, the Majority Leader operates in a more shadowy environment than does the President.

An instance of this power, but one which paraded more than usual in the public consciousness, was Majority Leader Harry Reid's yanking of the comprehensive immigration bill from Senate consideration after failure to shut off debate on it in 2007. Proponents of the bill argued that compromises and more time on the floor would have enabled the bill to pass. But Reid, D-NV, used his power to terminate the process at least temporarily. In doing so, he called the measure "the president's bill," and some observers claimed he was primarily interested not in solving the immigration mess but in denying President Bush a success. A seasoned observer reported that Reid was "being disingenuous when he said the Senate needed to move on and take up energy legislation. Instead, he plans to bring before the Senate today a motion censuring Attorney General Alberto Gonzales."[3]

Further examples of Majority Leaders' use of this power are legion.

Another power of the Majority Leader is that if he and other Senators are competing for recognition by the presiding officer, he will be the first to obtain the floor. Thus, he can be the first to offer arguments and motions. Robert Byrd, D-WV, former Majority Leader (1977-81, 1987-89), called this primacy "the most potent weapon in the Majority Leader's arsenal."[4]

A Majority Leader can exploit his powers to prevent some amendments to a bill. One method involves "cloture," the three-fifths vote that prevents unlimited debate. After a successful cloture vote, no non-germane amendments are permitted.[5]

The second method is "filling the amendment tree." That's a tactic available in slightly different forms to both the Majority Leader and the Speaker. The rules of each chamber, and of parliamentary procedure more generally, allow only certain numbers and types of amendments to be pending simultaneously. Consider the text of a bill as a tree trunk and that there are only a few branches to which an amendment can attach. Through the power flowing from first recognition, the Majority Leader or supportive Senators can offer all the permitted amendments to a bill, thus blocking later amendments from opponents.[6]

Results of this single Senator's power can be interesting and can provide money-making opportunities for insiders. Suppose, as may have been the case with a bill in 2006 to establish a trust fund to pay asbestos sufferers, that a particular bill would financially impact a set of companies. As prospects for the bill's passage wax and wane, the stock prices of the companies may advance and decline. If traders or Members have advance knowledge that the Majority Leader will or will not bring the bill to floor, they can profit.[7]

Congressional leaders usually must operate to enhance their party's reputation with voters, "to protect the collective electoral interests of their fellow partisans."[8] But a leader may push his or her own, more limited, even non-majoritarian, goals. For instance Harry Reid, as the new Senate Majority Leader promised to prevent any floor vote to make Yucca Mountain, Nevada, a national depository for nuclear waste. He favors keeping the waste at reactor sites in over half of U.S. states. That's a radioactive problem for many politicians whose voters worry about the interminable dangers of such debris. Some Yucca Mountain advocates say Reid is giving parochial interests a higher priority than national needs. They say he's abusing his power as Majority Leader and should recuse himself from Senate involvement. Refusing to step aside, Reid said, "Yes, the responsibilities I have are broader now. I have more to do than before, but Nevada comes first."[9] It may be that it was actually Reid's re-election chances in 2010 that came first.

A Majority Leader cannot always put his own or his party's desires completely ahead of the wishes of the Senate minority—especially if his majority is fewer than sixty. As recently explained, "In the Senate, unlike the House, a majority is not sufficient to act; to keep the Senate functioning requires supermajorities, and this almost always requires that the Majority Leader accommodate the minority to some extent."[10]

Speaker of the House

The Speaker is often called the second most powerful person in the U.S. government. Great power for her or him is indeed necessary in a body charged with important responsibilities and made up of 435 Representatives, five Delegates, and one Resident Commissioner. Yet, it's fair to examine whether too much authority is lodged in this office and whether needed authority is abused by improper use.

Of course, the leader of a majoritarian group holds power at the will of the majority and can be restrained or removed by that majority. Thus, in theory and to some extent in practice, as long as the Speaker is allowed by the majority to continue in office, any alleged abuses would seem to be sanctioned by that majority. The limit on the practical application of the theory is that the Speaker wields some powers that can inhibit hostile actions by dissatisfied members of the majority—powers such as appointment to undesired committees, removal of earmarks from bills, refusal of recognition in debate, and encouragement of someone to be an opponent in a primary election.

An otherwise valuable book incorrectly asserts that "the Speaker's role as presiding officer is an impartial one."[11] Of course, some actions by a Speaker are impartial, but in many respects she or he is an extreme partisan, leading her troops in battle to achieve a policy or an electoral advantage for the party.

In not requiring that the Speaker be a Representative, the Founding Fathers contemplated a Speaker who would be "above normal party politics." Later House traditions held that the Speaker rarely participated in debate, seldom voted, and did not go to the floor to lobby. Those traditions are now only lightly honored. Recent Speakers have embraced a more active role.[12]

Among the Speaker's powers, sometimes subject to formal approval by his or her party caucus—and always subject to continuing support by a sufficient number of the party's majority—are the following: [13]

● Presiding in the House.

● Recognizing Members to speak on the floor of the House. That is an absolute, unappealable right.[14] Usually, the Speaker may ask a Representative seeking recognition, "For what purpose does the (gentleman or gentlelady) rise?" Depending on the answer, the Speaker may or may not recognize the person. That gives the Speaker control of what motions will be offered and what business the House will consider.[15]

● Ruling on points of order.[16]

● Referring bills and resolutions to appropriate committees. That power technically resides in the Speaker but is normally exercised by the House parliamentarian.[17] Bills are often worded so they will be referred to a particular committee, and lobbyists even have influence in that process.[18]

● (Usually) designating one committee as having primary jurisdiction when bills, in parts or in sequence, are referred to more than one committee.[19] Referring a bill to multiple committees allows the Speaker to dictate a date by which the bill must be reported by each committee.[20]

● Scheduling floor action on bills and resolutions. "The power of the Speaker of the House is the power of scheduling,"[21] That authority is largely exercised through the

Committee on Rules, which the Speaker influences by controlling its majority composition.[22] A bill's special rule as reported by the Rules Committee typically states that "at any time after the adoption of this resolution" the Speaker may provide for consideration of the bill by the Committee of the Whole.[23] Thus, the Speaker decides when, or even if, the bill will be dealt with further.

• Postponing votes on accepting rules reported from the Rules Committee.[24]

• Removing a bill from House consideration after it has been scheduled or even after debate on it has begun.[25]

The Speaker's power to yank a bill from the floor rests on the House's adoption of an ad hoc rule (a "special rule") setting the procedures for consideration of that bill. Typically, one of those rules says, "During consideration in the House . . . the Chair may postpone further consideration of the bill to such time as may be designated by the Speaker."[26]

• Postponing a recorded vote for two legislative days.[27]

• Choosing bills to be designated H.R. 1 through H.R. 10 in each Congress.[28]

• Appointing majority party Representatives to the Rules Committee.[29] The Speaker may "use his authority over the House Rules Committee to have his preferred version of a bill sent to the floor under debate and amendment procedures that advantage the majority party."[30]

• Designating particular Members as chairs of committees, including the powerful Rules Committee.[31]

• Choosing members of select, joint, and conference committees.[32] House Rule I, 110th Congress, states that in appointing conference committees, "the Speaker shall appoint no less than a majority who generally supported the House position as determined by the Speaker" [emphasis added]. That language allows the Speaker plenty of wiggle room to select conferees who will support what the Speaker desires, even to the point of naming conferees who opposed a major part of a bill but supported its general thrust.[33]

• Regarding standing committees other than the Rules Committee, their memberships "shall be elected by the House within seven calendar days after the commencement of each Congress, from nominations submitted by the respective party caucus or conference."[34]   Each party has a committee assignment panel, the Republicans' Steering Committee and the Democrats' Steering and Policy Committee."[35] In practice, however, each party's leadership can often dictate who gets a committee assignment. For instance, in 2008, Minority Leader John Boehner bypassed anti-earmarker Jeff Flake in favor Jo Bonner, a Republican with less seniority, the reported reason being that Bonner generally voted for earmarks while Flake did not.[36]

• Creating ad hoc committees (if the House approves) to deal with bills that otherwise would fall under the purview of more than one standing committee.[37] The Speaker can also create task forces to circumvent standing committees; to generate ideas, publicity, and bills; or to generate increased support for a bill—and for the leadership—by giving more Members a chance to help craft the bill.[38]

• Controlling House members of conferences by (1) refusing to appoint conferees until receiving assurances that they will work for the Speaker's goals in the conference, (2) appointing more conferees after House conference membership has been constituted, and (3) removing conferees.[39]

• Imposing "sanctions against uncooperative chairs or partisan colleagues."[40] "'The truth is, if you don't always vote with [the GOP] leadership,' said Rep. Jeff Flake, R-Ariz., 'you'll often get a primary challenge from somebody who will walk in lockstep with them.'"[41]

• Influencing Members by doling out favors. For instance, the Speaker may give a Member the prestige of chairing the Committee of the Whole or of being the Speaker Pro Tem, grant an interview with important people from a Member's district, or help solve a district problem.[42] And when the President and the Speaker are of different parties, the Speaker probably also has some influence on the selection of a Representative or the challenger of an incumbent to give a response to the President's State of the Union speech or his Saturday radio talk. Additionally, the Speaker may aid a Member's re-election effort or appoint a Member to the board of some outside body such as the Smithsonian Institution.

A shocking exercise of the latter power is detailed in the book Charlie Wilson's War. Speaker Tip O'Neill had authority to appoint three Representatives to the board of the Kennedy Center for the Performing Arts, and Wilson had been seeking one of those plum assignments for several months, partly to get free entertainment and impress women. In 1981 O'Neill offered the position to Wilson on condition that Wilson become a member of the House Ethics Committee in order to protect Representative John Murtha from the fallout of an FBI attempt to bribe him during the ABSCAM sting operation. Wilson initially told O'Neill that he was not an Ethics Committee sort of guy, but he accepted after O'Neill informed him it was "a package deal." Shortly after Wilson joined the Ethics panel it closed down the Murtha investigation, and "a teary Murtha . . . confided to a colleague that Wilson's effort had saved his life."[43]

• Instructing "committee chairs to deal with certain bills."[44]

• Acting as party spokesperson. That is more crucial when the President is of the other party.[45]

• In the case of catastrophic circumstances, the Speaker now gets to decide, following a quorum-failure report from the Sergeant-at-Arms and following consultation with the majority and minority leaders, the number and names of Representatives who are incapacitated and no longer need be counted for achievement of a quorum.[46]

• If the Speaker declares the existence of at least 101 House vacancies due to catastrophic circumstances, special elections will be held to fill the empty positions.[47]

• Changing the rules of the House, although that of course requires support from the majority. The House has a long history of changing its rules, often for the better. Criticism of some changes, however, may be legitimate when they're done for merely partisan reasons, as in the following recent instances.

In 2007 Speaker Nancy Pelosi allegedly sought to change House rules relating to recommittal, germaneness, and the new pay-go rule. Recommittal provides that just before a final vote on passage of a measure there shall be an opportunity for a Member who opposes the measure to move to recommit the measure to the committee it came from. The mover has the option of including or not including instructions to the committee. With instructions, the motion provides minority Members an opportunity to put the majority on record about a proposal it wants to avoid. Recommittal instructions, however, must be germane to the bill for which recommittal is sought. That procedure has existed unchanged in the House for nearly two centuries.[48]

But Democrats in the 110th Congress became increasingly uncomfortable with Republican recommittal motions that attempted to force votes on tax increases that were not mentioned in bills but were implicit in them. House Rule XXI, clause 10, added to the rules by the Democrats near the start of the 110th Congress, "prohibits the consideration of any legislation proposing direct spending or revenue changes that would increase the budget deficit within a five-year or a ten-year time frame ('Pay-as-You-Go' point of order)."[49] The Democrats had opened the door to more far-ranging instructions that would be considered germane in recommital motions because of their "pay-as-you-go" rule requiring that new spending be offset by spending cuts in other programs or by tax increases. Republicans used that open door on several occasions.[50] An Internet blogger explained the situation thusly: "The Democrats were attempting to pass bills without cutting other expenditures, so the only way they were going to be able to fund the new spending under their own rules was by eventually raising taxes – and they refused to tell the public that in the bills."[51]

Those Republican recommittal efforts using expanded germaneness arguably led Pelosi to seek their end. According to Roll Call, The Newspaper of Capitol Hill Since 1955 the Democratic plan was to use a Rules Committee rule on consideration of the budget "as a vehicle to change the chamber's rules on motions to recommit." The Democrats did not make any formal presentation of the leadership's plan, and few rank-and-filers knew about it, although senior staff did know, one even writing, "I totally concur that this is a BIG deal and the leadership has to thoroughly understand what they are taking on before going forward."[52] In response to Pelosi's alleged scheme for altering the rules, Republicans slowed House business through procedural tactics that are permitted but seldom used. Pelosi then supposedly scrapped her effort to take away the long-standing minority right to offer recommittal motions.[53] But in January 2009, the Democratic majority in the new 111th Congress adopted a new rule that restricted recommittal. [54]

In April 2008, Speaker Nancy Pelosi again stepped over a line when she short-circuited the long-standing procedure for fast-track trade-promotion authority by inducing the House to pass a resolution that certain fast-track procedures would not apply to the U.S.-Colombia Trade Promotion Agreement, thus postponing House consideration of, and probably killing, the pact negotiated by the President. That was permissible because the most recent fast-track law (P.L. 107-210), dealing with procedures that the executive branch and legislative branch had to follow, did not contravene the Constitutional right of either the Senate or the House to change its rules at any time. Aside from the arguments whether the substance of the Colombian deal was advantageous or injurious, critics of the President's and Pelosi's <u>procedural</u> actions competed for acceptance of their positions. An impartial assessment may be that the House's action will harm future attempts at trade pacts.[55]

The Speaker has several additional powers, some of which are in Rule I; and Rule XX, clauses 1-4 and clause 5(a), 110th Congress.

CORRECTIVE SOLUTIONS

The Senate should adopt a rule that in each session every bill reported favorably by a Senate committee or coming from the House directly to the floor of the Senate must be accorded an up or down vote before the session ends. Same for Presidential nominations. Same for bills that neither come from the House nor from a committee, as was the case with the comprehensive immigration bill in the spring of 2007, which was yanked by Majority Leader Harry Reid before it was brought back to the floor, only to finally fail. Such rules should be self-enforcing, i.e., the Senate should not be able to adjourn sine die until final votes have occurred on all such bills and nominations.

Some way should be found to make the Speaker an impartial presiding officer, as is the Speaker of the British House of Commons. A former Speaker of the Commons said, "Our democracy owes more than words can say to the clash of ideas and the rough and tumble of party political debate, but it also owes an enormous amount to the fact that the Speaker is completely impartial in the political controversies."[56]

How the Speaker could be made impartial in the American system, or at least be made less partisan, is an issue of difficulty even for people who think the change would benefit the nation. And, of course, there are many who would completely oppose the innovation.

One improvement would be to change the rules of the House to provide that no bill which has been scheduled for House consideration or which is already under consideration can be withdrawn by the Speaker. A second good change would be a rule that the Speaker must appoint the House members of conference committees within a certain number of calendar days after the House's refusal to agree to Senate changes in a bill passed by the

House; and that the Speaker may not appoint additional conferees after House membership has been constituted save in cases of resignation, death, or incapacitation; and that the Speaker may not remove conferees. A third advance might be a rule that House rules cannot be changed other than during the first, say, three months of a new Congress.

To those who will say that the above rules would be subject to motions to suspend them, I point to Senate rules which include these words: "No motion to suspend this rule shall be in order, nor shall the Presiding Officer entertain any request to suspend it by unanimous consent."[57] Would the House be any less capable than the Senate of including and abiding by similar words in some of its rules?

However, the Senate has a procedure, little known to outsiders, for changing or suspending its rules. It can be done by a so-called standing order, which can be created in a variety of ways: (1) Adoption by simple majority as a stand-alone resolution at any time but often at the beginning of a yearly session, (2) Adoption through unanimous consent, or (3) By inclusion in the body of a bill, as when Public Law 106-554, Section 903 (2000), stated that "the reading of conference reports is no longer required, if the said conference report is available in the Senate." That provision annulled long-standing Senate precedents that enabled a single Senator to effectively filibuster a bill by asking that it be read out loud on the floor.[58]

We thus find that a standing order can be defined as a Senate procedure modification that has the same effect and enforceability as a Standing Rule of the Senate and that may change a Standing Rule without altering its words. As the name indicates, a standing order "stands" until repealed or until a time stated therein.

For standing orders there's no compilation similar to the Standing Rules of the Senate. Such orders adopted by resolution, however, are in the Senate Manual. Those created by unanimous consent can be found in the Congressional Record for the date of their adoption. Those embedded in laws can be found in each law.[59]

Notes: Chapter IX. Great Power: Senate Majority Leader and
Speaker of the House

[1]Cases in point: ●In late July 2008, Speaker Nancy Pelosi publicly announced that she would refuse to allow a vote on opening more offshore areas to oil drilling. ●At about the same time Majority Leader Harry Reid prevented Republican offshore-oil-drilling amendments to be voted on. ● Bill Frist refused to bring an enhanced rescission measure to the floor of the Senate in 2006; see the chapter on Insufficient Oversight of the Executive Branch

[2]Wm. Holmes Brown and Charles W. Johnson, House Practice: A Guide to the Rules, Precedents, and Procedures of the House (Washington: USGPO, 2003), p. 638.

[3]See Fred Barnes, "Who Killed the Immigration Bill?" The Wall Street Journal, June 11, 2007, p. A13.

[4]Found on the Internet under "Majority Leader's powers."

[5]Senate Rule XXII. Further, the leader can bring a bill to the floor, then immediately ask for cloture on it, then remove it from the floor until just before the cloture vote, and then bring it back later.

[6]Barbara Sinclair, "The New World of U.S. Senators," in Lawrence C. Dodd and Bruce I. Oppenheimer, eds., Congress Reconsidered, 8th edition (Washington: CQ Press, 2005), p. 14; Walter J. Oleszek, Congressional Procedures and the Policy Process, 7th edition (Washington: CQ Press, 2007), pp. 172-74 (for the House), 230-32 (for the Senate). Carroll J. Doherty, "Why Democrats Can't Get a Foothold On the 'Amendment Tree,'" CQ Weekly, May 8, 1999, p. 1056; this refers to the second tactic as "one of those arcane Senate procedures that only parliamentary wizards understand."
And the Speaker, through influence over the Rules Committee, can also "fill the tree, i.e., leave no branch for another Representative's amendment.

[7]Brody Mullins, "Hedge Funds Hire Lobbyists To Gather Tips in Washington," The Wall Street Journal, December 8, 2006, pp. A1, A15. See also this book's chapter on Violations.

[8]Randall Strahan, "Studying Leaders and Leadership in Congress," found on the Internet.

[9]Steve Tetreault, "Yucca Coalition Presses Reid on 'Abusing' Powers," Las Vegas Review-Journal, December 2006, found on the Internet.

[10]Sinclair, "The New World of U.S. Senators," p. 14.

[11]Brown and Johnson, House Practice, p. 637. The paragraph immediately preceding the quoted words makes it clear that "presiding officer" does not merely refer to actions while chairing a session. In support of the 'impartiality' of the Speaker, this work cites Congressional Record, [permanent edition], June 4, 1963, pp. 10151-65; but see especially pp. 10161, column 2, and 10165, column 1, which make it clear that a few Representatives stated their appreciation of the Speaker's impartiality in just one particular debate on that date.

[12]Thomas E. Mann and Norman J. Ornstein, The Broken Branch: How Congress Is Failing America and How to Get It Back on Track (New York: Oxford University Press, 2006), pp. 8-9.

[13]For lists of the Speaker's powers see Walter J. Oleszek, Congressional Procedures and the Policy Process, 7th edition (Washington: CQ Press, 2007), p. 20, Box 1-2; and Brown and Johnson, House Practice, pp. 639-40.

[14]House Rule XVII, clause 2, 110th Congress. Oleszek, Congressional Procedures, 7th edition, p. 116.

[15]James V. Saturno, "The Speaker of the House: House Officer, Party Leader, and Representative," CRS Report for Congress, updated January 29, 2007, pp. CRS-4 and CRS-5.

[16]Oleszek, Congressional Procedures, 7th edition, p. 20.

[17]Ibid., pp. 20, 82, 135; House Rule XII, 110th Congress.

[18]Oleszek, Congressional Procedures, 7th edition, p. 85.

[19]House Rule, XII, clause 2(c), 110th Congress; Oleszek, Congressional Procedures, 7th edition, pp. 87-88.

[20]House Rule XII, clause 2(c)(5), 110th Congress; Barbara Sinclair, "The Speaker as Party Leader," in The Speaker: Leadership in the U.S. House of Representatives, edited by Ronald M. Peters, Jr. (Washington: Congressional Quarterly, Inc., 1995), p. 45.

[21]Oleszek, Congressional Procedures, 7th edition, p. 113, quoting Speaker Thomas O'Neill, Jr. "If all measures have to be taken up in the order in which they are listed on the calendars, as was the practice in the early nineteenth century, many major bills would not reach the House floor before Congress adjourns. Instead, major legislation reaches the floor in most instances because it has been granted precedence through a special order (rule) obtained from the Rules Committee"; ibid. pp. 125-26. Following approval of a rule, the Speaker consults members of his or her leadership team and decides when the bill will reach the floor, where it is usually then dealt with by the Committee of the Whole before action by the House itself.

[22]Valerie Heitshusen, Congressional Research Service, Memorandum on "Scheduling Powers of the House Speaker," October 6, 2006; Saturno, "The Speaker of the House," January 29, 2007, pp. CRS-5, CRS-10. Sinclair, in Peters, p. 48: "By making the Rules Committee an arm of the leadership, the reformers gave the Speaker true control of the flow of legislation to the floor and provided the Speaker with a powerful and flexible tool for structuring members' floor choices."

[23]The Committee of the Whole is all members of the House operating under more relaxed procedures, and only 100 are necessary for a quorum. A special rule may provide for consideration by the House rather than its Committee of the Whole; Christopher M. Davis, "How Measures Are Brought to the House Floor: A Brief Introduction," CRS Report for Congress, updated April 16, 2008. See also Richard S. Beth, "How Special

Rules Regulate Calling up Measures for Consideration in the House," CRS Report for Congress, updated December 5, 2005.

[24]House Rule XX, clause 8, 110th Congress. "Under a 1977 procedural change, the Speaker may postpone votes on rules and permit them to be voted on at five-minute intervals later in the day or any time within the next two days. . . . There are occasions, too, when the majority leadership will either not take up a rule or yank it off the floor if the House appears likely to turn it down"; Oleszek, Congressional Procedures, 7th edition, p. 142.

[25] Ibid., pp. 115, 147.

[26]Congressional Record, daily edition, May 9, 2007, p. H4647. A perusal of the Record will unearth numerous other examples.

[27]House Rule XX, clause 8, 110th Congress.

[28]Section 217 of House Resolution 6, Congressional Record, daily edition, January 4, 2007, pp. H20, H27. That continues an earlier practice.

[29]Those appointments are subject to approval by the Democratic caucus or Republican conference (Saturno, "The Speaker of the House," January 29, 2007, pp. CRS-5 and CRS-6; Sinclair, "The Speaker as Party Leader," p. 45; Oleszek, Congressional Procedures, 7th edition, p.124. "As a GOP Rules vice chairman said about the panel's relations with the Speaker: 'How much is the Rules Committee the handmaiden of the Speaker? The answer is, totally'"; Ibid., p. 125.

[30]Ibid, p. 109.

[31]House Rule X, clause 5(c)(1), 110th Congress, stipulates that the chair of each committee "shall be elected by the House, on the nomination of the majority party caucus or conference"; the Speaker's influence therein allows her to make the actual appointment. See also Saturno, "The Speaker of the House," January 29, 2007, p. CRS-5; Oleszek, Congressional Procedures, 7th edition, pp. 125, 321. "Today, because of party rule and other changes made by Democrats and Republicans in each chamber, all committee chairs (and ranking minority committee members) are subject to secret ballot election within the confines of their party caucus or conference"; ibid., 92.

[32]House Rule I, clause 11.

[33] Oleszek, Congressional Procedures, 7th edition, p. 265.

[34]House Rule X, clause 5(a)(1), 110th Congress. For the Rules Committee see below in its chapter.

[35]Oleszek, Congressional Procedures, 7th edition, p. 92.

[36]"GOP Flake Out," Wall Street Journal, February 19, 2008, p. A18.

[37]Oleszek, Congressional Procedures, 7th edition, p. 86.

[38]Ibid., pp. 15-16, 87, 321; Sinclair, "The Speaker as Party Leader," pp. 47-48.

[39]Oleszek, Congressional Procedures, 7th edition, pp. 263-64.

[40]Ibid., p. 321.

[41]Ibid., p. 322.

[42]Saturno, "The Speaker of the House," January 29, 2007, p. CRS-7, quoting Tip O'Neill as reported in Michael J. Malbin, "House Democrats Are Playing With a Strong Leadership Lineup," National Journal, Vol. 9, June 18, 1977, p. 942. See also Sinclair, "The Speaker as Party Leader," pp. 46-47.

[43]George Crile, Charlie Wilson's War: The Extraordinary Story of the Largest Covert Operation in History (New York: Atlantic Monthly Press, 2003), pp. 81-85; John H. Fund, "John Murtha and Congress' 'culture of corruption,'" Jewish World Review, November 15, 2006, pp. 5-6 of 7 on the Internet.

[44]Oleszek, Congressional Procedures, 7th edition, p. 321.

[45]Saturno, "The Speaker of the House," January 29, 2007, p. CRS-6.]

[46]See Public Law 109-55 (August 2, 2005), Title III—Continuity of Representation, Section 301; and House Rule XX, clause 5(c); and Mann and Ornstein, Broken Branch, pp. 207-09. See also below in the chapter on Unrelated Items in the Same Bill.

[47]Public Law 109-55, Title III, Section 301.

[48]The House's germaneness rule has existed unchanged since 1822; it is now Rule XVI, clause 7, 110th Congress; Brown and Johnson, House Practice, pp. 526-27; Asher C. Hinds, Hinds' Precedents of the House of Representatives of the United States . . . (5 vols.; Washington: GPO, 1907), vol. V, pp. 388-89, section 5767; ibid., p. 264, section 5529: "It is not in order to do indirectly by a motion to commit with instructions what may not be done directly by way of amendment." See also EricCantor.com, "Alert: Shutting Down the Floor" on the Internet, Cantor being a Representative from Virginia; RS Insider, "Nancy Throws Out Thomas Jefferson's Procedures—Rejects Procedural Issue On Books Since 1822," [May 16, 2007] on the Internet.

[49]U.S., Congress, House, Rules Committee, "Summary of House Rules Package Opening Day of the 110th Congress," on the Internet.

[50]Here are some examples. Congressional Record, daily edition, March 7, 2007, p. H2263; ibid., March 8, 2007, p. H2328; ibid., March 9, 2007, p. H2374; ibid., p. H5351. See also "Republicans Ready to Commit," CQ Weekly, March 26, 2007, p. 900.

[51]Patrick Casey, "Pelosi Loses Power Grab, For Now," May 17, 2007, on the Internet . By late March, Republicans averred that less than half of their recommittal efforts had involved the pay-go rule; Susan Ferrechio, "Pay-As-You-Go Change Planned to Limit GOP's Motions to Recommit," CQ Weekly, April 2, 2007, p. 967.

[52]Susan Davis and Jennifer Yachnin, "GOP Halts Rules Change," Roll Call, May 17, 2007, pp. 1, 43.

[53]Casey, "Pelosi Loses Power Grab, For Now"; Allahpundit, "Pelosi proposes, then quickly withdraws, rule change to shut out GOP minority," May 16, 2007, on the Internet.

[54]See House Rule XIX, clause 2(b), 111th Congress. It states that motions to recommit may only instruct a committee to report one or more amendments back to the House.

[55]See House Resolution 1092, Rules Committee Report 110-574, April 9, 2008, stating "that section 151(e)(1) and section 151(f)(1) of the Trade Act of 1974 shall not apply in the case of H.R. 5724." The resolution passed on April 10 by a vote of 224 to 195. See also Timothy R. Homan, "Colombia Free-Trade Pact Held Up As House Democrats Block Action," CQ Weekly, April 14, 2008, p. 949; Greg Hitt and Martin Vaughan, "Bush Team Reassures Trade Partners," The Wall Street Journal, April 11, 2008, p. A2; David J. Lynch, "Rule change hits Colombia trade deal," USA Today, April 11, 2008, p. 1B; Carl Hulse, "House Votes to Put Off Trade Deal Bush Sought," The New York Times, April 11, 2008, p. C1. In what would doubtless be considered by many as an excessively extreme reaction, an editorial in The Wall Street Journal ("Pelosi's Bad Faith," April 10, 2008, p. A14) referred to "Ms. Pelosi's cheating."

[56]George Thomas, "The Speakership, House of Commons, Westminster," The Parliamentarian, Journal of the Parliaments of the Commonwealth, January 1978, p. 3.

[57]See Senate Rule XII, clause 1, 110th Congress, and Senate Rule XIX, clause 7, 110th Congress.

[58]Martin B. Gold and Dimple Gupta, "The Constitutional Option to Change Senate Rules and Procedures: A Majoritarian Means to Over Come the Filibuster, Harvard Journal of Law & Public Policy, Volume 28, No. 1 (Fall 2004), pp. 270-272.

[59]Thomas P. Carr, "Parliamentary Reference Sources: Senate," CRS Report for Congress, updated July 27, 2001, p. CRS-11.

X. The Untrue Amount of the Official Federal Deficit—and the Federal Debt Problem

EPIGRAPH: Blessed are the young, for they shall inherit the national debt.
                 ---Herbert Hoover.

EPIGRAPH: This 110th Congress will commit itself to a higher standard: pay as
                 you go, no new deficit spending. Our new America will provide
                 unlimited opportunities for future generations, not burden them with
                 mountains of debt.
                        ---Representative Nancy Pelosi as she became Speaker
                        of the House, January 2007.

A. The Federal Deficit.

Year by year, and sometimes several times during one year as federal deficit estimates change, we learn of the magnitude of that fiscal year's official deficit. It's usually huge. And the annual deficit must not be confused with the federal debt. The deficit is the amount by which one year's spending exceeds that year's income. The debt is the total amount of money owed by the federal government and is an accumulation from many years of deficits.

The difference is illustrated by reference to your own finances. If your income in the present year is $60,000 but you spend $61,000 during the year by borrowing the excess, your deficit for the year is $1,000. On the other hand, your debt is much larger because it includes all the money you owe, such as on your home mortgage, your auto loan, your student loan, your credit cards, etc.

The early estimate for the official federal deficit for fiscal 2007, which started on October 1, 2006, was almost $300 billion. By late August 2007, as an increasing torrent of tax revenue poured into the federal treasury, the Congressional Budget Office reported that the fiscal year 2007 deficit would be about $158 billion.[1]

But the <u>official</u> deficit vastly understates the true deficit, which may be twice as large. This deception is accomplished in two ways: One, by government borrowing some of the money for its excess spending from its own trust funds, such as the Social Security Trust Fund. The rest is borrowed from the public, both foreign and domestic.

Two, by Congress partially or completely not funding some vital programs so that at least for a while the money for them is not taken into account. The appropriation is provided later as an "emergency" action. As a prominent American explained, "These 'emergency' supplementals are not part of the regular budget. They're a way to portray the deficit as smaller than it really is."[2]

In September 2006, a prize-winning business journalist wrote this: "Let me share a dirty little secret with you; the real federal deficit isn't $260 billion. It's more than double that."[3]   Supposing that to have been true at that time, it meant that the federal government had to borrow just over $1.4 billion every day. But by late August 2007, as the deficit projection declined, the feds then had to borrow about $433 million a day—or way more than that to meet the obligations of the true deficit.

Reference is sometimes made to the federal "primary deficit." That refers to all excess spending but takes no account of interest payments.[4]

Because the government borrows from its trust funds, there's not real cash in them, only U.S. government bonds, what some people call federal IOUs. Take Social Security: Until recently, but still usually, more money is paid into Social Security than is paid to beneficiaries. The "unspent" balance, including even the interest earned on the federal bonds, is actually spent by the government on unrelated expenses.

One could argue that all the benefits paid to current Social Security recipients are derived from the current Social Security taxes. But under federal budgeting and accounting rules, S.S. taxes count as general government revenues, and S.S. payments are part of general government expenses.[5]

Either way, there's no accumulation of unspent money in the so-called Social Security trust fund. There are only federal bonds—or at least bookkeeping entries denoting such bonds. Now, if someone points out that any federal bonds owned by you represent real money, that's true—but it's not a fair analogy to compare your investment to the bonds held by the S.S. trust fund. The reason it's inaccurate is that if you cash in your bonds, you get the money from an outside entity, and you gain real money; but if the trust fund were to cash in its bonds, there would simply be an internal transfer of federal money or obligations. There would be no real gain for the trust fund. Consider it this way: If you owe yourself money, and you pay yourself the amount owed, you have gained nothing.

Thus, all the money alleged to exist in the Social Security Trust fund has already been spent. The benefits owed to elderly Americans—and they are only one of many groups of Social Security recipients—are being paid with the money deducted from the wages of current employees, not with money taken from a real trust fund or from earnings on it.

A classic fraud consists of paying money owed to first investors with funds coming from later suckers. It's called a Ponzi Scheme. Eventually, there's not enough money from new contributors to pay what's owed, and all the later suckers lose their investments. Charles Ponzi went to prison in the 1920s for that eponymous fraud. Social Security is widely considered to be a Ponzi Scheme. It pays old obligations with new income from future beneficiaries, not with earnings on old income.

It happened recently and will happen more often in the future that fewer dollars will be contributed to Social Security than are going out. That may happen regularly in about 2017. Even then Social Security will not be broke. Neither a person nor Social Security is broke if possessed of assets and the ability to borrow to cover the income shortfall. Social Security has U.S. government bonds as assets, and they will be redeemed through a combination of Social Security taxes and general revenue income. One would have to think that the bonds have no value to consider that the Trust Fund has no money and is a fiction. On the contrary, many people assert that the absolute safest investment is federal bonds; they will be paid off unless the nation ceases to exist. Were that to happen, the Social Security Trust Fund would be among the least of people's concerns.

At some still later time, Social Security outlays will have exceeded income for several years and all the bonds in the Trust Fund will have been "cashed" to pay benefits. According to some estimates, that will occur in about 2040.[6] But, unlike those whom Ponzi tricked, the later investors in Social Security will not lose their investments, because it would be political suicide for Congress to permit that. Instead, the government will find other ways of paying benefits, perhaps by simply printing more money. That would create new problems, such as mega-inflation, but that's another story.

In 2006 there was great publicity and controversy about President Bush's plan to strengthen Social Security by allowing Americans to control and invest part of their Social Security contributions in the stock market. Some of the arguments in support had merit, as did some of those in opposition. But the plan went nowhere and eventually died, partly because opponents demagogued it as scheme to "privatize" Social Security, as if that entire government program was going to be turned over to the private sector.[7] Some opponents, abandoning common sense in favor of partisan posturing, even asserted that Social Security is financially sound and needs no fixing.[8]

When Social Security outgo regularly exceeds income in about 2017,[9] the official federal deficit will skyrocket because the government will no longer enjoy the luxury of using billions and billions of Social Security dollars for other programs.

In the meantime, the true amount of the government's deficit is masked by the plundering of federal trust funds.

CORRECTIVE SOLUTIONS

Eliminate unnecessary spending. Pass a law mandating a yearly publicized disclosure of how much cost lurks in the future because of existing federal programs. That should be a year-by-year cost for, say, the next twenty-five years. A law should require that the annual deficit figure include all borrowing from federal trust funds such as Social Security. It's simply dishonest to do otherwise. If a business had expenditures in excess of its income, it would be guilty of fraud if it reduced its reported loss by claiming money borrowed from itself as income.

Of course, getting rid of unnecessary spending is fraught with difficulties. Many are the people seeking election to Congress who pledge to work against excessive spending. But in the end more is said than done. The determination of "unnecessary" is controversial. Nevertheless, the effort must be made.

B. The Federal Debt.

By early 2012, the debt owed by the federal government was just over fifteen trillion dollars.[10] That's the unpaid amount accumulated from the deficits of many years. To get an understanding of how much just one trillion is, consider that it takes almost 32,000 years for one trillion seconds of time to pass. One way of expressing fifteen trillion is that it's fifteen thousand billions. If the federal government stopped running deficits and began to pay off a fifteen-trillion dollar debt at the rate of 100 billion dollars a year, it would take 150 years to pay all of it, not counting interest on the debt. Of course, there's no prospect of that happening. With the spending and commitments occurring recently, the debt will increase far beyond what anyone was imagining only a few years ago.

It's often alleged that the U.S. is the richest nation on the planet. In some ways that's true but in other ways not. Greater emphasis on how much we owe might lead to clearer thinking about actions we need to take in the future. The U.S. government's outsized debt is bad enough, although the Hamiltonian idea that some federal debt is beneficial is correct. But there are also the state debts, county debts, city debts, special improvement district debts, school district debts, corporate debts, partnership debts, and individual debts. A country so mired in debt is not so rich. And it's especially not so rich when it claws its way deeper into insolvency every year by borrowing more billions of dollars.

And when one considers that much of American debt, especially that of the federal government, is held by foreigners, the problem looks, and is, worse. So long as we need foreigners to buy our bonds, we live under a financial guillotine—if people abroad drop the blade by ceasing to buy our debt, the government and economy as we know them will die.

CORRECTIVE SOLUTIONS

The needed action is to reduce our debt by reducing spending and eliminating deficits. We must reorder our priorities so that we cease to fritter away resources on nonessentials. Of course, there will be enormous controversies about what is or is not essential. Some people, for example, will argue that human stations on the Moon and Mars are extravagances that have enraptured NASA and its enablers, that spending billions on such space ventures is foolish given the state of federal finances and the many unmet needs here on Earth. Others will say that space exploration is vital to the human psyche and its yearning for discovery; some argue it may even be necessary for human survival. That will not be the only dispute; there will be many.

One danger is that disputation will lead to inaction and greater financial hazard. But increasing the publicity that warns of our fiscal vulnerability can perhaps convince enough Americans that their druthers must be set aside in favor of national survival. As of late 2011, many Americans seem to be opening their minds to that belief.

The federal debt can be looked at in two ways. One is to see it only as what is presently owed. The second is to view both present debt and debt that will accumulate in the future because of entitlement obligations already created. The first method is now more prevalent. And it conceals lurking expenses. More attention must be paid to the second—because it exposes what will be needed later.

The Social Security, Medicare, and Medicaid programs require such huge outlays in the future that the government, now struggling in chest-high water, will be forced into the deep end of the debt pool. The present deficits are financed by increasing the debt. When untold additional trillions are needed to pay for more entitlements in a few years, and when there are still deficits that prevent total expenses from being paid out of current income, the debt will leap upward at a rate far beyond its present problematical ascent.

One could claim that all of the projected entitlements will not have to be paid. Indeed, the government is not legally obligated to pay them. In Flemming v. Nestor (1960), the Supreme Court ruled that entitlements created by Congress are not contracts and that people expecting payments are not guaranteed anything even if they have paid entitlement taxes.[11] Congress can give and Congress can take away.

Even though Congress might eventually pass legislation reducing or eliminating some entitlements and thereby lessen the now-projected debt, we should not refuse to make the projection about future costs and debt. There are at least two reasons for this: (1) would Members of Congress dare incur the political penalty of depriving people of a financial benefit they think they are guaranteed?, and (2) if people refused to plan for the future just because things might change, they would never get anything done.

Therefore, all discussions about the magnitude of the federal debt should include its future growth due to overly generous entitlements. Federal spending for Medicare and Medicaid totaled $515 billion in 2005, which was $21 billion greater than outlays for defense. By mid-2011 the annual rate for Medicare and Medicaid spending was $992 billion.[12] At present growth rates, by about the middle of the 21st century, federal spending on health care and Social Security will consume all federal revenues, leaving no money for anything else.[13] There must be enlightening publicity to convince people that the future crisis needs to be addressed now. That fiscal future is here now.

To that end, one vital contribution is the article "The Perfect Demographic Storm: Entitlements Imperil America's Future," by Laurence J. Kotlikoff and Scott Burns, in The Chronicle of Higher Education, March 19, 2004, pages B6-B10. Not only does it explain a coming gap between projected federal income and obligations of 45 trillion dollars, largely due to Social Security, Medicare, and Medicaid—plus $6 trillion for the Medicare prescription drug benefit enacted in 2003—but it also proposes "some immediate and very painful sacrifices to protect our descendants and save our nation" [emphasis added]. The analyses and remedies in that article may not all be what are needed; for example, the authors' negativity about President Bush's tax cuts ignores the argument that they have increased tax revenues by stimulating the economy. Further, it is unclear what length of time produces the fiscal imbalance of $45 or $51 trillion.[14] But at least most of the article is exactly on point, and it should receive new and wider dissemination to WAKE UP AMERICA, especially because the fiscal imbalance is already several trillion dollars greater due to the lack of corrective action since the article's publication.

Articles about that problem are not producing acted-upon solutions from Congress or the President. Candidates for office often downplay the problem. Perhaps they fear that if they tell the public about the painful adjustments needed, their electability will suffer.[15]

Notes: Chapter X. The Untrue Amount of the Official Federal Deficit—and the Federal
        Debt Problem

[1]"How To Raise Revenue," The Wall Street Journal, August 24, 2007, p. A14.

[2]Mortimer B. Zuckerman, "Hypocrisy on Stilts," U.S. News & World Report, May 22, 2006, p. 60. For an interesting account of "emergency" and off-budget spending and other accounting gimmicks see Joseph E. Stiglitz and Linda J. Bilmes, "The $3 Trillion War," Vanity Fair, April 2008, pp. 147-48, 150, 153.

[3]Allan Sloan, "D.C.'s Deficit Math Doesn't Add Up," Newsweek, September 18, 2006, p. 24.

[4]Alan S. Blinder, "Four Deficit Myths and a Frightening Fact," The Wall Street Journal, January 19, 2012, p. A15.

[5]Allan Sloan, "The Surplus Shell Game," Newsweek, January 19, 1998, p. 28.

[6]Steve Forbes, "Fact and Comment," Forbes, December 25, 2006, p. 23.

[7]That's still going on; see "Home-Owners' Lament" letter, The Wall Street Journal, September 1, 2007, p. A5, where the writer refers to Bush's "arguments for phasing out Social Security in favor of 'private accounts.'"

[8]See Joseph E. Stiglitz, "Progressive Dementia," The Atlantic Monthly, November 2005, p. 42: "It is not at all clear that Social Security is in deep trouble."; Michael Hudson, "The $4.7 Trillion Pyramid," Harper's, April 2005, p. 35: "Bush himself offers two reasons for the present boldness. The first—that Social Security is 'in crisis'—is easily dismissed. Government actuaries, backed by economists from across the political spectrum, insist there is no funding problem." On February 5, 2005, on FoxNews, Senator Harry Reid was shown saying, "Just because there's less money coming into the program than is going out does not mean there's anything wrong with the program." Senator Edward Kennedy argued, "We have an administration that falsely hypes almost every issue as a crisis"; see Karen Tumulty and Eric Roston, "Social Security: Is There Really a Crisis?" Time, January 24, 2005, p. 25.

[9]Forbes, "Fact and Comment," p. 23.

[10]There is sometimes a distinction between the "gross" federal debt and the "net" debt. The former is all of the debt while the later excludes debt that the government owes to its own entities such as its various trust funds. See "On the Down Grade," National Review, February 21, 2011, p. 8. Another way of expressing the difference is to refer to the "marketable" and "nonmarketable" debt, the latter being intragovernmental, like the Social Security trust fund; Cait Murphy, "Debt Is Not A Four-Letter Word," Fortune, March 19, 2001.

[11]"Uncle Sam's Halloween," The Wall Street Journal, October 30, 2006, p. A12.

[12]See Robert J. Samuelson, "The Monster At Our Door," Newsweek, September 18, 2006, p. 51, for the 2005 statistics; Dennis Cauchon, "Medicare, Medicaid tab keeps growing," USA Today, August 3, 2011, on the Internet, for the 2011 statistic, citing the Bureau of Economic Analysis.

[13]"Entitlements Will Consume all Tax Revenue by 2049," The Heritage Foundation, 2011 Budget Chart Book, on the Internet.

[14]But the Gokhale and Smetters study which is the basis for much of the article indicates a time that extends well into the out-years beyond 2080, and it states that fiscal imbalance "measures the aggregate financial shortfall from all generations – past, living, and future"; p 8 (p. 19 of 51 on computer printout). See also pp. 27 of 51, 34 of 51, 43 of 51. Jagadeesh Gokhale and Kent Smetters, "Fiscal and Generational Imbalances: New Budget Measures for New Budget Priorities" (2003); on the Internet.

[15]See Geoff Colvin, "The $34 Trillion Problem," Fortune, March 17, 2008, p. 30, which focuses on Medicare.

XI. The Revenue Problem

EPIGRAPH: Tax rates were only an average of 3% under the tyranny of
King George III. One of the blessings of democracy is average
tax rates that are ten times as high.
          ---Bill Bonner, in "The Idea of America," Daily
          Reckoning, on the Internet.

Congress spends other people's money—largely from taxes and loans. But it's a bad mix
of those two. Many people agree that the U.S. borrows too much. And whether the bad
mix is aggravated by tax rates that are too low or too high is a controversy filled with
partisan land mines, camouflaged traps, and tactical deceptions. The Democrats
generally want higher tax rates, arguing that they produce greater revenue, and usually do
not admit their own social-leveling goal. Republicans generally claim that lower tax rates
stimulate the economy and thereby bring greater revenue, and they usually do not admit
their goals of rewarding certain groups such as risk takers, self-starters, or the
beneficiaries of old money. Agenda-driven people find one side's position appealing, the
other appalling.

You can set aside the unadmitted goals and concentrate simply on which tax rates bring
the most money to the government. There's much literature touting each case.

That conflict is part of the revenue problem: There's no totally convincing argument on
either side, no reliable guide for the unbiased—because the unadmitted goals are never
set aside by the politicians and their acolytes in the media. Therefore, with pre-existing
mindsets, each side disputes or minimizes evidence supporting the opposition and
selectively cherry-picks whatever bolsters its own position.

For proof about government officials acting on their preconceived notions, just look at
Supreme Court decisions in recent years: One justice swings back and forth between the
same four Justices who usually vote liberal and the other four who generally vote
conservative. With those fairly consistent stances, this raises questions about whether the
Justices vote on ideology or on the merits and facts of cases. Is ideology trumping
impartial justice?

Another prime example of nonobjective analysis reared up during the Florida mess in the 2000 Presidential election: Virtually every liberal or Democrat in the media interpreted the situation to Al Gore's benefit, and virtually all conservatives or Republicans did it to the benefit of George W. Bush.

An impartial solution of the revenue problem is needed so other problems can be reduced, problems such as, but not limited to, crumbling infrastructure, a flawed educational system, out-of-control Medicare expenses, excessive reliance on Middle Eastern oil, and the burgeoning national debt.

Each of those needs solutions, but here I'll concentrate just on the debt. It's a real danger. For many years, interest payments on the debt have been a huge part of yearly federal spending—$413.9 billion in fiscal 2010. The interest payments will grow each year because of the annual deficits, as indicated by the increase to $454.4 billion in FY 2011. And the debt-service <u>percentage</u> of federal spending will increase or decrease— probably increase—every year the debt grows depending on whether there are offsetting rises or declines in other spending. Interest and defense expenditures plus the mandatory spending of over one and a half trillion dollars per year on entitlements account for such a huge portion of federal spending that the money left for other outlays may not be enough to meet many needs.[1]

Stating it somewhat differently, debt increase may lead to a decrease in funds available for things other than debt service.

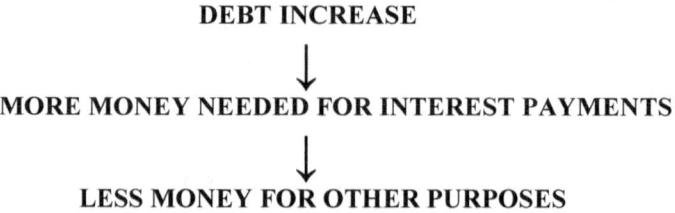

DEBT INCREASE

↓

MORE MONEY NEEDED FOR INTEREST PAYMENTS

↓

LESS MONEY FOR OTHER PURPOSES

And every time Congress expands the entitlement programs it aggravates the problem. Sometimes the supposed experts in the executive and legislative branches ignore or completely fail to see predictable results of such actions: When catastrophic care was added to Medicare in 1988, one official later explained that an unanticipated increase in cost occurred because the original estimates were based on the assumption "that there would be no significant change in utilization as a result of expanded coverage."[2] Huh? An unversed layman could have predicted the opposite.

And where will the feds get the additional money that will be needed in the future when Social Security and Medicare payments skyrocket as the population ages? Will there be enough revenue? Or will there have to be more borrowing? Or a combination of increased revenue and additional debt? Whatever the answer, the dollars involved are in the tens of trillions. The disparity between anticipated federal income and expenditures, known as the "fiscal gap" or "fiscal imbalance," was estimated as early as 2003 by one study at $45 trillion. Some other guesses are vastly higher.[3]

Congress keeps piling up new entitlements. The prescription drug bill it enacted in 2003 added trillions of dollars of commitments. A top official said that that law "increased the existing Medicare obligations nearly 40 percent over the next 75 years."[4] Many Senators and Representatives see the future so selectively that they propose costly new programs without looking at the fiscal harm that will result. For example, the current chair of the Senate Finance Committee proposed in 2007 that the federal government provide free college tuition for math and science majors as part of a $25 billion education bill.[5]

And why won't Congress take the necessary steps to prevent the impending Social Security and Medicare disaster? Could it be that the preventative is tough measures that might harm Members' re-election chances? One of the tough changes would be a benefits reduction. But how many Americans who have been counting on those benefits would vote for the Member who reduces them? Not many under current attitudes, because the disaster is several years away, and it's so easy to postpone action when the debacle won't affect anyone this year or the next or the next.

In early 2007, Senator Kent Conrad, D-ND, explained why something is not being done about this: "It's always easier not to. Cause it's always easier to defer, to kick the can down the road, to avoid making choices. You know, you get in trouble in politics when you make choices."[6] Ah! Re-election considerations again.

Another tough change would be increases in the separate, dedicated taxes that provide income for the Social Security and Medicare trust funds.[7] Again, would electoral success come to lawmakers who took more money from taxpayers? That's iffy, and Members know it.

It's just so much easier for today's incumbents to let the day of reckoning damage future Members. Never mind that every delay compounds the eventual damage that will be inflicted on most Americans—because waiting necessitates deeper future benefit cuts and/or painful fiscal fixes. Thus, millions of people, instead of only 535 Members of Congress, will take a major hit. We will pay now or later, but the cost would be lower now.

David Walker, interviewed in early 2007 on the CBS program "60 Minutes" while he was still Comptroller General of the United States, said, "If nothing changes [by 2040], the federal government's not going to be able to do much more than pay interest on the mounting debt and some entitlement benefits. It won't have money left for anything else—national defense, homeland security, education, you name it." The interviewer reported, "As Walker sees it, the survival of the republic is at stake."[8]

The federal government cannot indefinitely keep paying on its debt with more loans. That way leads to the Ponzi-scheme trap: Someday there's not enough new money to take care of existing obligations.

Another part of the revenue problem is that after Congress passes a tax increase, it's difficult to get rid of it. Case in point: In 1898 federal legislators enacted a telephone tax to help pay for that year's Spanish-American War. It was still in effect over 100 years later and was only eliminated in 2006, thus prompting the headline "News Flash: The Spanish-American War Is Over."

A more shocking example is the Alternative Minimum Tax, enacted in 1969 to prevent rich people with multitudes of deductions from avoiding income-tax payments. The unanticipated and bad consequence has been that inflation has caused hordes of less wealthy Americans to have a greater tax liability. The AMT has begun to assault the non-wealthy middle class. AMT taxation is very complex, and many Americans have no advance warning that they are about to become its victims. Without waivers, it was estimated that it would hit 19 to 23 million U.S. households for 2007 taxes, though it only applied to 3.4 million for 2006 taxes.[9] For 2010 the AMT was projected to affect 27 million taxpayers if no fix was applied.[10]

Tax lovers in the executive and legislative branches oppose elimination of the AMT because it's bringing in much-desired revenue and because they would be flayed for making a gift to the wealthy. Some Members of Congress, however, are now looking at ways to reduce its impact on ordinary Americans. We can hope they will succeed. So far, they succeed on a year-by-year basis by enacting a temporary fix.

Already noted above is how difficult it is to get rid of a tax. But it's much easier to abandon tax-rate decreases. Many of the reductions enacted early in George W. Bush's presidency included dates for their termination (sunset provisions). Thus, they were due to expire at the end of 2010, but Congress re-enacted them for about a year. Many Democrats in Congress are on record as wanting to eliminate at least a large portion of the decreases.

When a Democrat became President in January 2009, the pressure ramped up for tax increases and for ending the decreases. Hillary Clinton, for example, in June 2004 publicly stated, "We're going to take things away from you on behalf of the common good." That was not a careless or thoughtless statement. She has continued that assertion.[11] A pledge of selective tax increases was important in President Obama's campaign. Of course, what constitutes the common good is disputed.

CORRECTIVE SOLUTIONS

Much money owed under whatever tax rate is evaded by tax cheaters. Congress should provide additional enforcement funds to the Internal Revenue Service so that taxes fairly owed but evaded can be collected. A Senate report in 2006 estimated that tax cheaters with hidden offshore money are depriving the Treasury of about $70 billion a year. Further, two Senators "have proposed applying financial sanctions to nations with tax laws that encourage fraud in the United States, and requiring American financial institutions to automatically file 1099 reports to the IRS if they know the owner is a U.S. taxpayer."[12]

Notes: Chapter XI. The Revenue Problem

[1]For federal "outlays by agency: 1962-2012," "percentage distribution of outlays by agency: 1962-2012," and "outlays for mandatory and related programs: 1962-2012" see Office of Management and Budget, Historical Tables, Budget of the U.S. Government, Fiscal Year 2008 (Washington: USGPO, 2007), pp. 78, 84, 142; Supt. of Documents number PREX2.8/8:2008. The largest entitlements are Social Security and Medicare, but there are several others.

[2]Kenneth H. Bacon, "'Catastrophic' Medicare Insurance Plan Generates Skyrocketing Cost Overruns," The Wall Street Journal, September 18, 1989, p. A18; "Catastrophic Disaster," The Wall Street Journal, September 20, 1989, p. A24.

[3]For the $45 trillion figure see Lawrence J. Kotlikoff and Scott Burns, "The Perfect Demographic Storm: Entitlements Imperil America's Future," The Chronicle of Higher Education, March 19, 2004, p. B7; it's a report on that study and lists the Internet address for accessing the study. This report does not indicate how far the figures were projected into the future, but the study seems to deal with 75 years. For one of the higher guesses—$66 trillion—see the January 24, 2007, remarks made by Tom Campbell, dean of the Haas School of Business at UC-Berkeley and former Republican U.S. Representative, to Commonwealth Club of California, available on the Internet.

[4]Interview of David Walker, Comptroller General of the United States, on TV program "60 Minutes," 2007.

[5]"Baucus proposing free college tuition," Billings Gazette, August 20, 2007, p. 2C.

[6]"60 Minutes," CBS television, rerun on 7-8-07, also earlier in 2007.

[7]Here I don't deal with general tax increases or decreases because whichever of those two stimulates the economy has the effect of producing more employment and thus a larger number of people whose wages contribute to the two trust funds.

[8]"60 Minutes," rerun on 7-8-07.

[9]Ford Fessenden, "Alternative Tax Hits Home the Hardest," The New York Times, April 15, 2007, Sec. 14WC, p. 3.

[10]"Growth of the AMT," in Wikipedia, "Alternative Minimum Tax."

[11]There are numerous Internet entries for this.

[12]Michael Crowley, "Tax-Cheating Tycoons," <u>Readers Digest</u>, April 2007, pp. 33-35; the quotation is on p. 35.

XII. Earmarks: Good, Bad, and Ugly

EPIGRAPH: Some people say the government spends money like a bunch
                   of drunken sailors. That isn't fair. At least the drunken sailors
                   spend their own money.
                             ---Attributed to Ronald Reagan. Variants are from
                             numerous other people.

"Congress often is thought of as a kind of sugar daddy doling out goodies."[1] Would that
it were thought of as solving the nation's problems.

An issue that's been much in the news lately is the dollars and cents of earmarks. Critics
see much of it as dollars and nonsense. Earmarks are individual federal expenditures for
the benefit of lobbyists, businesses, universities, interest groups, small geographic areas,
or even individuals—and for Members of Congress, because at re-election time an
incumbent can brag about them as benevolences he or she has bestowed and for which
the reward should be more votes. Two Congressional scholars have called earmarks "this
most important advantage of incumbency."[2]

Even if projects are deemed justifiable, the earmarking process by which many of them
are funded and become law is so suspect that it created an uproar in 2006 that has not
ended. Earmarks are often inserted by a Member into an appropriation bill without any
scrutiny and sometimes in secret. And it requires an act of Congress to transfer
earmarked money to other projects.[3]

Only some earmarks are parts of the laws passed by Congress. Many are in the
committee reports that accompany bills. A bill sent by a committee to the full House
must travel with a written report that, among other things, describes what the bill is
intended to do.[4] The fellow-traveling report does not become law even if the bill passes.
Therefore, earmarks in the report can be ignored by executive agencies—but they do so
at their peril, because of the "veiled and not-so-veiled threats from appropriations
committee members regarding the agencies' future budgets."[5]

Another type of report that has the effect of law without being law is the non-bill part of a
conference report that comes from the joint committee of Senators and Representatives
that creates one bill out of two non-identical bills passed on the same topic by the two

chambers. That non-bill part is often called the statement of managers or joint explanatory statement. If you read about some provision but can't find it in the enacted law, you may find it lurking in the statement of managers. Such statements sometimes have hundreds upon hundreds of pages. Not only does length obscure the "transparency" that some politicians have crowed about recently, but the average concerned citizen may have great difficulty finding a copy. For instance, the Consolidated Appropriations Act of 2005 conference report contains 1,641 pages, of which 977 are the "Joint Explanatory Statement of the Committee of Conference."[6] Why are bills written so unclearly that explanations are needed? Often an explanatory statement contains a list, but no explanation, of projects being funded. As nothing in the list is being explained, why not require that such information be in the bill? Shouldn't any verbiage that relates to a bill and that has the effect of law be in the law?[7]

Some reports and bills deal with classified (secret) matters. Because they are therefore not part of the public record they can be used to hide Members' favors for campaign contributors or other special interests. That's how felonious Representative Randy Cunningham helped some of the people who were bribing him.[8]

This is the sort of Congressional self-serving long called pork-barrel spending. A dictionary definition says it "supplies funds for local improvements designed to ingratiate legislators with their constituents."[9]

Some people see an appropriate distinction between pork and earmarks, with the former meaning wasteful and unnecessary government projects and the latter having the wider meaning of any Congressionally directed spending whether wasteful or not.[10] The word "earmarks" as now widely used seems to be equated with pork.[11] The distinction between the two terms could continue to be useful; so the phrase "pork-barrel earmarks" should perhaps become widespread.

Despite operating inside the Beltway, Congress seldom cinches in its expansive waste. That fault is dangerous. In an attributed quotation, Alexis de Tocqueville, the famous 1830s observer of the U.S., said, "The American Republic will endure until the day Congress discovers that it can bribe the public with the public's money."[12] Pork-barrel earmarking is moving the nation closer to the fulfillment of that prediction.

And another sage is alleged to have said that a democracy "can only exist until the voters discover that they can vote themselves largesse from the public treasury. From that moment on, the majority always votes for the candidates promising the most benefits from the public treasury with the result that a democracy always collapses over loose fiscal policy, always followed by a dictatorship."[13]

For many years, the House of Representatives recognized the danger of pork-barrel earmarks. It created a House rule in 1914 stipulating that "it shall not be in order for any bill providing general legislation in relation to roads to contain any provision for any specific road." That directive lasted for seventy years[14]—until Members must have decided that their need to be seen as "bringing home the bacon" took precedence over careful stewardship of the public's money.

Members of Congress know that much of the public votes for the candidate "promising the most benefits from the public treasury." As noted observer George Will wrote, "The theory is that election to Congress is tantamount to being dispatched to Washington on a looting raid for the enrichment of your state or district."[15] Especially during their re-election campaigns, incumbents boast about the many federal dollars they've brought to their states or districts. Their efforts to "bring home the bacon" encourage wasteful spending. The Wall Street Journal reported in 2006 that multimillionaire Charles Taylor, R-NC, a powerful member of the House Appropriations Committee, "says using his clout to bring money to his district is nothing to apologize for. He warns that the largess [sic] might dry up if . . . [his novice opponent] is elected."[16] Despite Taylor's warning, the novice, a Democrat, won in the 2006 Republican debacle. Perhaps Taylor's defeat flowed partly from public disgust generated by reports that "every one of Congressman Taylor's earmarks in the last transportation bill was for a project near property that either he or one of his companies owns."[17]

Such "Taylorizing" of the public's money illustrates that some earmarks are passed to fatten Members' wallets. In a case that deserved greater publicity, Speaker of the House Dennis Hastert, R-IL, created a $200 million earmark for construction of a highway near land he and others owned. He allegedly then sold his share for a profit of 500 percent.[18]

Earmarks, even the pork-barrel sort, used more wisely may not backfire on the Member. At least two reasons for Robert Byrd, D-WV, becoming the longest-serving Senator in U.S. history have been his ability to "transfer much of the federal government"[19] to his home state and to attach his name to the plethora of West Virginia projects he induced Congress to fund. These activities are referred to in some quarters as "Byrd droppings."[20]

If they did not lard on the pork, some Members seem to think they could not argue effectively that they should be kept in office. Indeed, that may be true for some with otherwise vacuous records.

In one of the more Alice-in-Congressland actions, a solon may try to get credit for an earmark he or she opposed. In one reported instance, Phil Gramm, R-TX, announced the bestowal of $1.2 million on Southwest Texas State University for drug prevention even though he had not supported the grant.[21]

And, while portions of the public affect outrage over pork-barrel earmarks and other excessive federal spending, they will complain about any attempt to curtail an outlay that is for their own benefit. Examples abound. In 1999, as controversy raged about further funding for the National Endowment for the Arts, an actor was asked what the relationship should be between government and the arts; he replied, "Hands off," meaning there should be no restrictions on what recipients could do with publicly-provided funds. Of course, his "hands off" did not include eliminating federal money for the arts.[22] Also, local efforts to preserve federal outlays for local military bases resulted in such huge conflicts and lobbying efforts that the government had to work for base closures through a special process involving a Base Realignment and Closure Commission (BRAC). You can find a plethora of further information about this simply by entering "base closings" in an Internet search engine.

Many Members' spending proposals seem to be in the public interest and should be funded, but many are arguably a waste of federal money or are of such limited benefit or of such blatant self-serving that they should receive no appropriation. The most notorious recent example is the $223 million for 2005's "bridge to nowhere" in Alaska.[23] It was to be a new way to go from Ketchikan (8,000 people) to its airport on Gravina Island (50 people). Nevermind that the two are already connected by a seven-minute ferry ride. That proposed boondoggle produced such opposition that the bridge funding was removed as a specific item from the 2005 transportation bill—but the money was included as general discretionary funds for Alaska, which meant the state could still build the bridge. And could it be that one reason for this notorious pork-barrel earmark was that the family of Senator Lisa Murkowski, R-AK, owns property on Gravina Island, property whose value would ascend if the bridge is built?[24] Perhaps finally, in late September 2007, Alaska governor Sarah Palin ordered abandonment of the bridge project.

In another shocking example, Senator Daniel Inouye, D-HI, obtained an appropriation in 1987 that did nothing for his constituents in the Pacific Ocean nor, arguably, for other parts of the U.S.A. He somehow thought that eight million dollars for building schools in France for Algerian Jews would be an appropriate expenditure.[25]

Similarly, in 2007, a bill for spending $5 million on a museum about Jews in Poland achieved House approval by a vote of 407-13. An Internet posting criticized the thirteen Republicans who voted against the expenditure: "And if not as a political game, what other absurd reason could anyone possibly have to refuse funding for the preservation of Europe's largest Jewish community until the Holocaust?!"[26] Well, how about the non-absurd idea of fiscal responsibility?

In 2008, the Polish museum bill added to the burden of the deceptively named Advancing America's Priorities Act, as if it was a U.S. priority to consign $5 million to Poland for a museum. (Incidentally, a bill merely introduced in Congress often has the word "Act" in its title, so that media reports about it may give the misimpression that it became law.) This Priorities "Act" was actually a Senate conglomeration of almost forty bills that had passed the House but faced obstruction in the upper chamber. Total projected cost: Just over $11 billion. Among the grand-sounding bill titles was a clunker called "Melanie Blocker Stokes Mom's Opportunity to Access Health, Education, Research, and Support for Postpartum Depression Act." Majority Leader Harry Reid, D-NV, assembled the behemoth, perhaps in the belief that its variety and its inclusion of a few provisions likely to attract Republican votes would enable it to achieve a critical mass of supporters. As the bill never became law, it produced instead a combination of opponents.[27]

Some earmarks go to federal and state agencies,[28] but many, often providing for unnecessary spending, are directed to private entities that can be expected to support a Member's re-election. People with a limited-government and fiscally conservative bent may wonder why our government is allowed to give money to private entities. Too many earmarks are arguably for the financial benefit of a Member, as in the case of the aforementioned Representative Charles Taylor. Shouldn't even one qualify as too many?

One recent example of a supposedly wasteful earmark was $1.5 million for an Anchorage, Alaska, "transit intermodal depot," which some sources denigrated as a "bus stop."[29] Another was $480,000 for restoration of an historic warehouse in Lyons, NY. The latter was among the nearly 6,000 earmarks burdening a transportation bill in 2005.[30]

Also in the version of that bill that became law was a pork-barrel earmark so shocking in its association with bribery and unconstitutional trickery that it became notorious. See the Violations chapter for the $10 million pushed by Alaska Representative Don Young for studying a proposed Interstate highway interchange in Florida. One reason for its infamy is that Young ignored the precept explained by Representative John Murtha years earlier to an undercover FBI agent involved in the ABSCAM sting that fatally wounded the careers of five other Representatives and a Senator. Murtha said, "So I want to avoid that [the appearance of being on the take] by having some tie to the district. That's all. That's the secret to the whole thing."[31]

When William Proxmire, D-WI, was a Senator during the second half of the twentieth century, he issued 168 monthly Golden Fleece awards highlighting wasteful federal spending. The Associated Press reported a list of the ten most shocking as compiled by Taxpayers for Common Sense. Number 9 was millions in "payments to psychiatrists for unscheduled, coincidental meetings with patients who were attending basketball games, sitting on stoops, etc." Number 6 dealt with the "$25,000 grant in 1977 to study why people cheat, lie and act rudely on local Virginia tennis courts." Number 5 went to the "Office of Education for spending $219,592 in 1978 to develop a curriculum to teach college students how to watch television." And the champion waste was the "millions of dollars in 1975 to find out if drunken fish are more aggressive than sober fish, if young rats are more likely than adult rats to drink booze in order to reduce anxiety and if rats can be systematically turned into alcoholics."[32]

Yet Senator Harry Reid, D-NV, when he was Minority Leader said earmarks are a prerogative of Members and that they must be maintained to avoid any diminution of Congressional authority. Putting a partisan veneer on the issue, he said the effort to limit earmarks "is part of the Bush administration trying to take away the power of Congress."[33] His double standard was revealed when he sermonized about excessive earmarking by Republican Congresses!

It's a genuine concern, however, that banning Congressional earmarks would simply allow anonymous executive branch bureaucrats to still spend the same amount of money while deciding what projects to fund. Senator McConnell, R-KY, argued in late 2010 against an earmark ban, saying "Every president would like for us to appropriate all the money and send it to them and let them spend it in any way they want to."[34] Surely, there's a two-fold counter to that concern: Congress could appropriate less money, and there would be less incentive for Members to appropriate the same amount.

One reason for the sometimes lopsided vote in favor of a bill loaded with earmarked pork is that if a Representative wants to constrain that sort of waste and does not go along with the proposed spending, the leadership will kill that Member's own earmarks.[35] An instructive instance of that supposedly occurred in 2007 when Representative Mike Rogers, R-MI, introduced an amendment to kill a $23 million earmark sponsored by John Murtha, D-PA, chair of the Defense Appropriations Subcommittee under the Democrats' revived control of the House. Murtha then allegedly bludgeoned Rogers with this threat: "I hope you don't have any earmarks in the defense appropriations bill because they are gone, and you will not get any earmarks now and forever."[36] If Murtha actually said that, then his words clearly violated a new ethics rule created by the Democrats just over four months earlier stipulating that Members "may not condition . . . funding for a congressional earmark . . . on any vote cast by another Member." Yet that alleged violation received the endorsement of almost every House Democrat when they voted without debate against Rogers' resolution to reprimand Murtha for his transgression. Some voted against the reprimand because there was no proof that Murtha actually uttered the threat. [37] Others may have supported Murtha because of his power over defense appropriations and because of his having donated tens of thousands of dollars from his leadership PAC to the election campaigns of fellow Democratic Members.[38]

If the federal government were awash with excess income, projects such as the thousands of earmarks in transportation bills might seem justifiable. After all, they often provide improvements, unlike some of the notorious wastes of the past such as the $5 million added to a Defense Department bill in 1991 to design and erect a parliament building in the Solomon Islands, an independent nation in the western Pacific Ocean, or the spacey millions flown to Alaska for an effort to generate energy from the aurora borealis.[39]

But with the current federal financial problems, Members should put the long-range interests of the U.S. ahead of their short-term selfish desire to win another two or six years of "public service." By general election day on November 2, 2010, the ever-growing national debt had reached 13.7 trillion dollars. A year later it was almost fifteen trillion. That burden edges the nation ever closer to the hyper-inflation that can destroy the finances of most Americans. Remember the eye-opener that just one trillion is such a huge number that it takes almost 32,000 years for one trillion seconds of time to pass.

Hyper-inflation may occur because Congress and the President will not let the government go bankrupt. If it cannot fund its obligations, such as Medicare and Social Security, from income or borrowing, it will simply issue more paper money. And a significant increase in the money supply—without a corresponding increase in the supply of goods and services—will inevitably produce higher prices. In the Germany of 1923 the money supply got so large that it took millions of German marks just to buy a loaf of bread. There are more than enough examples from more recent monetary disasters, such as in Yugoslavia in 1994 and Zimbabwe in 2008.[40] Economist Ludwig von Mises taught that sound money is "an instrument for the protection of civil liberties against despotic inroads on the part of governments. Ideologically it belongs in the same class with political constitutions and bills of rights."[41]

Granted that U.S. war costs and general military spending are huge causes of the increasing debt, but they should be reasons to reduce other expenditures, not excuses for no fiscal discipline at all. It's a false argument that one project of, say, $500,000 should be funded because that "piddling amount" will not break the budget. By the time a bill with thousands of "trifling" earmarks becomes law, it may be fiscal insanity.

Senator John Danforth, R-MO, emphasized the problem when he said, "I think the major cause [of Senatorial discontent] is that deep down in our hearts we believe that we have been accomplices to doing something terrible and unforgivable to this wonderful country. . . . we know that we have bankrupted America and that we have given our children a legacy of bankruptcy. . . We have defrauded the country to get ourselves elected."[42]

The waste of money on pork-barrel earmarks is only part of the problem. Another part is the reduction of funds for genuinely necessary programs, such as national security. Pork inserted into the Department of Defense budget is often paid for by slicing dollars from a different part of that budget. A former Congressional staffer of many years explained this:

> "Huge cuts are extracted out of what is called the 'Operations and Mainte-nance' (O&M) budget. O&M is almost certainly the most important part of the budget, especially when it come to fighting a war. O&M pays for training for troops going into combat, weapons maintenance, spare parts, military exercises, and combat operations themselves
>
> Reluctant to make obvious what it is cutting to pay for pork, Congress puts the O&M cuts not in the O&M part of the bill but in the back, in the 'General Provisions' section, which most observers, including the press and the experts, pay little attention to. . . .
>
> . . . And, just so no one in DoD would get confused, the Appropriations Committee also left instructions that 'congressional items'—i.e., pork— are not to be reduced without specific permission from Congress, even if DoD is forced to cut programs that support military readiness."[43]

In an effort at concealment, Congress sometimes lists a pork-barrel earmark in an appropriation bill in such a way as to prevent the public from knowing who will get the money. A report in 2006 said, "Appropriators will even go to elaborate lengths to mask the intended recipient by stipulating conditions that restrict eligibility to a single entity without naming that entity."[44] That sort of secrecy exists in additional governmental areas. A well-researched book gives this example:

> "Consider a clause buried in paragraph two of Section 621(f) of the Internal Revenue Code, which gives a tax break to two companies that are identified only as being owned by 'a Texas resident whose birthday is May 16, 1931, and a Michigan resident whose birthday is November 16, 1941.' Journalists have long attempted to crack the mystery, but thus far no one has determined

the names of the companies or their owners, how much the loophole costs
the government, or who inserted the clause into the tax code."[45]
Although the mystery may still exist, that book lays the fault on Congress for slipping
"new loopholes into the law as quietly as possible."[46]

In 2006, negative publicity about earmarks and deviant Members caused Republican
leaders in the House to try to protect their majority by actions that could be touted as
solving problems. With votes from some Democrats, they passed a rule for disclosure of
earmarks and earmark sponsors in bills.[47]

That didn't work. During the remainder of the 109th Congress not one earmark was
disclosed.[48] And public revulsion against pork-barrel earmarks is credited as one of the
reasons Republican majorities in Congress disappeared after the 2006 elections. The
Democratic-controlled new Congress in 2007 promptly passed an omnibus spending
bill—for appropriations which should have been enacted before October 1, 2006—that
did not include porky earmarks.[49] Anti-waste hawks could cheer and the public could
imagine that Congress was actually engaged in beneficial reform. Realists long versed in
Congressional chicanery no doubt wondered if they were seeing only window dressing
that would vanish with the fading of voters' furor.

It soon transpired that the solons were abandoning pork-barrel earmarks only publicly
and temporarily. Many Members began to pressure agencies in the executive branch to
spend appropriated money on specific pet projects. That sort of arm-twisting had long
been an alternative to legislated earmarks and was often an effective back-door method
because bureaucrats would be fearful that noncompliance might result in reduced funding
in the next appropriation. Blocked from including their "re-election credits" in the
omnibus bill, Members stampeded to the back door. As reported by The Wall Street
Journal, "Members have been speed-dialing executive branch officials and asking them to
fund their specific earmark requests out of agency budgets even though they were purged
from the larger budget bill."[50] The Journal further noted that an appropriations lobbyist
"was gleefully . . . noting that congressional calls were so far being answered by agencies
wholly in 'the affirmative.'"[51] Senators and Representatives were acting as lobbyists.

Then came the irony that the Bush administration, regularly flayed by the Democrats for
excessive spending, issued orders to rein in the Congressional spendthrifts. In February
2007, Robert Portman, head of the Office of Management and Budget, directed all federal
agencies not to honor any Congressional spending requests that are not part of any law,
i.e., not "specifically identified in statutory text."[52]

None of that, of course, will end pork-barrel earmarks. The reform that budget limiters
are touting so loudly is "transparency," a 2006 law's requirement that earmarks will have
to be exposed on a searchable public website listing all sorts of information, such as
dollar amounts and recipients.[53] Also, during the first session of the 110th Congress each
chamber adopted a new rule for identification of Congressional requestors of earmarks.[54]
Presumably, Members will not pursue outrageous earmarks in the future because of fear
of negative publicity.

The newly created "transparency" was publicized as a great earmarks reform. The idea was that if the earmark requests of every Member were made public, they would be shamed into making fewer such proposals. That may be half good. The effective half will supposedly make Members reluctant to be seen as directing millions of tax dollars to projects for big campaign contributors. But the ineffective half is that most Members are not ashamed to be known as the sugar daddies who bring lots of federal dollars to the home folks. On the contrary, a major part of their re-election campaigns is publicity about their successes in doing just that. A conservative author says, "If reformers really wanted to cut down on earmarks, they would outlaw disclosure: If politicians could not take credit for bringing federal money to their districts, they would bring a lot less."[55]

Some Members made an unsuccessful effort to water down the 2006 law with so many loopholes it could masquerade as Swiss cheese. For instance, earmarks for non-federal government entities or institutions of higher education would not have been included.[56] The final product was not perfect but at least was a halting step forward.

Another came with a 2007 law providing that earmarks not passed by either chamber but added by a House-Senate conference, the so-called "airdropped" items, can be removed from an appropriations bill by a point of order. How strange that Members felt the need for that when each chamber already had a rule that nothing may be added to a bill during conference that was not in the version passed by either House or Senate.[57] The strangeness is dissipated by noting that if points of order against airdropped provisions were sustained under the old rules, the entire conference report would be rejected. That allowed most airdrops to survive because Senators usually did not want to massacre an entire bill just to get rid of one provision. The reform in 2007 permitted Senators but not Representatives to kill an airdropped clause without it being a death blow to the entire bill. However, if sixty Senators voted for a waiver, the offending provision would remain in the bill despite a sustained point of order. As for the House, it commonly sets aside its rule against airdrops by disallowing points of order against conference reports.[58]

Additional advances may occur after Congressional gaming of the new system produces new excesses and public concern. Those will happen. Already, in February 2009, after President Obama alleged (falsely?) that the hundreds of billions of dollars in the stimulus bill did not go to one single earmark, Senator Charles Schumer, D-NY, referred to "little, tiny, yes, porking amendments" and said (definitely falsely), "The American people really don't care."[59] If Americans don't care when there are earmarks, then what were the concerns, rules changes, and earmark-harm to Republicans during the previous three years all about?

One little porky earmark may not be ruinous by itself, but when Congress pigs out on pork it moves us closer to fiscal disaster. We should all reject the argument that one million or several million dollars are practically meaningless amid federal expenditures of trillions. It's subtraction by addition when Congress adds questionable spending that takes away from fiscal sanity. More is less. How many little holes are needed to destroy a dam that holds back catastrophe?[60]

And in early March 2009 when Congress was about to belatedly pass a spending bill for fiscal year 2009 with eight thousand five hundred or so earmarks, and White House spokesmen were asked if that wasn't counter to President Obama's anti-earmark policy, their response, so obviously planned ahead of time and so obviously false, was that the bill was "last year's business," a holdover from the Bush Presidency. But since Congress was then on the verge of passing the pork-laden monster but had not yet done so, it was very much "this year's business."[61]

When President Obama finally received the bill from Congress, he was apparently embarrassed by its departure from his anti-pork campaign pledges, not embarrassed enough to veto it, but so embarrassed that he signed it in private.

Many earmarks are inserted into bills at the behest of lobbyists, a group that regularly served as a whipping boy in the 2008 Presidential campaign. Nevermind that lobbying is protected by the U.S. Constitution's First Amendment which prohibits Congress from abridging the right of the people "to petition the government for a redress of grievances." And the second most senior Representative in 2007 referred to "the importance of lobbying to responsive and effective congressional and executive decision-making."[62]

Of course, some lobbying goes beyond the bounds of what is reasonable, and therefore Congress passed a law 2007 that regulates it somewhat.[63] For example, Members of Congress may not accept sit-down meals from lobbyists, but food consumed while standing is OK if eaten with fingers or spoons, not with knives or forks.[64] Such rules seem to some people like addressing what's minor and ignoring what's major. They are reminiscent of the old British enclosure laws that allowed poor people's rights on common lands to be abolished so that rich people could become individual owners of those lands:

> "The law locks up both man and woman
> Who steals the goose from off the common,
> But lets the greater felon loose
> Who steals the common from the goose."[65]

The loopholes that allowed, for example, Members of both parties to be wined and dined at the lavish parties thrown by lobbyists at the Presidential conventions in 2008 are so bad it's like using a chicken-wire fence to stop a flood. Among the Members attending were some who had been bombastic critics of lobbyists. And they appear to have been complicit in police actions such as the Denver rousting of a photographer away from public sidewalks outside one venue so there would be no photographic record of attendees.[66]

In the words of Senator Tom Coburn, a prominent earmark critic, "Lobbyists aren't the problem. Members of Congress are the problem. . . . We are going to say you can't take a meal from somebody, but you certainly can deliver on a couple-million-dollar earmark."[67]

Although the transparency reform may work against pork-barrel earmarks that are too obviously outrageous, it may actually function as more protective armor for incumbents—because they can use it to show voters that they are "bringing home the bacon." The searchable public data base will help incumbents trumpet their ability to obtain government funds for their states or districts.

The pressure in favor of pork-barrel earmarks is enormous. News reports in June 2007 told of 30,000 to 32,000 earmarks already submitted to the Appropriations Committee of the 110th Congress that only began about five months earlier. Even after that news, the number increased.

The gaming quickly began. In a transparent attempt at secrecy in early 2007, the head of the Congressional Research Service, Daniel Mulhollan, directed his agency to cease responding to Members' requests for information about earmarks. Why was he ending this years-long service? His directive stated that further research was not appropriate because the House and Senate were creating definitions of earmarks and because each chamber's appropriations committees as well as the executive branch's Office of Management and Budget were compiling lists of earmarks. An article in The Wall Street Journal exposed the "sophistry" of each of those reasons. CRS may incur Members' wrath if it says some directed spending is an earmark when appropriations committees don't list it as such. That may be a reasonable concern, but there is surely a legitimate way for CRS to continue its earmark service. And the new departure reeks even more of subterfuge because of Director Mulhollon's additional new rules that all CRS employees must report any media contacts within twenty-four hours and that approval must be obtained [from him?] before any CRS report can be released to the public.[68] People concerned about the allegedly excessive secrecy of the Bush administration might consider this evidence that the executive branch is not unique in cloak and smoke concealments.

An important book summed up Congressional pork action this way:
> "Americans like to think our system of government is one that runs by laws, not men, and that keeps itself under control through a system of checks and balances. The pork system is a system where things happen because people want them to happen, and parliamentary rules and U.S. statutes, such as the Budget Act, are circumvented or ignored when they pose an impediment. It is also a system that avoids review by outside or objective parties. Meaningful checks and balances simply do not exist in this system."[69]

The rot in the system is revealed in a study of the 7,000-plus earmarks in the twelve appropriation bills passed by the House for fiscal year 2008.[70] With Democrats in charge of the process for the first time in many years, the Representatives getting the most earmarks fell mainly into four categories: (1) Members of the Appropriations Committee; (2) House leaders, committee chairs, and ranking minority members of committees; (3) Democratic and Republican Members at risk of defeat in the next election; and (4) whites.

Those in group (1) got 45 percent of the $4.2 billion in earmarks requested by only one Representative. The cost of earmarks garnered by group (4) white Democrats averaged nearly twice as much as for black Members and over twice as much as for Hispanics.[71]

As for race, the question arises of whether black and Hispanic Members experience deliberate discrimination or an indirect, non-purposeful result that flows from their under-representation in groups (1), (2), and (3). A report on the study that generated these data says, "No one familiar with the numbers suggests that black and Hispanic lawmakers suffer discrimination in the awarding of earmarks. Other factors—seats on the Appropriations panel, leadership positions, political alliances and close election contests—appear to determine who does best."[72]

With 32,000 or so requests for earmarks reaching the Appropriations Committee in 2007, there was not enough money for all of them; so power, position, and electoral vulnerability were the main determinants for which requests move forward. A poor district whose Representative had none of those attributes got low funding. As one analyst explained, "This is a process about almost anything but need." [73]

According to that study, the most extreme earmarker was John Murtha, D-PA, chair of the Defense Appropriations Subcommittee. He gathered in four percent of all individually sponsored earmarks. If the largesse had been spread evenly among the 440 Members, Delegates, and Resident Commissioner, Murtha's share would have been .0227 percent, a decline of almost 98 percent. Or, put another way, if all the single-Member earmarks had been awarded at the same percent of the total that Murtha got, only twenty-five Members would have received any.

Murtha's place on the Defense Appropriations Subcommittee throne allowed him to be the top porker in the House. For fiscal year 2008 he awarded his own projects about $167 million, which is more by cost—notice, not by value—than any other Representative, even without adding in Murtha's haul from the eleven additional spending bills. Murtha also channeled large amounts to his cronies and toadies. Earmarks in the Defense bill cost far more than those in any other appropriations bill, and Murtha was the sole arbiter of who gets those earmarks.[74]

The following Representatives were the top ten earmarkers of the twelve appropriations bills for fiscal year 2008. Notice that eight of the ten were on the Appropriations Committee.
1. John Murtha (see above).
2. C. W. (Bill) Young, R-FL; most senior House Republican; ranking minority member (and former chair) on Defense Appropriations Subcommittee; member of Military Construction and Veterans Affairs Appropriations Subcommittee.
3. Jerry Lewis, R-CA; minority member on Appropriations Committee; minority member (and former chair) on Defense Appropriations Subcommittee
4. David Obey, D-WI; chair of the Appropriations Committee.
5. Peter Visclosky, D-IN; chair of Energy and Water Development Appropriations Subcommittee; on Defense Appropriations Subcommittee.

6. Nancy Pelosi, D-CA; Speaker of the House.
7. Marcy Kaptur, D-OH; most senior woman in Congress; on Defense Appropriations Subcommittee; on Agriculture Appropriations Subcommittee; on Transportation, Housing and Urban Development Appropriations Subcommittee; on House Budget Committee.
8. David Hobson, R-OH; on Defense Appropriations Subcommittee; ranking minority member on Energy and Water Development Appropriations Subcommittee.
9. Todd Tiahrt, R-KS; on Defense Appropriations Subcommittee; ranking minority member on Interior and Environment Appropriations Subcommittee.
10. Steny Hoyer, D-MD, House Majority Leader, former member of Appropriations Committee.[75]

The House passed rules in early 2007 mandating that committees disclose earmarks, costs, and sponsors in bills they advance to the floor. That's really great—except for all the ways it's not great. There's no requirement that Members' <u>applications</u> for earmarks be disclosed. There's nothing to prevent committees from listing costs separately from names of sponsors. There's nothing to make published lists electronically searchable. There's nothing to reveal why one request is approved but another isn't. There was nothing preventing someone like Murtha from scattering the projects and their costs throughout his committee report on the Defense bill, and when a reporter asked Murtha about the difficulty presented by that maneuver, Murtha spat out, "So, you have to work. Tough shit." [76]

CORRECTIVE SOLUTIONS

Ways must be found to stop Congress from bribing us with our own money.

Each chamber could add to its rules a provision that all earmarks in a particular bill will have to be in a separate section labeled "Earmarks." But can we really believe that Representatives and Senators, with their sometime penchant for secrecy and self-serving, would go for that? How would earmarks be defined? And it would later be ever so easy to repeal that reform, perhaps with no publicity. Or the reform might simply be violated. Even now, various House and Senate rules are occasionally ignored or waived (see the later chapter on Violations). As he planned a mass violation of the rule that nothing new can be added at conference, Appropriations Chairman David Obey, D-WI, trumpeted in May 2007 that he doesn't "give a damn if people criticize me or not" for ruling that Representatives may add earmarks only at the conference stage. A national commentator explained that this was a way that Democrats had found "to make the earmarks process more secretive."[77]

In a demonstration of the public and media power that this book advances as a way to make Congress tread the straight and narrow, there was such negative publicity about Obey's plan that he changed it in mid-June and announced that the appropriators would slog through the 32,000 or so proposed earmarks and create a list of them before the House passed the upcoming bills.

Even when a House or Senate rule is not ignored or waived there may be no way to enforce it. Consider the following. The Honest Leadership and Open Government Act of 2007 (P.L. 110-81) imposed in Senate rule XLIV a requirement that "the Senator who proposes an amendment containing any congressionally directed spending item ensure as soon as practicable that the list of such items be printed in the CONGRESSIONAL RECORD." But when Senator Cornyn, D-TX, asked the presiding office to rule that an amendment violated rule XLIV, he was told, "The provision is not enforceable and no point of order lies," i.e., is neither admissible nor sustainable.[78]

Reporters in the print and broadcast media sometimes give publicity to Senators and Representatives who criticize pork. Too many of those Members, however, pose as pork busters but do almost nothing toward real reform. Such poseurs, as an experienced observer reported, have made their stance a "spectacularly successful" political operation; "the press eats it up."[79] Therefore, reporters should find out and report whether the smoke emanating from self-appointed pork busters is accompanied by any real fire.

Halting a bad proposal may not always happen; therefore, perhaps certain types of earmarks should be prohibited by law rather than rule. What types? Maybe any earmark proposed by one Member but for which the majority of spending is in another Member's district or state. Of course, a law can be repealed, but doing so would be more difficult than rescinding a rule and would probably generate more publicity and opposition.

A reform that might go partway toward reducing the earmark onslaught was suggested by Representative Chris Chocola (R-IN): Just as committee chairs in the House have been term-limited, so should members of the Appropriations Committee.[80] That idea did not save him from defeat in 2006. And the idea may be half-baked anyway in that many Representatives not on Appropriations would love to work in that "favor factory" in order to have more power to direct pork-barrel earmarks to their districts.

Alternatively, and perhaps more possible of realization, the President should have the power of impoundment (deferral and rescission) or the line-item veto. The first of those two reforms means that the President could simply not spend some of the money earmarked by Congress. That's a power once held by Presidents, but Congress put limits on it under provisions of the Congressional Budget and Impoundment Control Act of 1974.[81]

The second reform means that the President could veto parts of bills while allowing the remainder to become law. Congress gave that power to the President under terms of the Line Item Veto Act of 1996, but the Supreme Court threw it out as unconstitutional in 1998. However, President George W. Bush's signing statements appear to accomplish the same purpose but rest on shaky ground as being constitutionally suspect. See above in the chapter on Insufficient Oversight of the Executive Branch.

Notes: Chapter XII. Earmarks: Good, Bad, and Ugly

[1]Jeffrey H. Birnbaum and Bruce Ingersoll, "Rightly or Wrongly, Pennsylvania Rep. Schulze Has Gained a Reputation as a Man Not to Cross," The Wall Street Journal, July 22, 1991, p. A10.

[2]Thomas E. Mann and Norman J. Ornstein, The Broken Branch: How Congress Is Failing America and How to Get It Back on Track (New York: Oxford University Press, 2006), p. 176.
While earmarks are understood to deal with spending, they have a cousin in provisions that are occasionally inserted in bills to exempt a person or group from some law. Some such insertions may arguably be good policy, but others seem clearly questionable. For example, in 1951 Louis B. Mayer of Metro-Goldwyn-Mayer fame obtained a clause that saved him $1.7 million in taxes because it classified his retirement payout as capital gains instead of regular income. For the law which gave Mayer the benefit see Public Law 183 (October 20, 1951), Section 329 [re-enacted as part of the Internal Revenue Code of 1954; Public Law 591 – Chapter 736, section 1240 (68A Stat.)]. After a second person took advantage of that benefit, Congress repealed it in 1976 [see Public Law 94-455, Title XIX, section 1901(a)(139)]. See also L.S., "'Five eight and bald-headed,'" Forbes, June 1, 1987, p. 86.

[3]Finnigan, All About Pork: The Abuse of Earmarks and the Needed Reforms (Washington: Citizens Against Government Waste, Policy Briefing Series, May 3, 2006) p. 9.

[4]Walter J. Oleszek, Congressional Procedures and the Policy Process, 7th edition (Washington: CQ Press, 2007), pp. 90, 105-07, 108. The Senate does not require such reports but its committees often produce them anyway; ibid., p. 106.

[5]Finnigan, All About Pork, p. 7.

[6]House Report 108-792 is its conference report. See also Rafael DeGennaro and Rachel Sciabarrasi, and ReadtheBill.org Foundation, "Monsters from Congress: How Republicans and Democrats allowed 13 inherently unreadable omnibus appropriations bills to devour deliberative democracy," October 2007, from the Internet.

[7]These issues are addressed in Brian Griffith, "Lobbying Reform: House-Cleaning or Window Dressing?" University of Cincinnati Law Review, Vol. 75, No. 2 (Winter 2006), p. 885: "Two potential paths are to either prohibit any language in a conference or committee report that does not conform to the text of the bill, or to enact a law that clarifies that conference and committee reports are informational only and that courts should afford them little if any weight."

[8]"Earmark Victory," The Wall Street Journal, January 18, 2007, p. A16.

[9]Random House Webster's College Dictionary (New York: Random House, 1991).

[10]Lately, earmarks and pork have become rather synonymous in public discourse. On the definitions, with an earmark being any spending authority for a specific purpose in a more general bill and pork being an appropriation inappropriately added to a bill for political reasons, see Finnigan, All About Pork, p. 4; and "pork" in dictionaries.

Citizens Against Government Waste, The Pig Book: How Government Wastes Your Money (New York: Thomas Dunne Books, an imprint of St. Martin's Press, 2005), p. xvi. This book relies on seven criteria, only one of which must be met for a project to be labeled "pork"; see pp. xvi-xvii.

[11]As in the definition of earmarks offered by the Las Vegas Review-Journal ("This little piggy," May 4, 2006, p. 8B): "the pork lawmakers slip into large spending bills to hijack federal money for projects that solidify voter support for incumbents."

[12]Quoted in Tom Clancy, The Bear and the Dragon (New York: Berkley Books, 2001), p. 210. Also as an "attributed" quotation in an Alexis de Tocqueville item on the Internet.

[13]Suzy Platt, editor, Respectfully Quoted (Washington: Library of Congress, 1989), p. 84, says this is unverified but attributed to Alexander Fraser Tytler, Lord Woodhouselee.

[14]Tom A. Coburn and John Hart, Breach of Trust: How Washington Turns Outsiders into Insiders (Nashville: WND Books, 2003), pp. 112-13.

[15]George F. Will, Restoration: Congress, Term Limits and the Recovery of Deliberative Democracy (New York: The Free Press, 1992), p. 31.

[16]John R. Wilke, "Bringing It Home: Seat in Congress Helps Mr. Taylor Help His Business," The Wall Street Journal, Oct. 11, 2006, pp. A1, A11.

[17]Wilke, "Bringing It Home," p. A11.

[18]Clive Thompson, "The See-Through CEO," Wired, April 2007, p. 137.

[19]Several references to this semi-joke can be found on the Internet under Byrd + "federal government to West Virginia."

[20]Leslie Paige, member of watchdog group Citizens Against Government Waste, uses that term; CBS Evening News, January 4, 2008, on the Internet.

[21]Bill Thomas, Club Fed: Power, Money, Sex, and Violence on Capitol Hill (New York: Charles Scribner's Sons, 1994), p. 30.

[22]Fox News, December 11, 1999, 4:50 P.M.

[23]Mann & Ornstein, Broken Branch, 218; "It's Super Pork!" Time, November 28, 2005, p. 25. The cost of the bridge and its earmark has been variously stated.

[24]Finnigan, All About Pork, p. 12. In what many people doubtless would consider an exemplar of one thing that's wrong with politics, Ms. Murkowski gained her Senate seat in December 2002 through appointment by her father, who had just vacated the position upon becoming governor of Alaska. When she ran for a full Senate term in 2004, Alaska's senior Senator, Ted Stevens, one of the Senate's most infamous porkmasters, warned voters that Alaska would probably get much less federal money if her Democratic opponent were elected.

[25]"Inouye Wins Aid for French Jews," The New York Times, December 28, 1987, p. A12.

[26]Rebecca Murow, "Why Don't These Republicans Want Funding for Museum of Polish Jewry?," posted on the Internet on November 27,2007; TrackBac, URL: http://www.typepad.com/t/trackback/642797/23708552. No longer there in 2011.

[27]"S. 3297 [110th]: Advancing America's Priorities Act (GovTrack.us)"; "Washington Times – Bill jeered as omnibus earmark full of pork," July 24, 2008, on the Internet. After the bill's introduction, Senator Reid threatened to "fill the amendment tree" so that opponents could not use amendments to delete or modify portions of it (see the Great Power chapter for more on that tactic).

[28]"Earmark Loopholes," The Wall Street Journal, May 19, 2006, p. A10.

[29]That was in a $388 billion spending bill passed by Congress in November 2004; Division H of the bill was the Transportation/ Treasury/General Government and Related Agencies bill for fiscal 2005; Public Law 108-447 (December 8, 2004), 118 Stat. 2809-3466. An Office of Management and Budget site gives some details on this; it can be found on the Internet by entering "transit intermodal depot" + "Anchorage Museum" and then clicking on the result item labeled Earmarks, and then clicking on the list item labeled Anchorage Museum/Transit intermodal depot, Alaska. See also Nicole Tsong, "Bus-stop fuss earns apology," Anchorage Daily News (adm.com), June 4, 2005, on the Internet; "Anchorage gets $1.5 million for bus stop," Associated Press, Billings Gazette, May 8, 2005, p. 4A; Citizens Against Government Waste, "2005 Pig Book Summary," on the Internet. The actual amount for the "bus stop" was $1,458,000 but news reports seem to have simply rounded it up.

[30]News Release from Representative Jeff Flake, July 29, 2005, on the Internet. That transportation bill (SAFETEA-LU) became law as P.L. 109-59 (August 10, 2005), 119 Stat. 1144-1978. For the warehouse see Section 1702, Item 369, 119 Stat. 1271.

[31]John H. Fund, "John Murtha and Congress' 'culture of corruption,'" Jewish World Review, November 15, 2006, p. 4 of 7 on the Internet.

[32]Associated Press, "Some Golden Fleece Recipients," December 15, 2005, on the Internet.

[33]"Senate votes to protect earmarks," Las Vegas Review-Journal, May 3, 2006, p. 13A.

[34]Janet Hook, "New Push to Ban Earmarks in Senate," The Wall Street Journal, November 9, 2010, p. A5.

[35]Daniel J. Mitchell, a senior fellow at The Heritage Foundation, "Earmarks: Good for politicians, bad news for America," Billings Gazette, July 8, 2006, p. 4A. "The promise of earmarks — and the threat of withholding them—has become one of the most powerful tools party leaders use to build legislative coalitions and enforce party discipline," Jonathan Allen, "The Earmark Game: Manifest Disparity," CQ Weekly, October 1, 2007, p. 2850, col. 1; "Rubbing colleagues the wrong way can mean less money for your constituents," ibid., col. 2.

[36]Stephen Spruiell, "From Abscam On: The career and m.o. of Rep. John P. Murtha," National Review, June 25, 2007, pp. 24, 26; Congressional Record, daily edition, May 21, 2007, pp. H5513, H5526-28; ibid., May 22, 2007, pp. H5584-85, E1118; ibid., May 23, 2007, p. E1127. The date of the alleged threat was May 17.

[37]Rule XXIII, clause 16, 110th Congress.

[38]Spruiell, "From Abscam On," pp. 24, 26.

[39]Citizens Against Government Waste, The Pig Book (2005), pp. 32-33, 45-46. For further info, see Noah Shachtman, "Sky Lab: A strange new Air Force facility creates enough energy to control the ionosphere—but not the conspiracy theorists," Wired, August 2009, pp. 70-76, 78.

[40]Elizabeth Spiers, "The World's Worst Inflation," Fortune, August 18, 2008, p. 36; Steve H. Hanke, "The Printing Press," Forbes, December 22, 2008, p. 106.

[41]Quoted by Steve H. Hanke, "Hyperinflation," Forbes, June 4, 2007, p. 200.

[42]George F. Will, Restoration, p. 144, from Congressional Record, daily edition, March 26, 1992, p. S4305.

[43]Winslow T. Wheeler, The Wastrels of Defense: How Congress Sabotages U.S. Security (Annapolis: Naval Institute Press, 2004), pp. 11-12; see also ibid., pp. 46-49, 93. In one example from the fiscal 2002 DoD Appropriations Conference Report, Section 8141, $3.5 million was taken from O&M "for a special needs learning center for the Central Kitsap School District in Washington state"; ibid., p. 47.

[44]Finnigan, All About Pork, p. 8.

[45]Charles Lewis and the Center for Public Integrity, <u>The Buying of the Congress: How Special Interests Have Stolen Your Right to Life, Liberty, And the Pursuit of Happiness</u> (New York: Avon Books, 1998), p. 244.

[46]Ibid.

[47]See House Resolution 1000, in <u>Congressional Record</u>, daily edition, September 14, 2006, p. H6615-16; Steven T. Dennis, "House Changes Its Rules on Earmarks," <u>CQ Weekly</u>, September 18, 2006, p. 2466.

[48]Steven T. Dennis, "House Adopts Budget, Earmark Rules," <u>CQ Weekly</u>, January 8, 2007, p. 125.

[49]Public Law 110-5 (February 15, 2007), 121 Stat. 8-60, "Revised Continuing Appropriations Resolution, 2007."

[50]"Earmarked for Death," <u>The Wall Street Journal</u>, February 17, 2007, p. A8.

[51]Kimberley Strassel, "It's a Trough Life: The secret new way of earmarks," <u>The Wall Street Journal</u>, February 9, 2007, p. A10.

[52]"Earmarked for Death," p. A8.

[53]Federal Funding Accountability and Transparency Act, Public Law 109-282 (September 26, 2006), Section 2. That law does not include the requirement that Congressional requestors be identified.

[54]House Rule XXIII, clause 17, 110th Congress; and Senate Rule XLIV, 110th Congress, which was added to the Senate Rules pursuant to the Honest Leadership and Open Government Act of 2007, Public Law 110-81 (September 14, 2007), Section 521, 121 Stat. 735.

[55]Ramesh Ponnuru, "Against the Porkbusters," <u>National Review</u>, May 28, 2007, p. 35. See also Edmund L. Andrews and Robert Pear, "With New Rules, Congress Boasts of Pet Projects," <u>The New York Times</u>, August 5, 2007, pp. 1, 18.

[56]"Earmark Loopholes," <u>The Wall Street Journal</u>, May 19, 2006, p. A10, and "Earmark Showdown," <u>The Wall Street Journal</u>, September 13, 2006, p. A18.

[57]See House Rule XXII, clause 9, 110th Congress, and Senate Rule XXVIII, 110th Congress. Although the Senate rule was amended because of P.L. 110-81 (September 14, 2007), the prohibition against adding new material during conferences existed earlier. That September 2007 law is the Honest Leadership and Open Government Act of 2007 (P.L. 110-81). Some sources refer to the bill's original 2007 Senate title: "An Act to provide greater transparency in the legislative process" (aka the Legislative Transparency and Accountability Act of 2007); see <u>Congressional Record,</u> daily edition, July 31, 2007,

pp. S10389-10401; ibid., August 2, 2007, pp. S10687-10719, S10723-24, for the Senate largely accepting the House version of the bill.

In other sources it's referred to as the Lobbying Accountability and Transparency Act (original House bill) or, again, as Legislative Transparency and Accountability Act (Senate bill; see "Lobbying Reform," Congressional Digest: A Pro & Con Monthly, May 2006), because those were the titles of similar bills in 2006 during Republican control of the 109th Congress; they never became law because the House refused to participate in a conference committee to resolve differences in House and Senate versions.

[58]Jonathan Allen, "Rules Change Would Give Senate More Say Over 'Airdropped' Items," CQ Weekly, August 6, 2007, p. 2368.

[59]Schumer's remarks "went viral" after he expressed them on the floor of the Senate on February 10, 2009.

[60]See Ponnuru, "Against the Porkbusters," pp. 34-36, for the argument that "conservatives should find another crusade" because "most of the time, getting rid of earmarks saves taxpayers no money."

[61]Emissions of Rahm Emanuel, White House Chief of Staff, on "Face the Nation," CBS TV, March 1, 2009, and Peter Orszag, Director of the Office of Management and Budget, on "This Week," ABC TV, March 1, 2009.

[62]Rep. John Conyers, D-MI, in Congressional Record, daily edition, July 31, 2007, p. H9204.   For another view see Robert G. Kaiser, So Damn Much Money: The Triumph of Lobbying and the Corrosion of American Government (New York: Knopf, 2009).

[63]The Honest Leadership and Open Government Act of 2007, Public Law 110-81, 121 Stat. 735. See Jack Maskell, "Lobbying Congress: An Overview of Legal Provisions and Congressional Ethics Rules," CRS Report for Congress, updated October 24, 2007.

[64]John Cochran and Martin Kady II, "The New Laws of the Lobby," CQ Weekly, February 26, 2007, pp. 594-95. See House Rule XXV, Limitations on Outside Earned Income and Acceptance of Gifts, 110th Congress; U.S. House, Committee on Standards of Official Conduct, "Highlights of the House Ethics Rules," Revised March 2007, on the Internet; Senate Rule XXXV, Gifts, 110th Congress; the Honest Leadership and Open Government Act of 2007, Public Law 110-81, 121 Stat. 735, sections 305, 541-43.

[65]William B. Willcox and Walter L. Arnstein, The Age of Aristocracy 1688 to 1830, 7th edition (Lexington, MA: D. C. Heath and Co., 1996), p. 192.

[66]Enter "ABC Reporter Arrested in Denver Taking Pictures" on the Internet to see the video of it. See also these Internet items" Mark Whittington, "ABC News' Asa Eslocker Arrested," August 28, 2008; "ABC Reporter's Attorneys Want All Charges Dropped," The Blotter from Brian Ross, August 28, 2008. On several days in August and September 2008 ABC TV also broadcast reports about the lavish parties and evasion of

Congressional ethics rules at the Democratic and Republican conventions; they can also be accessed on the Internet. See also Brody Mullins and Elizabeth Williamson, "Parties Skirt Rules on Gifts, Plan Lavish Conventions," The Wall Street Journal, August 16, 2008, pp. A1, A4.

[67]Congressional Record, daily edition, January 18, 2007, p. S746.

[68]John Fund, "Earmark Cover-Up," The Wall Street Journal, March 26, 2007, p. A15.

[69]Wheeler, Wastrels of Defense, p. 94.

[70]Allen, "Earmark Game," pp. 2836-51. Full cite is in note 34.

[71]Ibid.," pp. 2836-37.

[72]Ibid.," p. 2845.

[73]Ibid.,"p. 2838.

[74]Ibid.,"p. 2842.

[75]See ibid.," p. 2843, for the names. By looking at Members' home pages on the Internet, I have added the data about those Members' official positions in the House in 2007.

[76]Ibid.," pp. 2840-41, 2844.   The quotation is on p. 2844.

[77]Brit Hume, "Special Report" on Fox News, June 4, 2007.

[78]Congressional Record, daily edition, December 23, 2009, p. S13810. The first quotation is not from the rule but was said by the presiding officer.

[79]Wheeler, Wastrels of Defense, p. 13.

[80]John H. Fund, "Time for a Time-Out?" The Wall Street Journal, September 18, 2006, p. A19.

[81]Walter J. Oleszek, Congressional Procedures and the Policy Process, 7th edition (Washington: CQ Press, 2007), pp. 57, 69; Virginia A. McMurtry, "Presidential Rescission Authority: Efforts to Modify the 1974 Framework," CRS Report for Congress, December 2004. The 1974 budget act is Public Law 93-344. See also above in the chapter on Insufficient Oversight of the Executive Branch.

XIII. Budget and Appropriations Problems

EPIGRAPH: If we can prevent the government from wasting the labors of
the people, under the pretext of taking care of them, they must
become happy.
          ---Thomas Jefferson, letter to Thomas Cooper,
          November 29, 1802, in Suzy Platt, editor,
          Respectfully Quoted: A Dictionary of Quotations
          Requested from the Congressional Research Service
          (Washington: Library of Congress, 1989), p. 142.[1]

EPIGRAPH: No budget proposal coming out of the White House
      should ever be taken seriously.
          ---Alexander Cockburn, "The Third Obama,"
          The Nation, March 23, 2009, p. 11.

Federal budgeting and appropriations processes seem simple at first but are roiling with complexities, problems, and deceptions.

Although the federal budget is often in the news, its relation to reality is as insubstantial as smoke signals. So, let's begin with what the budget really is—a fantasy about the future. Or, as one writer explained, it's "that ultimate exercise in flimflam."[2]

The President is required by law to present a budget to Congress each year by the first Monday in February. It must show the condition of the Treasury at the end of the last fiscal year, the condition at the end of the current fiscal year, and the estimated condition at the end of the following fiscal year if the budget is implemented. But it's the Congress which appropriates money to certain purposes and provides the revenue to fund the appropriations, and Congress is not required to adhere to the President's budget.

Therefore, Congress creates its own budget by adopting a Congressional Budget Resolution, crafted separately by the Budget Committees of each chamber, proposed by each house, made identical by a conference committee of the two houses, and finally passed by both the House and Senate. As a concurrent resolution, it is not a law, only a guideline—that need not be followed—for the appropriation and revenue-raising measures that occur later. Thus far nothing about the budget is set in stone. Its guideposts can be ignored, demolished, or reoriented—except that the total budgeted amount is to be divided among the now-twelve appropriation areas.[3]

So it's curious that Congress and the media pay so much attention to something that can later be ignored without adverse consequences. Newshounds are treated to statements, counter-statements, and analyses of budget resolutions just proposed by the House. Partisans seeking to influence voters praise or criticize its provisions even though Congress ultimately enacts something different. These budgetary meteors-in-the-night attract brief attention and then disappear without impact.

To the extent that budgets do have influence, there's a built-in process that gets minimal publicity but exerts powerful upward influence on spending. It's so-called baseline budgeting. Here's how it works. If a federal program gets X amount of money one year, the amount which will be budgeted for it the next year will be larger because of (1) inflation (the Congressional Budget Act of 1974 says government services will continue to equal at least their existing level)[4]; (2) all built-in program expansions required by existing laws, (3) additional spending required by recent changes in laws; and (4) supplemental appropriations due to "emergencies" or due to deliberate underfunding in the original budget to make it look less extravagant.[5] Baseline budgeting causes avoidance of the huge amount of work that would occur if budgets were crafted anew each year from a starting point of no money (zero-based budgeting). Avoidance of that work—and of the accompanying policy battles—creates a bias in favor of baseline budgeting.

Article I of the Constitution mandates that "all bills for raising revenue shall originate in the House of Representatives; but the Senate may propose or concur with amendments." Because of past practice, that has been interpreted to apply also to all bills for spending revenue. In the House, the Committee on Appropriations deals with spending proposals, but most of its work is handled by subcommittees, such as Defense, Interior, and Transportation.

According to the rules of the House and Senate, money may be appropriated only to authorized programs, agencies, or purposes. Therefore, prior to appropriation, an authorization bill supposedly must be enacted into law.[6] A House or Senate rule can be enforced by a point of order during debate, but use of that parliamentary tactic can be waived (prohibited) by suspension of the rules, by unanimous consent, or by a special rule from the House Rules Committee. In fact, rules requiring previous authorization are often waived.

Does Congress ever appropriate funds to unauthorized programs? Silly question. Of course it does.[7] With each house sometimes violating its own rules, why would we think the authorization rules are sacrosanct? A 2007 report to Congress says, "Although the authorization of appropriations for the LSC [Legal Services Corporation] expired at the end of FY1980, the LSC has operated for the past 26 years under annual appropriations laws."[8] This unauthorized program received $348.6 million of federal money for fiscal year 2007.[9] Former Representative, now Senator Tom Coburn, R-OK, wrote in his 2003 book that "Congress spends more than $100 billion every year on well over two hundred programs that are not authorized by law."[10]

Each year's appropriation process begins with agreement in the Congressional Budget Resolution on the total sum that will later be appropriated. And U.S. law requires that the appropriations committees of each chamber suballocate that sum among their subcommittees.[11]

Following adoption of the budget resolution, Congress can pass, but is not required to do so, a budget reconciliation bill for the next fiscal year. That bill can include directives that legislation be created to achieve the budget's goals. In each chamber, relevant committees may then do that, and their recommendations are combined by the chamber's Budget Committee into one bill. Whether or not the provisions of each chamber's bill pass into law, the process often generates publicity and partisan posturing.

Reconciliation usually remains in the shadows but bounded into the news in April 2009 with reports that Democrats would try to use it to get health-care reform through the Senate. Most bills can be stalled in the Senate by a filibuster, a tactic by which a minority can talk a bill to death because of the Senate's ordinary practice of unlimited time to debate. There are, however, methods for preventing or ending a filibuster.

One is the reconciliation process. Another is called cloture, which allows debate to be ended by a vote of three-fifths (sixty votes) of the Senate's membership.[12]

Because getting sixty votes to invoke cloture may not be possible, the reconciliation procedure that requires only fifty-one votes has been increasingly used of late. It originated in a 1974 law,[13] which provided that a reconciliation bill can be passed that changes existing laws to fit the budget. The 1974 law prevents a filibuster of a reconciliation bill by limiting debate on it to twenty hours and by restricting amendments. Thus, if a budget resolution contains reconciliation instructions, the subsequent reconciliation bill can be passed by a bare majority after limited debate in each chamber.[14]

By taking filibuster power from the Senate minority, use of the reconciliation process is sometimes criticized as an unfair way to pass a measure that should not be subject to reconciliation and that could not otherwise pass.

When authorization exists the next step is appropriation of money. Bills to do that are introduced in the House and then sent to the Appropriations Committee, which then assigns them to the relevant subcommittees. That is where the process breaks down— because each subcommittee does its work without reference to what the others are doing and without reference to what the total effort will eventually produce. Higher spending often results.

The expenditures often flow from decisions made by a miniscule number of the House's 435 members. Each subcommittee's chair and its ranking minority member are the great powers here, along with their non-Member staff people. Other subcommittee members have some influence, but many of the major decisions are made informally by the top twosome before the subcommittee begins the bill's markup (the process for reviewing, possibly changing, and then finalizing a bill's provisions). With the "go-along-to-get-along" mentality in the House and the usual deference of junior Members to their seniors, there is little challenge to the judgments from "on high." Nor is there much objection from Members who fear retaliation and want their own projects funded so that they can be seen as "bringing home the bacon" and can get re-elected.

The bill next journeys to the full Appropriations Committee, where few changes are made. Most Committee members see it as bad form to question what a subcommittee has done, particularly since they don't want their own subcommittee's autonomy diluted, its presumed expertise questioned, and its work overturned. This paucity of change holds true when the bill is considered and passed by the full House.

Once passed, the bill, molded by so few Members, then goes to the Senate, where a similar pathway is followed—Appropriations Committee, subcommittees, back to the full Committee, and then to consideration by the entire Senate. Although changes are sometimes made during this progress toward enactment, the same forces as in the House are at work to place most decisions in few hands and to limit alterations.

Typically, appropriations bills passed by each house contain differences. Those are resolved by a conference committee. Such committees have about six each of Senators and Representatives, actually chosen by the chair of whatever standing committee dealt with the bill, but technically selected by the presiding officer of each chamber, who merely ratifies the names presented by the chairs. Most Members have little input about choosing conferees and scant knowledge of who they are, except for the expectation that the committee chair and senior majority and minority committee members have been anointed. Rarely, another Member is chosen if prominently identified with the bill's topic,[15] even if not on either appropriations committee.

Secrecy generally shrouds conference committee meetings, but the final products somewhat part the veils. See more on this in the chapter on the Conference Committee Problem. Members who care to do so can thus learn what has been added and deleted from a bill—if given enough time before having to vote on the conference report. Additions, especially earmarks, have become more common in recent years. Deletions sometimes are further instances of Congress not obeying its own rules, as when identical provisions from the two houses are dropped. One author forcefully reported, "It is not uncommon for these small secret meetings to strike from a bill identical language already approved by both houses, although this is strictly forbidden."[16]

Reposing so much power in a few Representatives and Senators about something so important may not square with some ideas about the democracy we supposedly have. Of course, efficiency militates against having large numbers in the decision process, but the informal code that works to reduce scrutiny and opposition by others is a regrettable addition.

Positions on the two appropriations committees are coveted because of the power and re-election potential that go with them. Commenting on his boss's position on the House's "Favor Factory" in the late 1980s, one of his staff wrote, "He knew that his seat on the Appropriations Committee virtually guaranteed his seat in Congress."[17] In the 2006 election campaign, minority leader Senator Harry Reid promised the Democratic Senate candidate in Montana, Jon Tester, an Appropriations seat "as soon as possible," knowing that voters would not want Montana to lose that spot if the Republican holding it were defeated. The media duly emphasized the promise but not the weasel words "as soon as possible." Within a week of the Democrat winning the election, Reid announced that Tester would not get the slot. Instead, that farmer from one of the most rural states would be on the Committee on Banking, Housing, and Urban Affairs, among other committee assignments. The conditional promise, having fooled many voters and worked its electoral magic, was set aside. Tester was finally appointed to Appropriations in January 2009.

When all the appropriations bills have finally become law, the dollar amounts are often far from those in either the President's or Congress's budgets.

In 1997 Congress passed a Balanced Budget Act mandating a mixture of decreased spending, increased outlays, and tax adjustments. It became a trick to mask reality. Congressional magicians crafted it so they could hide the elephant of irresponsible spending from their credulous audience. They would appear to set unbreakable spending caps while less obviously providing the escape hatch of "emergency" appropriations. That 1997 law put no limits on how much can be spent on "emergencies," nor indeed did it have any definition of an emergency.

Ludicrous results followed. For example, Congress deliberately omitted money for the 2000 Census from the regular appropriation process so it would not count against the spending cap. Did that mean there would be no Census? Of course not. The Constitution requires that there be one every ten years. So, Congress, as if unaware of this scheduled occurrence and of the Constitutional provision, decreed that Census spending was an emergency. It happened again for the 2010 Census. There have been numerous other instances of Congress busting the budget while adhering to the Balanced Budget Act. Therefore, "emergency" spending consumes huge amounts of federal dollars and is completely unregulated by prior laws or agreements. Congress can spew as much money as it wants to "emergency" projects. That makes a hoax of the entire budget process.

In a somewhat different charade, some supplemental appropriation bills also mock the budget limits. A House staffer offered this explanation:
> "One neat trick is deliberately to underfund something that has to be funded as, for example, veterans hospitals. This gives you breathing room to fit in less politically potent programs. After the start of the

fiscal year, warnings start coming in from, say, veterans hospitals about to close down, which activates the veterans lobby. They weigh in with their political muscle, and lo and behold, before long that sneaky little creature known as a supplemental appropriations bill begins to start wiggling its whiskers out from under its rock."[18]

A further problem is that after Congress appropriates emergency funds, the regular and supplemental amounts are added together as the baseline (starting point) for the next budget. The baseline is the sum from which Congress calculates the next year's spending. As the baseline moves ever upward, the process creates a propulsion toward increased outlays.

Off-budget programs are another deceit used to conceal what is actually happening. Social Security is partly off budget, ostensibly because its purpose is so important and because its funding through payroll taxes is non-standard, i.e., not having separate, annual appropriations. The Postal Service is off budget because its funding comes largely from charges for postal services.

Occasionally, other, more temporary, programs are also off budget. Spending on the Strategic Petroleum Reserve and part of the early '90s savings and loan bailout were among off-budget concealments.[19]

However, putting some items off budget invites abuse. That's been used by some companies engaged in fraud, Enron and the Baptist Foundation of Arizona for instance.

In 1968 the so-called unified federal budget began. It would reflect all federal income and expenditures. Later, however, Social Security and the Postal Service supposedly went "off budget." That made for the Alice-in-Congressland nonsense of those two programs being both on budget and off budget. Take Social Security. It's on budget when its receipts are melded into other federal income so that its surpluses reduce the federal deficit. It's off budget so that any federal spending restraints don't affect it.[20]

Hiding true deficit amounts and total spending is another degradation of democracy, and the mainstream media has often been complicit in the deception because it has concentrated its reports on Democrat versus Republican conflicts about spending priorities rather than on how the process itself is flawed.

Adding the totals from the various appropriations bills gives only a partial picture. Also needed are the amounts in the "emergency" spending bills upon which Congress increasingly relies. Virtually any funding proposal can be labeled "emergency." Billions of taxpayer dollars rush down the drain of real and purported emergencies, such as the census funding referred to above.

Reminiscent of the man who said, "Give me chastity and continency—but not yet,"[21] Congress often delays enacting appropriations bills for a fiscal year until after that fiscal year starts (October 1). Our lawmakers then frequently lump many usually separate appropriations together in one giant bill. Those so-called omnibus, or "ominous," bills defy easy analysis. Many spending details are in such bills but are hidden in the open amid the multitude of pages and provisions. Thus, waste and special-interest benefits sneak into law. As the following chart shows, for fiscal years 1983-2005 Congress treated us to fourteen of those bloated measures.

```
******************************************************************
******************************************************************
******************************************************************
**
```

**	Fiscal year (always designated by the year in which it ends)	Number of pages in each conference report (bill language & managers' statement)	Number of normally separate appropriations bills in the omnibus
**	1983	204	6
**	1985	420	8
**	1986	379	7
**	1987	808	13
**	1988	1,194	13
**	1996	571	5
**	1997	1,198	6
**	1999	1,602	8 and 1 emergency
**	2000	1,175	5
**	2001	1,103	3
**	2001 (yes; another 2001)	307	2
**	2003	1,507	11
**	2004	1,186	7
**	2005	1,645	9

**   I created this table from pages 16 & 17 in the source listed in note 22.

```
******************************************************************
******************************************************************
******************************************************************
```

For FY 2006 Congress actually passed most of the usual appropriation bills as separate measures. However, those were followed by a huge omnibus in February 2007 for FY 2007 (which began on October 1, 2006), another in December 2007 for FY 2008 (late again), and for FY 2009 the late-as-usual bill finally passed in March 2009 after controversy about the 8,500 or so earmarks in it.[23]

As an example of problems with omnibuses, the bill listed above as 1,602 pages was much shorter as merely a transportation appropriations measure before going into a House-Senate conference, but it emerged in October 1998 as the vastly expanded Omnibus Consolidated and Emergency Supplemental Appropriations Act of 1999. Besides the deadline failure of not being enacted by the start of the fiscal year (October 1,

1998), it appeared in the House as a Goliath of about 4,000 pages. Even worse, it reached the House at 4:00 P.M. for a scheduled up-or-down vote at 7:00 P.M. with no amendments permitted. Not even the fastest reading Member could have read, much less analyzed, the entire bill during that time. Yet many unprepared Members were prepared to pass it and thus foist on the U.S.A. that possibly dangerous mess from the heart of darkest Washington. And foist it they did as it passed at 7:45 P.M.[24]

Such fattened and mysterious monsters present problems dealt with below in the chapters on Unrelated Items in the Same Bill; Congress Misses Many Important Deadlines; and Violations of Rules, Procedures, Laws, and Regular Order.

It's not just omnibus bills that are so humongous they prevent easy understanding of the drains down which taxpayer dollars are disappearing. In the Statutes at Large a 2006 law for the Department of Justice covers 176 pages, and a Department of Defense law of 2006 fills 422 pages.[25]

Furthermore, citizens cannot be sure where all federal expenditures are really going. Two factors are at work here. One is the so-called "black budget," amounting to untold billions, mostly for military and intelligence operations. Money for those is hidden in the funding for other purposes. The basic principle of concealment of such activities from present or potential enemies is valid, but one wonders how much in fraud, favors, and waste is lurking in such dark corners.

The other obfuscation resides in the information about the thousands of details on spending. Few are those who trouble to find or publicize possible misspending amid the huge universe of federal outlays. A seemingly outrageous amount may be serendipitously discovered, like finding one particular grain of sand on a beach. But is that amount really excessive or is it a vehicle for part of the black budget?

Prominent New York banker Walter Wriston once said that if any corporation kept its books the way the federal government keeps its books, everyone would go to jail.[26]

And the Senators and Representatives don't advance public understanding when, for partisan advantage, they deliberately mischaracterize proposals and actions emanating from the other party. Such deceptions occur rather generally, not solely with budgets and appropriations. "For example, in 1995, when Republicans wanted to increase spending for federal school nutrition programs by 4.5 percent annually instead of 5.2 percent, they were accused of wanting to starve underprivileged children."[27]

In the fall of 2007 much misleading publicity attended the effort to reauthorize the State Children's Health Insurance Program. President Bush wanted to increase its funding by $5 billion over the next five years. Democrats—and some Republicans—passed a bill to hike the outlay by $35 billion. Because of wanting the lower increase and objecting to some of the bill's funding and expanded coverage beyond poor people, Bush vetoed it. Bush specifically and Republicans more generally then suffered from Democratic charges of being heartless and not caring about the welfare of poor people or kids. With the issue's one-sided publicity in much of the media, their suffering became more extreme at the polls in November 2008.[28]

The budget process is so dishonest that a 2012 magazine article has the title "The 8 Sneakiest Budget Gimmicks Congress Loves."[29]

CORRECTIVE SOLUTIONS

Will publicized examples of faulty processes and violations of rules cause enough embarrassment to produce improvements? One wonders. As a recent editorial explained, "It's hard to shame people who have no shame."[30] But Americans should not give up. They should rip a few more fig leafs off these flawed processes.

The responsible media should publicize, and not just once for each, all examples of appropriations that go to unauthorized programs.

Congress should start giving Americans a true understanding of budgets, appropriations, procedural flaws, and actual total amounts of federal spending. The projected out-year costs of each existing federal program should be publicized—along with the total future costs of all such projects. Businesses determine their future liabilities and so should Congress. And if Congress won't, then the media should do much more than it has.

Congress should eliminate the practice of adding regular and supplemental appropriations together to create new baselines which become the starting point for the next year's vastly increased spending. Or perhaps Congress should eliminate baseline budgeting entirely and adopt zero-based budgeting.

Congress should also end the off-budget evasion and require that all federal activities be on-budget.

Congress should abandon the deliberate underfunding and funding delays that result in "emergency" spending bills later. Such bills that flow only from the intentional tricks of Congressional magicians should be subject to points of order and to adverse publicity.

Congress should pass the regular appropriations bills on time so that there's never another monstrous omnibus spending bill.

Because the Congressional budget resolution each year is only a "concurrent" resolution and is not sent to the President and does not have the force of law, Congress should pass its yearly budget as a "joint" resolution, which does equal a law that must be followed. And because joint resolutions are sent to the President for approval or disapproval, use of them would let the chief executive influence the product—which may be exactly why Congress avoids that option.[31]

Numerous other sensible suggestions exist. For a list of them see "10 Elements of Comprehensive Budget Process Reform" by Brian M. Riedl, available on the Internet. It actually contains several ideas in each "element" so that it has about forty.

Notes: Chapter XIII. The Budget and Appropriations Problems

[1]This quotation was revised in a non-scholarly source as "I predict future happiness for Americans if they can prevent the government from wasting the labors of the people under the pretense of taking care of them"; Uncle John's Bathroom Reader. Colossal Collection of "Quotable Quotes" (Ashland, OR: Bathroom Readers' Press, 2004), p. 62.

[2]Ralph Kinney Bennett, "The Budget—America's Billion-Dollar Shame," Reader's Digest, March 1988, p. 49.

[3]Section 302(b) of the Balanced Budget Act of 1997 required that the total amount be divided among the thirteen appropriation bills that were supposed to be passed later. The number of appropriation bills now varies, mainly according to the number of subcommittees of the House Appropriations Committee. In 2005 when Jerry Lewis, R-CA, became chair of the full Committee, he reduced the number of subcommittees from thirteen to ten, resulting in eleven appropriation bills--eleven because the full Committee would craft the legislative branch bill. Joseph J. Schatz and Jonathan Allen, "A Challenging Year For Appropriators," CQ Weekly, May 9, 2005, pp. 1220-24. Next, in January 2007, the Democrats, once again in control of the House, changed the number of Appropriations subcommittees to twelve; Liriel Higa, "Democrats Restore Parallel Appropriations Jurisdictions," CQ Weekly, January 8, 2007, p. 126.

[4]See Section 605 ("Budget Data Based on Continuation of Existing Level of Service) of Public Law 93-344 (88 Stat. 297-339, at page 325), the Congressional Budget and Impoundment Control Act of 1974, commonly called the Congressional Budget Act, which states that the President's budget shall contain "estimated outlays and proposed budget authority . . . for the ensuing fiscal year if all programs and activities were carried on . . . at the same level as the fiscal year in progress and without policy changes in such programs and activities. . . . Accompanying these estimates shall be the economic and programmatic assumptions underlying the estimated outlays and proposed budget authority, such as the rate of inflation, the rate of real economic growth, the unemployment rate, program caseloads, and pay increases." This is also in the United States Code, 2006 edition, Volume Twenty, Title 31, Section 1109.

[5]Some basic sources on baseline budgeting are Allen Schick, The Federal Budget: Politics, Policy, Process (Washington: Brookings Institution Press, 2007); Davis R. Tarr and Ann O'Connor, Congress A to Z, 4th edition (Washington: CQ Press, 2003).

[6]House of Representatives, Rule XXI, clause 2(a)(1), 110th Congress. Senate Rule XVI, clause 1, 110th Congress, also deals with this. A previous authorization law may

have covered more than one year so that in a particular year no new authorization bill is required.

[7]Brian M. Riedl, "10 Elements of Comprehensive Budget Process Reform," June 15, 2006, pp. 4-5, on the Internet. "The Congress has appropriated about $159 billion for fiscal year 2006 for programs and activities whose authorizations of appropriations have expired" says "Unauthorized Appropriations and Expiring Appropriations," CBO Report, January 13, 2006, p.2, on the Internet.

[8]Carmen Solomon-Fears, "Legal Services Corporation: Background and Funding," CRS Report for Congress (Washington: Congressional Research Service, May 23, 2007), "Summary" page, on the Internet.

[9]Solomon-Fears, "Legal Services Corporation," "Summary" page and p. CRS-8.

[10]Tom A. Coburn and John Hart, Breach of Trust: How Washington Turns Outsiders into Insiders (Nashville: WND Books, 2003), p. 126. And Senator John McCain said, "It has become standard practice around here to forgo the authorizing process and simply do everything on appropriations. That is wrong and it needs to stop"; Walter J. Oleszek, Congressional Procedures and the Policy Process, 7th edition (Washington: CQ Press, 2007), p. 51.

[11]See amendment to Section 302 of the Congressional Budget Act of 1974 in Balanced Budget Act of 1997 (P.L. 105-33, Section 10106(b), 111 Stat. at p. 681).

[12]See cloture details in Oleszek, Congressional Procedures, 7th edition, pp. 240-45.

[13]Congressional Budget and Impoundment Control Act of 1974, Public Law 93-344 (July 12, 1974), Section 310, 88 Stat. 297; Title 2, U.S. Code, Section 641, 2006 edition.

[14]Reconciliation can be used only when its provisions are not extraneous to the budget process. That restriction is detailed in the so-called Byrd Rule of 1985 and its 1990 amendments that state limits on the reconciliation process and on budget provisions that do not expire after ten years. See Title 2 U.S. Code, Sec. 644, 2006 edition; Robert Keith, "The Budget Reconciliation Process: The Senate's 'Byrd Rule,'" CRS Report for Congress, updated April 7, 2005, on the Internet.

[15]Warren Weaver, Jr., Both Your Houses: The Truth About Congress (New York: Praeger, 1972), pp. 127, 129.

[16]Ibid., pp. 131-32.

[17]John L. Jackley, Hill Rat: Blowing the Lid Off Congress (Washington: Regnery Gateway, 1992), p. 127.

[18]Ibid., p. 112.

[19]National Priorities Project, "On Budget, Off Budget Federal Spending," 2005, on the Internet.

[20]For on-budget and off-budget confusions, see the following Internet sites among others: "Citizen's Guide to the Federal Budget: Fiscal Year 2001," updated March 30, 2004, from www.gpoaccess.gov; "Historical Tables of the FY 2007 Budget," which brings up Executive Office of the President of the United States, Historical Tables, Budget of the United States Government, Fiscal Year 2007 (Washington: USGPO, 2006) (see especially pp. 89 and 94); "Social Security Online—History—Budget Treatment of Social Security Trust Funds," which brings up "Agency History, Research Notes & Special Studies by the Historian's Office, Research Note #20, The Social Security Trust Funds and the Federal Budget," by Larry DeWitt, updated 6/18/07, from www.ssa.gov; David Stuart Koitz, "Social Security and the Federal Budget: What Does Social Security's Being 'Off Budget' Mean?" CRS Report for Congress, August 29, 2001; and "The Federal Budget: A Primer," in section on "Scope of the budget, Unified budget," no date other than one page updated on March 3, 2004, from TruthAndPolitics.org on the Internet.

[21]Saint Augustine of Hippo, Confessions (397-98 A.D., book 8 chapter 7, in Angela Partington, ed., The Oxford Book of Quotations, 4th ed. (Oxford and New York: Oxford University Press, 1992), p. 36.

[22]Rafael DeGennaro and Rachel Sciabarrasi, and ReadtheBill.org Foundation, "Monsters from Congress: How Republicans and Democrats allowed 13 inherently unreadable omnibus appropriations bills to devour deliberative democracy," October 2007, from the Internet. See ibid., p. 47, "Counting the pages," which explains why the number of pages in a bill coming from a committee as cited in debate varies from the number of conference-report pages cited in debate after the bill comes back from House-Senate conference, and why both of those numbers are larger than the enrolled bill which finally becomes law. One part of the explanation is that conference reports are composed of both the bill and the statement of the managers (Members) who represented their separate chambers of Congress during the conference; such statements are not included in the pages of enrolled bills.

[23]For FY 2007, see Public Law 110-5 (February 15, 2007), 121 Stat. 8. For FY 2008, see P.L. 110-161 (December 26, 2007), 121Stat. 1844.

[24]See Congressional Record, daily edition, October 20, 1998, pp. H11592-669, for debate and vote.

[25]Violence Against Women and Department of Justice Reauthorization Act of 2005, Public Law 109-162 (January 5, 2006), 119 Stat. 2960-3135, and National Defense Authorization Act for Fiscal Year 2006, Public Law 109-163 (January 6, 2006), 119 Stat. 3136-3557.

[26]McNeil-Lehrer News Hour, September 29, 1992.

[27]Coburn and Hart, Breach of Trust, p. 27.

[28]Because the House originally proposed a $50 billion increase but gave in to the Senate's $35 billion, the bill's proponents argued that the vetoed measure was "moderate" and a reasonable compromise. Thus, they said, the veto should be overridden, and Bush's offer to support a funding increase somewhat greater than $5 billion was an "insult."

[29]They are: 1. Expense Deferrals; 2. Bogus Emergencies; 3. Loan Guarantees; 4. Phony Rescissions; 5. "Step" Salary Increases; 6. Advance Appropriations; 7. Highway Fund Transfers; 8. "Hotlining." See Newsmax, January 2012, pp. 18-19.

[30]"Pork Project," The Wall Street Journal, June 22, 2007, p. A10.

[31]See one of the "bullet" items below in the chapter on Violations for the conflict between the Constitution's requirement about concurrent resolutions and Congressional practice.

XIV. Congressional Exemptions from Laws Applied to Others

EPIGRAPH: When the laws undertake to add . . . artificial distinctions,
                   to grant titles, gratuities, and exclusive privileges, to make
                   the rich richer and the potent more powerful, the humble
                   members of society . . . have a right to complain of the
                   injustice of their government.
                             ---Andrew Jackson, veto message on the
                             Bank Bill, July 10,1832.

Future President John Adams, writing in 1776, warned against a unicameral congress in these words: "A single assembly is apt to be avaricious, and in time will not scruple to exempt itself from burdens, which it will lay, without compunction, on its constituents."[1] Our history shows that this potentiality can be realized just as much with two chambers.

Over the years, Congress exempted itself from some laws the rest of us had to obey. That may sometimes be necessary and proper, but in other cases it may be merely Congressional self-esteem run amuck.

As for necessity, Congress often deals with national security information that should not be available to our enemies. Therefore, it's reasonable that the Freedom of Information Act cannot be used to obtain some Congressional data.

But what rationale other than elitism justified Congress putting the yoke on everyone but itself with exemptions from all or parts of the following laws?[2]
- Income tax provisions of the War Revenue Act of 1917 (see below).
- Social Security Act of 1935.
- National Labor Relations Act of 1935.
- Fair Labor Standards Act of 1938.
- Equal Pay Act of 1963.
- Civil Rights Act of 1964.
- Age Discrimination in Employment Act of 1967.
- Occupational Safety and Health Act of 1970.
- Equal Employment Opportunity Act of 1972.

- Title 9, Higher Education Act Amendments of 1972.
- Rehabilitation Act of 1973.
- Privacy Act of 1974.
- Age Discrimination Act Amendments of 1975.
- Ethics in Government Act of 1978.[3]
- Civil Rights Restoration Act of 1988.
- Worker Adjustment and Retraining Notification Act of 1988.
- Employee Polygraph Protection Act of 1988.
- Independent Counsel provisions of Title 28, Chap. 40.[4]
- Americans with Disabilities Act of 1990.
- Family and Medical Leave Act of 1993.
- Uniformed Services Employment and Reemployment Rights Act of 1994: Chap. 43 of Title 38, U.S. Code, Sections 4301-33, 2000 edition; Public Law 103-353, section 4314(c).
- Chapter 71 (Federal service labor-management relations) of Title 5, U.S. Code, 2000 edition.

The answer to the above question is that Congress exempted itself from those laws for two main reasons: (1) because of the Constitutional separation-of-powers doctrine: Congress should not be beholden to the executive and judicial branches, and (2) compliance with all the provisions of those laws would be too burdensome on Congress. It's funny-weird, not funny-ha-ha, that Congress didn't think those statutes would be too burdensome on millions of American individuals and businesses.

Even as far back as 1917, Congress used a bill-addition crafted in a secretive conference committee to exempt itself from the income taxes imposed by the War Revenue Act. The tax provisions including the Congressional exemption were enacted in a sneaky fashion that branded their manner as "almost as bad as the substance."[5] They were not in the bills passed by House and Senate but were added behind the closed doors of a conference by the House Majority Leader Claude Kitchin. Responding to that action a few days later, a leading Senator suggested in vain a rule against new insertions by conference committees. The product finally enacted received little attention because many Members were eager for adjournment and voted pretty much in the dark, partly because the "star chamber" conference made "the applicable provisions . . . so scattered in the bulky bill that only close study" revealed them.[6] That sort of obfuscation still occurs all too often.

Public outrage erupted. And although the House passed a repeal of the Congressional exemption in December 1917, Senate inaction pushed the issue into 1918. The tax avoidance for Members of Congress became moot in early February when the Internal Revenue Commission ruled rather strangely that they were not in the exempted category of officers or employees of the government.[7]

To the extent that any exemption had no reasonable basis, to that same extent Congress was failing our democracy. Members ought not to set off themselves as a privileged caste in American society—except as specified in the Constitution, which gives Members certain exemptions so that Congress can effectively do the people's business.

Representative Henry Hyde, R-IL, once said, "Congress would exempt itself from the law of gravity it if could."[8] And in 1991 Senate Majority Leader George Mitchell, D-ME, argued against applying the Civil Rights Bill to Congress with these revealing words: It's a "phony argument that we ought to be treated just like everybody else."[9]

Yet, "the principle that the laws should apply equally to all was at the heart of the American Revolution. The Fairfax County Resolutions, produced in a 1774 meeting chaired by George Washington, said England had denied the colonies a legal system with representatives 'chosen freely by themselves, who are affected by the laws they enact equally with their constituents.'"[10]

In Number 57 of <u>The Federalist</u>, James Madison, more than any other man the father of the Constitution, explained that one circumstance that would restrain the House of Representatives from oppressive measures would be "that they can make no law which will not have its full operation on themselves and their friends, as well as on the great mass of society. This has always been deemed one of the strongest bonds by which human policy can connect the rulers and the people together. It creates between them that communion of interests and sympathy of sentiments . . . without which every government degenerates into tyranny." He wrote that the main thing which would thus restrain the House would be "the vigilant and manly spirit which actuates the people of America" and that "if this spirit shall ever be so far debased as to tolerate a law not obligatory on the legislature, as well as on the people, the people will be prepared to tolerate any thing but liberty."

One change may require another, and Madison no doubt never envisioned the change represented by the Freedom of Information Act and the concomitant change that some government information, especially that which relates to national security, would have to be excluded from that freedom. Congress is privy to such information and therefore must be exempt from the FOIA. But, Congress, heedless of Madison's warning about loss of liberty, traveled beyond what was necessary and went into the realm of self-aggrandizement and privilege by needlessly exempting itself from a host of other laws. While some Members complained about the "imperial Presidency," they seemed not to worry about the "imperial Congress."

Additional instances of this are instructive.

When the federal government suspended most of its operations in November 1995 because of a budget and spending dispute between the Gingrich Republicans in Congress and the Clinton administration—and because Speaker Gingrich was miffed that Clinton had made him ride in the back of Air Force One on a trip—most federal employees were not paid. But, "as usual, Congress made a special exemption for itself," and all Members continued raking in their salaries.[11]

Federal law prohibits most Americans from using insider information when buying and selling stocks.[12] People even go to prison for insider violations—witness TV personality

Martha Stewart. Employees in the federal executive branch already labor under a ban on insider trading, and some may not even own stocks in companies that have business with their agencies. But neither the law nor Congressional ethics rules prohibit Members and their staffs from trading stocks based on advance knowledge gleaned from their legislative activities.[13]

That's a problem because an impending Congressional action could affect a company favorably or adversely and thus have the potential for a big change in its share price. Congressional insiders can profit from advance information—and doubtless they have. The general public cannot legally profit from inside information and may even be harmed if insider trading causes price movements, such as downside pricing before a stock sale by an investor, or a price rise before an investor's purchase. As Representative Louise Slaughter, D-NY, said, "Members of Congress and federal employees often know what is happening before anyone else. They have access to incredibly sensitive information that can have a dramatic effect on the stock market. The potential for the improper use of that information is very real."[14]

The value of such Congressional knowledge appeared in "a 2004 report from Georgia State University [that] showed that United States Senators received investment returns that were approximately 25% higher than what typical Americans were able to achieve."[15] Whether or not that's reasonably accurate, who will argue that no Member ever gains an investment advantage from nonpublic Congressional knowledge?

Misuse manifested itself with this disclosure:
"On November 15, 2005, the stock of a building materials company in Chicago (USG Corp) suddenly doubled, despite the fact that there was no publicly available news about the company, or industry, which explained the increase in volume. What the public didn't know yet, but what some investors discovered through back channels and political intelligence companies, was that then-Senate Majority Leader Bill Frist had quietly decided to move forward with legislation to relieve companies, such as USG Corp, of their liabilities in asbestos related lawsuits."[16]

The exemption of Congress from prohibitions on insider trading has produced occasional public concern:
"It remains perfectly legal for a Member of Congress to buy and sell stocks based on information that's not available to the public. . . . 'This is simply wrong that members of Congress can exchange information . . . and get rich on it,' says Rep. Brian Baird, D-Wash., who is co-sponsor of a bill to prohibit insider trading by members of Congress and their staffs. . . . We think Baird's right. Even if a congressional insider trading ban comes seven decades too late."[17]

A Baird press release of May 16, 2007, said, "Members of Congress and their staffs should not be above the law when it comes to profiting from sensitive information. . . . Privileging a select group of investors with confidential information about congressional activity is not only a misuse of a congressional office, it also undermines investor confidence about the fairness and integrity of the securities market."[18] Another of his press releases argued, "It violates any notion of fairness or common sense that Members of Congress or their staffs can legally share nonpublic information about current or upcoming congressional activity with a handful of investors outside of Congress for investment purposes, or can engage in their own trading of securities based on nonpublic information that they obtain by virtue of their position in Congress."[19]

The possibility of abuse is so great that Baird and Slaughter proposed the STOCK (Stop Trading on Congressional Knowledge) bill in March 2006.[20] It did not pass. Those two introduced a strengthened version in 2007. It also did not pass[21]

As of late 2011, no such bill had been passed. In 2010 and 2011 a few articles about stock trading by Members of Congress and their staffers appeared in the news.[22] Their impact was probably as small as their number. This special Congressional privilege to trade on inside information seemed to be of little public concern—until the TV program "60 Minutes" devoted a segment to it in November 2011. With that publicity, there was suddenly public outrage, much more media attention, and Members' support for passing the STOCK Act. After differing bills proposed by each chamber had been melded into one by a conference committee and then passed , the President signed it into law on April 4, 2012. [23]

More generally, the late 1980s witnessed a spate of publicity about exemptions. Stories in magazines and newspapers enlightened the public. In February 1988, "Nightline" on ABC TV used the entire program to examine the issue. Moderator Brit Hume began with this declaration: "In preparing for this broadcast, the people who ask guests to appear tried and tried and tried to find someone who would come on the program and defend this. And we couldn't find anybody who would do it, but obviously for many, many years, Members of Congress have been voting for laws which had these exclusions, so somebody must've been for it."[24]

Despite all that, Congress continued to favor itself with further exemptions on into the 1990s (see the list above).

By the early 1990s there was such adverse publicity about Congressional exemptions from laws that in 1995 the Congressional Accountability Act was passed. It applied to Congress eleven laws dating from 1935 to 1994. However, here's how one author described the new situation: "As usual, Congress made sure that when it came to laws its own members had to follow, there would be a cornucopia of loopholes. So Congress decreed that the Accountability Act would apply to Congress only as an exercise of its 'rulemaking power.' Thus, the provisions of the law can be changed at any time; and if that happens, Members who violate the workplace laws—for example, by sexually harassing or discriminating against an employee—might suffer no consequences."[25]

Despite that 1995 law, Congress made no attempt to place itself within all of the strictures of certain statutes, e.g., some sections of the Civil Rights Act of 1964.[26]

Therefore, the Congressional Accountability Enhancement Act was introduced in the House in 2004 to apply additional laws, or sections of laws, to Congress, but it was not passed.[27]

So, by the late 20th century, Congress had finally opened its eyes to the idea that federal legislators should live under the laws they imposed on the general populace, except for a few imperative exceptions. Why that awakening took so long and why such laws as prohibitions on insider trading do not yet apply to the legislative branch are questions still needing answers.

As mentioned above in the chapter on Ethics, Congress requires that most executive branch units must return to the Treasury money not spent at the end of each fiscal year, but doesn't apply that rule to itself. Unspent money appropriated to Congress gushes into discretionary accounts.   The House has such a slush fund jointly controlled exclusively by the Speaker and the chair of the Appropriations Committee. There's virtually no oversight of what they do with the money. In 1991, Speaker Tom Foley's chief-of-staff, his wife Heather (!!), used $314,000 to create in the Capitol a so-called policy office, complete with kitchen and bathrooms, for Democrats. There wasn't unused space available, so the agency providing the public with copies of bills was booted out and relocated to a "distant annex building."[28]

CORRECTIVE SOLUTIONS

Publicity about Congressional exemptions worked against some of them in the past. More is needed. If that fails to prevent unreasonable Congressional exemptions, the Constitution could be amended to state that Congress shall not exempt itself from any law other than provisions that protect executive-branch national-security information that comes to Congress or its Members.

Notes: Chapter XIV. Congressional Exemptions from Laws It Applied to Others

[1]Quoted in Richard N. Rosenfeld, "What Democracy? The case for abolishing the United States Senate," Harper's Magazine, May 2004, p. 38.

[2] Source for much of this list: Section 102(a), Congressional Accountability Act of 1995 (Public Law 104-1) [list repeated in Title 2, U.S. Code, Section 1302(a), 2000 edition]; "Congress's Wild Ganders," The Wall Street Journal, October 10, 1991, p. A14; "A New Political Ball Game, The Wall Street Journal, October 16, 1991, p. A16.

[3]"Congress has exempted itself from the conflict-of-interest provisions of the Ethics in Government Act"; "Farm Follies," The Wall Street Journal, April 17, 1990, p. A16.

[4]Prodigy, Internet Personal Services, James Boutelle, "UWSA-Connecticut," May 18, 1993.

[5]"The 8 Per Cent. Tax," The New York Times, February 2, 1918, p. 10.

[6]"Confirms Impost on Salaried Men . . . Congressmen Are Exempt," The New York Times, October 5, 1917, p. 1; "Kitchin Author of 8 Per Cent. Tax, Defends His Action in Exempting Salaries of Congressmen from the Impost," The New York Times, October 6, 1917, p. 1. Alex Mathews Arnett, Claude Kitchin and the Wilson War Policies (Boston: Little, Brown, 1937) makes no mention of this controversy.

[7]"House Votes To Tax Congress Salaries—Repeals Kitchin Joker and Passes Amendment—Makes President Subject to Impost," The New York Times, December 19, 1917, p. 2; "The 8 Per Cent. Tax," ibid., February 2, 1918, p. 10; "Congressmen Must Pay. Roper Holds That They Are Not Exempt from Occupation Tax," ibid., February 2, 1918, p. 11.

[8]"Outside the Law," The Wall Street Journal, May 18, 1992, p. A10.

[9]"Congress's Sweetheart Justice," The Wall Street Journal, November 1, 1991, p. A14; "Outside the Law," p. A10.

[10]Ronald Kessler, Inside Congress: The Shocking Scandals, Corruption, and Abuse of Power Behind the Scenes on Capitol Hill (New York: Pocket Books, 1997), pp. 248-49.

[11]Ibid., p. 144-45. Robert V. Remini, The House: The History of the House of Representatives (New York: Collins, a division of HarperCollins; Smithsonian Books, 2006), p. 486.

[12]See Title 15, U.S. Code, Sections 78t(d), 78t-1, 78u-1, and 78ff, 2000 edition.

[13]Representative Louise Slaughter press release of May 16, 2007, "Reps. Slaughter and Baird Introduce Legislation to Prohibit Insider Trading on Capitol Hill," from "Should Congress pass the Stop Trading on Congressional Knowledge (STOCK) Act?" on the Internet.

[14]Ibid.

[15]Rep. Brian Baird, press release "Reps. Baird and Slaughter Introduce Legislation to Prohibit Insider Trading on Capitol Hill," May 16, 2007, on the Internet. On whether or not such a figure is accurate, see Megan McArdle, "Capitol Gains," The Atlantic, November 2011, pp. 36-40, which reports on two studies of Members' stock trading; one saw outsized good results while the other did not

[16]Ibid.

[17]Seattle Post-Intelligencer editorial, "Insider Trading: Congress for Sale," posted online March 30, 2006.

[18]Rep. Brian Baird, press release, May 16, 2007, cited above.

[19]Brian Baird, press release "Rep. Baird Testifies before Rules Committee on Insider Trading and 72 Hour Proposals," March 30, 2006, from "Should Congress pass the Stop Trading on Congressional Knowledge (STOCK) Act?" on the Internet.

[20]Brody Mullins, "Bill Seeks to Ban Insider Trading By Lawmakers and Their Aides," The Wall Street Journal, March 29, 2006, p. A1; Congressional Record, daily edition, march 28, 2006, p. H1195.

[21]See the bill's details in Baird's cited press release of May 16, 2007. See also Congressional Record, daily edition, May 16, 2007, p. H5290.

[22]For some articles see Jason Zweig, Tom McGinty, and Brody Mullins, "Congress Members Bet on Fall In Stocks," The Wall Street Journal, May 4, 2010, pp. A1, A4; Zweig, Mullins, & McGinty, "Several U.S. Lawmakers Bet on Firms They Oversaw," The Wall Street Journal, June 17, 2010, pp. C1, C3; Mullins, & Zweig, "Congress Staffers Gain From Trading In Stocks," The Wall Street Journal, October 11, 2010, pp. A1, A16; McGinty & Mullins, "Lawmaker Vows to Outlaw Insider Trading on the Hill," The Wall Street Journal, October 12, 2010, p. A9; "Members of Congress Are Exempt from Insider Trading Law and Make 9% Per Year Trading on Inside Information," Economic Policy Journal.com, May 28, 2011; McArdle, "Capitol Gains."

[23]"60 Minutes" apparently relied in part on Peter Schweizer, Throw Them All Out: How Politicians and Their Friends Get Rich Off Insider Stock Tips, Land Deals, and Cronyism That Would Send the Rest of Us to Prison (Boston & New York: Houghton Mifflin Harcourt, 2011); it's a great book with many details. Who knows if the new law will really prevent insider trading by Members or will be amended after public interest evaporates. Or will Members find ways to skirt it? See Jonathan Macey, "Congress's Phony Insider-Trading Reform,: The Wall Street Journal, December 13, 2011, p. A21.

[24]"The Imperial Congress," The Wall Street Journal, February 16, 1988, p. 36.

[25]Kessler, Inside Congress, pp. 163-64. See Section 102(b)(3), 304(c), and 501 of Public Law 104-1; and Title 2, U.S. Code, Section 1301 et seq. and Section 1431, 2000 edition.

[26]The Office of Compliance was created by the Congressional Accountability Act of 1995. Its Section 102(b) Report in 2002 lists several laws which still did not "apply to Congress or to Legislative Branch instrumentalities." The biennial reports can be found by entering "Office of Compliance: Reports and Studies" on the Internet.

[27]The bill was H.R. 3963, 108th Congress, 2d Session. In the "List of Bills Enacted Into Public Law" in 118 Stat., it is not listed, nor have I found a later such law.

[28]"Congress's Slush Funds," The Wall Street Journal, May 19, 1992, p. A14.

XV. Falsified Records

EPIGRAPH: There are very few lovers of truth for truth's sake.
                        ---English philosopher John Locke, promoter of
                            several ideas later put in our Declaration of Independence.

EPIGRAPH: With equal care weigh well the record of the wisdom and the folly
                    of mankind.
                        ---Roscoe Conkling Ensign Brown,
                            Inscription for the wall of the
                            Central Library, Brooklyn, NY.

A. The <u>Congressional Record</u> Problem

U.S. law states that the <u>Congressional Record</u> "shall be substantially a verbatim report of proceedings."[1] "Substantially" is the weasel word that allows much falsification. Some sources, even official ones, propagate such misleading statements as "The <u>Congressional Record</u> is a verbatim report of the proceedings of both the Senate and the House of Representatives."[2] Not only is some of what was actually said in debate transformed into fiction in the <u>Record,</u> but much that was never said is printed. Sometimes words that were spoken do not appear.   And occasionally the <u>Record</u> leads the reader to believe that an absent Member was present.

For true history—and because what is said and done in Congress sometimes forms the basis for interpretations of law, for federal regulations, and for court decisions—it's important that the <u>Congressional Record</u> be accurate.[3]

Inaccuracies may not always be earth-shaking, but they are still falsifications. After a Representative got mixed up and said on the floor of the House, "I was elected to be part of the problem, not part of the solution," the <u>Congressional Record</u> printed a revised version that would look better.[4]

Aside from mistakes that are corrected in the <u>Record,</u> there's the dubious practice of the insertion of "speeches" not actually made. It used to be that the <u>Record</u> did not distinguish between the real and the false, and many of both even had parenthetical

insertions such as "great laughter" and "great applause." But a century or so ago the
suggestion to end the masquerade speeches brought the jest that it was "one of the most
radical and personally oppressive proposals now before Congress" and might prevent the
duping of the constituent who "imagines the House sitting spellbound as . . . [a
Representative] weaves the magic of his oratory." [5]

Insertions such as "applause," whether in delivered or in fake speeches, created a
problem that may seem silly but could gore two of Members' most sacred cows, their
egos and their re-election chances. In March 1945, responding to a complaint that such
insertions had been dropped from the <u>Congressional Record</u>, Speaker Sam Rayburn
explained the difficulty:

> In times past there appeared in the RECORD the word "Applause" where
> a Member spoke. In another place there was "Loud applause." In another
> place there was "Loud and prolonged applause." In another place there
> was "Loud and prolonged applause, the Members rising." If I had made a
> speech and had received "applause," and some Member had followed me
> immediately and had received "loud and prolonged applause, the Members
> rising," my opponent in the next primary might have called attention to how
> insignificant I was because I only received "applause" and the other Member
> had received "loud and prolonged applause, the Members rising."

Therefore, Rayburn announced, "The Chair has held that demonstrations in the House are
not a part of the RECORD, and shall continue to hold that until the rules of the House are
changed."[6]

That practice endures for actual speeches but is not always applied to "Extensions of
Remarks." For example, an insertion by Newt Gingrich in 1998 had one "Laughter" and
thirteen "Applauses."[7]

Starting in 1978, rules have required that speeches not actually made be identified in the
<u>Record</u> by a "bullet" (a solid black dot) or by a different typeface. [8] But Members are still
permitted to "revise and extend" with nothing flagging the changes. So some sham
speeches still appear in the <u>Record</u> as if actually spoken. For the House, "words inserted
or appended, rather than spoken . . . on the floor" are supposed to appear in the <u>Record</u> in
bold print; but even when that happens, perhaps only the experienced or careful reader
will note or understand the difference, especially when the unspoken insertion is worded
to make it appear as spoken on the floor, as when a Representative's fake speech begins
"Madam Speaker, I rise in strong support of the . . ."[9]

Furthermore, there's a gaping loophole: A Member who obtains the floor in either
Senate or House can enter words not spoken as well as portions of material from other
sources without the <u>Record</u> later identifying those insertions with a bullet and without
them appearing in the sections of Additional Statements or Extensions of Remarks. A
Representative accomplishes that by saying, "I request unanimous consent to revise and
extend my remarks" or by asking that all Representatives who speak during a particular
debate be granted that privilege. For a Senator it's even easier: After speaking only a bit
or a lot, he or she may append unlimited additions.[10]

Among the untutored, the Congressional Record has a sometimes undeserved reputation as a source for truth and accuracy. False material inserted in the Record has occasionally been publicized as factual, the alleged proof being that it was printed in the Record. One example from 1928 and another from 2006 illustrate the long existence of this problem. The latter will be presented later in this section.

In 1928 the Catholicism of Presidential candidate Al Smith was considered a threat by many Protestant Americans. They used anti-Catholic smears against Smith. Some people claimed that all Protestant babies would be declared bastards if Smith became President. Copies of a photograph showing Smith at the opening ceremony for the Holland Tunnel connecting Manhattan and New Jersey were circulated in some Protestant areas where less educated people "learned" that the tunnel went under the Atlantic Ocean all the way to Rome and that a Papal army would march through the tunnel and take over America if Smith won. And the purported "Knights of Columbus Oath" was taken from the 1913 Congressional Record as "proof" that Catholics were intent on persecuting Protestants in dreadful ways. The oath was actually a nineteenth-century forgery that had been created to harm the Jesuits. Later it was alleged to emanate from the Knights of Columbus, a Catholic laymen's organization. After it was used against a Catholic candidate for the House of Representatives in 1912, a House committee investigated and exposed it as a fraud. The oath and its fraudulence were printed in the Record, but some anti-Catholics of 1928 pulled out only the oath and asserted its legitimacy by citing its inclusion in the Record.[11]

That the Record is a faithful account of what occurred and what was said on the floors of the House and the Senate is partially true. Indeed, the Record has much correct information. But there's also much that is false. So much, in fact, that even a well-informed specialist may not be able to know where factuality yields to fabrication. So much, in fact, that a February 1983 article in Reader's Digest was titled "Congress's License to Lie," and little has changed since then.[12] So little, in fact, that perhaps the Record should be renamed Congressional Truths and Untruths.

A lawsuit in the mid-1980s sought injunctive relief to prevent publication of this "corrupt" record. It failed, however, at two levels of the federal judiciary. A district court cited the clause of the Constitution saying "for any speech or debate in either house, they shall not be questioned in any other place." A Court of Appeals relied on the separation of powers doctrine in saying it could not review "congressional practices and procedures when they primarily and directly affect the way Congress does its legislative business."[13]

When Senators and Representatives speak on the floors of their respective chambers, employees trained in shorthand try to write exactly what each Member says. The shorthand record is quickly transcribed and printed so that the Member can soon see a copy. The trouble is that after the Member "revises and extends" his or her remarks, the original copy is not available to the public. Thus, in revising and extending, what was actually said will sometimes disappear. Factual mistakes, bad grammar, and confused syntax journey to oblivion. In their places appear somewhat fictional compositions of greater literary merit. The author of the aforementioned Reader's Digest article averred that the "Record is probably the government's most untrustworthy official publication—up to 70 percent of what's in it was never spoken on the floor, and 10 to 15 percent of what *was* spoken doesn't get in." That article also said,

> "In the 1970s the late William A. Steiger, a Wisconsin Representative, began collecting examples of the wide variety of fiction and myth that appears in the Record as fact. His extensive findings included a 131-page issue of the Record that came out in 1977 for a day Congress was not even in session. (The issue contained 'floor remarks' by Sen. Hubert Humphrey, despite the fact that Humphrey was then some 1000 miles away in a Minneapolis hospital.) A 1972 issue had Rep. Hale Boggs delivering an address to the House two days after he took off in a small plane from an Alaska airport and disappeared forever. A single 1977 issue contained 24 speeches (all of them on the subject of Congressional ethics) —by absent members."[14]

Unfortunately, even the 1978 reform sometimes falls victim to the falsification goblin. The Congressional Record for December 22, 2005, has remarks by Minority Leader Harry Reid, D-NV, that are not flagged in any way, yet numerous sources indicate that John Warner, R-VA, was the only Senator present during the four-minute session on that date.[15] (See greater detail in the chapter on The Part-time Congress on Full-time Salary.)

Occasionally an outrageous section is slipped into a bill without notice to most Members, and to prevent later breach-of-trust charges the Record is manipulated to falsely show that the section was explained in a speech on the floor. When courts decide cases involving laws they will sometimes look at the history of that law's trip through the legislative body to determine legislative intent. For federal laws the Congressional Record may be helpful. Or harmful—because it is not an accurate record.

Consider this: In 2006 the Supreme Court heard arguments in the case of Hamdan v. Rumsfeld involving whether the Detainee Treatment Act of 2005 (DTA) was intended by Congress to apply retroactively to prisoners at Guantanamo.[16] The Congressional Record contained eight pages of a "colloquy" on December 21, 2005, on the floor between Senators John Kyl (R-AZ) and Lindsey Graham (R-SC) to the effect that Congress did intend the DTA to apply to cases filed before it became law.[17] In February 2006, Kyl and Graham filed a brief with the Supreme Court, saying that the purported dialogue between them was evidence of Congress's intent. The Justice Department's brief contained a similar argument. But that dialogue was never spoken on the floor. It was inserted into the Congressional Record after debate on the bill had closed. The Kyl-Graham brief argued that words not uttered on the floor are identified as such in the Record and that their dialogue occurred "live" because the Record contained no such identification. That was false. The rule that off-the-floor remarks by Senators be "bulleted" in the Record does not apply to remarks allegedly made on the floor.

In ruling that Congress had not intended for President Bush to authorize military trials for detainees at Guantanamo, Justice John Paul Stevens wrote for the majority that the Kyl-Graham statements "appear to have been inserted in the <u>Congressional Record</u> after the Senate debate."[18]

Aside from the issue of whether the debate words of a very few Senators truly reflect the legislative intent of the majority, the greater problem in the Kyl-Graham colloquy is the effort to use the <u>Congressional Record</u> to deceive the Supreme Court. The words inserted into the <u>Record</u> were structured for deception, to make a <u>post facto</u> insertion appear to have been live debate. Observe Kyl noting, "I see that my colleague, the senior Senator from South Carolina, is also on the floor," and Graham telling Kyl, "You are absolutely correct," and Senator Brownback (R-KS) saying, "If I might interrupt, I would like to add . . .," and Kyl advising, "I have just been handed a memorandum on this subject," and Graham addressing the chair, "Mr. President, if Senator Kyl would be so kind, could he explain how our amendment will affect ongoing litigation?" and Graham requesting unanimous consent to have a newspaper editorial entered in the <u>Record</u>, and Kyl stating, "Mr. President, I see that we are nearing the end of our allotted time." Unanimous consent cannot be given when the request occurs in fictional live debate. Also, the editorial was apparently never entered in the <u>Record</u>.[19]

Asked by a reporter if Senator Brownback's printed interruption occurred in live debate, an aide responded, "Yes, it was live." When the reporter said there was contrary evidence, the aide offered, "Let me call you back," but of course she did not.[20]

It's standard practice for Senators and Representatives to place unspoken words in the <u>Congressional Record</u>. After Senator Kyl was criticized for the fabricated debate, he resorted to the "we-all-do-it" defense. But what's not standard, and was apparently unprecedented, is for Senators to use a bogus debate to try to deceive a court about legislative intent. Of course, Senators Graham and Kyl suffered no civil or criminal penalties for this hoax.[21]

In another outrageous—and common—fabrication, Members can revise for publication in the <u>Record</u> what they really said on the floor. The press secretary of a Democratic Representative from Texas explained the process: Following a debate, a request will be granted for "all members to have five legislative days to revise and extend their remarks." A Member, presumably one who actually spoke, can look at the newspaper and TV reaction and recast what he or she said. The new language can rebut arguments appearing in the media, can make debate reasoning more persuasive, can create whatever changes will throw a more favorable re-election light on the speaker. If the alterations are made soon enough, the revised version will appear in the <u>Record</u> of the debate date, not the date when the revision was submitted.[22]

On February 7, 1990, Representative Robert Walker, R-PA, introduced a resolution directing the Committee on House Administration to make recommendations about the use of "revise and extend" to delete words spoken on the floor because "these omissions seriously threaten the integrity of the proceedings of the House." Walker was concerned that the video recordings of House sessions would show something different from what would appear in the Congressional Record. After brief debate, the resolution passed by a lopsided majority.[23]

Walker's efforts finally bore fruit in 1995 when House standing rules were amended to require that remarks on the floor would be subject only to "technical, grammatical, and typographical corrections authorized by the Member making the remarks involved."[24] However, as noted below in the section on committee records, that loophole is sometimes abused to change fact into fiction.

Another problem with the Record is that different page numbers sometimes exist for the same report of the proceedings. In the case of Walker's resolution, for example, one book cites the page numbers as H330-H332 rather than 1515-17.[25] The explanation for this is that there are two different editions of the Congressional Record, a daily edition and a permanent one. The former is published on the day after the proceedings it reports—or as close thereafter as possible—and its page numbers are prefixed with S (Senate), H (House), E (Extension of remarks), or D (Daily Digest). The permanent edition is a revision and has continuous page numbers without any prefixes such as H or S.[26] This can produce difficulties and perplexities: ●The careful researcher will sometimes have to check both versions to see if there are differences; ●The permanent edition may falsify what actually occurred; ●Because of differing pagination, a citation to one edition may create a problem for a researcher who has only the other readily available.

Another suspect use of the Record is that Members insert praise of campaign donors. Contributions quickly followed by laudatory remarks in the Record raise suspicions of quid pro quo. The Scripps Howard Foundation Wire studied donations and Congressional Record praise by leading Representatives and reported in April 2006 that it found numerous such combinations. Combinations, however, do not necessarily prove linkage. (A logical fallacy called post hoc, ergo propter hoc argues that because one event follows another it must have been caused by the first.) So much praise of non-donor individuals and organizations is inserted into the Record that Members can argue, as they do, that there's no ethical transgression relating to praise of donors. A contribution tied to an official House action, such as placing a statement in the Record, would violate House ethics rules. But the possible linkage is so vague that the Ethics Committee steers clear of that difficult road.[27]

On occasion, the Record is altered to eliminate offensive statements that were actually made, whether by mistake or deliberately. In 1991 Senator Ted Kennedy, D-MA, charged that Senator Arlen Specter, R-PA, was a White House puppet. Senator Orrin Hatch, R-UT, leaped to Specter's defense: "Anyone who believes that, I know a bridge up in Massachusetts that I will be happy to sell them with the help of Sen. Kennedy." This appeared to refer to Kennedy's notorious 1969 wreck on Chappaquiddick Island which killed his female companion. Hatch later apologized and said he intended to refer to the Brooklyn Bridge. The Record was altered to reflect that.[28]

During floor debate in 1974 House Majority Leader Tip O'Neill criticized another Member's tactic as "a cheap, sneaky, sly way to operate." That Member, Robert Bauman, R-MD, then demanded "that the gentleman's words be taken down," a way of asking that the words be noted as a violation of House rules. Speaker Carl Albert ruled that the words were "not parliamentary" and would be stricken from the Record. After further debate and maneuvering, that was done, and the offending words are not in the Record's report of O'Neill's remarks. Yet you can find them on the next page.[29]

CORRECTIVE SOLUTIONS

Adverting to the theme of this book, it's a failure of democracy for Members of Congress to falsify the official record of what they say and do. Congress could stop this malpractice by passing a law, not just a changeable rule, that all words reported in the Record as having been spoken on the floors of the two chambers must actually have been uttered and must be exact and unchanged. The British and Canadians have no trouble doing that, and American legislative bodies are surely just as able.

The problems caused by having two differing editions of the Record could be eliminated by having only the daily edition, and it could be bound into volumes just as is now done for the permanent edition. That would provide greater historical accuracy, reduce expenses, and present fewer hurdles for researchers. Of course, that would also provide fewer chances for Members to bamboozle the public and pad their re-election chances.

Another improvement: As House and Senate sessions are already videotaped, put the tapes, without added comments, on the Internet where anyone can access them.

B. Committee Records

Both chambers require their committees to keep records of their meetings, but the House allows reports of words spoken to be altered from what was recorded by stenographers. House Rule XI, 110th Congress, says the record shall include "in the case of a meeting or hearing transcript, a substantially verbatim account of remarks actually made during the proceedings, subject only to technical, grammatical, and typographical corrections authorized by the person making the remarks involved."[30]

Because "corrections" can be made, the transcript record may not reflect reality. A correction, as defined by dictionaries, is an accurate substitute for something previously inaccurate. In a definition reversal, the House sometimes uses "correction" to mean an inaccurate substitute for something previously accurate. Sometimes the revision is benign, sometimes malignant. Whether one or the other, it's a falsification. Congress should stop all the "corrections" in favor of truth.

In mid-1983, a scandal the Republicans called Altergate besmirched the House. The published transcripts of a committee hearing contained numerous important and material deviations from the original stenographic record. Further, changes made by another committee after it had approved a bill, increased allocated funds by 1.3 billion dollars.

Also, names of Representatives "associated with a suspect group" were deleted from a document attached to a committee report.[31]

The blame for the transcript changes was assigned to a staffer working for the Democratic majority.[32] So many of the alterations made Republicans look bad that they appeared to be partisan dirty tricks. Some examples:

- Robert Walker, R-PA, said he was "willing to take part in reasonable hearings." The altered version said he was not willing to do so.

- John Hiler, R-IN, said, "The majority had about one or two people here" [at a hearing]. The printed mutation said it was "the minority" that was lax in its attendance.

- Hiler also said, "We are unfortunately doomed to have to undergo, what has been an extraordinarily partisan hearing." The change had him merely say "We are unfortunately doomed."

- Judd Gregg, R-NH, wondered why the majority, with so many staffers, "did not have time to get back to us." The "correction" had him questioning why the numerous minority staff "did not have time to get back to us."[33]

The Democrats rejected Republican attempts to create an ad hoc investigating committee, and instead referred the issue to the Ethics Committee, where oblivion engulfed it.

Such changes can be momentous. They may prevent the true intent of Congress to be clouded when executive agencies and courts seek guidance.

Imagine the damage to justice and the legal system if the stenographic record of what is said in court could be altered. Jurors would be more likely to convict the innocent and acquit the guilty. Appellate courts could be misled. Surely, Americans would not permit such modifications. Yet, Congress allows committee words and activities to be falsified—just as it allows, even encourages, the Congressional Record to depart from truth and reality.

And it's still in House Rule XI that "incorrections" can be made.

The Senate also allows committee records to be falsified, though no Senate standing rule makes the practice blatant. In fact, Rule XXVI, 110th Congress, by newly providing for publicly available electronic recordings, makes "corrections" difficult. However, if such recordings are not made (which is permitted) or when they are no longer available (after "the end of the Congress following the date of the meeting"), then the printed transcript can still be fiddled.[34]

CORRECTIVE SOLUTIONS

Each chamber should require that reports of committee activities, including words spoken, be printed as they originally occurred—and that any "corrections," for whatever reason, be printed in an appendix to each report. People can then compare the two and make judgments about which is accurate. Because of the flimflams that Members sometimes commit, it might be best that all public committee proceedings always be taped and made available to the public via the Internet.

Notes: Chapter XV. Falsified Records

[1]US. Code, Title 44, Section 901.

[2]Government Information Services: "Using the *Congressional Record*," on the Internet.

[3]One of the best sources for information on this is N. David Bleisch, "The *Congressional Record* and the First Amendment: Accuracy is the Best Policy," Boston College Environmental Affairs Law Review, Vol. 12, No. 2 (Winter 1985), pp. 342-79.

[4]Robert Cwiklik, House Rules: A Freshman Congressman's Initiation to the Backslapping, Backpedaling, and Backstabbing Ways of Washington (New York: Villard Books, 1991), p. 226.
One must, of course, be careful using secondary sources because they may have misinformation. For instance, a respected book reported that Speaker Tip O'Neill said some remarks by New Gingrich were the "lowest thing" he had seen in his 32 years in Congress, and that in "an embarrassing move for the Speaker," the Congressional Record eliminated O'Neill's statements; Julian E. Zelizer, On Capitol Hill: The Struggle to Reform Congress and Its Consequences, 1948-2000 (New York: Cambridge University Press, 2004), p. 215. But if you look at the Congressional Record, permanent edition, May 15, 1984, p. 12201, you will see O'Neill's offending words, for which he received what amounted to a reprimand.
There's an issue about whether quotations should be rendered exactly as said or can be cleaned up a bit. See Jay Nordlinger, "Quotin'Obama," National Review, October 31, 2011, pp. 28, 30. For example, should President Obama be quoted precisely when he says of Jeremiah Wright "He married Michelle and I," or when he goes before a black audience and drops "g's," as in "Stop complainin"?

[5]"Cruelty to Congressmen," The Outlook, June 10, 1911, p. 272.

[6]Congressional Record, permanent edition, March 6, 1945, p. 1789; Lewis Deschler, Deschler's Precedents of the United States House of Representatives, continued by Lewis Deschler and Wm. Holmes Brown, Deschler-Brown Precedents of the United States House of Representatives (16 vols.: Washington; USGPO, 1977-2002), Vol. I, pp. 361-62.

[7]Congressional Record, daily edition, October 21, 1998, pp. E2291-93.

[8]Senators' insertions, identified by bullets at beginning and end, are included in the Record as "Additional Statements" preceding the adjournment information near the end of a day's report of Senate activity. Starting in September 1985, bullets were dropped for many of the additions by Representatives, which instead would be in bold-face type in the main body of each day's Record, thus [allegedly] giving the unuttered speeches "more typographical prominence in the pages of the Record"; James F. Clarity and Warren Weaver, Jr., "Briefing: Chasing Bullets," The New York Times, September 20, 1985, p. A14; "House Approves Changes in *Congressional Record*, Congressional Quarterly Weekly Report, August 10, 1985, p. 1615. Other additions by Representatives are in the "Extensions of Remarks" section at the end of the report on each day's House proceedings.

[9]The first quotation is from the disclaimer appearing near the bottom of each first page of the Record's report of a day's House proceedings. The second is from one of the recent examples showing that it's sometimes hard to see the difference between the regular and bold typefaces: Congressional Record, daily edition, July 31, 2007, p. H9208. See also ibid., May 13, 2008, pp. H3713-14, H3719.

According to one source, "Senate staffers say you scrawl 'live' on a written statement, hand it over, and usually no one is the wiser. (Heads up: The 'bullets' in the **Congressional Record** denoting testimony that's not live are entirely discretionary.)"; Emily Bazelon, "Not Live From Capitol Hill," Slate Magazine [online], June 29, 2006.

[10]James Nathan Miller, "Congress's License to Lie," Reader's Digest, February 1983, pp. 74.

[11]Bruce L. Felknor, Dirty Politics (New York: W. W. Norton, 1966), p. 53.

[12]Miller, "Congress's License to Lie," pp. 72-77. See also Richard Neuberger, "The Congressional Record Is *Not* a Record," The New York Times, April 20, 1958, Sec. 6, p. 14, reprinted in Congressional Record, permanent edition, April 21, 1958, pp. 6816-18; and Howard N. Mantel, "The *Congressional Record*: Fact or Fiction of the Legislative Process," The Western Political Quarterly, December 1959, pp. 981-95.

[13]Gregg v. Barrett, 594 F.Supp. 108 (1984); Gregg v. Barrett, 771 F.2d 539 (1985).

[14]See also William A. Steiger, "'Say,' the Senator Asked, 'Read Any Fiction Lately?' 'Yes. The Congressional Record,'" The New York Times, August 29, 1977, p. 27. Steiger wrote, "The Record is a deliberate distortion of what actually happens in the House and Senate."

The claim that Hale Boggs spoke in the House after having disappeared while on an airplane ride in Alaska rests on an entry in the Record for October 18, 1972 (permanent edition, pp. 37160 et seqq.). But that entry, for the day Congress adjourned sine die, says, "(Mr. Boggs asked and was given permission to extend his remarks at this point in the Record and to include extraneous matter.)" Those words indicate that he asked permission before he embarked on his final trip.

[15]<u>Congressional Record</u>, daily edition, December 22, 2005, pp. S14423-25.

[16]<u>Hamdan v. Rumsfeld</u>, 548 U.S. 557 (2006).

[17]<u>Congressional Record</u>, daily edition, December 21, 2005, pp. S14260-S14268. While dictionaries define "colloquy" merely as conversation or dialogue, there's a more specific and limited Congressional usage, i.e., that it's a scripted, often pre-written, dialogue designed for clarification of Congressional intent.

[18]<u>Hamdan v. Rumsfeld</u>, 548 U.S. at 580 (2006).

[19]Under "New York (NY) Times" in <u>Congressional Record Index</u>, December 6 to December 30, 2005; ibid., January 3 to January 27, 2006; and January 30 to February 17, 2006; ibid., February 27 to March 16, 2006, there is no entry that the editorial was entered.

[20]"Anonymous Liberal," "The fictitious Kyl/Graham 'floor debate,'" March 28, 2006, on the Internet, quoting Emily Bazelon of the online site Slate.

[21]See this interesting item: Vagabond Scholar, "Will GOP Senators Face Consequences for Lying to the Supreme Court?" on the Internet.

[22]John L. Jackley, <u>Hill Rat: Blowing the Lid Off Congress</u> (Washington: Regnery Gateway, 1992), p. 32. See also ibid., pp. 279-80 for the racist remarks of Gus Savage, D-IL, a black Representative, being 'deleted and toned down.'

[23]<u>Congressional Record</u>, permanent edition, February 7, 1990, pp. 1515-17; "House Will Review Cuts From Record," <u>Congressional Quarterly Weekly Report</u>, February 10, 1990, p. 374.

[24]That was in Rule XIV (Decorum and Debate), clause 9, in 1995. Since the recodification of House rules by the 106th Congress, it has been in Rule XVII (Decorum and Debate), clause 8.

[25]Jackley, <u>Hill Rat</u>, p. 342, n. 7, gives the page numbers as H330-332.

[26]On the Internet at <u>http://thomas.loc.gov/home/abt.cong.rec.html</u> see "About the *Congressional Record.* A revision example is that "a detailed description of homosexual love-making, inserted by Rep. William Dannemeyer (R., Calif.), was carried in the day's edition but erased from the permanent record. It has become a collector's item"; Milton Gwirtzman, "Congress's Daily Advertisement for Itself," <u>The Wall Street Journal</u>, October 8, 1992, p. A14.

[27]Michael Malik, "Is Congressional Record for sale?" Scripps Howard Foundation Wire, April 18, 2006, on the Internet.

[28]"Sen. Hatch rewrites the 'Record' book," <u>USA Today</u>, October 17, 1991, p. 5A. <u>Congressional Record</u>, permanent edition, October 15, 1991, p. 26306.

[29]Mark J. Green, <u>Who Runs Congress?</u>, revised edition (New York: Bantam/Grossman, 1975), pp. 203-04. <u>Congressional Record</u>, permanent edition, August 21, 1974, pp. 29652-53. See House Rule XVII, clause 4(a), 110th Congress, different number earlier.

[30]House Rule XI, clause 2(e)(1)(A)(i), 110th Congress. That language is a revision of the original rule made in 1953.

[31]Joseph P. Shapiro, "Behind Furor Over Altering Records," <u>U.S. News & World Report</u>, August 1, 1983, p. 30.

[32]"House Official Says Aide Altered Transcripts, <u>The New York Times</u>, September 3, 1983, p. 24.

[33]"Altered States: A House probe of transcripts," <u>Time</u>, July 11, 1983, p. 13; Shapiro, "Behind Furor Over Altering Records," p. 30.

[34]Winslow T. Wheeler, <u>The Wastrels of Defense: How Congress Sabotages U.S. Security</u> (Annapolis: Naval Institute Press, 2004), p. 101: "Before printing, staffers will have gone over it [the transcript] word by word. Each raw (verbatim) transcript is delivered to senators' staffs with an admonition to make only minor changes; the caution is routinely ignored."

XVI. Unrelated Items in the Same Bill

EPIGRAPH: Laws are like sausages. It's better not to see them being made.
                 ---Otto Von Bismarck.[1]

EPIGRAPH: This many-headed monster.
                 ---Philip Massinger, The Roman Actor (1629),
                 Act III, Scene 2.

Congress often unites many unrelated items in a single bill. If you look at the titles of bills, you will see that the last part often reads "and for other purposes."[2] Those words indicate the profusion of topics that may be in a single bill. That has some justification on grounds of efficiency, and it avoids the disputes that would arise about whether provisions were of sufficient closeness to travel together on one omnibus bill.

But several bad results can occur. One is that when a bad proposal is included in a larger and vital bill, the President cannot veto the bad part without also killing the more important sections. Appropriations bills that give a free ride to irresponsible pork-barrel spending are a favorite vehicle used by Congress to bypass a potential veto. The recent Congressional practice of failing to pass appropriation bills before the new fiscal year begins and then lumping them together in a giant omnibus bill, presents the President with the choice of approving the bloated measure or shutting down much of the government by use of the veto. As one book reported, "In this manner one of the principal checks and balances in our system of government is effectively eliminated, and Congress knows it."[3]

Part of that first bad result is that a scheme unable to obtain passage on its own may pass when tacked on to a larger measure. It's a defeat for democracy to allow ideas to become law when they could not pass on their own if voted on separately. A disliked provision can be added—by majority leadership, committee chair, or conference—to a guaranteed-to-pass bill that enjoys wide support or is deemed vital to the national interest. The abhorrent "free rider" thus sneaks into the statute books on the merits of something unrelated.

For instance, in 1981 a provision to give Members of Congress about a $19,000 yearly income-tax deduction for their D.C. homes was sneaked into a bill to provide benefits to people suffering from black-lung disease. See the chapter on Thief-in-the-Night Pay Raises.

Secondly, when a popular idea is grafted onto another proposal, it fails if the entire colossus is defeated. In 2006 Ron Wyden, D-OR, and Charles Grassley, R-IA, succeeded in getting 84 of their fellow Senators to vote in favor of ending "secret holds" (explained in the chapter on "Holding" the Senate Hostage). Did that mean the abolition of secret holds? Of course not—because the potentially victorious proposal was part of a larger ethics bill that never passed. And in September 2006, Speaker Dennis Hastert refused to allow a bill for military pay raises and other national defense priorities to move forward in the House unless certain immigration and court-security provisions were attached. One newspaper headline was "Unrelated items delay defense bill."[4]

A recent example relates to the desire for Congressional continuity after a terrorist attack leaving numerous Members dead or incapacitated. Many people concluded that the hijacked United Airlines Flight 93 that crashed in Pennsylvania on 9-11-2001 would have struck the Capitol Building but for the heroic efforts of its passengers. Had that happened, Congress might not have had enough living or functioning Members to meet the Constitutionally mandated quorum of a majority of the membership of each chamber to do business. (Each chamber, however, habitually violates that requirement by assuming the existence of a quorum unless a challenge occurs; see the chapter on the Part-Time Congress.) Then government might have been paralyzed or Caesarized. Therefore, many thoughtful people began to seek ways to achieve Congressional continuity after such a calamity.[5]

After several years of proposals, contention, and foot-dragging, one flawed idea became law in 2005. But it did so only because of dubious shenanigans by Speaker Dennis Hastert and his minions. After the House passed continuity bills in both 2004 and 2005, the Senate, with astounding lack of concern, refused to act on them. Therefore, in 2005 Speaker Dennis Hastert violated House norms by ordering the chair of the Appropriations Committee to add the continuity proposal to the legislative appropriations bill. As explained below in the chapter on Violations, it has long been Congressional policy that legislative riders on appropriations bills are forbidden. When the appropriations bill, heavy with the unrelated and precedent-breaking addition, reached the Senate, Hastert blackmailed the Senate into accepting it by threatening that the larger bill would not be passed by the House if the continuity provisions were excluded. So, the entire bill became law after the Senate knuckled under.[6] No doubt the continuity part would not have advanced to the statute books on its own.

In a further outrage, Hastert and his abettors created a new House rule to allow the Speaker to decide if some Members are incapacitated and to then declare, in violation of the Constitution, that a quorum of the House is no longer a majority of the Representatives but is instead a majority of the "provisional number of the House."[7] To those who would claim that to be a sensible and practical method to deal with a catastrophic circumstance, ask them why a revision of the Constitution was accomplished by rule rather than a Constitutional amendment. Indeed, an effort to amend was attempted but it failed.[8]

The final appropriations/continuity bill provided for special elections to fill House vacancies not more than 49 days after the Speaker declared the existence of at least 101 House vacancies.[9] (Special elections for Senators were not included because the 17th Amendment already provides for them and for governors to appoint temporary Senators.)

The bill ignored all sorts of problems:
- What about unaddressed conflicts with state laws and other federal laws?
- What about too little time for primary elections (because candidates would have to be selected not later than the tenth day of the 49 allotted)?
- What about selection of candidates by party bosses?
- What about the question of whether the ten-day period would start with the Speaker's declaration or only after a five-day delay caused by a lawsuit disputing the existence of a particular vacancy? (The law seems to specify the Speaker's declaration regardless of such a five-day delay.)
- What about the limited time for programming election machines, training poll workers, and finding polling places?
- What about the limited time for printing and distributing ballots after the selection of candidates?
- What about the limited time provided for voting by absent members of the armed forces and overseas voters?
- What about other absentee voting?
- What if a district held its election on the 50th day?
- What about the possible 75-day delay if a general election is already scheduled to be held within 75 days of the Speaker's declaration? (In that case, the law says no emergency special election need happen.)
- What about the unaddressed issue of Members not dead or missing but only incapacitated because of a terrorist attack (see below)?

Some Members and scholars pointed to these flaws as reasons for a different solution, but the Republican leadership bulldozed the bill through the House.

With the problems not addressed by these continuity provisions and with all the other problems that would flow from a major terrorist attack, there is a high probability of 49 or 75 days of chaos and possible martial law. And surely it's not a desirable part of the democratic process that something becomes law as a rider on another measure when it could not do so on its own merits.

And what about alive but incapacitated Members? The answer appeared in a new House rule passed in January 2005. After 72 hours of failed attempts to obtain a quorum following a disaster, the Sergeant-at-Arms or his designee will list the dead, missing, or incapacitated Members in a "catastrophic quorum failure report." The Speaker will then consult with the majority and minority leaders about the report's content and will announce said content to the House. After a further 24 hours pass without a quorum of "the whole number of the House," then the reduced, "provisional number of the House," meaning Representatives who had responded to the most recent quorum call, will constitute a quorum.[10]

That produces several issues.

- The Constitution, Article I, Section 5, states that a majority of the members in each chamber "shall constitute a quorum to do business." Many people argue that the House cannot alter the Constitution by a mere rule, and indeed, as noted above, there was an effort to launch a Constitutional amendment about continuity, but Senate and House leadership scuttled it.
- This Constitution-change-by-rule may be cited in the future as a precedent for further tinkering.
- What if the Speaker and/or the majority and minority leaders, all given roles under the new rule, are dead, incapacitated, or missing?
- How can a non-Member, the Sergeant-at-Arms, have a say-so about turning Members into non-Members?

CORRECTIVE SOLUTIONS

What can be done about the perversion that permits unpassable ideas to become law as part of something more popular or necessary? A process for judging whether various provisions can be lumped together in one bill might bring in a different set of problems— who would decide?—what criteria would apply? And there can hardly be a rule that every part of a bill must be passable on its own. Some proponents of an allegedly unpopular provision will argue that there's no certainty of its stand-alone rejection; so the issue becomes largely subjective.

At least three correctives are possible. One is to turn the light of publicity on the problem so that public pressure may occasionally prevent it. The give-and-take of open and publicized discussion has at least the chance of producing a good result. Second, passage of a Constitutional amendment to require single-subject bills. To avoid evasion of such single-subject requirement, the amendment should prohibit any legislative provision tying the fate of one bill to the fate of another.

Second, some state constitutions have provisions requiring that all bills deal with only one subject, and that sort of rule could be applied to Congress. When some Maryland legislators launched a move in 2000 to rid that state's constitution of its single-subject rule, the successful opponents of the change used the example of lawmaking in the U.S. Congress "and the mischief that is a central part of that process" as one of their telling arguments.[11] How do those states' legislatures manage to function when Congress can't seem to do so without bills that contain multiple unrelated topics? Allowing late introduction and having expedited hearings seem to work. And to the argument that the federal government is vastly more complicated and has greater needs, the proper response might be that if Congress reformed some of the other problems addressed in this book, it could deal with single-subject bills. The negatives about this change might be more than balanced by the positives:

- Prohibiting non-germane amendments might help assure that bill provisions would be dealt with in public hearings. That is sometimes avoided under the existing system, which allows such amendments after a bill has left committee.
- This improvement would help prevent conference committees from violating the rules by adding new provisions to bills. See the later chapter on Violations.
- This reform would lessen the pressure for giving the President a line-item veto. Opinions would vary on whether that is positive or negative. A line-item veto might still be desirable in appropriations bills because a pork-barrel provision in a transportation spending bill could be considered part of the single subject of transportation.
- The public could more easily understand what Congress does.
- It would become harder for Congress to conceal something buried in a lengthy bill on an unrelated topic.
- This change would help in court cases involving interpretation of laws and the intent of Congress.
- It would reduce the public's cynicism about Congressional trickiness and subservience to special interests.

Current House practice differs from that of the Senate. A House committee may report a bill dealing with multiple subjects, but Rule XVI, clause 7, 110th Congress, prohibits motions in the House "on a subject different from that under consideration." Thus, amendments must be germane to the pending proposition. Interpretations of what is or is not germane are complex, as indicated by 27 pages in the notes to Rule XVI, clause 7, on the Internet's PDF version for the 110th Congress. Enforcement is through points of order, but they may be waived by resolution or by special order from the Committee on Rules. The Senate has no rule against non-germane amendments except for appropriation bills and three other unusual situations. Thus, improvement in this procedure requires rule changes in both chambers.

Liberals, a term now being euphemized into "progressives" by those it referred to, long defended the Senate non-germaneness practice as a way to permit passage of bills that had been blocked by conservative-dominated committees. A bill stalled in committee could simply be added as an amendment to a bill that had reached the floor. That, of course, sometimes meant that no hearings occurred on the blocked measure. And the discharge procedure was available for prying a bill out of committee but was seldom used. Further, a bill passed by the House could be considered directly on the floor of the Senate without going to a committee.[12]

The third corrective is to give the President a line-item veto. See above in the chapter on Insufficient Oversight of the Executive Branch.

Notes: Chapter XVI. Unrelated Items in the Same Bill

[1]This version is from <u>Forbes</u>, October 13, 2003, p. 34.

[2]For some examples, see Congressional Record, daily edition, March 29, 2007, S4159-61.

[3]Randall Fitzgerald and Gerald Lipson, Porkbarrel: The Unexpurgated Grace Commission Story of Congressional Profligacy (Washington: Cato Institute, 1984), p. 110. Page 111: In such cases "the president's constitutional veto power is practically worthless."

[4]"Unrelated items delay defense bill,"Billings Gazette, September 26, 2006, p. 3A. See also Jonathan Weisman, "House-Senate Disagreement Could Halt Defense Bill," The Washington Post, September 25, 2006, p. A6. Other examples are legion, for instance: Adrianne Kroepsch, "Senate Farm Bill Quickly Bogs Down Over Unrelated Amendments," CQ Weekly, November 12, 2007, p. 3409; John M. Donnelly, "Defense Authorization Conference Stalls Over Hate-Crimes Provision," CQ Weekly, November 19, 2007, p. 3483.

[5]For lengthy detail on this, see Thomas E. Mann and Norman J. Ornstein, The Broken Branch: How Congress Is Failing America and How to Get It Back on Track (New York: Oxford University Press, 2006), Chapter Six, pp. 192-210.

[6]Ibid., pp. 209-10. See Public Law 109-55, Title III—Continuity in Representation, pp. 588-90 in 119 Stat. 565-90.

[7]See House Rule XX, clause 5 (c), 110th Congress.

[8]Mann and Ornstein, Broken Branch, pp. 195-96, 197, 200, 203, 204-07, 209-10.

[9]Public Law 109-55, Title III, Section 301(2).

[10]See House Rule XX, clause 5(c), 110th Congress.

[11]Maryland State Bar Association, "2002 Final State Legislative Program," available on the Internet; click on Table of Contents, then on Core Issues, then on Single Subject Rule.

[12]Senate discharge of committees is mentioned in Rule XVII without explanation or stated procedure. Judy Schneider, "House and Senate Rules of Procedure: A Comparison," CRS Report for Congress, February 10, 2005, p. CRS-5, on the Internet, says, "Other Senate procedures for bypassing committees, such as the motion to discharge a committee . . . are employed so infrequently they are not discussed here." For details see U.S., Congress, Senate, Riddick's Senate Procedure: Precedents and Practices, 1992 edition (Washington: USGPO, 1992), "Discharge of Committees."

XVII. Travel Allowances

EPIGRAPH: There used to be a Representative who flew back to his
                   South Philly district every night "to hold office hours
                   from 9 P.M. to 1 A.M."
                             ---Mark J. Green, Who Runs Congress?, revised
                                edition (New York: Bantam/Grossman, 1975),
                                p. 250.

EPIGRAPH: When new Vice President Joe Biden was a Senator he
                   commonly commuted by train to and from his Delaware home.

In addition to enjoying salaries that increase with almost metronomic regularity,
Members are allowed to receive additional payments, some of which are reasonable as
advancing their representational duties. Others, however, may be viewed as perks of
office for the financial well-being or re-election chances of Members. Expenses for
travel between a Member's state or district and Washington, D.C., are abundantly funded
by taxpayers, most of whom probably have no awareness of their generosity. (See the
previous chapter on Members' Perks.)

For Representatives, there's an Official Office Expenses Allowance composed of a base
allowance plus money for one or more offices in the district plus a sum for travel to and
from the farthest point in the district. The latter varies among Representatives and is
based on this formula: "64 times the rate per mile . . . multiplied by the mileage between
Washington, DC, and the furthest point in a Member's district, plus 10%."[1] Thus, the
taxpayers finance 32 roundtrips per year. Well, what's the extra ten percent for? Is it for
taxi fares to and from airports? Is it for meals? Is it just an elitist generosity? But,
Wait!—the situation is even worse, because funds from a Representative's Personnel
Allowance and Official Mail Allowance may be used for expenses normally covered by
the Official Office Expenses Allowance.[2] Thus, if 32 trips back home aren't enough,
even more can be taken on the backs of taxpayers.

Each Senator gets an Official Office Expense Allowance which can be tapped for travel
to and from the home state, among other expenditures. The allowance amounts vary, one
factor being the distance of the state from D.C. Senators are free to decide how to use the
fund. Thus, the number of taxpayer-funded Senatorial trips is not set.[3]

Ah; so now we understand the financing that allows each federal lawmaker to make scores of trips back home every year. They can afford the trips because we taxpayers can afford them. Or can we?

Listing Members' travel funds under "office expenses" seems, at least to this author, to be another Congressional subterfuge to make voter knowledge more difficult to obtain. It looks like a concealment from penny-pinching Scrooges among the public.

Although some people may allege that the travel allowances promote good interactions between the governed and the governing, others will reasonably charge that the amount is excessive, especially considering the ease of communication by letter, phone (old style and cell), email, teleconferencing, radio, and TV. And some of the supposedly good interactions may reek of the sort epitomized by long-ago Senator Tom Connally of Texas. When asked by a farmer during a re-election campaign, "How do you stand on the cotton issue?" Connally blandly replied, ""I'm okay on that one. Are there any other questions?"[4]

When an ordinary person takes a job that involves commuting, does he or she expect the employer to pay for that travel? The answer is usually and obviously "No." But many Members of our present part-time Congress are commuters who arrive in D.C. on Tuesday and leave for home on Thursday—and they do it on the taxpayers' dime. When a newly elected Senator from the West, as recently occurred, trumpets that he will come back to his state "nearly every weekend," he does not also say, "And by the way, you suckers will be paying my travel expenses." Oh, sure, he will counter that he's tending to the needs of his constituents, and some of that no doubt occurs, but a portion of us will maintain that more self-interested forces are also at work—fund raising, re-election efforts, or personal reasons, such as going home to take care of a farm. Some of the travel therefore relies on public funding for private advantage.

If Congress were to maintain a normal Monday through Friday work week, how much time would a member have back home if a round trip of, say, four thousand miles had to begin on Friday evening and finish in the wee hours of Monday morning? Note that the round-trip distance D.C.-Hawaii-D.C. is about 9,800 miles.

So, we have here two bad results contending with one good one. It's bad that taxpayers are shouldering a huge financial burden for excessive travel. And it's pernicious that the travel desires of Members are a major cause of Congress not meeting with enough frequency or duration to tend properly to creating good legislation. Are the Members' contacts with constituents of sufficient good to balance the two bads?

CORRECTIVE SOLUTIONS

Voters should deluge Congress with demands that travel funds be sharply curtailed and that they be listed as separate appropriation items with headings more realistic than "office expenses." Just as Roman senator Cato the Elder said time after time, "Carthage must be destroyed," so a continuous drumbeat of media publicity must destroy excessive Congressional perks. If Members won't respond favorably, constituents should not re-elect them.

Notes: Chapter XVII. Travel Allowances

[1]Paul E. Dwyer, "Congressional Salaries and Allowances," CRS Report for Congress, January 26, 2004, pp. CRS-2 through CRS-4; the quotation is on CRS-3.   See also Title 2, U.S. Code, Sections 57b, 57(c) [Committee Order No. 30], and 58, 2000 edition, and rules promulgated by the Committee on House Oversight and the Committee on Rules and Administration of the Senate.

[2]Dwyer, "Congressional Salaries and Allowances," p. 2.

[3]Ibid., pp. 6-7.

[4]Paul Boller, Congressional Anecdotes (New York: Oxford University Press, 1991), pp. 104-05.

XVIII. Failure to Devote Enough Time to Legislation

EPIGRAPH: With indignation I survey
                   Such skill and judgment thrown away;
                   The time profusely squandered there.
                        ---William Whitehead, in his poem "The Youth and
                        the Philosopher" (1774).

Writing laws is often difficult. Bills created for consideration by Congress are sometimes long and complex. They require the close attention of staffers with long experience, and they should get the same from Members. But as Lee Hamilton, formerly a Representative for thirty-four years, explained, "We are more dependent on staff than we used to be. That is not good."[1]

Unfortunately, Members frequently do not carve enough legislative time from their busy lives. That has at least three bad results: (1) they often vote in the dark or as someone else suggests, (2) errors pass into law, and (3) staffers have perhaps too much influence on legislation.[2]

So many Members are often not in D.C. that one wonders how much attention they can be devoting to their legislative duties. With thousands of bills introduced during each session, no single Member can be knowledgeable about each, so how much perusal does each one get? Of course, some deserve more scrutiny than others, but do even the bills at the top of the importance heap get proper vetting? Members often rely on their staffs to craft legislation, analyze bills, and make recommendations. But there's an additional set of "cues" that Members use as guideposts to action. That's information from fellow Members, from the leadership, from the party, from constituents, and from lobbyists.[3]

One cue is a little card which a Senator can get upon entering the chamber. It has a brief description of what's up for a vote. Those summaries are separately prepared by the staffs of the two party leaders and may have partisan variations along with suggestions on which way to vote. The cards "are never made available to the public," and for some Senators these "cheat sheets" may be "the first, and last, they learn of what they are about to vote on."[4]

The cues are helpful and save time. But they don't necessarily prevent excesses and mistakes.

Federal judge Charles Richey, having dealt with many cases involving interpretations of federal laws, said, "The staff writes the bills and the members spend so much of their time raising money, they don't know what they're doing."[5] Former Representative, now Senator, Tom Coburn, R-OK, wrote, "On a few occasions, my own staff sent letters or made agreements with other members without my knowledge. . . . Staff also have the ability to control the agenda by not giving a member or committee member timely or complete information they might need to make a proper choice. . . . staff are very capable of inserting their own philosophy in lieu of the district's desires or constitutional limits."[6] Coburn also reported, "On several occasions I confronted members of the Appropriations Committee with questionable spending items their staff had inserted into bills without their knowledge or consent."[7]

One staffer, after running afoul of the law for having his unleashed dog in a D.C. park, inserted a requirement in an appropriation bill that a dog run be constructed in that park. His Representative boss didn't know of the earmark's existence until columnist Jack Anderson wrote about it.[8]

Most staffers join with the Members in not knowing all the details of bills. When a bill contains hundreds or thousands of pages with a myriad of detailed provisions, no single person is going to be familiar with all of them. As a staffer of long experience wrote, "The members virtually never take the time to read, let alone comprehend, what is before them. Neither do most staff. When these bills are presented to the Senate for final approval, the text of the bill and the conference committee report to explain it are often unavailable or available only in the form of one copy for all one hundred senators and a few thousand staff to read."[9]

This issue famously intruded on the public consciousness in early 2009 with the stimulus bill for boosting the economy. The measure came out of a House-Senate conference committee with just over one thousand pages and about $787 billion of spending. Both chambers passed it less than twenty-four hours after it emerged from the conference. Of course, not one Member read much of that bloat before voting on it. And the House did not even abide by its promise, made only three days before its roll-call vote, of allowing forty-eight hours for perusal of the final version before the vote.[10]

And don't forget Speaker Nancy Pelosi's infamous comment that the health care reform act of 2010 had to be passed so Members could find out what was in it.

When there are provisions like the one described in a law review article as "hideously complicated," it's persuasive that some Members don't take time to understand some of what they vote on.[11] You can be sure, however, that Senators were completely aware in 1992 that the following somewhat opaque language meant they would get a pay raise of 23.76 percent, from $101,900 to $125,100 per year:

The rate of pay for the offices referred to under section 703(a)(2)(B) of the Ethics Reform Act of 1989 (5 U.S.C. 5318 note) shall be the rate of pay that would be payable for each such office if the provisions of section 703(a)(2)(B) and 1101(a)(1)(A) of such act (5 U.S.C. 5318 note and 5305) had not been enacted.[12]

Some bills loaded with Rosetta-Stone language would take weeks to decipher. Rationality tells us that Members don't do that. If most of them have any awareness of those enigmas, it's likely to be merely an interpretive summary from a staffer—or lobbyist.

In late 2004, a perfect illustration of Congress's failure bubbled into view from its cauldron of secretive and misplaced priorities. With foot-dragging ineptitude—or, even worse, anti-majoritarian perversity driven by ideology—the House had not passed several appropriation bills for fiscal year 2005 when it began on October 1; so the House lumped them together in a later catch-all, or omnibus, bill that passed. Before the Senate could act on it, someone discovered a mistake of monumental importance among its plethora of pages: It would allow some Appropriations Committee staffers to view income tax returns and be free from current criminal penalties for publicizing them. Apparently, this was an error of benign motivation; the intent was merely to give those staffers access to IRS facilities for oversight purposes. The chairman of the relevant Appropriations subcommittee said he was unaware of the provision, which seems to have been inserted by a staffer who messed up the language. The offending provision was deleted.[13]

But there are greater lessons to be learned than that a mistake may sometimes be caught. One is that Congress has abandoned much of its proper role. It is supposed to adhere to what is called "regular order," meaning that committee members should analyze and discuss the details of bills, deadlines should be honored, there should be opportunities for the full House and Senate each to debate and improve bills, there should be adequate vetting by conference committees, each chamber should have plenty of time for consideration of conference reports before final passage, and appropriation bills should be passed separately and not be fused into monstrosities that defy understanding and become rush jobs. None of that occurred in this case—nor in many other cases. (See also the chapter on Violations.)

A further lesson is that too much of the real work on bills is done by staffers, with Members willfully or inadvertently in the dark. The public needs to become aware that the people elected to make the decisions often do not. For example, during the four years from 2002 to 2006, Senator Arlen Specter—or his staff—created thirteen earmarks worth $48.7 million for clients of American Defense International, a lobbying outfit whose president is Michael Herson, husband of Vicki Siegal Herson, Specter's legislative appropriations aide. The clients paid the firm almost $1.5 million for its help. Responding to the apparent conflict of interest, Specter said he was unaware that the earmarks would benefit clients of his staffer's spouse. He also explained, "I am advised that at no time did her husband lobby my office or seek appropriations from any member of my staff'—but he refused an interview on the topic.[14] Let's give Specter the benefit of the doubt and believe he really didn't know what was going on, but that only emphasizes the problem of Members not devoting enough time to their legislative duties. It's sad that giving a U.S. Senator the benefit of the doubt exposes a merely different failure.

Recurring to anti-majoritarian perversity driven by ideology, the Republican House leadership during the Clinton and George W. Bush years used last-minute, catch-all appropriations bills to enact provisions that could not pass separately.

"[They] learned that amalgamating such a massive amount of must-pass legislation into one package makes it possible to not only do most of the work of an entire session in one fell swoop but also pass numerous agenda items that do not have majority support – and which simply could not survive in any other form [emphasis added].

In other words, these omnibus appropriation bills have become a tool by which the democratic principles that underlie both Houses can be circumvented."

The author of that quotation points to another goal of this departure from regular order:

"[Republican leaders were insuring that] "legislation is consistent with a specific ideological criteria [sic] that is often not the will of a majority in the House.

They have committed to conservatives within the Republican Conference that legislation sent to the president will be consistent with the views of a majority of the Conference. On dozens of issues . . . the majority position in the Republican Conference is not the majority position of the full House. Preventing the House from producing legislation that reflects the views of its Members requires circumventing a body of rules and procedures developed in the past 215 years."[15]

In February 2006, Congress passed a budget reconciliation bill. Trouble was, one chamber's version was not identical to the other. Some reports estimated the difference as being worth about $2 billion. Speaker Dennis Hastert and Senate President Pro Tempore Ted Stevens then certified that the Senate's language was the correct version, but Hastert did not present the modification to the House for a vote. President Bush signed the bill into law.

That process, especially Hastert's non-voted action, was arguably unconstitutional. It is long-settled Constitutional law that enacted legislation is valid only if passed by the two parts of Congress in identical form. In this case, leaders in both chambers deliberately added a Constitutional violation to the original inadvertent error. They could have gone back to either house for a vote on language identical to that passed by the other chamber. It appears that their reason for not doing so was an unwillingness to devote the necessary time to the effort and a fear that one of the two chambers would not approve the revision. Then, scrounging around for an ex post facto justification, they unearthed an 1892 Supreme Court decision that was used to defend against a lawsuit initiated after the bill ostensibly became law. In August 2006, a federal judge dismissed the lawsuit and ruled that the certification by Hastert and Stevens met the Constitutional requirement.[16]

Here's another instance of Members not taking time to address problems: An amendment to the Voting Rights Act of 1965[17] mandates that if more than five percent of a state's or political subdivision's citizens of voting age "are members of a single language minority and are limited-English proficient," all voting directions and ballots must be printed in that language as well as English, and helpers who speak that language must be present at the voting places. That section resulted in lawsuits initiated by the Department of Justice, even when no complaint was lodged by a voter or potential voter in the affected jurisdiction. When Springfield, MA, was judged to have run afoul of that section, it had to hire additional Spanish-speaking poll workers and accept federal election observers. For Springfield's primary election in 2006, the feds sent in 49 observers, some from as far afield as Florida and the West Coast. They later reported that they gave assistance to 92 voters. With the tens of thousands of dollars expended on those monitors, each instance of help cost nearly $500. In the absence of complaints, the Justice Department ferrets out purported violations by looking at the ratio of supposed foreign-language voters to foreign language poll workers; if the ratio is deemed to be too low, Justice sues. In 2006, with many Members mindlessly unaware of this make-work enforcement history, Congress extended the life of the section for twenty-five years.[18]

A more recent blunder gave windfall millions of government money to some corporations to do what they'd already been doing for years without bounty from taxpayers. That happened because Congress modified existing law in 2007 to allow the blending of more types of alternative fuels with oil products. Additional companies qualified under the new rules and would receive a 50-cents-per-gallon tax credit. Congress didn't bother to determine all the new ingredients, processes, and industries that would qualify for the expanded tax credit.

One beneficiary of this oversight was the paper-making industry. For years it had produced a byproduct called "black liquor." The industry burned that sludge to power its factories. Under the new law the paper manufacturers qualified for the tax credit if they mixed black liquor with a small amount of diesel. According to industry leader International Paper, it got $71.6 million from this federal benefit in just one month in late 2008. It was projected to get about $1 billion in 2009. Another paper company latched on to almost $30 million for just one factory in a three-month period. Some estimates projected that the government would pay about $8 billion to the biggest paper companies in 2009 on this tax credit.

Most paper companies only mixed diesel with black liquor after Congress provided the incentive. So a law intended to reduce fossil fuel consumption is subsidizing increased usage. One analyst compared it to pouring a bit of gasoline into a toilet bowl and reaping fifty cents a gallon with every flush. Although some foreign paper companies and governments are complaining that the benefit amounts to an unfair trade practice, the main critics should be the U.S. taxpayers who are financing this red-ink result.[19]

Senate Finance Committee chairman Max Baucus, D-MT, said, "It's an unintended adverse consequence. It's very expensive and it should be closed."[20] But some

Members of Congress see this tax credit as a lifeline for companies and their employees in troubled times.[21]

CORRECTIVE SOLUTIONS

With many bills passed by Congress being so long that the Senators and Representatives who vote on them don't know much of what's in them, especially the bills that come out of conference committees near the end of a session with accompanying pressure to pass them quickly before adjournment, one wonders what's to be done? Already, both chambers require an explanatory statement about conference reports.[22] Maybe such statements should be more detailed. Perhaps there could even be a rule saying any section not summarized, or not sufficiently summarized, is null and void.

And with Members devoting so much time to the money-grubbing and voter-cultivation of the almost-permanent re-election campaign that they scant their other duties, one again wonders what's to be done? Taxpayer financing of campaigns would help, and was even suggested as early as 1907 by Theodore Roosevelt in his State of the Union message.[23] That reform would give legislators much more time to actually legislate. But wouldn't they still engage in the campaign-contributions quest in an effort to augment their funds? Not if another of Roosevelt's ideas became law, that being a prohibition on private donations.[24]

Opponents would, of course, argue that taxpayers would suffer another rip-off if they paid for campaigning.[25] But the benefit of public financing is worth more than the cost. Taxpayers already finance Members' campaigns in at least three ways. First, ordinary people suffer and pay with their taxes when Congress, beholden to the demands of big contributors, funds self-serving projects for fat-cat campaign donors, projects that benefit only privileged slivers of the populace. As prominent New Yorker Mark Green wrote, "When private money can purchase public policy, voters and consumers pay the price four times over." Second, taxes already fund the salaries and other expenses of staffers who ostensibly go to districts and states to perform only official business but who also work on campaigns. Third, taxes already finance the franking privilege for mailing millions of items, many of which are simply propaganda for Members' re-election. Further, Mark Green also observed, "If we rightly spend $900 million annually on democracy abroad through the National Endowment for Democracy, why not half that amount for democracy at home?"[26]

And would labor unions object to public financing of campaigns because they would then be unable to spend their members' dues to influence elections?

As for the free-speech contention against a ban on private campaign donations, we already have scads of limitations on free speech, and thus the courts might find that the public benefit would justify this additional limit.[27] If the courts did not accept that rationale, a Constitutional amendment would do the job.

The Fair Elections Now variant of public financing would require candidates to raise small amounts of money from a certain number of people in their states (Senate candidates) or House districts to "qualify for a grant large enough to run a competitive campaign." [28]

Yet, even if public financing of campaigns were to eliminate much of the bribery of Members, we still would need to ban or minimize the bribery by Members in the form of pork-barrel earmarks meant to snare votes. Term limits would help.

Finally, Members would have more time for unflawed bills to benefit people in the United States if they did not spend so much time meddling in the internal affairs of other countries. What business is it of the U.S.A. for an attempt in Congress that was "designed to encourage United States firms to locate in Northern Ireland and designed to encourage firms already there to comply with a series of fundamental nondiscrimination standards"? Those words appeared in a Representative's statement about his "Introduction of Northern Ireland Fair Employment Legislation." [29] And why would he and his co-sponsors want American firms to "locate in Northern Ireland" when unemployed Americans needed jobs?

That's not an unusual example of Members' meddling efforts. Take the "Sense of the House in Support of Efforts to Forge Political Compromise in Fiji. [30]

OK, complaint can be made that those two examples are from the late 1980s. But brief searches among some actions in the next two decades uncover further examples showing that such interference is ongoing. See the proposed 1998 resolution to express "concern over interference with freedom of the press and the independence of judicial and electoral institutions in Peru," and the 1999 bill to force Indonesia to provide "full compensation for material damage in East Timor." In 2010 there was a bill to reduce payments to U.S. cotton producers as part of an effort "to provide technical assistance and capacity building" in Brazil. [31]

Notes: Chapter XVIII. Failure to Devote Enough Time to Legislation

[1] Ronald Kessler, Inside Congress: The Shocking Scandals, Corruption, and Abuse of Power Behind the Scenes on Capitol Hill (New York: Pocket Books, 1997), p. 80.

[2] The infamous omission of thirty-four pages from a huge "farm" bill sent to President Bush in May 2008, as noted above in the chapter on Insufficient Oversight of Subordinate Congressional Operations, occurred at the so-called "enrollment" (printing) stage and perhaps outside of the immediate purview of Members and their staffers.

[3] David J. Vogler, The Politics of Congress (Boston: Allyn and Bacon, 1974), pp. 90-95, 203-04.

[4]Winslow T. Wheeler, The Wastrels of Defense: How Congress Sabotages U.S. Security (Annapolis: Naval Institute Press, 2004), pp. 107-08.

[5]Kessler, Inside Congress, p. 86.

[6]Tom A. Coburn and John Hart, Breach of Trust: How Washington Turns Outsiders into Insiders (Nashville: WND Books, 2003), p. 45. See also Wheeler, The Wastrels of Defense, p. 176.

[7]Coburn and Hart, Breach of Trust, p. 37.

[8]Tom Finnigan, All About Pork: The Abuse of Earmarks and the Needed Reforms (Washington: Citizens Against Government Waste, Policy Briefing Series, May 3, 2006), p. 8, on the Internet, citing James Bovard, Freedom in Chains: The Rise of the State and the Demise of the Citizen, St. Martin Press [sic], May 19, 2000, p. 113. Staffer: Jason Alderman. Representative: Sidney Yates, D-IL. Time: 1997.

[9]Wheeler, Wastrels of Defense, p. 176.

[10] Congressional Record, daily edition, February 10, 2009, pp. H1096, H 1101.

[11]Michael Botein and Edward Samuels, "Compulsory Licenses in Peer-to-Peer File Sharing: A Workable Solution? Southern Illinois University Law Journal, Vol. 30, 2005, p. 76.

[12]Public Law 102-90 (August 14, 1991), Section 6(a), 105 Stat. 450; see Eric Felten, The Ruling Class: Inside the Imperial Congress, , abridged edition (Washington: U.S. Congress Assessment Project, Heritage Foundation, 1993), pp. 8-9.

[13]Scott Lilly, "When Congress Acts In the Dark of Night, Everyone Loses," originally published in Roll Call, December 6, 2004, but available on the Internet; Thomas E. Mann and Norman J. Ornstein, The Broken Branch: How Congress Is Failing America and How to Get It Back on Track (New York: Oxford University Press, 2006), pp. 173-74, which also has much of the Scott Lilly op-ed from Roll Call; Dan Morgan and Helen Dewar, "Tax-Return Provision in Spending Bill Dropped," The Washington Post, December 7, 2004, p. A4, also on the Internet. The bill became Public Law 108-447 on December 8, 2004, without the offending provision.

[14]Matt Kelley, "Senate aide's spouse gets a windfall," USA Today, February 16, 2006, on the Internet; cited and quoted in Finnigan, All About Pork, p. 11.

[15]Lilly, "When Congress Acts In the Dark."

[16]John W. Dean, Broken Government: How Republican Rule Destroyed the Legislative, Executive, and Judicial Branches (New York: Viking, 2007), pp. 51-54;

Norman J. Ornstein, "Will Scalia Blow the Whistle on this Constitutional Farce?," Roll Call, March 15, 2006, but found on the Internet; Steven T. Dennis, "Democrats Mull Challenge to Budget Cuts Enacted With Glitch," CQ Weekly, February 13, 2006, p. 441; Steven T. Dennis, "Watchdog Group Files Suit to Overturn Budget Law," CQ Weekly, March 27, 2006, p. 854; Steven T. Dennis, "Details of Budget Reconciliation Law, CQ Weekly, April 17, 2006, p. 1036; Walter J. Oleszek, Congressional Procedures and the Policy Process, 7th edition (Washington: CQ Press, 2007), p. 284. For the suit's dismissal see "Suit to Block Deficit-Reduction Bill Is Ended," The New York Times, August 12, 2006, p. A11.

[17]See Title 42 U.S. Code, Section 1973aa-1a, 2000 edition.

[18]Edward Blum, "Se Habla Lawsuit?" The Weekly Standard, March 26, 2007, pp. 13-14. Is it a coincidence that the great majority of such suits have occurred since 2003, after Supreme Court decisions that reduced the workload of lawyers in the voting enforcement division of the Justice Department; ibid., p. 14. See Title 42, U.S. Code, Section 1973aa-1a, 2000 edition.

[19]The original law providing tax-credit incentives for use of non-fossil fuels was the 2005 transportation bill called SAFETEA-LU (P.L. 109-59, 119 Stat. 1144-1978; see section 11113 [pp. 1946-49]). The 2007 amendments are in the Tax Technical Corrections Act (P.L. 110-172, 121 Stat. 2473, 2478-79; see section 5 that mentions "liquid fuel derived from biomass"; that was "part of a change in 2005 transportation legislation." See also Christopher Hayes, "Pulp Nonfiction," The Nation, April 20, 2009, pp. 6, 8; Kimberley Strassel, "Alternative Fuel Folly," The Wall Street Journal, April 17, 2009, p. A11.

[20]Brett Ferguson, "Baucus Pledges to End 'Black Liquor' Tax Credit for Paper Firms," April 24, 2009, Tax News From BNA Software / BNA Web Site, on the Internet. One theory about this boondoggle's origin is that paper-industry consultants figured out how their clients could benefit; Rortybomb, Paper Companies Gaming the Tax Credit System?," April 5, 2009, on the Internet; Environmental Paper Network, "Background on Billion Dollar Black Liquor Loophole," [April 2009?], on the Internet.

[21]Senator Olympia J. Snowe, "What black liquor tax credit means for Maine," Know County Opinions – Village Soup, May 5, 2009, on the Internet.

[22]See House Rule XXII, clause 7(e), 110th Congress, and Senate Rule XXVIII, clause 6, 110th Congress.

[23]Kessler, Inside Congress, p. 239.

[24]Ibid., p. 239.

[25]For some arguments pro and con, see Gary W. Copeland, "The House Says 'No' To Public Financing of Congressional Campaigns," Legislative Studies Quarterly, August

1984, pp. 487-504. For some recent ideas on this see Anna Quindlen, "Dialing for Dollars," Newsweek, October 29, 2007, p. 70.

[26]Mark Green, Selling Out: How Big Corporate Money Buys Elections, Rams Through Legislation, and Betrays Our Democracy (New York: ReganBooks, a HarperCollins imprint, 2002), p. 237 (first quotation), and p. 239 (second).

[27]The First Amendment states, "Congress shall make no law . . . abridging the freedom of speech." And the Fourteenth Amendment applies the First Amendment and the rest of the Bill of Rights to the states. Yet speech is legally limited in the following ways, among others: ● laws against false advertising, ● copyright laws, ● laws against seditious utterances, ● laws against revealing classified information, ● law against threats to kill the President, ● penalties for slander, ● penalties for libel, ● penalties for perjury, ● laws against sexual harassment speech, ● laws against hate speech, ● laws against transmitting gambling info across state lines, ● ban on child pornography, ● penalties for revealing companies' trade secrets, ● penalties for making false statements to police, ● penalties for contempt of court, ● the ban on words such as "no wheelchairs" in real estate ads, ● restrictions on words that are allowed on personal auto license plates ● limits on campaign activities in federal elections ● prohibitions on certain types of advertising (such as ads for hard liquor and, formerly, ads by lawyers) ● and, of course, that classic that you cannot yell "Fire" in a crowded theater where there is no fire. In June 2007 the Supreme Court added a further limit when it ruled that a student could be punished for displaying the sign "Bong Hits 4 Jesus" when he was not on school property but was watching an off-campus school event.

[28]Nick Nyhart and David Donnelly, "Fair Elections Now! The Nation, April 13, 2009, pp. 6-7. Those authors say, "As fundraising demands have steadily increased, lawmakers have spent more time dialing up well-heeled donors, the vast majority of whom live nowhere near the lawmakers' districts, and less time gaining in-depth understanding of leading issues, crafting effective legislation with their colleagues or listening to their constituents" (p. 6).

[29]Congressional Record, permanent edition, January 3, 1989, pp. 158-59.

[30]Ibid., permanent edition, October 27, 1987, pp. 29236-37.

[31]Ibid., daily edition, October 20, 1998, p. H11695; daily edition, October 27, 1999, p. H11067; daily edition, May 27, 2010, p. H4022.

XIX. Part-Time Congress on Full-Time Salary

EPIGRAPH: It's a damn good thing we don't get all the government we pay for.
                            ---Anonymous.

Many Members are so neglectful of their legislative duties that they spend less time in Washington than voters might think appropriate. They have sometimes been in the Tuesday/Thursday Club, flying in from wherever on Tuesday night and departing on Thursday afternoon. In the 1960s and '70s Congress averaged about 162 days of meetings per year. That declined to about 139 in the 1980s and '90s.[1]   ABC News reported that the House was scheduled to meet only 76 days in 2006 and that "even Members from Hawaii jet home for long weekends." Actually, the House's "days in session" in 2006 turned out to be 101 legislative days and 104 calendar days.[2] Yet, House ethics rules imply that being a Representative should be nearly a full-time job.[3]

In its first session, the 110th Congress, back under Democratic control, met much more frequently: The House had 167 calendar days in session in 2007, 119 calendar days in 2008, 158 calendar days in 2009, and 127 calendar days in 2010.[4]

While recognizing that Members often are working on the people's business when their chamber is not in session, the following two statistics are interesting. One hundred twenty-seven calendar days are 34.8 percent of a year's 365 days (34.7 percent in a leap year). A person in private employment who works five days a week with three weeks off for vacation is on the job for 245 days a year, which is 67.1 percent of a 365-day year.

The publicized numbers on how many Congressional days in session occurred in a particular year are reminiscent of Benjamin Disraeli's famous comment that there are lies, damned lies, and statistics. One Congressional deception involves what are called "pro forma" sessions, which count as legislative days. The official House historian reported about "pro forma Mondays" in a recent book: On those days "nothing gets done, nobody is present in the House. Frequently what happens is that the Speaker pro tem calls the House in session, approves the minutes of the previous day, and then adjourns."[5]

An authoritative source reports that in the first session of the 109th Congress (January 4, 2005-December 22, 2005) the Senate met for 159 days and the House for 140.[6] But if you go through all issues of the <u>Congressional Record</u> for that session, you find that the House met pro forma on fifteen of those days and that the Senate had two pro forma meetings, if we arbitrarily define a pro forma session as lasting ten minutes or less. This means the House met in only 125 "real" sessions out of the 140.

For the most recent full year, 2010, the House had sixteen pro forma meetings among its total of 127 days in session.[7]

It seems impossible that a pro forma meeting could last only six-tenths of one second. Yet, as reported in the <u>Congressional Record</u>, that's allegedly how long the Senate met on February 27, 1989.[8] With such overworking of our lawmakers, no wonder they want higher salaries.

Recent pro forma examples occurred during the Thanksgiving and Christmas breaks in late 2007. Majority Leader Harry Reid announced on November 16 that "the Senate will be coming in for pro forma sessions during the Thanksgiving holiday to prevent recess appointments." He did the same on December 19.[9] Sometimes referred to as "fake," "bogus," and "micro" sessions, they skew the number of sessional days away from reality. If you look at the more-or-less official number, you might want to do some research and find out how many pro forma days are included.[10]

I did that for the year 2007 and found that the Senate had twelve pro forma meetings and the House had eight. Those of the House were scattered from February 9 to December 10 with only October having as many as two. Other than one each in September and October, those of the Senate were all in November and December. After sessions lasting sixteen seconds, eight seconds, and nine seconds in late December, the Senate went all-out and met for a full minute on December 28![11]

In furtherance of his scheme to obliterate President Bush's constitutional right to make recess appointments, Senator Reid announced that after the first session of the 110th Congress adjourned sine die on December 31 there would be pro forma sessions [of the second session of the 110th Congress] on January 3, 7, 9, 11, 15, and 18, prior to a [real] session on January 22.[12]   For the first session's Senate to thus control several meetings of the Senate during the second session smacks of a dead hand grabbing the future, but it was not illegal.

The Constitution (Article II, Section 2) states, "The President shall have Power to fill up all Vacancies that may happen during the Recess of the Senate, by granting Commissions which shall expire at the End of their next Session."[13]   Such interim appointments have been common since the days of President Washington. However, the Democrats in control of the Senate in 2007 used pro forma sessions to deny that Constitutional power to the President. Majority Leader Reid even admitted that the purpose was to prevent President Bush from filling vacancies with "controversial recess appointments," i.e. Republicans or even Democrats not deemed ideologically pure.[14] Sham meetings to take away a clear Presidential right should be abhorrent to all who value the rule of law, foremost among whom should be the people entrusted with creating laws.

Deciding that the Senate is not really in recess during pro forma sessions, President Obama made a recess appointment of Richard Cowdray in January 2012 to head the new Consumer Financial Protection Bureau. At the same time he filled three vacancies on the National Labor Relations Board. Those appointments depart from over two hundred years of practice and precedent. They thus raise important constitutional issues. They also raise questions about politics and hypocrisy. As noted above, Senate Democrats embraced pro forma sessions to block Bush's recess power. Then-Senator Obama was part of that obstruction. Yet his White House now spews about his "practical, common sense approach" and that a "holiday session" is "just a gimmick."[15]

The constitutional issue is important, and not just because any President's claim of a different meaning in the foundational document of American government is important. There's the further problem that if pro forma sessions mean the Senate is not really meeting, then their future usage to pass important legislation no longer exists or is at risk. Doubts will also arise about the validity of all such past actions, as, for example, the passage in August 2010 of an emergency border security appropriation of $600 million in a thirty-minute pro forma session with only two Senators present. Another recent instance was the December 2011 passage of the continuation of the payroll tax holiday during a pro forma Senate session.[16] And Obama's action is already rearing up as a diminution of the Senate's constitutionally-granted power.

How do pro forma sessions not run afoul of the Constitutional requirement that in both chambers "a majority of each shall constitute a quorum to do business"? If "nobody is present in the House" except for the Speaker pro tem and, perhaps, a very few other Members, then the necessary majority of the membership must not be present. Each chamber gets around this problem by assuming that a quorum exists unless a quorum call is demanded and shows that a majority is not present. The House has a rule that "the Speaker may not entertain a point of order that a quorum is not present unless a question has been put to a vote."[17] As Walter Oleszek's excellent Congressional Procedures explains, "The House has determined . . . that the mere conduct of debate, where the Chair has not put the pending proposition to a vote, is not 'conducting business.'"[18]

That defies what many people may see as the clear meaning of the U.S. Constitution.

Rules in Congress are not self-enforcing, so if the House or Senate violates the Constitution by conducting business without a quorum, no action against that violation will occur unless a Member raises a point of order about it. In the case of the Senate passing an amendment to the Patriot Act with only one Senator present (see below), that single Senator would, of course, not raise a point of order against his own action.

To this author, it seems reasonable to believe that the men who created the Constitution meant that there would have to be a majority of the membership present for either house to begin a day's activity. Surely, they did not contemplate that a handful of Members could do so. The proof of this seems to lie in the fact that when the first Congress was scheduled to meet on March 4, 1789, there was a lengthy delay because neither house then had a majority of its membership present. The House did not achieve the necessary quorum until April 1 and the Senate did not get its required quorum until April 6. Only then could the two bodies open and count the electoral votes for the first President and Vice President.[19] If the present practice had been allowed back then, the eight Senators and thirteen Representatives who were present on March 4 could have begun doing the people's business. But, of course they did not.

Now we have the spectacle of actions taken by the few while the many are absent. It got so extreme that on December 22, 2005, Senator John Warner, R-VA, opened and chaired a pro forma session, asked for unanimous consent for several actions, achieved permission, and adjourned the Senate after a session of only four minutes even though he was the only Senator present. As chair he granted his own requests for unanimous consent, which required only his own agreement since no other Senator was there.

And the action Warner permitted himself was nothing trivial. It was to present to the Senate a House message that the House had passed, with a minor amendment, a Senate bill about the renewal of the terrorism-fighting Patriot Act. Warner said, "I ask unanimous consent that the Senate concur in the House amendment and the motion to reconsider be laid upon the table. Without objection, it is so ordered." Renowned Congress observer Bob Novak reported, "In 49 years of watching the Senate, I never before observed legislation passed with one senator present."[20]

If, however, you look at the relevant pages in the Congressional Record, you will see more than a full column of remarks by Senator Harry Reid.[21] Was Novak wrong, and was Reid really there? Both answers are "No." The New York Times and CQ Weekly both mention that Warner was the only Senator present.[22] The now-usual practice of the Congressional Record is that Senators' statements not added to remarks actually made by them on the floor appear in the Record with a black "bullet" at the beginning and at the end. No such bullets accompany Reid's words. But appearing on the same page and listed under "Additional Statements," are several paragraphs from Senator Baucus, and they are set off by bullets. Therefore, it appears that the Record falsely indicated Reid's presence. Was it just a mistake or was it part of the usual hocus-pocus that makes the Record inaccurate? (See the preceding chapter on Falsified Records.)

The two chambers were at odds over the Senate's attempted six-month extension of the Patriot Act versus the House's five-week extension, and the Act would have gone out of existence on December 31 without Warner's lonely action.[23]

It bears re-emphasizing that the Framers surely did not contemplate detours around the Constitution's provision that "a majority of each shall constitute a quorum to do business."

Yet, Congress still takes pro forma detours. On September 29, 2011, with only three Members present, the House passed a temporary extension of government funding. One

Representative asked for unanimous consent to pass the measure, and neither of the other two objected.[24] That action took all of five minutes and two seconds.[25]

Some Congressional procedures exist to support efficiency, such as giving great power to the Senate Majority Leader and the House Committee on Rules, and the requirement that conference reports must get strict up or down votes without amendments. But efficiency procedures would be less needed if Members spent more time on their legislative duties—and if they didn't waste some of their legislative time and energy on such unnecessary frivolities as resolutions for National Watermelon Month and National Grasslands Week.[26]

Shockingly, with little publicity many Members regularly violate a law designed to encourage their attention to their legislative duties. Title 2, U.S. Code, Section 39, 2006 edition, mandates that a federal lawmaker's pay must be reduced for each day of absence from Senate or House "unless such Member assigns as the reason for such absence the sickness of himself or of some member of his family." For many years absences because of traipsing the campaign trail, caused no pay deduction, and that was a violation. Even when two Representatives (Mel Reynolds, D-IL, and Walter Tucker, D-CA) were absent in 1995 to attend their trials for sexual assault, obstruction of justice, and solicitation of child pornography in the first case, and extortion and tax evasion in the other, no deductions occurred.[27] There have been numerous other occasions when Members were absent to attend court on criminal charges, and their pay was not docked.

In 2005 the law was modified so that absent Senators would lose no pay.[28] That became another perk for them. The original law, however, still applies to Representatives but is never enforced. Indeed, a note accompanying House Rule III, 108th Congress, says about this law, "Its general application is not practical under modern circumstances."[29] Oh, I get it: Representatives are not required to obey a federal law if the House simply decides that doing so "is not practical."

CORRECTIVE SOLUTIONS

Congress, responding to public and media pressure, should repeal the 2005 provision that allows Senators to be absent without any salary deduction. Then, any citizen living in the state or district of any Member whose pay has not been reduced for absences should file a lawsuit asking that the pay-docking law be enforced against that Member. Such legal cases might encounter two problems: (1) an individual's lack of "standing" to bring such a lawsuit,[30] and (2) the stone wall of separation-of-powers rulings that no punishment on a Senator or Representative could be levied by the courts, absent treason, felony, or breach of the peace. If so, the final recourse for people who care about the rule of law might be concerted publicity campaigns to defeat the scofflaw Members. And don't let Congress simply repeal the basic law that still requires salary deductions for Representatives.

And what's to be done about the Tuesday-Thursday Members who aren't really absent on Friday through Monday because Congress isn't in session on those days? One corrective could be incessant publicity about the amputation of sessional days from the available time. And with the adoption of public financing of campaigns suggested elsewhere in this book, the solons would not feel such need to be scrounging for donations back home or in the money centers and might be more willing to attend to the public's business they were elected to do.

Another part of public financing to shorten campaigns and keep officials on their legislative duties would be statutory clauses denying federal election funds to candidates before a certain date, and preventing the use of the funds for any expenses or loans contracted before that date.

The application of these suggestions to Presidential elections would limit the current "campaign-ad-nauseam" to something reasonable.

And a law should be enacted to prevent pro forma sessions.

Notes: Chapter XIX. Part-Time Congress on Full-Time Salary

[1]Tables that include "Days in Session" are in various yearly editions of CQ Almanac Plus (Washington: Congressional Quarterly), chapter 1. See also each year's last issue of Congressional Record, "Résumé of Congressional Activity."

[2]ABC News, July 29, 2006. "Résumé of Congressional Activity," Congressional Record, daily edition, December 27, 2006, p. D1173; and "Days in Session" (House & Senate) THOMAS (Library of Congress), on the internet. The days in session reports in the "Résumé" in the Congressional Record are "legislative days." The days in session in THOMAS show both legislative and calendar days, which are often different.

[3]The implication is in House Rule XXV, clause 1, 110th Congress: "Except as provided by paragraph (b), a Member . . . may not—(1) have outside earned income attributable to a calendar year that exceeds 15 percent of the annual rate of basic pay for level II of the Executive Schedule under section 5313 of title 5, United States Code, as of January 1 of that calendar year."
Senate Rule XXXVI, Outside Earned Income, 110th Congress, says it incorporates section 501 of the Ethics in Government Act of 1978 into the rules of the Senate; however, it you look at the original act (Public Law 95-521), you will see that its section 501 relates to post employment conflict of interest, not limits on outside earned income. Therefore, look at the amended version in Title 5, U.S. Code, sections 501 (outside earned income limitation) and 502 (limitations on outside employment), both of which apply to Members in both chambers [5 U.S.C. Appendix, Sec. 501, p. 524, and Sec. 502, p. 525, both in 2006 edition].

[4]Statistics are from and "Days in Session" (House & Senate) THOMAS (Library of Congress), on the internet.

[5]Robert V. Remini, The House: The History of the House of Representatives (New York: Collins, a division of HarperCollins; Smithsonian Books, 2006), p. 499.

[6]CQ Almanac Plus 2005, p. 1-8. Those figures are also available in the Congressional Record, daily edition, December 30, 2005, p. D1341.

[7]I developed the number of pro forma sessions by going through every issue of the Congressional Record for 2005, 2007, and 2010 and counting every meeting of ten minutes or less.

[8]U.S., Congress, Senate, Riddick's Senate Procedure: Precedents and Practices (Washington: USGPO, 1992), p. 251, citing Congressional Record, [daily edition], February 27, 1989, p. S1755. See Congressional Record, permanent edition, February 27, 1989, p. 2791.

[9]Congressional Record, daily edition, November 16, 2007, p. S14609, and p. S14661 for a unanimous consent request from Senator [Jim] Webb; ibid., daily edition, December 19, 2007, p. S16069.

[10]Statistics often considered reliable can be found in the various volumes of CQ Almanac.

[11]The sessions of November 20, 23, 27, and 29 were all part of the "legislative day" of November 16, 2007; Congressional Record, daily edition, November 29, 2007, p. S14669. Sessions on December 21, 23, 26, 28, and 31 were all part of the "legislative day" of December 19, 2007; ibid., daily edition, December 31, 2007, p. S16081.

[12]Congressional Record, daily edition, December 19, 2007, p. S16069.

[13]See also Henry B. Hogue, "Recess Appointments: Frequently Asked Questions," CRS Report for Congress, updated January 16, 2007, on the Internet. There's much controversy about what sort of breaks in Senate meetings should be considered as recesses as mentioned in the Constitution's Article II, Section 2; see Bill McAllister, "Recess Appointments: A Disputed Matter of Timing," The Washington Post, July 19, 1993, p. A13.

[14]"Gone in 60 Seconds," The Wall Street Journal, November 23, 2007, p. A12; "While You Were Sleeping In," The Wall Street Journal, December 31, 2007, p A12.

[15]"Contempt for Congress," The Wall Street Journal, January 5, 2012, p. A12; Bruce Ackerman, "Recess Appointments: Release the Legal Advice," ibid., January 11, 2012, p. A13; "Memo Says Steps Taken By Obama Are Legal," ibid., January 13, 2012,

p. A4. See also T. J. Halstead, "Recess Appointments: A Legal Overview," CRS Report for Congress, July 26, 2005.

[16]First example: Congressional Record, daily edition, August 12, 2010, pp. S6995-S7001; Naftali Bendavid, "How to Fix a Dysfunctional Senate: Cut 98 Senators," The Wall Street Journal, August 13, 2010, pp. A1, A4. Second instance: "Contempt for the Constitution," ibid., January 13, 2012, p. A12.

[17]Rule XX, clause 7(a), 110th Congress.

[18]Walter J. Oleszek, Congressional Procedures and the Policy Process, 7th edition (Washington: CQ Press, 2007), p. 153.

[19]U.S. Congress. Biographical Directory of the United States Congress 1774-2005 (Washington: United States Government Printing Office, 2005), p. 45n.

[20]Robert Novak, "Decline of Congress," December 29, 2005, on the Internet.

[21]Congressional Record, permanent edition, December 22, 2005, pp. 14423-25, with Reid's words on p. 14424.

[22]Sheryl Gay Stolberg, "Postponing Debate, Congress Extends Terror Law 5 Weeks," The New York Times, December 23, 2005, pp. A1, A24; Michael Sandler, "Only Brief Extension of Anti-Terrorism Law," CQ Weekly, December 26, 2005, p. 3394.

[23]Novak, "Decline of Congress," December 29, 2005.

[24]"Near-Empty House Passes Stopgap Spending Measure," The Wall Street Journal, September 30, 2011, p. A4.

[25]Andrea Seabrook, "It Took Only 5 Minutes? House Votes to Stay Funded," on the Internet, from National Public Radio.

[26]For National Watermelon Month see Congressional Record Index, June 18 to June 29, 2007, and July 9 to July 20, 2007. For National Grasslands Week see ibid., June 18 to June 29, 2007.

[27]Peter J. Sepp, "Congressional Perks: How the Trappings of Office Trap Taxpayers," National Taxpayers Union Foundation Policy Paper 131, in the section "Selective Enforcement—Paid to Play," on the Internet, on p. 30 of 47.

[28]That was done by Public Law 109-55, which appropriated money for legislative branch operations for fiscal year 2006. See that law's Title I, Senate, Administrative Provisions, Section 5, which revised Title 2, U.S. Code, Section 39, 2000 edition.

[29]Rule III, note under clause 1, Rules of the House, 108th Congress; this was in Rule VIII, note under clause 1, before the recodification done by the 106th Congress.

[30]On lack of standing see below in the Violations chapter (just before the section on corrective solutions).

XX. The Multiplicity-of-Votes Problem

EPIGRAPH: Many things having full reference
             To one consent, may work contrariously.
                    ---Shakespeare, King Henry V, Act I, Scene 2.

An artful dodge by Members of Congress is the deceitful use of the many votes that occur on a single bill so they can trumpet a particular vote to their constituents at re-election time even though that one action may not be typical of their other votes on the same measure. Sometimes this deceit is used against a Member by an unscrupulous opponent seeking the seat. And a voting record may be distorted by reference to the votes cast by a Member on many different bills.

Typically, there are so many votes on a bill as it goes through what has been called "the tangle of Congressional procedure"[1] that it's easy for a Member, a supporter, or an opponent to misrepresent the Member's true stance on an issue.

Senator John Kerry's notorious 2004 statement of personal inconsistency, "I actually did vote for the $87 billion before I voted against it," is indicative of the many opportunities to vote different ways on the same issue.

After introduction, a bill is sent to a committee. There, it may be amended one or more times, and each amendment offers a chance to vote for strengthening or weakening, adding or reducing proposed benefits, and broadening or narrowing scope. Then there's the final committee vote on whether to approve or reject the amended bill. Although the votes in committee will be a matter of public record only if a record (roll call) vote is demanded, information about them may be cited in a campaign. In the case of a non-record vote, chances for incorrect reportage abound. Eventually, the bill may reach the floor to be voted on by the full House or Senate, if the bill has not been buried by the leadership or the Rules Committee. On the floor, there may be opportunities for many more votes—voting on a motion to table, voting on a motion to recommit the bill to the committee that reported it favorably, voting on a motion to eliminate the enacting clause, voting on final passage. Final passage of the bill is followed by it going to the other chamber of Congress. If that chamber passes the bill in modified form, even by so little as a comma, it goes back to the originating body, where there may be a chance to vote on whether to accept the other chamber's version. If the vote rejects the variation, there may be a vote on whether to appoint a conference committee to create a bill which can later be voted up or down in identical forms by both parts of Congress. Any of the above votes may be followed by a motion to reconsider. From the foregoing it is obvious that a Member has multiple chances to vote on a bill.[2]

And that leads to multiple chances for the Member's voting record to be portrayed in a favorable or unfavorable light.

If a proposal favored by a Member is in an unsatisfactory version in a bill, the Member may vote against it in that form with the intention of supporting an improved variation later. Then, the opponent in the next election campaign can publicize the "Nay" vote and gain a possible advantage by thus distorting the Member's true position.[3] Consider the vote on a motion to recommit a bill to the committee that reported it favorably. A Member might vote in favor of recommittal because of wanting to kill the bill or because of desiring to improve the proposal in some way. Depending on which alleged reason is emphasized, that vote can be depicted in opposite ways.

There are occasions when a lawmaker wants a bill to pass but votes against it. Huh? That may seem counterproductive and weird but it can be sensible. The explanation is that it may become obvious that the bill is about to be rejected by a majority vote, and parliamentary procedure allows reconsideration of a defeated measure but only on the motion of someone who voted with the prevailing side, in this case, against the measure. Thus, the Member who desires the bill's enactment will, in this situation, vote against the bill so he or she can later move reconsideration and perhaps get the measure finally passed. But a later electoral opponent can falsely claim that the Member opposed the bill by publicizing the vote against the bill without explaining the esoteric reason.[4]

Suppose that a Member favors a bill that is unpopular among voters back home; he or she may vote against it, knowing there are sufficient votes among other Members to pass or advance it. The reverse can occur with a bill that the Member opposes but that is popular with constituents; he or she can vote for it in the expectation that enough other Members will kill it.

Further, a Member can propose and vote for an amendment on a topic highly favored by the folks back home, and his chamber can pass it with everyone understanding that the measure will be tossed out by the later conference committee. During the next re-election campaign, that Member can posture as a local-interest champion whose efforts were defeated by uncaring and obtuse Members in the other chamber.[5]

With a bill that a Member supports or opposes, he or she can vote one way in a committee and then vote the opposite way on the floor. Later, whichever vote seems to be the one most in accord with re-election can be trumpeted during the campaign.

As Representative David Obey, D-WI, explained in 1972, "[With unrecorded votes in the Committee of the Whole] a member can vote for any number of amendments which may cripple a water pollution bill or render ineffective a civil rights bill or fail to provide adequate funding for hospital construction or programs for the elderly, and then he can turn around on final passage and vote for the bill he has just voted to emasculate by amendment." But, under a provision of the Legislative Reorganization Act of 1970, Members can demand a record vote in the Committee of the Whole.[6]

A dishonesty can occur through a misleading interpretation of what a vote actually meant. All history is interpretation. Interpretations change over time, and some may be efforts to present a truthful account while others may be ax-grinding or agenda-pushing. Robert F. Kennedy's campaign used the following distortion in its successful effort to defeat Senator Kenneth Keating in 1964. Kennedy's campaign claimed that Keating had voted in 1963 "to cut $600 million from the Aid to Higher Education bill." Keating had actually voted to substitute a three-year bill providing for greater annual aid dollars in place of a five-year bill with less annual aid. Keating had voted for a bill that was more generous for the time it covered, but Kennedy's campaign falsely made it appear that Keating was short-changing education. With that and other dishonest tricks, Robert Kennedy, of course, won. Robert's brother Senator Edward Kennedy had voted the same way Keating did on that issue.[7]

An additional interpretation example involved future Vice President Dick Cheney when he was a Representative from Wyoming in 1982. He voted in favor of a $9,100 pay raise for Members but argued that he was not really in favor of it and was only voting for it to prevent a $15,000 increase which would have occurred without passage of the amendment for the smaller amount.[8]

Furthermore, some votes become matters of record, while other don't. In the House, the requirement for roll-call voting, those votes recorded by Members' names, is limited: A vote by the "yeas and nays" is only automatic in certain situations.[9] But there can be other recorded votes if thus stipulated by a rule reported by the Rules Committee and approved by the House, or if demanded by one-fifth of a quorum, or in certain other situations.[10]

Cherry picking is also done by issue-oriented or partisan organizations that publicize Members' voting records as "conservative," or "liberal," or "pro-choice," or "pro-gun-control," or whatever. They can select the votes that will most support their agenda whether the selection is fair or not. Candidates can and do engage in the same sort of distortions against their opponents.

In 1950 the Nixon campaign to make him a Senator from California, portrayed his opponent Helen Gahagan Douglas as soft on Communism and issued pink-colored flyers linking her votes in the U.S. House of Representatives with those of the notorious left-wing Representative Vito Marcantonio of New York. The flyers noted, with impressive detail, that the two had voted the same way 354 times. Unmentioned was that most of the votes were on minor issues and that indisputable anti-Communists, like Representative Nixon himself, had often voted identically. Partly due to such trickery, Nixon, of course, defeated the "Pink Lady."[11]

Another sly maneuver designed to fool constituents about a Member's voting record is the introduction of two (or more) bills or resolutions on the same basic topic. One is written to favor something while the language of the other opposes it. Neither is expected to garner enough votes to pass, but a lawmaker can vote for the one most likely to be favored by constituents. To illustrate: In 1994, the House addressed the term-limits issue with one proposal for a limit of three terms and another for a six-term limit. As new Representative Tom Coburn later wrote, "In the end, leadership rigged the vote to make sure that every Republican could go on record voting for term limits of some kind while ensuring that no measure received a majority of votes. The freshmen were outraged by their deceptive tactics."[12]

Here's an additional example from the 1982 squabble about the proposed Constitutional amendment for a balanced budget:
> The Democratic leadership firmly opposed the amendment, which
> required Congress to adopt a balanced budget each year. President
> Reagan was lobbying hard for it.
>   The leadership did not want to appear to be preventing a vote on the
> measure, so the Rules Committee constructed a rule that allowed the
> amendment onto the floor but increased its chances of defeat.
>   The rule provided for a vote first on an alternative opposed by the
> administration that required the president to submit a balanced budget
> to Congress. As expected, that amendment was soundly defeated, 77-346,
> with no Republicans voting for it.
>   When the Reagan-backed amendment came up for a vote, it fell 46 votes
> shy of the two-thirds majority required. Fifty-six of the 77 Democrats who
> had voted for the first version voted 'no,' but their earlier vote enabled them
> to tell constituents they had voted for a balanced budget.[13]

Another part of the multiplicity-of-votes problem is that it's sometimes hard to learn what proposals have actually become law—because what finally emerges as a statute can be very different from earlier highly publicized actions by House or Senate. The first several months of the 110th Congress (2007) illustrate the problem. There was much publicity about proposals for Congressional ethics reforms. The House proposed one version, the Senate another. After the attempt to have a House-Senate conference failed, and after final votes by both chambers on a consensus bill created by the Speaker and the Majority Leader, what finally became the Honest Leadership and Open Government Act of 2007 (P.L. 110-81) was different from what each chamber had originally "passed."[14] A concerned citizen may have received a misimpression from seeing a report about one of the original bills but not anything about the final product.

CORRECTIVE SOLUTIONS

There is no complete solution to the problems of multiple votes on single issues and the unfair distortion of voting records. As various people have observed, "A lie gets halfway around the world before the truth can get its pants on."[15] A partial remedy is publicity from impartial observers. In these days of instant global communication by television and the Internet, truth can give a close race to misrepresentations and lies. Occasionally truth wins. We can hope that newspapers, magazines, TV news programs, and Internet bloggers will expose distortions. But we cannot rely on the various organs of the media to perform the function of impartial reportage because the media is populated by partisans with their own agendas, no matter how much they may protest to the contrary.

Another part of the solution is that the media should avoid headlines such as "Senate Passes Bill X." Even worse is "Senate Passes X Act," as if the measure, as an "act" rather than a bill, has become law. The word "passes" implies that final action has taken place when that's often not true. If one of the two chambers "passes" a bill, it will not become law unless it's also passed in identical form by the other chamber and approved by the President (or his veto of it is overridden). Better headlines are "Senate Approves Bill X," "House Adopts Bill Y," or "Senate Advances Bill Z."

Notes: Chapter XX. The Multiplicity-of-Votes Problem

[1]Bruce L. Felknor, <u>Dirty Politics</u> (New York: W. W. Norton, 1966), p. 181. "One congressional report identified more than 100 specific steps that might mark a 'bill's progress through the Congress.'"; Walter J. Oleszek, <u>Congressional Procedures and the Policy Process</u>, 7th edition (Washington: CQ Press, 2007), p. 19, citing [U.S., Congress, House], Committee on House Administration, <u>The Bill Status System for the United States House of Representatives</u>, July 1, 1975, p. 19.

[2]See Felknor, <u>Dirty Politics</u>, pp. 177-78.

[3]Ibid., p. 129.

[4]Additionally, the Senate allows a motion to reconsider from someone who did not originally vote; Oleszek, <u>Congressional Procedures</u>, 7th edition, p. 337. Bills that have passed are generally subjected to reconsideration motions, followed by motions to table the motion to reconsider; when the motion to table is passed, the rules do not permit reconsideration; thus the passed bill is protected.

[5]Warren Weaver, Jr., <u>Both Your Houses: The Truth About Congress</u> (New York: Praeger Publishers, 1972), p. 135.

[6]Oleszek, <u>Congressional Procedures and the Policy Process</u>, 2d edition (Washington: CQ Press, 1984), pp. 140-41; for the Obey quotation see p. 140, cited on p. 148, n.25, as from <u>Congressional Quarterly Weekly Report</u>, January 22, 1972, p. 153. This is not in Oleszek's 7th edition (2007).

[7]Felknor, <u>Dirty Politics</u>, p. 186.

[8]Editorial, "Congressional pay hike unconscionable," Billings Gazette, December 20, 1982, p. 4-A.

[9]Those situations are on passage of bills and resolutions, adoption of conference reports, general appropriation bills, bills to raise income tax rates, the final adoption of the annual budget resolution., and on overriding a Presidential veto. See House Rule XX, clause 10, 110th Congress; U.S. Constitution, Article I, Section 7, clause 2; Charles W. Johnson, "How Our Laws Are Made," revised edition (2003), p. 34 (House Document 108-93, 108th Congress, 1st Session).

Although the vote cast by each Member is recorded for a vote by the yeas and nays, a so-called recorded vote does the same; the difference lies in the number of Members who must demand one or the other type of vote. For the yeas and nays it's one-fifth of Members present in the House, but Senate practice stipulates eleven (one-fifth of 51); for recorded votes it's 44 Representatives (one-fifth of a quorum) in the House; 25 Representatives (one-fourth of a quorum in the House's Committee of the Whole); or the so-called automatic recorded vote in the House, which is obtained by a Member saying "I object to the vote on the ground that a quorum is not present, and I make a point of order that a quorum is not present"; Oleszek, Congressional Procedures, 7th edition, pp. 177, 338, 341.

In the Senate, recorded votes are called "yea and nay votes" or "roll-call votes" and occur upon the demand of any Senator if supported by at least ten additional Senators; Judy Schneider, "House and Senate Rules of Procedure: A Comparison," CRS Report for Congress, updated February 10, 2005, pp. CRS-11, CRS-12. Further, votes to invoke cloture must be decided by roll-call votes; Betsy Palmer, "Ordering a Rollcall Vote in the Senate," CRS Report for Congress, updated March 28, 2003, p. CRS-2; and Senate Rule XXII, clause 2, 110th Congress.

[10]See U.S., Congress, House, Committee on Rules, Majority Office, "Floor Procedure In The U.S. House Of Representatives," January 1999, Section XIV, on the Internet.

[11]Felknor, Dirty Politics, p. 80. See also Greg Mitchell, Tricky Dick and the Pink Lady (New York: Random House, 1998), passim, but especially pp. 65, 80, 104, 106, 126, 135, 138, 149-41, 143, and 231.

[12]Tom A. Coburn and John Hart, Breach of Trust: How Washington Turns Outsiders into Insiders (Nashville: WND Books, 2003), p. 52.

[13]Andy Plattner, "New Rules Committee Head Expected to Carry Forward In Tradition of Rep. Bolling," Congressional Quarterly Weekly Report, November 6, 1982, p. 2804.

[14]Congressional Record, daily edition, August 2, 2007, p. S10688.

[15]This has been listed in various forms as a Middle Eastern proverb and as attributed to Winston Churchill, Mark Twain, Henry Stimson, and others.

XXI. Unrecorded Votes

EPIGRAPH: Isn't that the real genius of democracy?
                        The voters are ultimately to blame.
                                    ---A cartoon in Reader's Digest, October 2008, p. 139.

EPIGRAPH: The Recording Angel, as he wrote it down, dropped a
                        tear upon the word, and blotted it out for ever.
                                    ---Laurence Sterne, The Life and Opinions of
                                        Tristram Shandy Gentleman, Book VI, Chapter 8.

Unrecorded votes prevent Members from getting blame.

Unrecorded votes are those for which the names of Members voting for and against a motion are not listed. Voting in each chamber can be conducted by several methods: Voice votes, divisions, and recorded votes.[1] On voice votes, all who vote for a motion say so at about the same time, followed shortly by all those voting no. With a division, all who favor a motion stand and are counted, but not noted by name, followed in the same way by all who oppose. Use of division voting is rare, and in the Senate can be done by raising hands rather than standing up.[2]

Only on recorded votes (also referred to as record votes) is a Member listed by name as having voted one way or another. Therefore, if there is no recorded vote on an issue, constituents who care about it have no sure way of finding out how their Senators or Representative voted on it. The great majority of Members will be honest of course in listing their votes, but some may fudge the record for presumed electoral gain, particularly when a series of procedural and substantive votes on one issue allows a Member to emphasize only the one that will look best to most voters.

Both chambers allow the "pairing" of a Member present with an absent one who would have voted the opposite way. That's a so-called "live pair." In the House, the Member present casts a recorded vote and then withdraws it and announces the pairing. Pairs are shown in the Congressional Record immediately following the list of those who voted.[3] The Senate has no formal rule about pairing, which is voluntary on roll call votes, but the procedure is much the same as in the House, except that the Senate permits "dead pairs" (those in which both Senators are absent).[4] The original reason for pairs was to give a collegial courtesy to the absent Member and to allow the absentee to indicate most prominently how he/she would have voted.

Some observers consider this a pernicious practice because the Member who cancels his or her vote is essentially allowing the opposition on that issue to appear stronger. Also, the Member seems to have little conviction about which way to vote.[5]

At the start of the 106th Congress (January 1999), the House began an alternative to pairing by permitting Members to enter a statement in the Congressional Record on how they would have voted if present.[6]

A good Congressional practice is that proxy voting is not permitted on the floor of either chamber. In the House it is no longer allowed in committees.[7] The Senate prohibits proxy voting in committees except under certain conditions.[8]

CORRECTIVE SOLUTIONS

Because a recorded vote can be demanded by a small number of Members in either chamber, no change is needed in the methods for requiring recorded votes. The real problem is that the multiplicity of votes on one issue can lead to duplicity, and for that I see only a limited chance for a solution because the rules of parliamentary procedure, developed for good reasons over many centuries, would have to suffer unacceptable disturbance to lessen the number of votes. The "limited chance" would be simply for Members to demand more recorded votes and for there to be publicity about how they voted. Technology allows all House votes to easily be recorded votes.

As for pairing, it can be eliminated because of the aforementioned alternative established in January 1999.

Notes: Chapter XXI. Unrecorded Votes

[1]A record vote can be accomplished in the House by electronic device, but not in the Senate. In both chambers a record vote can done by roll call or by the "yeas and nays," which differ only in certain technical respects. The former House practice of teller voting, by which Members would be counted by walking past other Members designated as tellers, or by signing a tally card, was abandoned for most purposes when voting by electronic device began in the House in 1972.

[2]There is no Senate rule controlling division or voice voting; Judy Schneider, "House and Senate Rules of Procedure: A Comparison," CRS Report for Congress, February 10, 2005, p. 11n.

[3]House Rule XX, clause 3, 110th Congress. Note in PDF format for 108th Congress, Rule XX, clause 3, on the Internet: "While this clause permits the announcement of a

'live' pair, the practice of general pairs found in former clause 2 of rule VIII was deleted in the 106th Congress."

[4]Walter J. Oleszek, <u>Congressional Procedures and the Policy Process</u>, 7th edition (Washington: CQ Press, 2007), p. 235. A Senate roll call vote by less than a quorum is valid if enough paired Senators are present and announce their votes; Betsy Palmer and Stanley Bach, "Voting and Quorum Procedures in the Senate," CRS Report for Congress, updated June 16, 2003, p. CRS-8, footnote.

[5]Warren Weaver, Jr., <u>Both Your Houses: The Truth About Congress</u> (New York: Praeger Publishers, 1972), p. 110.

[6]Richard C. Sachs, "Pairing in Congressional Voting: The House," CRS Report for Congress, updated July 21, 2003, p. CRS-2.

[7]House Rule XI, clause 2(f), 110th Congress.

[8]Senate Rule XXVI, clause 7 (3), 110th Congress.

XXII. Thief-in-the-Night Pay Raises

EPIGRAPH: Shall the throne of iniquity have fellowship with thee,
                which frameth mischief by a law?
                ---The Bible, Psalms, xciv, 20.

Before addressing the shameful subterfuge by which Members now often get annual pay raises, some historical context is helpful.

The U.S. Constitution, Article I, Section 6, states that "Senators and Representatives shall receive a compensation for their services, to be ascertained by law and paid out of the treasury of the United States." That gives Members the right to set their own pay, which, under the separation of powers, may be preferable to having it set by the executive or judiciary branches of the government. But it also creates two problems: (1) members have a conflict of interest in passing any law about their own salaries, and (2) even reasonable pay raises may cause a public backlash.

In 1789 the first Congress set Members' pay at $6 for each session day that a member attended.[1] Congress changed the pay to $1,500 a year in 1816. An ostensible reason for the revision was greater Congressional efficiency by Members not prolonging sessions just to get more per diem compensation. But voters were outraged, and several incumbents resigned or suffered defeat in the next election. Therefore, the next Congress repealed the $1,500 yearly wage and replaced it with an $8-a-day stipend. That lasted until 1855, when a $3,000 yearly wage was passed without much public reaction, and that was changed to $5,000 a year in 1865.

In 1873 Congress passed what became known as the Salary Grab, a raise to $7,500. Public rancor erupted because of the 50 percent increase and because the hike was retroactive for two years, even for Members who had retired or failed of re-election. That resentment produced defeat for many incumbents in 1874; so the next Congress repealed the increase. Having learned a bitter lesson, Members did not get another increase until a salary of $7,500 went into effect in 1907.

In 1917 a conference committee inserted an income tax exemption for Members. Part of a report about it in The New York Times revealed this: "Hidden meanings of the complicated provisions of that portion of the war revenue law relating to excess profits continue to come to light. Today the discovery was made that although . . . a provision applying the excess profits tax of 8 per cent to all earnings of individuals in excess of $6,000 a year [was inserted], care was taken to see that members of Congress were not subject to this provision, as far as it applied to their official salaries."[2]

Of course, freeing Members from a tax was tantamount to a salary increase.

Actually, the exemption applied to all members of federal, state, and local governments, but few of them, other than Members of Congress, had salaries high enough to benefit from it. The Times quoted an Internal Revenue official as guessing that "the exemption of members of Congress was the thing aimed at and to accomplish that it was necessary to take in with them all officers of the government."

Several Congressional procedures facilitated this greedy effort: The secrecy cloaking conference committee activity, the ability of conferees to inject entirely new provisions into bills with neither house ever having considered them, and the lack of careful vetting of bills in their final form. As The Times explained, "Those responsible for the provision had an easy time of it . . . as the Senate and the House were in the throes of agitation over the prospect of an early adjournment and were not disposed to scrutinize carefully the agreement reached by the conferees."[3]

That outrage enraged the public so much that Congress quickly repealed it. As one Representative said, Members came to "fear for our political skins."[4]   Further fallout from this debacle occurred when the Senate adopted a rule in 1918 against conferees adding new matter to bills and against striking provisions identically agreed to by both.[5]

In 1925 salaries bounded up to $10,000, but went down to $9,000 in 1932 and $8,500 in 1933 because of economizing during the Great Depression. As conditions improved, however, the $10,000 pay was restored in 1935 and was raised to $12,500 in 1947.

When Congress voted Members an 80% increase in 1955 there was little public criticism, perhaps because Americans were enjoying flush economic times. However, an effort for a raise to $32,500 in 1964 failed on a roll-call vote, but a hike to $30,000 was passed after the primary elections were over.

In 1967 Congress began a "thief-in-the-night" dodge for higher salaries. To get more money while insulating themselves from public revenge, Members created an outside "Quadrennial Commission" whose every-four-years salary recommendations, subject to changes made by the President, would go into effect automatically unless either chamber voted against them within thirty days of the President presenting his budget containing his recommendations.[6] (Procedural adjustments occurred in 1977, 1985, and 1989.[7]) The process was explained as "an attempt to remove politics from pay raises,"[8] but it was more like an attempt to remove voters from pay raises.

That dodge resulted, February 1969, in salaries of $42,500, a nearly 42 percent hike from the immediately preceding $30,000.[9] Next, Congress actually rejected a proposed increase in 1974, perhaps because it was an election year.

In 1975 a new law provided Members with the same annual cost-of-living adjustment (COLA) as for other federal workers.[10] However, Members could be held accountable for giving themselves more money because they would have to vote each time to appropriate funds for the COLA. Congress soon did so, producing salaries of $44,600 in October 1975. But just as Congress can repeal or modify any existing law, so it can pass legislation denying itself any year's COLA. Public revulsion about the first COLA caused Congress to reject the 1976 COLA.

However, in early 1977, a non-election year, the salaries surged to $57,500 after the third Quadrennial Commission recommended that amount, and neither house of Congress disapproved. The methods used to avoid disapproval were surely offensive to honesty and true democracy: The House deliberately delayed until the rejection deadline had passed, and the Senate used parliamentary trickery, as follows: Majority Leader Robert Byrd recessed rather than adjourned the Senate from January 19 through February 1, so that no new legislative day began during that time, which meant that no disapproval resolution could be considered during that time because of a Senate rule that a resolution cannot be considered on the same legislative day it's introduced. And a disapproval resolution offered as an amendment to another measure was killed by tabling.[11]

Thus, from 1967 to 1977 Congress could get pay increases without voting for them, but Members might have to expose themselves by a recorded vote on whether to reject the raises. The procedural change in 1977 provided that a recommendation from the Commission and the President would go into effect if both chambers approved it within sixty days of the President submitting it in his budget.

The COLA for 1977 was declined.[12] The COLA was again rejected in 1978 but accepted in the non-election year 1979, causing pay to ascend to $60,662.50.[13] Perhaps because there were elections in 1980, the COLA was rejected that year.

Members lusting for both higher salaries and re-election needed a method for exalting the first without endangering the second. They found it in 1981 in a law making COLA funding a permanent appropriation needing no annual vote.[14] Yet, strangely, the COLA was declined that same year and again in 1982 and 1983.[15] We can perhaps discover the reason for the 1982 rejection by noting that Congress separately enacted a 15 percent pay raise in December of that year, but only for Representatives, not Senators.[16] (The Quadrennial Commission process did not prevent Congress from voting itself additional and separate pay increases.) The reason for the disparity, which lasted only a few months, was a deal that permitted Senators to earn unlimited amounts of outside income, such as honoraria for speeches, while outside income of Representatives was capped at 30 percent of salary.[17] When a limitation was again imposed on Senators' outside earnings in mid-1983, their Congressional salaries were elevated to the same level as for Representatives ($69,800).[18]

COLA increases caused salary hikes in 1984, 1985, and 1987 (effective on January 1 of each of those years).[19]

Additionally, on January 5, 1987, in responding to the report of another Quadrennial Commission and submitting his budget to Congress, President Reagan recommended an increase of 15.6 percent. Then came the all-too-familiar Congressional trickery. Congress had modified the Quadrennial Commission law in 1985 to make pay hikes harder to kill: The augmentation would take effect unless both houses voted against it within 30 days of the budget's submission.[20] The Senate did so on January 29, 1987, and the House followed suit on February 4, just hours after the deadline of midnight February 3. So Members got the increase, to $89,500.

Early 1989 brought a huge fight about a jump to $135,000, which was recommended by another Quadrennial Commission and by President Reagan. Members were pitted against other Members and large sections of the public. Congress had voted against a four percent COLA in June 1988, but House Members who coveted more money advanced a plan to get the $135,000 without a vote. Speaker Jim Wright and other high-ranking Democrats thought they could get enough support in the House for the raise by promising a later vote to ban honoraria, which fattened some Members' wallets by tens of thousands of dollars. (For honoraria, see later in this chapter.) Although Senators passed a resolution opposing the increase on February 2, 1989, many expected to get the additional money anyway because the hike would occur if the House did not also vote against it before February 8.

It turned out that the public cared little about honoraria—until pay-hike advocates identified abolition of the speaking fees as an ethics issue that would separate Members' financial concerns from special interest groups. But the public cared greatly that each Member might receive a salary increase greater than the average American worker's yearly income. Amid overwhelming public opposition, the House finally also voted against the raise one day before it would have taken effect.[21]

When Vic Fazio, D-CA, introduced the disapproval resolution, he intoned his disappointment: "The media in general did a very poor job. They provided, in some cases, biased coverage. We became cartoon cannon fodder for trash television and for talk radio. . . . We fell prey to the deception of the rabble rousers."[22]

Perhaps Members realized that one argument in favor of the raise, that it was needed to attract better people to Congress, should cause voters to reject most incumbents at the next election.

One regret of Fazio and like-minded Members about the rejection of the pay raise was that thousands of officials in the executive and judicial branches would not get higher salaries. That happened because Congress, ever mindful of its self-esteem, refused to approve compensation recommendations for higher pay than Representatives and Senators for "comparable" officials in the other two branches.[23] Senator Thurmond expressed a belief common to many Members when he said, "I do not feel we should relegate the Congress to a lower status."[24] The salaries for comparable federal employees had become hostages.

Fazio and others expressed concern that people with expertise were leaving federal service or would not accept federal jobs to start with because they could make more money in the private sector.[25] Of course, there was a simple solution to that problem: Congress could uncouple the executive and judicial salaries from those of its own Members and allow them to be higher than Members' pay. Will pride ever permit something so beneficial to the nation? The House Judiciary Committee approved a bill in December 2007 to raise the salaries of U.S. District Court judges to $233,500 a year.[26] The bill did not become law. And while salaries for Supreme Court justices and for judges on U.S. courts of appeal are higher than those of ordinary Members of Congress, salaries for U.S. district court judges are still the same as for Members.

After COLAs were rejected in 1988 and 1989, Congress passed the Ethics Reform Act in late 1989 that gave Representatives a stair-step pay increase (including COLAs and an outright raise) by January 1, 1991, to $125,100 while eventually banning honoraria for them. That law also ratcheted up Senators' pay to $101,900 but only reduced, rather than eliminated, their allowable honoraria.[27] The law also provided for automatic future COLAs but changed some details of their computation.[28]

 Members sought cover through obfuscation by refusing to refer to the bill as a pay raise, preferring instead "ethics bill," and by limits on honoraria and by linking increases for Members to additions for Executive and Judicial pay—but at least they allowed recorded votes in both houses.

Leaders in the House had been so worried that the bill would cause opposition that they kept its details secret until only a week before its consideration on the floor. That suspect effort to ram something through before the American public would have a fair chance to respond was not new; the 1975 plan to provide Members with COLAs, crafted by a cabal of Executive and Legislative functionaries, also creeped out of secrecy and was passed "only five days after most members had even heard of it. [29]

Sometimes, as with the Ethics Reform Act of 1989, COLA pay raises previously denied have been restored by catch-up legislation.[30] Therefore, pity the deluded taxpayer who thought Members had permanently rejected some COLAs and whose faith in Members of Congress had been thereby somewhat restored.

The Ethics Reform Act of 1989, as amended, remains in effect and has resulted in COLA raises in fourteen of the twenty years 1990-2009 inclusive. COLAs were blocked for the other six years.[31] The last COLA received raised Members' pay to $174,000 per year in January 2009. COLAs were blocked for 2010, 2011, and 2012.[32]

A legislative appropriations law in August 1991 banned Senatorial honoraria and bumped up Senators' pay to make salaries in both chambers equal.[33] Since then there have been only COLA increases in Congressional pay.

In another obfuscation, House leaders of both parties crafted a maneuver in 1999 to prevent the rank and file from blocking COLA salary hikes: The only vote would be on whether the House would "foreclose the possibility of an amendment that would nullify the coming pay increase during debate on the annual spending bill that governs civil service pay."[34] Not only would that issue be little noticed, but if it were publicized, it could be presented as a humanitarian effort to make sure the salaries of ordinary federal workers would be protected from inflation.

* *
* *
* *
* *

**
**   Pay-Raise Trickery in the Late 1900s
**
**   1967: A raise recommended by the Quadrennial Commission and the
**   President would go into effect unless either the Senate or the House
**   voted against the recommendations within thirty days of the President
**   submitting them.
                      ---Public Law 90-206 (December 16, 1967), Section 225(i)(1);
**   and Title 2, U.S. Code, Sections 351-61, 1970 edition.
**
**   1975: Members would get annual COLAs.
**   ---Public Law 94-82 (August 9, 1975), Section 204 (a),
**   89 Stat. 421, referencing P.L. 79-601, Section 601
**   (Legislative Reorganization Act of 1946); and Title 5,
**   U.S. Code, Section 5305, 1976 edition.
**
**   1977: Raises recommended by the Quadrennial Commission and the
**   President would go into effect if both chambers voted approval within
**   sixty days of the President submitting them.
**   ---Public Law 95-19 (April 12, 1977), Title IV, Section 401;
**   and Title 2, U.S. Code, Section 359, 1982 edition.
**
**   1981: Permanent COLA funding without an annual vote.
**   ---Public Law 97-51, Section 130(c), 95 Stat. 966; & Title 2,
**   U.S. Code, Section 31, 1982 edition (p. 23); and Congressional
**   Quarterly Weekly Report, October 3, 1981, p. 1892.
**
**   1985: Recommended raises (non-COLA) would take effect unless
**   both chambers voted against them within thirty days of their submission

**   by the President.
**   ---Public Law 99-190 (December 19, 1985), Section
**   135(e). 99 Stat. 1322; and Title 2, U.S. Code, Section 359,
**   1988 edition.
**
**   1989: Representatives were awarded COLAs that had been rejected in
**   two earlier years. They also were given a new COLA. As a result of
**   those three COLAs, the announced pay raise of 25 percent actually
**   became an increase of 39.77 percent, as salaries ascended from $89,500
**   to $125,000. Automatic COLAs will occur every January except that
**   Congress can vote yearly to prevent one.
**   ---Public Law 101-194 (November 30, 1989), Sections
**   702 and 703, 103 Stat. 1767-68.
**
**   1989: Senators got three COLAs, two of which had been previously
**   Rejected, but got no other pay raise.
**   ---Public Law 101-194 (November 30, 1989), Section
**   1101, 103 Stat. 1781-83.
**
**   1989: The Quadrennial Commission was abolished and was replaced
**   by the Citizens' Commission on Public Service and Compensation. But
**   it has never met.
**   ---Public Law 101-194 (November 30, 1989, Title VII,
**   Section 701, 103 Stat. 1763.
**
**   1999: The House, as explained above, would vote yearly on whether
**   to "foreclose the possibility of an amendment that would nullify the
**   coming pay increase during debate on the annual spending bill that
**   governs civil service pay." If that mumbo jumbo were ever questioned,
**   its alleged humanitarianism would be emphasized.
**   ---See below, note 34.
**

****
****
****
****

By 2006 Congressional pay was $165,200 per year. Meantime, although getting several salary increases Congress allowed the federal minimum wage to languish at $5.15 an hour from September 1997 to July 2007.

With a vote of both chambers required to block a Congressional COLA, the effort in June 2007 to do so failed in the House.[35] Result: In January 2008 all Members got a boost to $169,300, an increase of $4,100. However, partly because the House's action was not a direct vote on the pay hike but was only an obscure procedural vote, there was minimal publicity.[36]

In January 2009 another COLA (2.8%) caused Members' salaries to rise to $174,000 with little public knowledge or reaction.

Some Americans complain that such COLAs violate the Constitution's 27th Amendment, which says "No law, varying the compensation for services of the Senators and Representatives, shall take effect until an election of Representatives shall have intervened." Of course, between the House action of June 2007 and the effective date of the COLA increase in January 2008 there was no election of Representatives. But Congress fiddled the system so effectively that it can be argued that numerous elections of Representatives intervened after the original Congressional COLA law was passed in 1975, and after a 1981 law made COLA funding a permanent appropriation needing no annual vote, and after the modification made by the Ethics Reform Act of 1989. COLA advocates can argue that the 27th Amendment is not violated because Congress does not pass any new law to get the COLAs. Members get the COLA if either chamber does not vote to block it. Non-action trumps the 27th Amendment.

Almost immediately after the Amendment's ratification a lawsuit was initiated to prevent retiring and defeated members of the old Congress, who were scheduled to get a COLA on January 1, 1993, two days before the end of their terms, from receiving the increase. Not only would they benefit from a last-minute cash infusion, they would further gain from increased pensions, which were determined by their three highest years of pay. In December 1992, federal district judge Stanley Sporkin dismissed the suit. He ruled that the 27th Amendment would not be violated in letter or in spirit because an election of Representatives had actually intervened. But one wonders if the plaintiffs got a fair shake because Judge Sporkin issued his fifteen-page opinion only an hour after the completion of oral arguments, thus showing he had already decided the case regardless of plaintiffs' presentation—or was he just the world's fastest thinker and writer? In an appeal from Sporkin's decision, the D.C. circuit court also ruled that the 27th Amendment was not contravened. Dealing with a similar suit filed in 1999, the Supreme Court affirmed decisions of District and Circuit courts and reached the same conclusion.[37]

Despite the rancor about Congressional pay raises in the 1980s and '90s and the supposed fixing of the system, salaries for Members continue upward, separating them increasingly from most Americans. Indeed, the system has been fixed, as in the corruption cliché "the fix is in." Sometimes one house votes against the COLA but the other does not, so the increase occurs. Then some Members can tell their constituents that they opposed the added money—yet they knew they would get it because of the virtually certain inaction of the other house. Often, Members up for re-election oppose pay hikes, while those not soon facing the voters support them.

It's not democracy when voters cannot hold government officials responsible for the actions of government, one of which is setting government salaries.

It's fair to refer to those COLAs as "thief-in-the-night" pay raises and shameful subterfuges because (1) Members receive COLA pay raises automatically unless both houses vote not to do so in a particular year, (2) COLAs are included as part of vastly larger appropriations bills, so they are often not subject to a separate vote, (3) these COLAs allow Members to reject blame by pointing out that the basic provisions were enacted long before they were first elected, and (4) the leadership will sometimes resort to parliamentary-procedure trickery to prevent a vote on a prospective COLA-blocking amendment. The latter maneuver happened on September 17, 1997: House leadership suddenly advanced an appropriation bill from its announced place on the calendar to immediate consideration, and Rep. Tom Coburn, R-OK, who planned to offer an anti-COLA amendment was reportedly caught unawares and could not get to the floor in time to do so.[38]

After the House did not spurn the COLA in September 1997 and the Senate rejected it, both in larger appropriations bills, a conference committee had to resolve the differences. An anti-COLA amendment on instructions to conferees was indirectly defeated by a motion for the "previous question," which was passed.[39] This procedure, little understood by ordinary voters, brought the following analysis from Congressional Quarterly Weekly Report:

> The leaders in effect had given lawmakers a way to vote themselves a pay raise without appearing to vote themselves a pay raise. After all, those who voted for the [previous question] motion could claim they were simply voting on a technical motion dealing with instructions to conferees, not on a pay raise. The vote offered members crucial cover, a plausible way of obscuring their actual position on the issue.

Of course, the conference committee dropped the Senate's anti-COLA provision, and thus Members' pay was raised from $133,600 to $136,700 (effective January 1, 1998).[40]

Some Members continue to carp about their alleged low pay, $174,000 as of this writing in late 2011, the most recent COLA having awarded Members a raise of $4,700.[41] While most Americans struggle along on much lower incomes, Congressional pay does seem low if compared to the costs of re-election campaigns. Senator Wendell Ford, D-KY, delivered this shot as he got ready to jump off the money-go-round in the late 1990s, "I do not relish, in fact I detest, the idea of having to raise $5 million for a job that pays $133,000 a year."[42]

Despite the poor-mouthing about "low" salaries, many Members never raked in so much money in their private-sector jobs.[43] One former Texas Representative touched on this when explaining his decision to seek re-election: "Congress voted themselves 125,000 bucks. I can't make that around here."[44] In perhaps the most extreme recent case, a California Representative ascended from a pre-Congressional yearly income of $2,262 in unemployment pay in 1992.[45]

Many Members consider themselves overworked and underpaid,[46] yet most of them seek re-election. And they aren't just mild seekers—they order virtually their entire lives around the goal of staying in Congress. Figures for recent elections are proof: In 2010, an unusually large number of thirty-eight Members in the House did not seek re-election, but sixteen of those left to seek a different political office, including some who wanted to remain in Congress as Senators. Of those thirty-eight, seventeen were Democrats; and only three of them sought another office, compared to twelve of the twenty-one Republicans. Also in 2010, twelve Senators retired, half from each party.

In 2008, retirement numbers, although still indicating a small minority of Representatives, were again larger than usual, mainly because many Republicans decided not to push against what looked to be a strong Democratic tide. Thus, twenty-eight Representatives retired, only three of whom were Democrats; and five Senators whose terms would expire at the end of the 110th Congress retired, all of them Republicans.[47]

In 2006, only four Senators and eleven Representatives retired, although there was a larger number of open House seats in the general election due to Members who sought other offices or were defeated in primaries or resigned because of scandals.[48] In 2004, only sixteen Representatives and six Senators actually retired, but there was a larger number of open seats in that year's general election because some Members sought other offices or resigned before their terms ended.[49] In 2002, eighteen Representatives and five Senators retired, but again there was a larger number of open seats at election time because of expulsions, deaths, resignations before end of term, and attempts to win election to other offices.[50]

The sixty-five retirements from the House in 1992 were exceptionally numerous.[51] Several unusual factors influenced the decisions to leave: Redistricting, fattened pensions flowing from recent pay raises, involvement in the scandal at the House bank, and the money-lust of some Representatives who got a last chance to take their unspent campaign contributions and put that money to whatever personal use they desired. Senate rules banned personal use of campaign money, but two laws affected House incumbents: (1) the 1979 amendments to the Federal Election Campaign Act included a provision that only Members serving on the date of that law's enactment, January 8, 1980, could convert unused campaign funds to personal use; (2) the Ethics Reform Act of 1989 provided that only a pre-January 9, 1980, Member who retired prior to the convening of the 103d Congress in January 1993 could convert leftover campaign money to personal use, "other than to defray any ordinary and necessary expenses incurred in connection with his or her duties as holder of Federal office."[52] That resulted in a few retiring Members jacking up their personal wealth by over a million dollars. Many others added hundreds of thousands.[53] Some announced that they would donate all the surplus funds to charities—but who knows what actually happened?

Other, more common, reasons for not seeking re-election include old age or ill health, death, or running for another office such as Senator or governor.

In Congress, partisanship frequently rides roughshod over fairness or the national interest. But the desire for higher salaries trumps party advantage and everything else except re-election. Consider this: Democrats who disliked Republican Newt Gingrich put up a strong candidate, David Worley, against him in 1990. Under a November 1989 law,[54] Representatives were scheduled to receive a massive pay hike in January 1991, and to lessen the chance of a public outcry leaders of both parties made a bipartisan pact to withhold campaign funds from any challenger making an issue of the pay raise. When Worley began heavy criticism of Gingrich for voting in favor of the increase, the Democratic Congressional Campaign Committee cut off its contributions to Worley even though polling indicated he might win. Worley eventually failed to unseat Gingrich by only 974 votes. By their collusion with the Republicans and by stabbing their own candidate in the back, the Democrats lost a great opportunity to defeat the future Speaker of the House and to prevent his later successful attack against them.[55]

Actions for Indirect Pay Hikes

Members have occasionally had other ways to increase their incomes. A 1974 law limited to $15,000 per year their age-old outside earnings from "honoraria," the payments Members could get for speeches, published articles, and mere appearances.[56] That limit was so corseting it was relaxed to $25,000 per annum in 1976.[57] New ethics rules adopted by both chambers in 1977 and effective in January 1979 imposed a limit of fifteen percent of Congressional salary on total outside earned income.[58]

In what Congressional Quarterly Weekly Report called "a skillfully executed surprise attack,"[59] the House changed its rules in December 1981 to permit Representatives to receive up to 30 percent of their Congressional salaries in outside earned income rather than the previous limit of 15 percent.[60] This related mainly to honoraria but also to professional fees such as income from a law practice or serving on a board of directors. The "surprise attack" happened when few Members were present in the House chamber. Representative John Murtha, he of greater and more recent fame ("infamy" to some), asked for unanimous consent to approve House Resolution 305 to make the change in the rules. No Member objected, and the revision occurred. Congressional Quarterly Weekly Report said, "The entire process took about 10 seconds."

Back on October 28, 1981, a recorded-vote resolution had been defeated that would have raised the limit to 40 percent of a Member's salary—Members had then been afraid to be identified with such a self-serving proposal.[61]

Not satisfied with the 30 percent limit, in 1986 Representative Murtha and the House leadership of both parties devised another ambush maneuver to raise the cap to 40 percent. With few Members on the floor—again!—Murtha introduced a cap-raising resolution, but its language must have been like the bikini that concealed what was vital because one Member asked "what the gentleman's resolution is about." On receiving Murtha's response that the "intent . . . is to change the current 30-percent limitation to 40 percent" and that it had "been cleared by the leadership on both sides," the questioner dropped the issue, and the resolution passed. [62] The next day, however, after most Representatives learned what had been done, they were so frightened about adverse electoral consequences that the House repealed the resolution for the 40-percent cap.[63]

The limit then remained at 30 percent until January 1, 1991, the effective date of a ban on honoraria for Representatives that was part of a deal to increase salaries[64] (see earlier in this chapter).

As for the Senators, in what they must have seen later as excesses of rectitude, they had limited themselves, as mentioned above, first to $25,000 per year in honoraria and later to total outside earned income at a maximum of fifteen percent of Congressional salary. Seeming to regret those restrictions on honoraria, they fiddled around for several years with various postponements, an exemption, and a repeal.[65] Then, further tinkering from January 1984 into the early 1990s produced caps of varying amounts on how much of their honoraria Senators could keep.[66]

Finally, as with the House, honoraria for Senators were banned as of mid-1991.[67]

There was a bit of Congressional law evasion during some of the time when Members could receive honoraria: A rule stipulated that they could keep only $2,000 of each payment. If more was paid, the excess above $2,000 had to be donated to charity. Federal law required that anyone directing someone else to contribute to a specific charity had to report the donation as part of his or her own income. In what one lobbyist called "sort of the ultimate form of the shell game," he said that this trickery worked as follows: "A member tells you, 'I'd like $2,000 sent to my office, but it would be a good idea if you donate another $3,000 to a charity. We won't tell you which charity, but we really like the third one on that list.' If you want to play ball with that member, you know damn well you'd better make the contribution."[68]

Alternatively, a Member could accept the entire $5,000 and donate the excess to charity himself. So why would he or she go for the "shell-game" trick? Answer: "The lower figure keeps his total at a more respectable level, and because the interest group makes the charitable donation, it is easier for the member to keep his contributions to a sum that is still tax-free."[69] The solon might want to keep the "total at a more respectable level" because "lawmakers know these fees are seen as little more than legalized bribes or 'dishonoraria.'"[70]

A further backdoor increase in Congressional pay was crafted in 1981 when Congress removed a 1952 limit of $3,000 for Members' income-tax deductions for District of Columbia living expenses and got instead per-diem deductions for each "congressional day," which amounted to somewhat over $19,000. That was accomplished by a typical maneuver-in-the-shadows, as follows: In October, Congress passed a revision giving Members an increased income-tax deduction for Washington living expenses, starting with 1982 tax returns. Next, on December 11, Congress allowed the larger deduction for 1981 taxes as well. Then, having discovered an overlooked conflict with a 1976 tax law, the House passed a corrective measure. The Senate, however, on the last day of the session (December 16, 1981), modified the tax break and made it an unrelated part of a bill to benefit victims of black-lung disease. The House concurred. The final version directed the IRS to set an "appropriate" per-diem deduction for the increased tax break, for which Members would not have to prove actual expenses. Some Members said they

were unaware of this when they voted for the bill. Senator Dole, R-KS, indicated that
$75 per day would be appropriate but said that no specific per-diem amount was included
in the bill "because the press will add up $75 times so many days in session and they will
interpret it in some ways as looking like a tax credit or a pay raise."[71] Indeed, one of
Dole's own colleagues, Senator William Proxmire, D-WI, later said this was a "sneaky"
way for Members to give themselves a pay raise.[72]

It should be no surprise that in early 1982 the IRS came up with the same figure
suggested by Senator Dole. It ruled that the unsubstantiated deduction could be $75 "for
each 'congressional day,' which includes among other things the four-day weekends that
Congress regularly schedules."[73] Well, who could have predicted that the IRS would
settle on the exact same amount suggested by the chairman of the Senate Finance
Committee? Public outrage led to the scheme's repeal in July1982, but the repeal was
not retroactive; so Members were able to apply the huge deduction against their 1981
income tax liability and thus have to pay virtually no tax on their $60,662 salaries.[74]

CORRECTIVE SOLUTION

Members should not receive a COLA in a year when inflation exists but is so low that
Social Security recipients don't get one. That idea, in somewhat different wording, is
already law,[75] except that it still takes a vote in both chambers to prevent the salary
increase. In the other years Members should get COLAs, for without them Congressional
salaries suffer decreases in real purchasing power, and eventually the Members propose a
catch-up in the form of a massive pay increase that looks to many voters like greed run
amuck. But each yearly COLA should only occur after an open, recorded, positive vote
on the COLA as a stand-alone issue, not after an automatic grant of money that can only
be stopped by a negative vote. Because so many other Americans, Social Security
beneficiaries for example, get COLAs, they can be reasonably defended to the voters—
but only if no sneaky method is used. Any covert, underhanded process simply proves to
many voters that the result is bad and indefensible.

The public is more likely to accept COLAs than large pay hikes. COLAs may seem like
pay increases, but they really just keep recipients from losing ground through inflation.
Indeed, a court ruled that a Congressional COLA is not a pay raise.[76] The latter are seen
by much of the public as rapacious elitism by people who fail to meet the nation's needs.
COLAs don't generate as much opposition. Congressional incumbents who get them
should not fear being frank and honest about them if the process is frank and honest. But
it's hard to defend something as legitimate when it's achieved by illegitimate means.

Yet, Members might laugh at the proposal to require a positive COLA vote each year.
They might say, "The public doesn't seem to object to the current system since almost all
of us get re-elected anyway, so why should we change it?"

Notes: Chapter XXII. Thief-in-the-Night Pay Raises

[1]"In the First Congress, members received $6 a day, which for the long 1789 session of 210 days meant $1,260"; Warren Weaver, Jr., Both Your Houses: The Truth About Congress (New York: Praeger, 1972), p. 196. At least one source converts the $6 per diem to $1,500 per year "based on a hypothetically possible 250-day session" after 1789; Paul E. Dwyer, "Salaries of Members of Congress: A List of Payable Rate and Effective Dates, 1789-2006," CRS Report for Congress, updated April 18, 2006, pp. CRS-4; CRS-6, note b.

[2]"Confirms Impost On Salaried Men . . . Congressmen Are Exempt," The New York Times, October 5, 1917, p. 1.

[3]Ibid.

[4]Weaver, Both Your Houses, 132; "House Votes To Tax Congress Salaries: Repeals Kitchin Joker and Passes Amendment—Makes President Subject to Impost," The New York Times, December 19, 1917, p. 2.

[5]"Senate Amends Its Rules," The New York Times, March 9, 1918, p. 4.

[6]The panel was named Commission on Executive, Legislative and Judicial Salaries but was commonly referred to as the Quadrennial Commission. See Public Law 90-206 (Dec. 16, 1967), Section 225(i)(1); and Title 2, U.S. Code, Sections 351-61, 1970 edition. The law actually said the President's recommendations "shall become effective at the beginning of the first pay period which begins after the thirtieth day following the transmittal of such recommendations in the budget" if "neither House of the Congress has enacted legislation which specifically disapproves all or part of such recommendations" (emphasis added); Title 2, U.S. Code, Section 359, 1970 edition. That, however, appears to have been interpreted so that a disapproval by either chamber had to take place within thirty days of transmittal regardless of when the next pay period would begin.

[7]Legislation in April 1977 changed the 30 days to 60 days and made it clear that the 60 days started with "the submission of the President's recommendations to the Congress" and that both chambers had to approve rather than one disapproving (see Public Law 95-19, Title IV, Section 401, and Title 2, U.S. Code, Section 359, 1982 edition).
Amendments in 1985 reverted the time period to 30 days after submission and provided that the recommendations would go into effect unless disapproved by both chambers passing a joint resolution (see Public Law 99-190, Section 135(e); Title 2, U.S. Code, Section 359, 1988 edition). Joint resolutions are sent to the President for action and have the force of law if approved; thus, the new procedure avoided the "legislative veto" that the Supreme Court ruled unconstitutional in INS v. Chadha, 492 U.S. 919 (1983); see Congressional Quarterly Almanac . . . 1989 (Washington: Congressional Quarterly, 1990), p. 59.
The process was further tweaked by the Ethics Reform Act of 1989, which abolished the Commission on Executive, Legislative, and Judicial Salaries and created the Citizens'

Commission on Public Service and Compensation (see Public Law 101-194, Title VII; Title 2, U.S. Code, Section 351, 2000 edition), but it has never met; thus, the Act's revised procedures that would follow the Commission's recommendations have not applied.

[8]"Federal Pay Raise," Congressional Quarterly Weekly Report, November 13, 1976, p. 3191.

[9]The Commission had recommended $50,000, but LBJ recommended $42,500; Mike Mills, "Raising Members' Pay: A 200-Year Dilemma," Congressional Quarterly Weekly Report, February 4, 1989, p. 211.

[10]That was provided by the Executive Salary Cost-of-Living Adjustment Act, Public Law 94-82 (August 9, 1975), Section 204(a), 89 Stat. 421, referencing Title 5, U.S. Code, Section 5305 [1976 edition; not there in 2000 edition].
Members, however, could deprive themselves of the COLA in a particular year by refusing to appropriate the funds for it.

[11]Thomas P. Southwick, "Senate Defeats Allen Move to Kill Federal Pay Raise; Approves Committee Plan," Congressional Quarterly Weekly Report, February 5, 1977, p. 196.

[12]Paul E. Dwyer, Salaries of Members of Congress, 1789-2003 (New York: Novinka Books, 2003), p. 38. This book is perhaps the most accurate and detailed exposition on its topic.

[13]Congressional salary increases based on percentages have usually been rounded to the nearest $100, but language in the law creating the 1979 pay hike prevented that; "Pay and Perquisites of Members of Congress," TheCapitol.Net on the Internet. The 1979 COLA could have been 7 percent, but Congress approved only 5.5 percent; Dwyer, Salaries, p. 38.

[14]"Public Law 97-51, Section 130(c), 95 Stat. 966; Irwin B. Arieff, "Congress Votes Itself New Pay Benefits," Congressional Quarterly Weekly Report, October 3, 1981, p. 1892.

[15]Dwyer, Salaries (Novinka Books), p. 38.

[16]Ibid., pp. 5, 38, 64.

[17]"Most Senators Over Proposed Income Limit," Congressional Quarterly Weekly Report, June 4, 1983, p. 1124.

[18]Dwyer, Salaries (Novinka Books), pp. 5, 38, 64. Paul E. Dwyer and Frederick H. Pauls, "A Brief History of Congressional Pay Legislation," Congressional Research Service, Library of Congress, January 8, 1987, p. CRS-23: Public Law 98-63, approved

on July 30, 1983, made the Senators' pay increase effective on July 1, 1983, but their honoraria limit of 30 percent of salary would not begin until January 1, 1984.

[19]Dwyer, Salaries (Novinka Books), pp. 5, 38, 64.

[20]See Title 2, U.S. Code, Section 359, 1988 edition; Congressional Quarterly Almanac . . . 1989, p. 59.

[21]Janet Hook, "Pay Raise Is Killed, but the Headaches Persist," Congressional Quarterly Weekly Report, February 11, 1989, pp. 261-63; Janet Hook, "How the Pay-Raise Strategy Came Unraveled, ibid., pp. 264-67.

[22]Congressional Record, permanent edition, February 7, 1989, p. 1709.

[23]For detail on this see Russell R. Wheeler and Michael S. Greve, "How to Pay the Piper: It's Time to Call Different Tunes for Congressional and Judicial Salaries," (Washington: The Brookings Institution, 2007), on the Internet. Ibid., p. 6: "The practical reason for linkage is . . . Congress can raise the salaries of all three groups, as a package, more easily than it can raise its own, standing alone," but (p. 2) "data are at best inconclusive on whether linkage serves" that purpose.
Some linkage of Congressional salaries to those of federal circuit or district judges has existed since 1890, but was not mandated by statute until the Ethics Reform Act of 1989 became law; ibid., pp. 3-4. (That requirement seems to have related only to the recommendations made by the new Citizens' Commission on Public Service and Compensation, which has never met, and to the President's recommendations in response to those of the Commission; see Title 2, U.S. Code, Section 362, 2000 edition. Thus, one interpretation holds that there has recently been legal linkage.)
In 1987 Senator John Glenn quoted the recent Quadrennial Commission to the effect that the linkage was created so that pay raises for the other two branches would increase Congressional pay and insulate Members from criticism about salary hikes for themselves. But the reverse occurred: Congressional reluctance kept all the relevant salaries down, and Members hoped that public pressure for pay raises in the other two branches would be like the "rising tide that lifts all boats" and would create "public support for across-the-board salary increases"; Congressional Record, daily edition, January 29, 1987, p. S 1349.
For further detail see American Bar Association (Denise Cardman) and Federal Bar Association (Bruce Moyer), "Federal Judicial Pay: An Update on the Urgent Need for Action" (May 2003), on the Internet.

[24]Congressional Record, daily edition, January 29, 1987, p. S 1362. That argument soon lost force: "One might conclude that Congress meant to reduce its stature in 1989 by matching its salary with district judges' salaries, rather than maintain the member-circuit judge match that had been in place off and on since 1965"; Wheeler and Greve, "How to Pay the Piper," p. 8.

[25]Congressional Record, permanent edition, February 7, 1989, p. 1708. et seqq.

[26]"Chief Justice Backs Legislation That Would Raise Judges' Pay," The Wall Street Journal, January 2, 2008, p. A4.

[27]Dwyer, Salaries (Novinka Books), p. 6, note e. Effective August 14, 1991, Congress eliminated the salary difference between Senators and Representatives; P.L 102-90 (August 14, 1991), 105 Stat. at 450; Dwyer, Salaries (Novinka Books), pp.5; 6, note e.

[28]Ethics Reform Act, Public Law 101-194 (November 30, 1989), Section 704, 103 Stat. 1769.   Various other sections of that law gave raises to holders of top jobs in the executive and judicial branches, and changed each chamber's rules about financial disclosure, receipt of gifts and travel expenses paid by outside groups, and certain other money matters, including a limit on retention of unused campaign funds.

[29]Congressional Quarterly Almanac . . . 1989 (Washington: Congressional Quarterly, 1990), pp. 57, 59.

[30]Paul Dwyer, "Salaries of Members of Congress: Current Procedures and Recent Adjustments," Report for Congress, received through the CRS Web, updated February 6, 2003, pp. CRS-4, CRS-11, CRS-26, and [CRS-27] note e. Example: for Representatives the somewhat misnamed Ethics Reform Act, P.L. 101-194 (November 30, 1989), 103 Stat. 1716-83, restored the rejected COLAs of 1989 and 1990 by compounding them to 7.9 percent ($7,070.50) of the previous base salary of $89,500 to produce a new salary of $96,600 (rounded up from $96,570.50) to which was then grafted a 25 percent pay increase of $24,150, producing a newer salary of $120,750, to which was added another COLA of 3.6 percent ($4,347) thus creating a salary of $125,100 (rounded up from $125,097). Combining this law's 25 percent pay hike and the three COLAs, we see that the actual pay increase was $35,600 (39.77 percent).
For Senators, that law restored three rejected COLAs by compounding them to 9.9 percent ($8,860.50) of the previous base salary of $89,500 to produce a new salary of $98,400 (rounded up from $98,360.50). Because that law allowed Senators to continue receipt of honoraria, it provided no other augmentation for them; Dwyer, "Salaries of Members of Congress: Current Procedures and Recent Adjustments, updated February 6, 2003, p. [CRS-27] note e.

[31]During 1990-2008 COLAs were denied for 1994, 1995, 1996, 1997, 1999, and 2007. For 2007 see "Congressional Pay Freeze in Fiscal 2007 Spending Bill," CQ Weekly, February 5, 2007, p. 394.

[32]For the COLA that would have taken effect on January 1, 2010 see the FY 2009 Omnibus Appropriations Act (H.R. 1105, which became Public Law 111-8), Division J, Section 103.
For the COLA that would have occurred in January 2011, see ibid., Congressional Record Index [to the daily edition], Vol. 156, No. VI, April 26 to May 7, 2010, p. H.B. 33, column 3, for legislative history; see also Congressional Record, daily edition, April

22, 2010, p. S2544, for the Senate on that date passing a bill identical to the House measure; but that Senate action is not reflected in the legislative history.

Ida A. Brudnick, "Salaries of Members of Congress: Recent Actions and Historical Tables," September 7, 2011, CRS Report for Congress, p. 3, explains the 2012 denial: "P.L. 111-322, which was enacted on December 22, 2010, prevents any adjustment in GS base pay before December 31, 2012. Since the percent adjustment in Member pay may not exceed the percent adjustment in the base pay of GS employees, Member pay is also frozen during this period. If not limited by GS pay, Members could have received a salary adjustment of 1.3% in January 2012 under the ECI formula."

[33]Dwyer, Salaries (Novinka Books), p. 6, note e; see Janet Hook, "Senate's Ban on Honoraria Marks End of an Era," Congressional Quarterly Weekly Report, July 20, 1991, p. 1955, for the change being in a legislative appropriations bill, and ibid., p. 1956, for Members still being able to charge for speeches but having to make charities the recipients of the payments.

[34]"Congressional Pay Freeze in Fiscal 2007 Spending Bill," CQ Weekly, Feb. 5, 2007, p. 394. That would work as follows: The House Rules Committee would report a rule for the procedure under which the House would consider a bill providing the appropriation for the next COLA. The rule would include a provision preventing an amendment to block the COLA and waiving (prohibiting) points of order that the COLA would violate House Rule XXI, clause 2, which states, "An amendment to a general appropriation bill shall not be in order if changing existing law." Next, upon consideration of the rule by the full House, the "previous question" would be moved, and there would be no debate on the rule if the motion was adopted. Thus, no amendment to block the COLA could be offered. See explanations of this in Dwyer, "Salaries of Members of Congress: Current Procedures and Recent Adjustments," Report for Congress, pp. CRS-17, CRS-19, CRS-20, CRS-22, and CRS-23.

[35]See Congressional Record, daily edition, June 27, 2007, pp. H7277-84.

[36]One of the few media stories was a small item in USA Today: "Congress, justices get cost-of-living raises," January 10, 2008, p. 5A. I didn't even find a January report about it in CQ Weekly, but the House's refusal to block the COLA was dealt with in Jonathan Allen, "House Members Protect Pay Hike," CQ Weekly, July 9, 2007, p. 2033.

[37]Laura Michaelis, "Judge Upholds Hill Pay Raise; Old, New Congresses Benefit," Congressional Quarterly Weekly Report, December 19, 1992, p. 3880. For Sporkin's decision see Boehner v. Anderson, 809 F. Supp. 138 (D.D.C. 1992); an Internet blogger, in "Bad Judges Make Bad Law" (8-23-06) wrote that it tied with one other as the worst decision he had seen in 36 years as a lawyer. For the decision of the D.C. Circuit Court see Boehner v. Anderson, 30 F.3d 156 (D.C. Cir. 1994). See also Adrian Vermeule, "The Constitutional Law of Official Compensation," Columbia Law Review, March 2002, pp. 501-38. The court responses to the 1999 lawsuit (Schaffer v. Clinton) are in 54 F.Supp.2d 1014 (D. Colo. 1999); 240 F.3d 878 (10th Cir. 2001); and 534 U.S. Reports 992 (2001) (certiorari denied).

[38]David Hosansky, "Harried Treasury-Postal Bill Dodges Ban on Pay Raise," Congressional Quarterly Weekly Report, September 20, 1997, p. 2202. But see Congressional Record, permanent edition, September 24, 1997, p. 19972 (daily edition, p. H7766), where Rep. Hoyer claimed the bill had been on the floor for over forty-five minutes; and where Rep. Kolbe said there had been plenty of notice and of time.

[39]Ibid., daily edition, September 24, 1997, pp. H7760-H7769. Dwyer, Salaries of Members of Congress, 1789 (full cite in note 12 above), pp. 21-22, explains what happened: ". . . the House voted to order the previous question on a pending motion to instruct conferees on an issue unrelated to the pay issue. Because the House permits only one motion to instruct conferees, and ordering the previous question precludes amendment to the pending question, this vote in effect foreclosed the possibility of instructing conferees to omit the pay adjustment from the conference report."
For further information about the "previous question" see below in the chapter on the House Committee on Rules.

[40]"Congressional Pay Raise," Congressional Quarterly Weekly Report, December 20, 1997, p. 3117.

[41]Jordy Yager, "With economy in shambles, Congress gets a raise," TheHill.com, December 17, 2008, on the Internet.

[42]Helen Dewar, "Sen. Ford Announces He Will Retire," The Washington Post, March 11, 1997, p. A4.

[43]Peter Egill Brownfeld, "For Most House Freshmen, Salaries Bring Boost in Pay," The Hill, June 23, 1999, p. 1.

[44]National Taxpayers Union, "Sex, Lies and Videotape," 1990, quoted in Peter J. Sepp, "Congressional Perks: How the Trappings of Office Trap Taxpayers," National Taxpayers Union Foundation Policy Paper 131, November 2000; it was Bob Price.

[45]Bill Thomas, Club Fed: Power, Money, Sex, and Violence on Capitol Hill (New York: Charles Scribner's Sons, 1994), p. 100; it was Dan Hamburg, elected in 1992 and defeated for re-election in 1994. See his "Politics and Spirituality: A Personal Journey," on the Internet.

[46]John E. Yang, "They're Underpaid And Overworked—Or So They Say," The Wall Street Journal, January 13, 1988, p. 50.

[47]Bob Benenson, "Muscling Up the Majorities," CQ Weekly, October 27, 2008, pp. 2866, et seqq. (obtained online). Thirty-three Senators' terms expired in January 2009 as the 110th Congress ended (twelve Democrats and twenty-one Republicans).

[48]"Departing Members of the 109th Congress," CQ Weekly, November 13, 2006, p. 3066. (This shortened title of the former Congressional Quarterly Weekly Report became effective with the issue of April 18, 1998.)

[49]"Departures: the 108th Congress," CQ Weekly, November 6, 2004, p. 2629.

[50]"Departing Members of 107th Congress," CQ Weekly, November 9, 2002, p. 2943.

[51]The sixty-five includes those who left to run for other offices.

[52]The 1989 law totally banned Members' personal use of unspent campaign funds as of the start of the 103d Congress in January 1993; see Public Law 101-194, Section 504.
There's a problem with that provision in that it said it was repealing part of Section 313 of the Federal Election Campaign Act of 1971 (P.L. 92-225, which became law on February 7, 1972)—but there was no Section 313 in that 1971 law. Finding the reason for that discrepancy involves tedious work going through amendments to P.L. 92-225, which are listed in Title 2, U.S. Code, Section 439a, 2000 edition. After several amending laws that renumbered some sections and added new sections, P.L. 96-187, Section 113 (which became law on January 8, 1980), amended P.L. 92-225, Section 313, so that anyone not a Member of Congress on the enactment date of P.L. 96-187 was prohibited from converting unused campaign funds to personal use.
Finally, P.L. 101-194, Section 504 (which became law on November 30, 1989), deleted part of Section 313 and added the proviso that Members serving on January 8, 1980, or during earlier Congresses, could only convert to personal use unused campaign money in amounts greater than the "unobligated balance on hand on the date of the enactment of this Act," which turned out to be November 30, 1989.
Members of both House and Senate, however, could still use unspent campaign money for political or charitable contributions; see P.L. 101-194, Section 504, which did not delete that part of Section 313 (of amending law P.L. 96-187, Section 113). See also Charles W. Hucker, "House Members Excused From Campaign Fund Bill," Congressional Quarterly Weekly Report, December 29, 1979, p. 2965, and Congressional Quarterly Almanac . . . 1989, pp. 52, 55.
Congress could improve clarity and understanding by wording bills to read something like "Federal Election Campaign Act of 1971 as amended." P.L. 101-194, Section 504, did include a reference to "2 U.S.C. 439a," which opened the window to the amendments.

[53]In 1989, Representatives Stephen J. Solarz, D-NY, and Dan Rostenkowski, D-IL, had $1.17 million and $1.04 million respectively; "Campaign-Cash Loophole Closed," Congressional Quarterly Almanac . . . 1989, p. 55.

[54]The Ethics Reform Act of 1989 (Public Law 101-194, 103 Stat. 1768-1769).

[55]Eric Felten, The Ruling Class: Inside the Imperial Congress (Washington: Regnery Gateway, 1993), pp. 7-8.

[56]Public Law 93-443 (October 15, 1974), Section 101, 88 Stat. 1263 and 1268, which add Section 616 to Title 18, U.S. Code.

[57]That was done by the Federal Election Campaign Act Amendments of 1976, Section 112, which added new Section 328; P.L. 94-283 (May 11, 1976), 90 Stat. 486 and 494.

[58]Thomas P. Southwick and David Loomis, "Financial Disclosure: New Rules Will Have Impact," Congressional Quarterly Weekly Report, July 23, 1977, pp. 1507-08.

[59]Irwin B. Arieff, "Congress Votes Itself New Income Tax Break, Doubles House Outside Income Limit," Congressional Quarterly Weekly Report, December 19, 1981, p. 2480.

[60]Done by Public Law 94-283; "Honoraria Limit Takes Effect Jan. 1," Congressional Quarterly Weekly Report, December 4, 1982, p. 2961.

[61]Arieff, "Congress Votes Itself New Income Tax Break," p. 2480. To give the House due credit for an improvement, its 15 percent limit had gone into effect in January 1979.

[62]"House Reverses Itself on Outside Income Lid," Congressional Quarterly Weekly Report, April 26, 1986, p. 914. Congressional Record, permanent edition, April 22, 1986, p. 8328.

[63]"House Reverses Itself on Outside Income Lid," p. 914. Congressional Record, permanent edition, April 23, 1986, pp. 8442-43, 8474-75.

[64]This was done by the Ethics Reform Act of 1989 (Public Law 101-194) .

[65]The postponement of the fifteen percent limit, to January 1983, was in early 1979; see Congressional Record, permanent edition, March 8, 1979, p. 4314 (Senate); Irwin B. Arieff, "House Turns Back Effort To Loosen Its Restrictions On Outside Earned Income," Congressional Quarterly Weekly Report, October 31, 1981, p. 2126; and "Senate Income Limit," Congressional Quarterly Almanac . . . 1979 (Washington: Congressional Quarterly, 1980), pp. 578-80. That left in place the $25,000 limit, but in October 1981 it was repealed; House Joint Resolution 325 (Oct. 1, 1981); Irwin B. Arieff, "Congress Votes Itself New Pay Benefits," Congressional Quarterly Weekly Report, October 3, 1981, p. 1892; Arieff, "House Turns Back," p. 2126. That left in place the prospective fifteen percent limit scheduled to take effect on January 1, 1983; "Honoraria Limit Takes Effect Jan. 1," Congressional Quarterly Weekly Report, December 4, 1982, p. 2961. However, in late 1982, Senate Resolution 512, effective on January 1, 1983, repealed the fifteen percent limit that had resided in Senate Rule XXXVI (Congressional Record, permanent edition, December 14, 1982, pp. 30641-43; Andy Plattner, "House, Senate Again at Odds Over Limits on Pay Increases," Congressional Quarterly Weekly Report, Dec. 18, 1982, pp. 3049-50); that left Senatorial honoraria temporarily unlimited.

[66]They could retain honoraria up to 30 percent of salary (effective January 1, 1984 [Public Law, 98-63] until late 1985), 40 percent (effective in 1985), and 27 percent (effective in 1990). For the 30 percent limit see Judy Sarasohn, "Senate Backs Salary Increase, Delays Speech Income Limit," Congressional Quarterly Weekly Report, June 18, 1983, pp. 1201-02, and Steven Pressman, "Detailed Listing of Senators' 1982 Finances," ibid., December 3, 1983, p. 2563. For the 40 percent limit see Nadine Cohodas, "$368.2 Billion Omnibus Spending Bill Cleared," Congressional Quarterly Weekly Report, December 21, 1985, pp. 2665-68. For the 27 percent limit see Congressional Quarterly Almanac . . . 1989, p 52.

[67]In what amounted to an amendment to 1989's Ethics Reform Act, the legislative appropriation implemented the change. See Janet Hook, "Senate's Ban on Honoraria Marks End of an Era," Congressional Quarterly Weekly Report, July 20, 1991, pp. 1955-56; Phil Kuntz, "Byrd's One-Month Juggernaut Won Grudging Votes on Pay," ibid., pp. 1957-61.

[68]Bill Whalen, "With a Salary Study Comes the Honorarium Furor Again," Insight, December 19, 1988, p. 22.

[69]Ibid.

[70]Eleanor Clift, "It's Back! The Return of the Pay Raise," Newsweek, July 3, 1989, p. 22.

[71]Arieff, "Congress Votes Itself New Income Tax Break," p. 2480.

[72]"Proxmire blasts 'outrageous' tax," Billings Gazette, January 18, 1982, p. 6A.

[73]Leonard M. Apcar, "By Letter and Song, Voters Hit Tax Gift Congress Gave Itself," The Wall Street Journal, May 11, 1982, pp. 1, 20.

[74]"Compromise 'Urgent' Funding Bill Cleared," Congressional Quarterly Weekly Report, July 17, 1982, p. 1700; Andy Plattner, "Pay Raise Decision Facing Congress Again," Congressional Quarterly Weekly Report, December 4, 1982, pp. 2959; [No author], "Members' Pay: $6 a Day to $60,662 a Year," ibid., p. 2960; "Proxmire Seeks Repeal Of Congress Tax Break, The New York Times, January 18, 1982, p. B6; "House Votes Plan to Repeal Its $75-a-Day Tax Deduction," The New York Times, June 10, 1982, p. B8. For a history of this, see John R. Hibbing, "Washington on 75 Dollars a Day: Members of Congress Voting on Their Own Tax Break," Legislative Studies Quarterly, May 1983, pp. 219-30. "Members could deduct even more than $75 per day if they were able to provide the Internal Revenue Service with supporting documentation"; ibid., p. 221.

[75]See Section 704, P.L. 101-194, November 30, 1989 (the Ethics Reform Act).

[76]Statement by Rep. Vic Fazio, D-CA, <u>Congressional Record</u>, daily edition, September 24, 1997, p. H7765; ibid., permanent edition, p. 19972..

XXIII. Lavish Pensions

EPIGRAPH: Pension never enriched a young man.
                        ---George Herbert, Jacula Prudentum [1651], Number 515.

Pensions for Members are closely related to their salaries and are another example of patricians ensuring their undemocratic separation from the masses. Five years of Congressional service qualify a former Member for a pension at age 62 regardless of age at end of Congressional service. Twenty years of service and age 50 also produce a pension. There's a plethora of other Congressional pension situations.[1]

Congress first attempted pensions for its Members by a law passed in 1942, but hostile public reaction led to its repeal only two months later. Pensions became permanent with a 1946 law that allowed Members the option of joining the existing Civil Service Retirement System but with larger contributions and benefits than other recipients. Their advent was one more indication of how careerist attitudes had departed from the Framers' idea that service in Congress would be a temporary interruption of a different vocation. A 1946 Senate report saw Congressional pensions differently: Paid retirements "would contribute to independence of thought and action, [be] an inducement for retirement for those of retiring age or with other infirmities, [and] bring into the legislative service a larger number of younger Members with fresh energy and new viewpoints concerning the economic, social, and political problems of the Nation."[2]

The Congressional pension system is complex, with some Members qualifying under one program, others under another, some under both, and with options that may lead to different payouts for Members with the same years of service. Perhaps the best easily accessible source for information on this topic is CRS Report for Congress, "Retirement Benefits for Members of Congress," by Katelin P. Isaacs, January 7, 2011. The most basic calculation, and the one that applies to most Members, is that benefits are figured as 2.5% of the average of a Member's three highest years of salary multiplied by the number of years served in Congress.[3] Because pension amounts are tied to salaries, every pay increase for Members produces a pension increase for subsequent retirees.

A further benefit, not usually available in private pensions, is that Congressional pensions are indexed for inflation.[4]

The complexities of the system and the secrecy surrounding pension amounts for individual beneficiaries are such that when reports of a former Member's pension are mentioned by the media or even by watchdog groups such as the National Taxpayers Union, the annual pension figure is often accompanied by words like "estimated" or "about." But shouldn't the amounts that taxpayers are doling out to former lawmakers be public information? What privacy right trumps the right of the people to know about those expenditures? Here's a possible answer: Members of Congress, ever worried about public perceptions of the extravagant perks they have created for themselves, favor this concealment so that public outrage will not reduce their own future pension benefits.

Nevertheless, the following figures, while perhaps not exactly applicable to any one individual, give a reasonable approximation.

Thus, to take a mid-level example, a three-term Senator retiring at the end of 2006 would get an annual pension starting at $72,810 and increasing every year.[5] That was about 51 percent higher than annual US median household income of $48,201 in 2006. (The median household income was barely higher in 2011 at $49,900).

In the extreme, Robert Byrd of West Virginia, a Member of Congress since January 3, 1953, would get, prior to a salary increase as President Pro Tempore of the Senate in January 2007, a pension of $214,385 per year—if only the most basic calculation is used, but the actual amount may be somewhat different. This figure, however, gives at least a general idea of what the system can produce in a non-standard case.

The first former Member to receive over $1,000,000 in cumulative Congressional pension was Margaret Chase Smith, R-ME, who reached that height in May 1988. Her annual benefit then was about $80,715 even though her highest Congressional salary was $42,500.[6]

If you're not a corporate bigwig, good luck finding such gold-plated retirement benefits for yourself.

Sadly, former Members of Congress in prison for acts committed in office (other than espionage, treason, and other offenses against national security) still got their pensions while doing time—until Congress bowed to adverse public reaction in early 2007 and changed the law. Now, Members who violate several anti-corruption parts of federal law while serving in Congress will not receive any Congressional pension.[7] It's also sad that our federal lawmakers were so ethically blind that they didn't take such action until public outcry made it seem politically advantageous. At least this is evidence of a curative emphasized often in this book: Public pressure can make Congress do what it should have done anyway.

But because the Constitution ostensibly bans ex post facto laws,[8] a convict such as former Representative Randy Cunningham continues receiving a yearly sum that exceeds the median U.S. household income.

CORRECTIVE SOLUTIONS

Eliminate the secrecy cloaking the precise pension amounts received by former Members. As former <u>public</u> servants, so-called, their payouts from the <u>public</u> purse should be <u>public</u> knowledge. Because everything about their pensions, except the individual amounts, depends on things public, the privacy right they claim should fail to apply. And we know, don't we, why they claim privacy about this? It's surely because they don't want to put their lavish retirement money at risk of being scaled back because of the people's outrage.

Increase the number of Congressional service years required for pension qualification. Five years in Congress should not provide a pension at age 62—or at any age. And should a former Member get retirement pay as early as age 50?

Reduce the pension amounts. The argument against this is that Members of Congress get a greater amount per year of service than most other federal retirees "because of the uncertain tenure of congressional service." People may argue about the validity of that reasoning.

Notes: Chapter XXIII. Lavish Pensions

[1]For them see Katelin P. Issacs, "Retirement Benefits for Members of Congress," CRS Report for Congress, January 7, 2011. This is a continuation of earlier editions by Patrick J. Purcell. See his "Retirement Benefits for Members of Congress," CRS Report for Congress, February 9, 2007; another edition was produced in 2008.

[2]Purcell, p. [CRS-1].

[3]Ibid., pp. CRS-7 & CRS-8.

[4]Ibid., p. CRS-11.

[5]That amount results from $158,000 (salary effective on Jan. 1, 2004) plus $162,100 (salary effective on Jan. 1, 2005) plus $165,200 (salary effective on Jan. 1, 2006), which yields an average of $161,800 (rounded up to the nearest hundred), multiplied by 18 years of service, which totals $2,912,400, multiplied by .025, which equals $72,810.

[6]Glenn Simpson, "Pension Plan Makes First Millionaire," <u>Insight</u>, October 3, 1988, p. 27.

[7]Jack Maskell, Memorandum: "Lobbying and Ethics Rules Changes in the 110th Congress," Congressional Research Service, September 24, 2007, pp. CRS-14-15, available on the Internet. Felonious Members subject to the 2007 change can retrieve their own contributions to the retirement system; ibid., p. CRS-15.

[8]Despite the clear Constitutional language, court-created change applies the ban only to criminal laws. That's how an ex post facto law can raise your taxes for times before the law was enacted. See Steve Selinger, "The Case Against Civil Ex Post Facto Laws," The Cato Journal, Vol. 15, Nos. 2-3 (Fall/Winter 1995/96), seventeen pages on the Internet.

XXIV. Gerrymanders: Beastly House Districts

EPIGRAPH: There's a new pinnacle in formless, shapeless art. For ingenuity, it
                 rivals the fascinating intertwined drips of Pollock, the extraordinary
                 slashes of Franz Kline, the splashed stains of Helen Frankenthaler,
                 the drifting masses of Mark Rothko. It's the accomplishment of
                 brilliant circumscribers of the democratic process who design new
                 congressional districts after every decade's new census. Their
                 gerrymandering art, though, should be judged by the courts."
                        ---Malcolm Forbes (1983), quoted in Forbes,
                            September 1, 2008, p. 120.

EPIGRAPH: Out of good still to find means of evil.
                        ---John Milton, Paradise Lost, Book 1, line 165.

Shown on the next page is House District 18 in Texas in the 1990s. Responding to such
twisted creations, The Wall Street Journal wrote that "American democracy is being
drawn and quartered" and that "the politicians win, and the voters lose."[1] That district's
boundaries are an extreme example, but numerous other House districts then and now
show disdain for compactness and sensible democracy. They have been
"gerrymandered."

A gerrymander is any electoral district with boundaries drawn to give an electoral
advantage to a particular political party, candidate, or group. The term was created in
1812 when a person noted that Governor Elbridge Gerry's party had devised a district in
Massachusetts that looked like a salamander and someone else retorted that it was a
"Gerrymander." (The hard-g, as in "guns," correct for Gerry's name, has been
superseded for "gerrymanders" by a soft-g, as in the pronunciation of words such as
"jams.") Such electoral beasts concentrate like-minded voters together to produce a
desired result.[2]

As has been well said, "With gerrymandering, the voters don't choose their politicians—
the politicians choose their voters."[3] After the 1990 census, one architect of districts said
he could have more impact on elections than campaigns, candidates, or voters.[4]

****
****

U.S. HOUSE DISTRICT 18 IN TEXAS IN THE 1990s

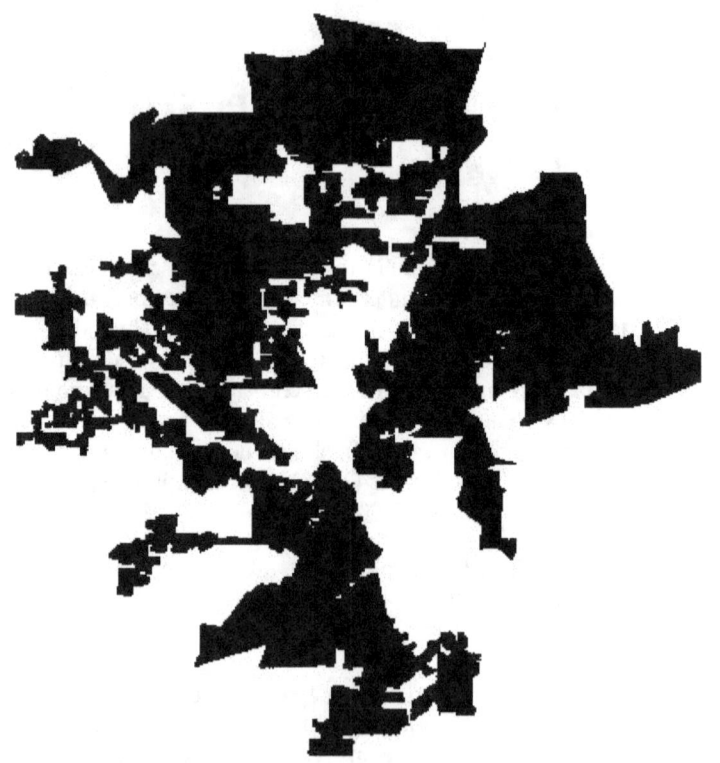

Source: Bush v. Vera, 517 U.S. 952 (1996) at p. 987.

Some small illustrations of large areas are not completely accurate because they cannot show tiny separations among parts of the large area. That's the case here. But the district's outline is sufficient for presenting the anti-democracy results of such grotesque creations. For full details of the 1990s districts see Bureau of the Census, Congressional District Atlas, 103rd Congress of the United States (2 vols.; Washington: USGPO, 1993); SuDoc number: C3.62/5:103.

****
****

The illustrated district was a more extreme Rorschach-like ink blot than most House districts. And some of the more bizarre creations of the 1990s were later eliminated, but many survived or were newly created after the 2000 and 2010 censuses.[5]

More recently, the editor of Forbes magazine explained, "The public be damned; the objective is to create safe districts that guarantee lifetime jobs to incumbents. Gerrymandering has made congressional elections into a farce in which only one district in seven is competitive. Democracy? Even a politician in Zimbabwe would be embarrassed to call it that."[6]

In some districts sizable bodies of water and even land separate disconnected parts. New York had several after the 2000 Census, such as District 8, where the lower Manhattan section was about three and one-half miles from the closest part of the section in Brooklyn, and with one of the four separated regions of District 12 and part of the Atlantic Ocean intervening. As one report says, "District boundaries are [sometimes] drawn to connect distant disjoint [sic] areas with thin strips of land running through unpopulated areas such as industrial parks and cemeteries, down highways and railroad tracks, and through bodies of water such as rivers, lakes, and the ocean."[7]

Supreme Court decisions have established the "districting principles" of compactness, contiguity, respect for political subdivisions, and respect for "communities defined by actual shared interests."[8]

District compactness is an amorphous concept. Neither courts nor commentators have agreed on how to define it or on how much deviation from perfect closeness is acceptable. Even the concept of "functional compactness" has intruded, replacing any notion of shape with the more recent notion of community of interest.[9] Although compactness is undefined, anyone exercising common sense should be able to see when a district is not compact and amounts to political pornography. It's like the problem of defining sexual pornography when Supreme Court Justice Potter Stewart said, "I know it when I see it."[10]

Contiguity means that no part of a district is physically separated from another. A person might think that contiguity is violated if two land areas in single district are separated by several miles of water, but courts have held that bodies of water are equal to land areas in determining contiguity.[11]

Respect for political subdivisions is also problematical. Which subdivisions are to be respected? Counties? Cities? Townships? Special improvement districts? School districts? Precincts? If they can be split, how much splitting is permissible?

Communities of interest can be identified in myriad ways permitting disputation and conflict. They can be whatever a biased decider wants them to be. As a federal district court concluded in 1996, their "cohesiveness may arise . . . [from] numerous sources, both manifest and obscure, that include geography, . . . history, tradition, religion, race, ethnicity, economics, and every [other] conceivable combination of chance, circumstance, time and place."[12] The subjectivity shrouding this concept has generated so many different guideposts from the courts that people charged with creating districts are scarcely led from this "political thicket" to a common destination.

And, finally, which criterion deserves primacy when adherence to one of the four may cause conflict with another, as when a community of interest is so dispersed as to lie in different political subdivisions and not be compact?

Gerrymanders of U.S. House districts have usually been perpetrated by state legislatures. Sometimes, however, they have been done by federal judges or ostensibly "nonpartisan" commissions. In California, with no U.S. House races deemed competitive in recent elections, the redistricting after the 2000 Census was the handiwork of Michael Berman, brother of Howard Berman, a Democratic member of the U.S. House for over two decades.[13]

Many House districts are redrawn every ten years because of population data generated by the decennial U.S. censuses. And there was some gerrymandering in the 1800s and most of the 1900s. But the extremes of the districts shown above became much more common after the 1990 census because computers allowed crafty politicians to more easily identify voting patterns by blocks and even houses and then use that information to "kidnap" certain types of voters from an old district and pack them into a new one. That process is sometimes used to create a constituency rich with voters of one party and thus ensure the election of that party's candidate.[14] Other times it is used to take voters of an incumbent's party away from him or her and divide them among several districts so that the incumbent has little chance of winning re-election. Or it may be used to lump several incumbents into a smaller number of districts, thus getting rid of some of them, as when a Republican gerrymander in 2001 forced six Michigan Democrats into three new House districts.[15]

And, of course, the gerrymandering of one district necessarily twists and distorts nearby districts. A district such as the illustrated number 18 in Texas contorts those nearby.

Some of what looked like partisan gerrymandering occurred because the Supreme Court mandated in 1964's Wesberry v. Sanders the achievement of "one person, one vote" by outlawing extremes of population variation among districts. The case arose in Georgia, where the redistricting after the 1960 Census had the 5th District (Atlanta) with 823,680 people, while the neighboring 9th District had only 272,154.[16] At the same time, the greatest intrastate disparity in the nation was in Texas, where the 4th District, a "rotten borough" maintained for the benefit of longtime Speaker of the House Sam Rayburn, had 213,374 residents, and the next-door district (Dallas) was the nation's largest at 951,527.[17] The redistricting required by Wesberry often resulted in less populous big-city districts and more populous rural ones.

Some people will argue that what appears to be gerrymandering is merely legitimate compliance with the Voting Rights Act of 1965 and its later amendments and Justice Department interpretations, which mandated that minority voters, first blacks but later Hispanics, be accorded the right to elect candidates who represent their interests.[18] And, while that view is correct to some extent, that does not mean that mere political gerrymandering has somehow vanished. It is alive and robust.[19]

Its strength was shown in 2003 when new Republican majorities in the Texas legislature sought to abolish the Congressional House districts created after the 2000 census and create new ones favoring Republicans. First, 51 Democratic members of the Texas House fled to Ardmore, Oklahoma, in May to prevent passage of the Republican plan by denying the House the quorum necessary to conduct business. That action temporarily stopped the Republican effort; but when the legislature met in special sessions called by the GOP governor, eleven Democratic members of the state Senate decamped to Albuquerque, NM, in another quorum-busting effort. After several weeks, one of the runaways returned, thus providing a quorum during the third special session. The remaining truants then came back, and the Republican redistricting was passed and signed by the governor. Result: Four incumbent Democrats were defeated in 2004, and Texas's U.S. House delegation, which had been 17-15 in favor of Democrats, became a 21-15 Republican majority.[20]

Another mid-decade reconfiguration occurred in Georgia in March 2005 when the Republicans were newly in control of both houses of the legislature and got rid of the boundaries gerrymandered by Democrats. The impartial publication CQ Weekly analyzed the changes as not likely to increase the GOP's 7-6 majority of House Members but as making the GOP districts more likely to elect Republicans.[21]

Compliance with the requirements of the 1965 Voting Rights Act as amended in 1982 so that Rorschach districts are created violates the earlier tradition that districts be compact, but that was never a legal requirement for U.S. House districts. Race-based districts, i.e. minority-interest districts, need not be compact, but some observers argue a negative result, that such constituencies encourage racial polarization and "reduce the incentive for politicians to form coalitions by reaching across racial lines."[22]

After passage of the original Voting Rights Act in 1965, activists in and out of government saw "that simply removing formal barriers to registration and voting would not, by itself, realize the civil rights movement's broader goals of electing impartial and responsive officials, dismantling racial oppression, and establishing a progressive politics. . . . Accordingly, the 'second generation' of voting rights activity addressed the problem of racial vote dilution rather than outright disenfranchisement. . . . The standard remedy for this dilution through submergence [the inclusion of black voters in districts dominated by whites] has been the creation of one or more majority-black districts."[23] Thus, the Voting Rights Act as amended in 1982 was construed by activists in and out of government as requiring that certain racial and ethnic groups (blacks and, later, Hispanics) be given House districts virtually guaranteed to elect members of those minorities.

One result of such "minority-majority" districts was shapes that defied compactness and common sense, such as North Carolina's Congressional District 12, created after the 1990 census. It was the ultimate in skinnyness.[24]

A secondary result was numerous legal challenges and court decisions invalidating some districts and allowing others to stand.[25]

Although federal district boundaries are set at the state level, state legislative leaders usually follow the wishes of the state's senior members of the U.S. House.[26] Representatives and their stooges in state legislatures have gamed redistricting so outrageously that most House members face little or no opposition in the general elections. Primaries can be more threatening to them. It may be a matter of opinion on whether a House race is a real contest, but a standard measure is that an election was competitive if the winner got less than fifty-five percent of the vote.[27]

Reports indicate a declining trend for real competition in House contests—except when unusual circumstances intrude, as in 2006, 2008, and 2010.   One reckoning says the "the average number of competitive races from 1982 through 2000 was seventy-two," i.e., between sixteen and seventeen percent.[28] The elections of 2000, 2002, and 2004 reflected reduced competition. In 2000, 12.87 percent were competitive; 10.57 percent in 2002, and 7.35 percent in 2004.[29] In 2000 only six incumbents lost in the general election; in 2002 only eight Representatives failed in the general, and only seven in 2004.[30]

In early September 2006 it looked like about 46 of 435 House races would be competitive in November[31]—until Representative Mark Foley was exposed in late September as a homosexual who sent sexually inappropriate emails to House pages. Foley immediately resigned from his safe seat, but his dalliances tainted Republicans in general as well as House leaders suspected of not acting on early Foley knowledge. Suddenly, more safe seats were in play. As voter dissatisfaction mounted because of Foley and other Republican errors it became more difficult to be accurate about the number of competitive House races. Several open seats formerly held by Republicans began to look safe for Democrats. It was hardly reasonable to list those races as competitive. And some formerly safe Republican incumbents looked ready to get the boot.[32]

The November 2006 election results showed an increase to 15.6 percent in competitive House races (sixty-eight seats) and wiped out twenty-two Republican incumbents, thus giving the Democrats control of the House (and they also won control of the Senate).[33]

By mid-to-late summer 2008 it looked like about fourteen percent of House races (sixty-one or so), including those for open seats, would be competitive.[34] Estimates varied, of course, and some people saw approximately seventy-five real contests.[35]   The election results, again disastrous for Republicans, showed that fifty-eight House winners (13.3 percent) got less than fifty-five percent of the vote.[36]

The House was designed by the Founders to be closer to the people than the Senate; it was to be the mirror that most quickly and accurately reflected alterations of voters' desires. But the semi-permanent aristocracy of incumbents need not be responsive to the general will; those grandees are more likely to heed the party extremists who dominate voting in primaries. And as more and more Americans have realized that it's pointless to vote in an election already decided by the primary and by gerrymandering, larger numbers of those disfranchised millions simply don't vote.

It's not democracy when so few House elections are competitive. Despite the aberrational results of the 2006 elections, the vast majority of incumbents seeking re-election were successful—95 percent of them. Fair elections are essential and indispensable for a representative democracy, but we don't have them in many districts because of gerrymandering.

CORRECTIVE SOLUTIONS

A new Voting Rights Act is needed to replace the one enacted in 1965 and amended later, which seeks to ensure the opportunity for one racial minority and several language minorities to elect people of their choice.[37] With the U.S. being the diverse society that it is, are those really the only minorities deserving consideration? What about economic minorities, ideological minorities, policy minorities, political party minorities, educational minorities, religious minorities, and ethnic minorities not distinguishable by race or language? As one minority is advantaged another may be disadvantaged. And the effort to ensure the election of representatives of specified minorities, with the district boundary contortions thus required, keeps the door open for gerrymandering in general, keeps alive the principle of boundary manipulation for nefarious purposes, such as the protection of incumbents. One surely unacceptable result of gerrymandering is the current situation which makes the great majority of U.S. House seats electorally non-competitive.

Therefore, it's at least arguable that a new Voting Rights Act should abandon the Balkanization inherent in the current law and should require a general and specific adherence to compactness and contiguity. The idea that House district boundaries ought to respect political subdivisions should be abandoned, because the lines defining those subdivisions often change, and because, as mentioned above, it's unclear which subdivisions deserve respect—indeed we already have the precedent in the monstrosities of recent years that often ignored subdivision borders. Further, "respect [for] the geographical integrity of any city, county, and region boundary . . . gives politicians too much flexibility to manipulate district boundaries by selectively following odd-shaped city, county, and region boundary lines."[38]

I'm suggesting that we at least consider rejecting the current guarantee of U.S. House seats to certain minorities—while ignoring others. "So long as the group-specific goals of the VRA remain . . . the American voting rights dialogue will remain unresolved."[39] In adopting compact and contiguous districts we can allow the electoral chips to fall where they may. That would be more in accord with democracy than the present system that identifies some minorities as more deserving than others.

Could that be accomplished with a new Voting Rights Act? If we look at the possibility of districts that don't continue the present advantage enjoyed by incumbents, we might doubt that those very incumbents would favor the change. Sufficient public pressure however, might bring the improbable to realization. And no Constitutional provision prohibits the reform, because Article I, Section 4, says that the "times, places and manner of holding elections for Senators and Representatives shall be prescribed in each State by the legislature thereof; but the Congress may at any time by law make or alter such regulations, except as to the places of choosing Senators." Nevertheless, a Constitutional amendment might be desirable to give permanence to the change and thus prevent self-serving solons from fiddling with it.

Who would construct the new districts? As has been famously said, "Ah, therein lies the rub." Finding people who would do the work in a non-partisan, non-incumbent, impartial manner is difficult. Some states create commissions to do the work. My own state of Montana created a commission in 1999 to revise the legislature's senate and house districts, but the supposedly non-partisan commission got a Democratic majority when its appointed chair became a person with a background in the Democratic party,[40] and the result was districting that favored Democrats.[41]

The suggestion that commissions be composed of retired federal judges has merit. Judges, however, whether retired or not, can be partial, as with a "Democrat-friendly map that was implemented by a panel of judges" in one state.[42]

One scholar offered this:
> "The only way to prevent gerrymandering is to create an effective system of rules and constraints, and possibly a computer program that automates an objective mathematical algorithm, to draw fair unbiased election district maps. Ideally, control of the redistricting process will be taken away from incumbent politicians. They have a conflict of interest, and historically, they have severely abused the redistricting process to promote fraud and corruption. In a bipartisan gerrymander, the incumbents of all parties cooperate and collaborate to give themselves safe, noncompetitive election districts.
>
> As a minimum, any proposed redistricting map should be validated, ranked, and either accepted or rejected by a computer program using various compact-ness and fairness metrics computed for each election district and for the entire collection of districts. The best of multiple proposed district maps should be selected based on which has the best values for these metrics.[43]

And while the American people are at it, they might include provisions about voter identification to prevent the fraud that sometimes occurs now.

Notes: Chapter XXIV. Gerrymanders – Beastly House Districts

[1]"Monster Map," The Wall Street Journal, October 18, 1991, p. A14; the map published there is incomplete; the complete map reproduced in this chapter is from Bush v. Vera, 517 U.S. 952 (1996) at 987. Several other mind-blowing monstrosities are in ibid., pp. 988-89, 1042-44.

[2]The complete bestiary can be seen in Deirdre A. Gaquin and Katherine A. DeBrandt, The 109th Congressional District Atlas (Lanham, MD: Bernan Press, 2005; or U.S., Bureau of the Census, Congressional District Atlas: 109th Congress of the United States (Washington: U.S. Department of Commerce, Bureau of the Census, 2005), CD-ROM, Superintendent of Documents Number C3.282/5:109; or entering Printable Maps – Congressional Districts on the Internet brings up maps of the House districts of the 110th Congress, from nationalatlas.gov.

[3]This saying is so common it can be found in numerous places. One is Michael D. Robbins, "Gerrymander and the Need for Redistricting Reform," revised version, July 25, 2006, p. 4 of 71, on the Internet.

[4]Juliet Eilperin, "The Gerrymander That Ate America," Slate Magazine, April 17, 2006, on Lexis-Nexis, adapted from Juliet Eilperin, Fight Club Politics: How Partisanship Is Poisoning the House of Representatives (Lanham, MD: Rowman & Littlefield, 2006). For a good explanation of theory and practice about the distribution of the 435 House seats among the states see Carl Bialik, "Bad Math = Mad Politics," The Wall Street Journal, April 25, 2008, p. A10.

[5]See examples such as Georgia Districts 8 and 13, Illinois Districts 4 and 17, Maryland Districts 2 and 3, North Carolina District 12, Pennsylvania Districts 6, 12, and 18, and Tennessee District 7 in Deirdre A. Gaquin and Katherine A. DeBrandt, The 109th Congressional District Atlas (Lanham, MD: Bernan Press, 2005); or U.S. Bureau of the Census, Congressional District Atlas: 109th Congress of the United States (Washington: U.S., Dept. of Commerce, Bureau of the Census, 2005), CD-ROM, Supt. of Doc. Number C3.282/5:109. An Internet source is Printable Maps–Congressional Districts from nationalatlas.gov.

[5]William Baldwin, "DIY Democracy," Forbes, September 1, 2008, p. 16. "DIY" seems to refer to Do It Yourself.

[7]Robbins, "Gerrymander and the Need for Redistricting Reform," revised version, July 25, 2006, p. 2 of 71. For an example of a district with "skinny" parts see North Carolina district 12 in the 1990s (illustration in Miller v. Johnson, 515 U.S. 900 (1995) following p. 949.

[8]See Shaw v. Reno, 509 U.S. 630 (1993), and Miller v. Johnson, 515 U.S. 900 (1995); the quotation is from the latter (pp. 901, 916).

[9]See Richard L. Engstrom, "The Political Thicket, Electoral Reform, and Minority Voting Rights," in Fair and Effective Representation? Debating Electoral Reform and Minority Rights, edited by Mark E. Rush and Richard L. Engstrom, (Lanham, MD: Rowman & Littlefield, 2001), pp. 22-24.

[10]Stewart used this now-famous line in a different context in Jacobellis v. Ohio, 378 U.S. 184 (1964) at 197.

[11]Engstrom, "The Political Thicket," pp. 20-22.

[12] Engstrom, "The Political Thicket," p. 26; this source imperfectly quotes Scott v. United States Department of Justice, 920 F.Supp. 1248 (1996), at p. 1254, as indicated by my brackets.

[13]Jackie Calmes, "California's Slim Congressional Pickings," The Wall Street Journal, September 20, 2006, p. A6.

[14]"A classic example of incumbent-protection redistricting came in Virginia in 2002. Republican congressman Frank Wolf's district bordered on the district of Democrat Jim Moran. The state legislature redrew the lines, giving Wolf some of Moran's Republican and Moran some of Wolf's Democrats—leaving both candidates safer. This goes on all over the country"; Laura Ingraham, Power to the People (Washington: Regnery Publishing, 2007), p. 115.

[15]"The Gerrymander Scandal," The Wall Street Journal, November 7, 2001, p. A22.

[16]Andrew Hacker, Congressional Districting: The Issue of Equal Representation, (Washington: Brookings Institution, 1963), p. 117, and "Congressional District Dataset" on the Internet. Wesberry et al. v. Sanders, Governor of Georgia, 376 U.S. 1 (1964).

[17]"Seeking the Mantle," Time, January 5, 1962, p. 15, and "Congressional District Dataset" on the Internet.

[18]See "Birth of a Gerrymander," The Weekly Standard, February 20, 2006, pp. 14-16. An issue that will not be addressed in this book is whether black interests are better represented by a white Representative who votes "black," i.e. Democratic, or a black person who votes Republican.

[19]For this problem see Charles Backstrom, Samuel Krislov, and Leonard Robins, "Desperately Seeking Standards: The Court's Frustrating Attempts to Limit Political Gerrymandering," PS: Political Science and Politics, July 2006, pp. 409-15.

[20]See Steve Bickerstaff, Lines in the Sand: Congressional Redistricting in Texas and the Downfall of Tom DeLay (Austin: University of Texas Press, 2007); League of United Latin American Citizens et al. v. Perry, Governor of Texas et al., 548 U.S. 399 (2006); Gregory L. Giroux, "Texas Completes Unusual Redistricting and Readies for GOP Stampede Next Year," CQ Weekly, October 11, 2003, p. 2502; Jeffrey Toobin, "Drawing the Line: Will Tom DeLay's redistricting in Texas cost him his seat?" The New Yorker, March 6, 2006, pp. 32-37; Jeffrey Toobin, "The Great Election Grab: When does gerrymandering become a threat to democracy?" The New Yorker, December 8, 2003, pp. 63-80.

[21]Gregory L. Giroux, "Georgia Republicans Clear State Remap: Redrawn districts lock in GOP seat, weaken Democratic odds," CQ Weekly, March 28, 2005, p. 792.

[22]George Will, "The Voting Rights Act at 30," Newsweek, July 10, 1995, p. 64. The Wall Street Journal, April 2, 1992, p. A14, headlined such districts as "America's 'Segremanders.'"

[23]Pamela S. Karlan, "The Impact of the Voting Rights Act on African Americans: Second- and Third-Generation Issues," in Voting Rights and Redistricting in the United States, Mark E. Rush, ed. (Westport, CT: Greenwood Press, 1998), p. 122.

[24]It's illustrated in Miller v. Johnson, 515 U.S. 900 (1995) following p. 949.

[25]Among the voluminous literature on that see David T. Canon, Race, Redistricting, and Representation: The Unintended Consequences of Black Majority Districts (Chicago: University of Chicago Press, 1999); Gary W. Cox and Jonathan N. Katz, Elbridge Gerry's Salamander: The Electoral Consequences of the Reapportionment Revolution (Cambridge, England, and New York: Cambridge University Press, 2002); Mark Monmonier, Bushmanders & Bullwinkles (Chicago: University of Chicago Press, 2001); several contributions in Mark E. Rush, editor, Voting Rights and Redistricting in the United States ; Will, "The Voting Rights Act at 30," p. 64; and several of the sources cited in other footnotes in this chapter.

[26]Calmes, "California's Slim Congressional Pickings," p. A6.

[27]On fifty-five percent as the generally accepted dividing line between competitive and non-competitive races see sources such as "No Contest," The Wall Street Journal, November 12, 2004, p. A12; and "True Competition a Rarity in House Races," CQ Weekly, November 9, 2002, p. 2936. The fifty-five percent dividing line is usually meant to show competition between the winner and his or her main opponent; that, however, may not be the case when there are three or more strong candidates seeking one seat, and the principal competition involves the eventual losers, as seems to have happened in Minnesota's 4th district in 2000, where the winner got 48.0 percent, defeating candidates with 30.9 percent, 20.6 percent, and 5 percent; and it's also been misleading in several elections in Louisiana, where the requirement that the winner get an absolute majority sometimes attracts multiple office seekers.

[28]Gary C. Jacobson, "Modern Campaigns and Representation," in The Legislative Branch, edited by Paul J. Quirk and Sarah A. Binder (New York: Oxford University Press, 2005), pp. 112; 143, n. 7.

[29]I calculated the 12.87 percent getting less than 55 percent of the vote in 2000 from "Senate, House, Gubernatorial Results," CQ Weekly, November 11, 2000, pp. 2694-2703. For 2002, I figured the 10.57 percent getting less than 55 percent from "True

Competition a Rarity in House Races," CQ Weekly, November 9, 2002, p. 2936; see also CQ Almanac Plus 2002 (Washington: Congressional Quarterly, 2003), pp. F-3 through F-12. For 2004, I computed the 7.35 percent as getting less than 55 percent from "Senate, House & Gubernatorial Results," CQ Weekly, November 6, 2004, pp. 2653-60; CQ Almanac Plus 2004 (Washington: Congressional Quarterly, 2005), pp. 18-25 through 18-34.

[30]Looking at "Senate, House, Gubernatorial Results," CQ Weekly, November 11, 2000, pp. 2694-2703, and biographical information on the Internet, it appears that seven incumbents lost in the general election and that two lost in primaries. Numbers cited elsewhere differ; e.g., Gary C. Jacobson, "A House and Senate Divided: The Clinton Legacy and the Congressional Elections of 2000," Political Science Quarterly, Spring 2001, p. 6, says six incumbents lost; Gregory L. Giroux, "House: GOP Maintains Thin Edge," CQ Weekly, November 11, 2000, p. 2652, says three incumbents lost in primary elections. These two discrepancies are explained by Representative Michael P. Forbes being defeated in the Democratic primary in New York and then running and losing (with only 2.6 percent of the vote) as candidate of the WFM (Working Families) Party in the general election. Thus, the more reasonable numbers are six losses in the general election and three in primaries.

For eight incumbent general-election losses in 2002, see CQ Almanac Plus 2002, p. A-16; another eight incumbents lost in 2002 primaries. For seven general-election losses in 2004, see CQ Almanac Plus 2004 (Washington: Congressional Quarterly, 2005), pp. 18-22; also, two incumbents suffered primary defeats. Of the seven 2004 losses, four were Texas Democrats who were unfavorably gerrymandered by a Republican legislature; "No Contest," The Wall Street Journal, November 12, 2004, p. A12.

Of course, turnover due to election results is not as great as total turnover of Representatives, for which see above in the chapter on American National Democracy.

[31]Danielle Knight, "House of Horrors,"U.S. News & World Report, September 11, 2006, p. 54, citing Cook Political Report.

[32]Two articles by Donald Lambro ("Incumbency is clear winner in House midterms; With most seats safe, battle for control comes down to a few dozen," The Washington Times, October 15, 2006, p. A2, and "Hill control reality check," ibid., October 19, 2006, p. A17) reported several estimates of number of competitive seats ranging from about 30 to 62 and concluded there was a "relatively small universe of 30 to 40 competitive House seats." By November 5 The New York Times said "only about 10 percent of House races could be considered even remotely competitive"; Adam Nagourney and Robin Toner, "G.O.P. Glum as It Struggles to Hold Congress," p. 1.

On "Measuring and Evaluating Changes in the Number of Competitive Districts" [a subheading] see Michael P. McDonald, "Drawing the Line on District Competition," PS: Political Science and Politics, January 2006, pp. 91-94. For changes in the number of competitive House races (toss-ups and leaners) as 2006 progressed, see David B. Magleby and Kelly D. Patterson, "War Games: Issues and Campaign Finance in the Battle for Control of Congress," in David B. Magleby and Kelly D. Patterson, editors,

The Battle for Congress: Iraq, Scandal, and Campaign Finance in the 2006 Election (Boulder, CO: Paradigm Publishers, 2008), pp. 12-15, especially Figure 1-2 on p. 14.

[33]"Senate, House & Gubernatorial Results," CQ Weekly, November 13, 2006, pp. 3068-75. Also, two House incumbents lost primary elections in 2006: Cynthia McKinney, D-GA, and Joe Schwarz, R-MI.

[34]CQ Politics / 2008 House Ratings Chart, no date, on the Internet. This source lists 61 seats as no clear favorite, leans Democratic, or leans Republican.

[35]June Kronholz, "Not All Democrats Want to Ride Obama's Coattails," The Wall Street Journal, July 14, 2008, p. A4.

[36]"Presidential, Gubernatorial, Senate and House Results," CQ Weekly, November 10, 2008, pp. 3043-52.

[37]Richard L. Engstrom, "The Political Thicket, Electoral Reform, and Minority Voting Rights," in Rush and Engstrom, Fair and Effective Representation?, p. 10.

[38]Robbins, "Gerrymander and the Need for Redistricting Reform," revised version, July 25, 2006, p. 32 of 71.

[39]Mark E. Rush, "The Hidden Costs of Electoral Reform," in Rush and Engstrom, Fair and Effective Representation?, p. 73.

[40]After the two Democrats and two Republicans appointed to the commission by legislative leaders could not agree on a choice for the fifth member, the Montana Supreme Court made the choice in a meeting closed to the public; "Supreme Court names Indian fifth member of apportionment commission," Helena Independent Record, August 4, 1999, p. 3A. A Republican legislative leader said the fifth member (and chairwoman) "had applied to be a Democrat appointee"; Roy Brown letter to editor, "Democratic plan disenfranchises voters," Billings Gazette, February 2, 2003, p. 11C. An Associated Press story refers to the "three Democratic commissioners" and to "Democrat Janine Pease Pretty on Top, commission chairwoman"; "Redistricting plan goes to court," Billings Gazette, February 6, 2003, p. 4B. A biographical article about her says, "She was chairman [sic] of the Democratic Central Committee in Big Horn County for eight years" and quotes her thusly: "I certainly was a Democrat, and I'm not even a closet Democrat"; David Crisp, "Still fighting the fight," The Billings Outpost, May 31, 2007, p. 7.

[41]Mike Dennison, "Analysis: Redistricting favors state Democrats," Billings Gazette, December 1, 2007, p. 1C.

[42]CQ Almanac Plus 2004 (Washington: Congressional Quarterly, 2005), 18-17 [chapter 18, page 17], state not given.

[43]Robbins, "Gerrymander and the Need for Redistricting Reform, p. 32 of 71.

XXV. Large Campaign Contributions as Legalized Bribery

EPIGRAPH: Politics has become so expensive that
               it takes a lot of money even to be defeated.
                    ---Will Rogers.

EPIGRAPH: Much of Congress is owned (through campaign contributions)
               by the banks and brokers whose wealth depends on fending
               off the financial police.
                    ---Jane Bryant Quinn, Newsweek, April 14, 2008, p. 82.[1]

A person running for the U.S. House or Senate faces the task of raising the huge amounts of money necessary for an effective campaign. Often, the greatest expense is TV ads. If the candidate, especially the less-well-known challenger of an incumbent, cannot buy numerous television spots, he or she will simply not be competitive and will have little chance of winning. Of course, any political campaign has further expenses—such as the notorious $400 and $1250 haircuts for John Edwards when running for President in 2007.

In House and Senate elections, office seekers spend hundreds of millions of dollars. Where does the money come from? Aside from multimillionaire candidates who use many of their own dollars and basically seek to buy membership in Congress, the money comes from donations large and small.

Federal election law controls and limits direct contributions. Examples: Except for an exception mentioned later, an individual may not donate more than $2,500 to one candidate for a federal primary or general election. Corporations and labor unions may not contribute any money to campaigns. Such limits on allowable "hard-money" donations would make campaigns much less visible were it not for "soft money." The latter is unlimited if spent by a so-called "501 organization," more fully a 501(c)(3). That number refers to a section of the Internal Revenue Code that exempts certain entities from some federal taxes. Those organizations—often charitable, non-profit, or educational—may spend unlimited dollars on non-partisan information about issues. Thus, a 501(c)(3) may "educate" voters in a way that conforms to the tax-exempt requirements while actually promoting by indirection the election of a particular candidate.

The exception mentioned above is that individuals' campaign contributions to any candidate for Congress are capped at $6,900 per election rather than $2,500 if that candidate's opponent self-finances his or her campaign at more than $350,000. Further, those extra-large donations don't count against the donor's total contribution limit for a two-year period. Also, the candidate opposed by the $350,000 or more of a self-financing opponent is allowed to receive unlimited political party campaign funds rather than the normal limited amounts. Those incumbent-protecting deviations are the so-called "millionaires' amendment" to the McCain-Feingold Act.[2] One result is that incumbents may feel more beholden to people who make larger donations while the self-financing opponent is beholden only to himself.

Let's not kid ourselves that many big donors expect nothing in return. Contributors of small amounts surely know their few dollars will not get them a quid pro quo if the candidate wins. They are probably content that they are helping a like-minded person. But many big givers are more like investors expecting to make money from their expenditure. And they often do—because the campaign-contribution process is legalized bribery. Noted American businessman Stanley Marcus once wrote, "Legislators' dependence on monetary gifts to support their campaigns makes a mockery of the democratic process."[3]

And many years ago Senator Paul Douglas (D-IL) explained, "The vast majority of the big donors want something in return for their money. Their gifts are in a sense investments. After election, if their candidates are victorious, they will come around to collect. They will want contracts, insurance policies, jobs for friends and relations, loans, subsidies, privileges[,] legislation, and so on. Woe betide the officeholders and the party which ignores [sic] their claims, for if they do, then the next time the money is likely to be shut off."[4]

As one staffer explained, "Don't kid yourself about the 'no-strings attached' to a contribution. There's always a string attached . . . and some day it's going to get pulled."[5]

Some years ago a Member was shown on TV saying that he did not think contributions ever influence the way a Member votes. Either he was terribly naïve or he believed in the gullibility of listeners and voters. We should tell people who spout such falsehoods to "keep that bull in the pasture."

It's a severe brain strain to think that money controls most human activity but not the actions of Members of Congress. As Henry Adams wrote, "Knowledge of human nature is the beginning and end of political education."[6]

Actually, "campaign contributions can be among the strongest influences on congressional decision-making."[7] Of course, donations are not the only determinant of elections and later voting by Members, but they do have a huge impact. The political class has media apologists who try to sanitize campaign contributions. Robert J. Samuelson, writing in <u>Newsweek</u> some years ago, is a prime example: His piece had the subtitle "Campaign contributions haven't corrupted Congress" and had a statement set off in larger type saying "Money is a necessary evil in elections. It doesn't buy votes."[8] Even if it was true then, would we fall for that today? More realistic interpretations come from New York's Mark Green: "It is difficult to represent the little fellow when the big fellow pays the tab," and it's "against the laws of human nature . . . [to] conclude that congresspeople accept money from petitioners but don't let it affect them."[9]

Green also reported a persuasive observation from Senator William Proxmire:
"Anyone who has been around Congress or a state legislature or a city council knows that over time the payoff by public officials for the PAC contributions they receive is as real and sure and certain as the sunrise. Oh, sure sometimes the public action by the elected official may not come immediately. It may not come in a vote. It may come in a speech not delivered. The PAC payoff may come in a colleague not influenced. It may come in a calling off of a meeting that otherwise would result in advancing legislation. It may come in a minor change in one paragraph in a 240-page bill. It may come in laying off or transferring a staff member who is unsympathetic to a PAC. . . . The contributions constitute gilded corruption that has no . . . smoking gun or even an empty cartridge to prove the crime. This is one reason why it is so insidious. The other reason is that everybody does it, or almost everybody."[10]

Former Louisiana Representative Billy Tauzin seemed to try to mislead the gullible when he said, "No one can determine the intent of the donor."[11] Longtime Senator Bob Dole was more candid about this in saying, "When these political action committees give money, they expect something in return other than good government."[12]

Large campaign contributors often make their desires perfectly clear to the recipients. Even if a big-bucks donor is not explicit about expectations, anyone smart enough to get elected also has enough brainpower to see which way to vote to keep the money gushing in.

Contributions do not have to take the form of money. If an organization sends its members around to knock on doors, make phone calls, and do other tasks for a candidate, those are contributions—as are cajoleries or directives to its members to turn out and vote a certain way. Big Labor commonly does that for the Democratic Party. After candidates endorsed by Labor win an election, they know which way to vote. They know that they have to bring back the prize when Labor says "fetch" or Labor's support will go elsewhere in the next election.

A perfect example occurred in early 2007 when Democrats regained control of Congress with Labor's election support. One of Labor's goals was passage of the deceitfully named Employee Free Choice Act, which would end secret ballots in many but not all union-recognition elections at companies and would further the intimidation of workers by union organizers and management. With many Members eager to repay Labor for its support, the House passed the bill. In this, there was great hypocrisy—and abandonment of principle for the purpose of rewarding a special-interest—by some of those Democrats because in 2001 sixteen of them signed and sent a letter to the Mexican government urging that Mexico adopt a policy of secret ballots in its own union-recognition elections. The letter stated, "We feel that the secret ballot is absolutely necessary in order to ensure that workers are not intimidated into voting for a union they might not otherwise choose." Representative George Miller took the lead in both the letter and the recent bill, "which means," as The Wall Street Journal explained, "the same person lecturing Mexican officials on the primacy of secret ballot elections has been heading up the effort to end them for 140 million U.S. workers."[13]

Making expectations clear is not limited to contributors. Politicians are also sometimes frank about the obligations of their—dare we say it?—clients. Yes; we can say that as meaning someone who uses the professional services of a politician. Here's one instance: "After the 1982 election, Tony Coelho, then head of the Democratic Congressional Campaign Committee, met with groups of corporate PAC directors and explained that access to Democratic lawmakers required contributions to Democrat House members, not to Republican challengers. As a result, by the 1990 election cycle, more than half of the contributions of corporate PACs went to Democratic incumbents, and only 8 percent were given to Republican nonincumbent candidates."[14]

More recently, during Republican control of both houses of Congress, one aspect of the so-called K Street Project was the blunt directive to Washington lobbyists that their access would be enhanced if they pink-slipped their Democratic employees. This signal that obligations flowed two ways became notorious and was another straw that in 2006 broke the back of Republican domination of Congress. And it worked against democracy by limiting the ideas presented to Congress. Democrats now do much the same.

As the House Democrats took control in January 2007, they passed a rule that "prohibits Members from threatening official retaliation against private firms that hire employees who do not share the Member's partisan political affiliation." That's an improvement, and one hopes it will not just be ink growing dim on an ethics page while not reflecting actual practice.

Despite such tweaking of the system, the money chase by Members and the influence chase by lobbyists will continue. Campaign money is the lifeblood of political careers. Members seek it almost constantly. They lobby lobbyists for it. As mentioned earlier in this book, a former Representative at a top firm explained, "The dirty little secret is that the biggest lobby in town is members of Congress lobbying us.[15]

Of course, the other lobbyists will still seek influence. In late 2006, as they foresaw the Republican election debacle, firms began hiring well-connected Democrats. And in many cases former lobbyists were assuming high staff positions in the 110th Congress. Does anyone seriously imagine that a new committee chief of staff who was a company's lobbyist for several years will not have a bias in favor of that corporation in the committee's relevant work?[16] Republican lobbyists were not necessarily being dumped, because some companies that saw themselves as targets of the Democrats needed at least 41 Republican votes in the Senate to block adverse bills.

And lobbyists will continue buying access and favorable treatment through campaign donations. With freedom of speech and with court rulings that legal contributions are a form of free speech, these "bribes" cannot be made illegal.

CORRECTIVE SOLUTIONS

The problem can be corrected by public financing of campaigns. That has been suggested by reformers for decades, but nothing has been done aside from the Presidential campaign check-off on income tax returns, which produces only a limited fund. A Presidential candidate whose campaign avails itself of taxpayer financing for the general election cannot also resort to private funds from other people. The 2008 campaign exposed the flaw in that regulation when one candidate accepted public financing while the other gained a huge monetary advantage by accepting gazillions in private donations after breaking his promise to use public financing. See the chapter on Failure to Devote Enough Time to Legislation for greater detail on taxpayer financing of campaigns.

Notes: Chapter XXV. Large Campaign Contributions as Legalized Bribery

[1]There's actually much controversy about whether contributions influence the way Members vote, and I address that issue in the text of this chapter. See Janet Grenzke, "Money and Congressional Behavior," in Money, Elections, and Democracy: Reforming Congressional Campaign Finance, edited by Margaret Latus Nugent and John R. Johannes (Boulder, CO: Westview Press, 1990), pp. 143-64; Larry J. Sabato, PAC Power: Inside the World of Political Action Committees (New York: W. W. Norton, 1984), pp. 135-40 .

[2]See the Bipartisan Campaign Reform Act, Public Law 107-155, 116 Stat. 81 through 116, Sec. 304 (relates only to Senators and does not lend itself to a brief summary) and Sec. 319 (for House candidates); George F. Will, "McCain and the Oath," Newsweek, March 10, 2008), p. 64.

[3]"Congress can't have it both ways," Dallas Morning News, June 13, 1989.

[4]Warren Weaver, Jr., Both Your Houses: The Truth About Congress (New York: Praeger, 1972), p. 211.

[5]Mark J. Green, Who Runs Congress?, revised edition (New York: Bantam/Grossman, 1975), p. 12.

[6]Henry Adams, The Education of Henry Adams, Chapter 10.

[7]Weaver, Both Your Houses, p. 144.

[8]Robert J. Samuelson, "The Price of Politics," Newsweek, August 28, 1995, p. 65. Although pursuing the money takes time away from other activities, what is the "evil" if the money doesn't buy votes?

[9]Mark Green, Selling Out: How Big Corporate Money Buys Elections, Rams Through Legislation, and Betrays Our Democracy (New York: ReganBooks, a HarperCollins imprint, 2002), pp. 16, 240.

[10]Green, Selling Out, p. 240.

[11]I made a note of this statement when I heard it on TV on February 22, 2002.

[12]Mark Green, Selling Out, p. 239.

[13]"'Secret Ballot Is Absolutely Necessary,'" (editorial), The Wall Street Journal, March 8, 2007, p. A16.

[14]Paul S. Herrnson and Clyde Wilcox, "Not So Risky Business: PAC Activity in 1992," in Risky Business? PAC Decisionmaking in Congressional Elections, edited by Robert Biersack, Paul S. Herrnson, and Clyde Wilcox (Armonk, NY: M. E. Sharpe, 1994), p. 241, quoted in Green, Selling Out, p. 142.

[15]Massimo Calabresi, "When the Democrats Take Back K Street," Time, December 4, 2006, p. 49.

[16]The new chief of staff of the House Energy and Commerce Committee was Dennis Fitzgibbons, who "has worked for Daimler Chrysler since 2000 and before that was on the committee's staff for 12 years. The panel's new chief counsel, Gregg Rothschild, is also a former congressional aide and was a lobbyist for Verizon for two years"; Jeffrey H. Birnbaum, "Democrats' victory is felt on K Street," TheWashington Post, November 23, 2006, on the Internet.

XXVI. Other Briberies

EPIGRAPH: When their lordships asked Bacon
                   How many bribes he had taken
                   He had at least the grace
                   To get very red in the face.
                        ---Edmund Clerihew Bentley (1875-1956), Baseless
                           Biography, in Angela Partington, editor, The Oxford
                           Dictionary of Quotations, 4th edition (Oxford and New
                           York: Oxford University Press, 1992), p. 64.

It's laughable that Members deny that campaign contributions influence their actions but effectively admit that free lunches and rides on private airplanes do. How do they admit it? By the recent outlawing of such "donations" as free rides and meals. Could it be that their prohibition is an effort to fool the public into thinking that a total cure has occurred—despite the continuation of large campaign contributions? Do arrests of a few street-level pushers eliminate the illegal drug problem?

Influencing Senators and Representatives with packets of untraceable cash has apparently fallen from favor. How common it used to be is hard to assess. One book says it "was not unusual" as recently as the 1960s and '70s and that "Members often retired as millionaires on their government salaries."[1] Let us, however, note that such statements are anecdotal and that we should not conclude that a few examples indicate typical behavior. It could be that such millionaires were frugal savers who invested wisely.

On the other hand, an illegality did not have to be typical to need publicity and reform. For instance, 1970 brought news that the Ford Motor Company had made cut-rate leases of its most luxurious cars, Lincoln Continentals, to powerful Members for about a decade. Most of those lawmakers were important members of committees that dealt with policy vital to Ford. The Historian of the House writes that "there were at least four criminal statutes that forbade members from accepting such gratuities" and that these were among "the regular revelations of improper conduct by members of Congress."[2] With the Historian not mentioning any investigations by ethics committees or any indictments, there was apparently nothing done about those transgressions. Was it because the criminality was minor or that the guilty were major?

There have been other somewhat indirect bribes of Members. On occasion, a Member would buy something such as land or cattle and the seller would later repurchase it at a much higher price. Or the provision of inside corporate information would enable a lawmaker to profit on stock trades. Or sexual favors would be provided as a reward or in expectation.[3] How much that still occurs is impossible to quantify, although, once again, we have felon Randy Cunningham as Exhibit A.

Even recently, there have been charges and investigations about the amazingly profitable real estate transactions of a few Members.

Numerous ways exist other than campaign contributions, property repurchases, stock tips, and sex to gain influence with a Member of Congress. Some people would argue that these amount to bribery. Examples include the following:

● Gifts to lawmakers. They, including travel and personal hospitality, are limited to maximums of $50, and $100 per year from one source. But even small ones may create a sense of obligation. Lobbyists and foreign agents may generally not make gifts to Members—unless, in the case of lobbyists, they lobby only for their own organization or its members' interests.

● Junkets. Travel costs suffer no gift limitation if incurred for official business. Here's a loophole large enough for jumbo-jetting to all sorts of exotic and expensive locales that ordinary people may consider vacation spots.

● Non-official travel on privately-owned airplanes even when done within the rules. For instance, in September 2006 Senator Conrad Burns, R-MT, flew to Bigfork, MT, to the 13th Annual Burns Classic Golf Weekend on a plane chartered by Vonage Holding Corp., an Internet phone company. Accepting such largesse is legal if the Member of Congress later pays the company an amount equal to first-class airfare, which a Burns staffer said he would do. A few days before the trip, the Senate passed a Burns amendment to provide Vonage and other Internet companies their long-sought access to the 9-1-1 emergency system and their freedom from liability therewith. Although some parts of Burns's amendment wanted by Vonage were not passed, Burns provided the company with a partial victory.[4] Spokesmen for Burns and Vonage alleged that relations between the two were not good because of the failed parts, but a reasonable person might wonder why Vonage took Burns to the golf fundraiser if that was true. And even if Burns did pay for the flight, does a reasonable person think there was no sense of obligation involved?

● Employment by lobbying or consulting firms of key people who were formerly on a Member's staff. Vonage said it did not lobby Burns, but in 2005 it had paid $75,000 for lobbying to a firm headed by Burns's former chief of staff. A Member may feel a special thank-you is owed to a firm that has given a former staffer a good job. The Member may react favorably to a legislative idea pitched by that former staffer.

- Jobs for relatives. When Majority Leader Tom DeLay's wife worked for the lobbying outfit run by DeLay's former chief of staff, she doubtless had a special ability to get her employer's ideas considered by her husband.[5] As with the former staffers, the Member may feel a sense of obligation when a relative is given high-salary and/or minimal-work employment.

- So-called "issue" ads run during campaigns. As mentioned above, federal election law prohibits campaign contributions (hard money) from corporations and labor unions but permits unlimited informative spending of an allegedly non-partisan nature by the 501 organizations. Clearly, however, if Candidate A has a strong stance on one side of an issue, and the "non-partisan" ads promote the same position, the 501 group is effectively campaigning for that candidate. Then, after Candidate A wins the election, would anyone seriously argue that he or she feels no sense of obligation to that 501 organization? Sure, they were already on the same side regarding that particular issue, but that sense of indebtedness may extend to other parts of that organization's agenda or personnel.

- Bribery of Members' staff people. Many of the staffers of Senators and Representatives wield influence with their employers. Thus, it may not be necessary for special interests to actually "turn" a Member of Congress. If key staff people can be reached, they can lead their bosses in certain directions. Or staffers themselves may be able to fulfill the desires of lobbyists because many have been given discretionary power in certain areas by their overburdened bosses. As the former chief of staff of disgraced Representative Bob Ney explained, "When I was on Capitol Hill, I was given tickets to sporting events, concerts, free food, free meals. In return, I gave preferential treatment to my lobbying buddies."[6] With such opportunities available, it's no wonder Washington contained almost 33,000 registered lobbyists in 2005, a number that had mounted to almost 35,000 by 2006.[7]

- If a Member wants to introduce legislation addressing an issue, much of the hard work of bill-drafting may be done by some lobbying group. Naturally, those people will craft provisions they favor. But, that aside, who will say that the Member then does not feel a sense of obligation to that group? And the feeling may run both ways, with the group wanting to support the Member's re-election. Thus, would it be too extreme to allege that while a few Members may be bribed, they are also doing some bribing by sponsoring or supporting legislation in exchange for campaign aid?

Of course, lobbyists perform some legitimate functions, and it would false to say that the American people, individually or in groups, cannot communicate with legislators, but as one Senator put it, "They should be kept on tap and not on top."[8]

- "The Senate decided in its 1968 ethics code to permit members to accept contributions to help meet the cost of travel, printing, radio and television reports to constituents, telephone, telegraph, postage, and stationery as they exceed the regular allowances."[9]

- Corporations, forbidden from donating directly to candidates, have many other spending opportunities that can influence lawmakers. Aside from the aforementioned payments for junkets and other travel, and the charitable donations for speeches made by Members (see the chapter on Thief-in-the Night Pay Raises), businesses can underwrite event expenses. <u>USA Today</u> reported in 2007 that "organizers of the Republican and Democratic conventions are offering companies access to power brokers and the chance to lobby them as they try to pick up their fundraising pace a year before the events." Corporate officials, for instance, can "golf with state and national GOP leaders for $2.5 million." At the Democrats' convention in Denver, "companies donating at least $250,000 can host talks with politicians on issues affecting their industries. Other private events with Democrats such as Rep. Diana DeGette also start at $250,000. DeGette said contributors aren't gaining special favors: 'A reception that donors attend . . . doesn't in itself show any undue influence.'"[10] Well, again, how stupid do politicians think the public is? Would anyone with a brain think that a lawmaker will give equal treatment to a non-donor and to someone who gave the party a quarter of a million dollars?

• The quid pro quo of logrolling, mentioned in earlier chapters, may arguably be bribery. "I'll vote for your bill if you vote for mine."

CORRECTIVE SOLUTIONS

Because some forms of communicating with lawmakers are legitimate and cannot be prohibited, only the "communication" called donations of money should be targeted. This leads again to government funding of election campaigns. If Members do not become beholden to the fat cats because private donations are prohibited, they will presumably not stroke the fat cats with special-interest legislation.

But what about "donations" of volunteer work? If a labor union encourages its members to work in a person's campaign, can that be stopped? I say no. Proving that the volunteer is only helping because of union pressure might be impossible in most cases. Besides that legal hurdle, a law against citizen involvement would run counter to American ideas about democracy—and counter to the oft-voiced desire for greater public participation in politics. We can hardly lament low voter turnouts and at the same time forbid people from working in campaigns. Therefore, people and organizations complaining about opposition volunteers working for candidates should simply mobilize their own volunteers.

Bill drafting by lobbyists can hardly be outlawed. How would the line be drawn between a legitimate legislative suggestion from a constituent or a good-government group and an illegitimate suggestion from a lobbyist?

Corporate—or union—underwriting of convention expenses could be replaced by government funding. To conservatives who would deplore that as a step toward bigger and more intrusive government, the winning response might be that government funding is preferable to making legislators hostage to people and organizations that seek to purchase undue influence.

Laws against bribery of staffers should be strengthened.

The law that imposes a waiting period between a Member's end of Congressional service and the start of his or her lobbying of current Members should be changed so it applies also to employment by a lobbying firm. The current situation is that a former Member can immediately get such a job but has to wait awhile before directly lobbying former colleagues who are still in Congress. The line between legal and illegal lobbying during the waiting period often becomes invisible to those involved—and even if it were bright and well-marked, what outsider could blow the whistle on it in all but the most flagrant cases? (See the information on lobbying restrictions in the chapter on Ethics.) There should be a long waiting period between Members' and staffers' Congressional service and their mere employment by lobbying firms.

 A federal law should also prohibit employment of Members' and staffers' relatives by lobbying firms. That law would no longer apply to the relative as soon as the Member's or staffer's Congressional service ends.

Issue ads should not be banned at any time. Though there are numerous restrictions on freedom of speech in the U.S., as noted earlier (see the chapter on Failure to Devote Enough Time to Legislation), such a ban would move the nation too far toward the sort of totalitarianism recently advancing in Venezuela. Such a ban would move us too close to Big Brother, who allows only the government's propaganda.

Notes: Chapter XXVI. Other Briberies

[1]Ronald Kessler, Inside Congress: The Shocking Scandals, Corruption, and Abuse of Power Behind the Scenes on Capitol Hill (New York: Pocket Books, 1997), p. 98.

[2]Robert V. Remini, The House: The History of the House of Representatives (New York: Collins, a division of HarperCollins; Smithsonian Books, 2006), p. 423, citing Congressional Quarterly Almanac . . . 1970 (Washington: Congressional Quarterly, 1971), p. 33.

[3]Kessler, Inside Congress, pp. 99-100.

[4]"Senator to reimburse plane trip," Billings Gazette, September 19, 2006, p. 3B.

[5]Dick Morris and Eileen McGann, Outrage: . . . (New York: HC, An Imprint of HarperCollins 2007), p. 115.

[6]Danielle Knight, "House of Horrors," U.S. News & World Report, September 11, 2006, p. 54.

[7]Ibid., p. 52, for 2005; Tom Finnigan, All About Pork: The Abuse of Earmarks and the Needed Reforms (Washington: Citizens Against Government Waste, Policy Briefing Series, May 3, 2006), p. 9, for 2006.

[8]Joseph S. Clark, <u>Congress: The Sapless Branch</u> (Westport, CT: Greenwood Press, 1964), p. 72.

[9]Weaver, <u>Both Your Houses: The Truth About Congress</u> (New York: Praeger Publishers, 1972), p. 235.

[10]Fredreka Schouten and Patrick O'Driscoll, "Conventions welcome corporate cash," <u>USA Today</u>, July 27, 2007, p. 3A.

XXVII. Out-of-State Campaign Contributions to Control Elections

EPIGRAPH: Government is everywhere to a great extent controlled
                    by powerful minorities with an interest distinct from
                    that of the mass of the people.
                              ---Goldsworthy Lowes Dickinson (1862-1932),
                                 The Choice Before Us, Chapter 4.

EPIGRAPH: Beware of strangers bearing gifts.
                    ---A common warning.

Many of the direct and indirect contributions to a candidate's campaign come from out-of-state or out-of-district donors. The flaw in this is that big contributions from such money centers as New York City and Hollywood may skew the vote in "fly-over country." That may be less objectionable in a Presidential campaign; after all, that election is national. But when people in the hinterlands are heavily influenced by "coastal" money in an election for Senator, Representative, or a position in state government the result may not reflect the unalloyed sentiment of the voters. Who is to say that any particular election result is not what the locals would have achieved if left alone—but does any reasonably astute observer think that a changed outcome never occurs or that the intrusive money is given without expectation of producing a certain result?[1]

In 2008 a tight U.S. Senate contest between Republican incumbent John Sununu and Democrat Jeanne Shaheen raised that issue as out-of-state money cascaded into New Hampshire. A television news report explained, "A single seat could swing the balance in the Senate, and because of that, Granite Staters have been bombarded with ads, many financed by national organizations looking to sway public opinion." The report then showed a video of University of New Hampshire professor of political science Andrew Smith referring to special interests spending millions to influence voters. He said, "And I think that's actually a bad thing for our political debate because now we do have groups from outside New Hampshire that really don't have that much tied to the issues in the campaign, and they kind of bring in these more general negative national issues from the campaign rather than focusing on issues that are of concern to voters here."[2]

In the case of out-of-state contributions to the campaign committees or leadership PACs of Senators and Representatives, the big donors may fall into either of two categories: (1) people who seek to influence who wins a competitive seat in Congress, (2) people who contribute to safe-seat Congressional Members because they want influence with that person. Contributors in that second category may not particularly care who is elected to a position in <u>state</u> government, but they influence that result anyway because their donations to the sage Member often end up in the hands of state or local party committees that help candidates.[3]

CORRECTIVE SOLUTIONS

Again, the main remedy may be public financing of campaigns. See the chapter on Failure to Devote Enough Time to Legislation for greater detail on taxpayer financing of campaigns.

Some Members have addressed this issue by introducing bills to prohibit or limit House candidates "from accepting contributions from individuals who do not reside in the district the candidate seeks to represent."[4] But those here-today-gone-tomorrow proposals have, of course, never become law.

Further ideas about the infiltration of funds from out-of-state, big-money cities are in an article cited below. Those suggestions include the requirement that candidates disclose every contribution or at least all donations of more than some low amount , that candidates report online all such receipts within twenty-four hours, and that state laws prohibit candidates from receiving out-of-state money. The article also deals with problems that might accompany that last remedy.[5]

Notes: Chapter XXVII. Out-of-State Campaign Contributions to Control Elections

[1]For the influence of outside money in some recent Congressional elections, see David B. Magleby and Kelly D. Patterson, editors, <u>The Battle for Congress: Iraq, Scandal, and Campaign Finance in the 2006 Election</u> (Boulder, CO: Paradigm Publishers, 2008), passim.

[2]Molly Line reporting from Concord, NH, on "Special Report" on Fox News, October 20, 2008.

[3]Brenarlo, "Out of State Money: How Out of State Interests Are Buying Local Elections," January 15, 2007, on the Internet, republished from the <u>Dakota Beacon</u> newspaper. This is valuable for data about out-of-state influence in North Dakota, where one assumes the situation is not unique.

[4]Examples were H.R. 449 and H.R. 450 in the 107th Congress; see <u>Congressional Record,</u> daily edition, February 7, 2001, p. H220.   Near the start of each new Congress from 1993 to 2007, Representative Wayne Gilchrest introduced two bills similar to H.R. 449 and H.R. 450, one to ban campaign contributions by PACs to all candidates for federal office, the other to prohibit contributions to House candidates from individuals living outside the candidate's district. They all died aborning.

Other Members, with equal futility, have introduced variants; see, for example, H.R. 715, introduced 2-11-1999, to limit contributions by individuals "not eligible to vote in the state or Congressional district" of a federal candidate; H.R. 1880, 5-20-1999, was similar. See also Richard S. Dunham, "Carpetbagger Cash Is Buying Elections," Business Week Online News Flash, May 19, 1997, on the Internet, reporting that Representatives Charles Schumer, D-NY, and Newt Gingrich, R-GA, were the two main recipients of outside money in the 1996 election cycle.

[5]Brenarlo, "Out of State Money," January 15, 2007.

XXVIII. Congress Misses Many Important Deadlines

EPIGRAPH: Politics is the art of postponing decisions
                until they are no longer relevant.
                       ---Henri Queuille, Radical Party three-time
                          prime minister of France's Fourth Republic
                          after World War II.

The twelve appropriations bills[1] that fund various parts of the federal government are supposed to be passed each year before the federal fiscal year begins on October 1. (Fiscal years are identified by the year in which they end; so fiscal 2011 began on October 1, 2010.) It has become quite common that some of those spending bills are not passed by that deadline. In those cases, Congress generally passes "continuing resolutions" that continue funding at the level of the previous fiscal year pending passage of new appropriation bills.

By the end of 2006 Congress had passed only two of the needed measures for FY 2007. In a conflict over reducing earmarked spending or increasing general funding levels, the Republican majorities in the two houses, along with some Democrats, could not agree. Another factor no doubt was that the last session of the 109th Congress lazily failed to meet for enough days to have a reasonable chance of doing its necessary work. Therefore, spending was temporarily set at the amounts for fiscal 2006, and the problem of passing the remaining specific appropriation bills was left to the new 110th Congress with its Democratic majorities. The 110th had to do double duty: Pass the needed bills for fiscal 2007 left over from the 109th Congress plus the appropriation bills for fiscal 2008. The Democratic plan for dealing with this mess was to pass an omnibus bill that set some funding at fiscal 2006 levels and increased some funding beyond those amounts.

Meanwhile, the people suffered because of Congressional irresponsibility. Not only were projects eliminated, some federal programs and agencies bled because of old dollar amounts not buying as much due to inflation and because of not getting requested additional money they claimed to need. So, if we think of government as existing to serve people's needs, it may fail when providing less service. Perhaps even more outrageously, Congress did pass a law continuing some important tax breaks for ordinary people but did it so late in 2006 that the IRS had already printed tax forms not reflecting that Congressional action; thus, many Americans may have prepared their tax returns without being aware of certain deductions they were legally entitled to. As The Wall Street Journal headlined, "Congress Restores Tax Breaks, But Public May Be Last to Know."[2] That last-minute action also saddled the IRS with extra millions in costs for reprogramming computers and for printing and distributing new directions and tax tables.[3]

Additionally, financial companies that usually send out 1099 forms in late January had to ask for time extensions or send out dividend reports that had to be revised later because of a late change in tax law. Again, a January 2007 headline in The Wall Street Journal highlighted the problem: "The Risk of Filing Your Taxes Early."[4]

Failing to learn an obvious lesson, Congress dillydallied until December 2007 on passing its usual one-year "patch" of the Alternative Minimum Tax to prevent it from clobbering about 23 million middle-class taxpayers. The result was that those millions could not file their taxes as early as usual—and therefore could not get their tax refunds as early as they expected—because the initial tax forms did not reflect the patch.

The delay flowed largely from a battle over whether Congress should enact $50 billion in tax increases to pay for the prospective revenue the AMT would have produced without the patch.[5] The $50 billion was the estimated one-year income the federal government would get from the AMT by imposing it on about 23 million Americans who didn't currently pay it. Democrats in Congress wanted other revenue increases to offset the imagined loss.

This supremely phony issue was hardly ever identified as such by the mainstream media. It was phony because no one seriously believed Congress, with its overriding political considerations, would ever allow the unpatched AMT to suck a $50 billion tax increase from the voters. Congress has never yet permitted the AMT to clobber middle-income Americans. Thus, there was never going to be a "lost" $50 billion that would have to be offset with other revenue increases under the "paygo" rule that House Democrats enacted on the first day of the 110th Congress in January 2007. "Pay-as-you-go" sounded sensible as meaning that any tax cut had to be balanced by an equal amount of tax increases or spending cuts. But it became nonsense when used as an excuse to increase taxes in order to offset a revenue decrease that was unreal and would never occur. It was as nonsensical as a man who never buys a lottery ticket saying he will be deprived of a $50 million lottery jackpot and deserves compensation for the loss.

That delay made it two years in a row that Congress did not pass tax legislation until it was too late for the IRS to make tax forms available on time.

With Democrats back in control of both chambers, and after their carping about the failures of Republican control, Congress had not passed even one of the normal appropriations bills by November 2007, a record not "achieved" in the preceding twenty years.[6]

Deadlines missed by Congress are so numerous that if you enter "missed deadlines by Congress" (without the quotation marks) on an Internet search engine, you get hundreds of thousands of results. They contain statements such as these:

- "Passing the budget is Congress' most basic responsibility. The fiscal year ended September 30 [2007], and not one appropriation bill landed on President Bush's Desk."[7]
- "The 1974 Budget Act . . . set targets and deadlines for Congress to meet. But now 25 years later, deadlines are routinely missed—and nobody worries. Provisions of the law are regularly waived—with the approval of budget hawks. And spending caps are evaded through myriad gimmicks and tricks."[8]
- "The congressional budget process is notorious for missed deadlines."[9]
- "The Senate has failed in meeting the deadline" of November 14, 2005, to provide a "status of Phase II investigation into the 9-11/WMD issues in re the intelligence."[10]
- "Congress has never been very good at deadlines, and the annual May 15 deadline for Members of Congress to file their financial disclosure forms is no exception. Dozens of Members missed the May 15 deadline this year."[11]
- "Congress Fails to Meet Budget Deadline for 20th Time in 23 Years . . . As Congress missed its April 15 budget deadline, Congressman Christopher Cox, along with more than 200 Republican and Democratic House colleagues, introduced legislation today to end more than two decades of 'budget lawlessness' in Congress."[12]
- "Legislators on the conference committee [on a Medicare prescription drug bill] have missed several deadlines."[13]
- "The 2002 Farm Bill technically expired Sept. 30 [2007], though Congress still has not managed to pass a replacement. . . . Many of [the] farm programs that would have expired Sept. 30 along with the farm bill will be extended to Nov. 16 under a continuing resolution passed by Congress and signed by President Bush."[14]

The House has a rule about its committees submitting reports of the past two years' activities no later than January 2 in each odd-numbered year. [15] Those reports don't appear in the Congressional Record and are therefore not easily accessible, if indeed they are submitted, and if indeed the deadline is met.

There's also a House rule requiring each committee to "submit its rules for publication in the Congressional Record not later than 30 days after the committee is elected in each odd-numbered year."[16] Judging by a perusal of the Record, that often seems not to happen.

The rule that the standing committees of the House "shall be elected by the House within seven calendar days after the commencement of each Congress"[17] is not completely followed. Nor does the Congressional Record make it easy to find out who has been elected to committees.[18]

CORRECTIVE SOLUTIONS

Thomas Jefferson once wrote, "Delay is preferable to error."[19] Unfortunately, with Congress we often get both. When people fail to do what they are supposed to do, someone may suffer. Children can get a spanking, a timeout, or a grounding. Adults can lose money, become ineligible for a benefit, be sent to jail, etc. But none of those behavior modifications or punishments can be applied to Congress or its Members. So, what's to be done? I offer two remedies.

The first is admittedly weak. The media should deluge Americans with stories about this type of Congressional failure and with the suggestion that voters should replace incumbents with candidates who promise to adhere to deadlines. That's a weak suggestion because (a) how could a new Member be held to the promise?, and (2) even when Congress is in low repute, polls show that most Americans are satisfied with their own Senators and Representatives.

Second is a Constitutional amendment with a limited list of mandatory deadlines, such as passage of all regular appropriation bills for a fiscal year by the start of that year, and a denial of salaries to all Members of Congress on a prorated basis for every calendar day that a deadline is missed.

Some writers criticize Constitutional tinkering. George Will, for instance, wrote that the 27th Amendment, relating to Congressional pay, is "misbegotten" and an "absurdity" because it "trivializes the Constitution."[20] But, I ask you, which is more important, correcting an otherwise intractable problem or refusing to make the Constitution slightly longer? Do we think the Constitution is so perfect or has created such a perfect government that no changes are needed? What if such thinking had prevented adding the Bill of Rights or any of the other important amendments?

Notes: Chapter XXVIII. Congress Misses Many Important Deadlines

[1]For variations in the number of regular appropriations bills, see note 2 in the chapter on Budget and Appropriations Problems.

[2]Tom Herman, "Congress Restores Tax Breaks, But Public May Be Last to Know," The Wall Street Journal, December 13, 2006, p. D2.

[3]Ibid.

[4]Tom Herman, "The Risk of Filing Your Taxes Early," The Wall Street Journal, January 24, 2007, pp. D1, D2.

[5]Sheryl Gay Stolberg and David M. Herszenhorn, "As Clock Ticks, Congress and White House Stand Firm," The New York Times, December 4, 2007, p. A28; Carl Hulse and Suevon Lee, "Tax Stalemate Threatens Chaos as Filing Season Nears," The New York Times, December 6, 2007, p. A33; David M. Herszenhorn, "Blue Dog Democrats

Try to Keep Pay-as-You-Go Promise," The New York Times, December 13, 2007, p. A36; "The Delta House Congress," The Wall Street Journal, December 14, 2007, p. A20; David M. Herszenhorn, "Congress Averts Higher Tax Bill for Middle Class," The New York Times, December 20, 2007, pp. A1, A30.

[6]Philip Burrowes, "Congress Can't Always Rush Home For the Holidays," CQ Weekly, November 5, 2007, p. 3305.

[7]Karen Kerrigan, "The Business of Congress: All Work, Low (Really Low) Approval Ratings," October 4, 2007, from the Internet.

[8]David Baumann and Richard E. Cohen, "Budget Breakdown," October 1, 2000, from the Internet.

[9]Ronald D. Utt, "Getting the Federal Budget Process Back on Track," March 18, 1996, from the Internet.

[10]"Remember the 14th," Constant's pations [a blog], November 28, 2005, from the Internet.

[11]Paul Singer, "66 House Lawmakers Late to File," Roll Call, June 17, 2008, from the Internet.

[12]"What the Budget Process Reform Act (H.R. 1372) Would Do," April 1997, from the Internet.

[13]Julie Rovner, "Medicare Drug-Benefit Bill Stalled in Congress," All Things Considered, NPR, October 26, 2003, from the Internet.

[14]"Farm Bill delayed, but for how long?" October 18, 2007, from the Internet.

[15]House Rule XI, clause 1(d)(1), 110th Congress.

[16]House Rule XI, clause 2(a)(2), 110th Congress. Do the words mean that the rules must be submitted within 30 days or that the rules must be published in the Record within 30 days? That's unclear.

[17]House Rule X, clause 5(a)(1), 110th Congress.

[18]Taking the Congressional Record's reports about the organization of the 110th Congress in January 2007 as a guide, I found the following: (1) the index volume for January 4-19, 2007, has citations to majority and minority "appointments" listed by House Resolution number, page number, and date under "Committees of the House; (2) the page numbers refer to the section "Public Bills and Resolutions" located near the end of the record of each day's proceedings rather than the section showing votes, nearly verbatim debates, etc.; (3) a typical entry is this: "H. Res. 7. A resolution electing

Members to certain standing committees of the House of Representatives; considered and agreed to," but that action is not in the votes and debates section; (4) the text of that resolution (nor any of the others of similar import) is nowhere in the Record; (5) the index volume does not have references to the "Daily Digest" section for each day's proceedings, yet that's the only part of the Record showing the names of Members elected to committees; (6) the Daily Digest section only reports on some, not all, of the resolutions electing Members; for January 4-19, 2007; resolutions 7, 8, 73, 74, and 75 are not in the Daily Digest, which does have resolutions 45,46, 47, 56, and 60 with names of elected Members; thus, you cannot find in the Record who was elected by resolutions 7, 8, 73, 74, and 75; (7) because House Rule X requires election within seven calendar days of the start of a new Congress, and because the 110th Congress began on January 4, the elections that occurred from January 11 onward (such as those reflected in resolutions 56 and 60 on January 12 and 73, 74, and 75 on January 19) violated that rule and are further examples of Congress not meeting deadlines.

[19]Letter to George Washington (May 16, 1792), John Bartlett and Justin Kaplan, Familiar Quotations, 16th edition (Boston: Little, Brown, 1992), p. 343, number 19.

[20]George F. Will, Restoration: Congress, Term Limits and the Recovery of Deliberative Democracy (New York: The Free Press, 1992), pp. 39-40.

XXIX. "Holding" the Senate Hostage

EPIGRAPH: These scoffers, these obstructionists,
                These fossils—who are they?
                    ---Bert Leston Taylor (1866-1921), So Shall It Be, Stanza 6
                    (Bartlett, Familiar Quotations, 13th edition, p. 831a).

Surely, protection of minority rights should not allow a single Senator to prevent action. But that ability does exist in two ways. One is the use of a so-called "hold." A second is that a Senator may object to a request for unanimous consent. The Senate expedites much of its work through consent to such requests.[1] Because action through unanimous consent is easily understood without further explanation, the arcane procedure involving holds will be emphasized here. Holds have only recently begun to enter the public's consciousness.

In issuing a hold a Senator requests notification from his/her party leader when a certain bill or nomination is about to be considered by the full Senate. That seems innocent enough. But lurking behind that apparently benign request is the threat that the "holder" will filibuster the bill, will talk it to death unless "cloture" is invoked to end the filibuster. A successful cloture vote ends unlimited debate and makes it possible to bring a pending motion to a vote, but it requires an affirmative vote of three-fifths (60) of all Senate members, not just those present and voting. However, the up or down vote on the pending motion will not occur immediately because each Senator may still speak for one hour, and germane amendments can still be offered, and a post-cloture filibuster may be waged. The latter involves delaying tactics such as repeated suggestions that a quorum is not present, recurrent roll calls, and word-for-word reading of proposed amendments.[2]

Because achieving cloture is difficult and because many of the Senate's actions are accomplished through unanimous consent, Senators usually want to prevent filibusters. Thus, the possibility of a filibuster causes avoidance and gives the hold great power.

Filibusters have a long Senate history. Their possibility has existed since 1806, when the Senate abandoned its practice of permitting debate to be ended by a motion for the "previous question."[3] Yet, the first resort to a Senate filibuster came only in 1841. Gradually, there were more.

When a merchant-ship armed-neutrality bill desired by President Wilson was orated to death in early 1917, he lashed out: "The Senate of the United States is the only legislative body in the world which cannot act when its majority is ready for action. A little group of willful men, representing no opinion but their own, have rendered the great government of the United States helpless and contemptible."[4] In the resulting special session called by Wilson, the Senate adopted a new rule that two-thirds of Senators present and voting could shut off debate. A successful vote to that effect became known as "cloture" (French for "conclusion" or "ending").

After changes to the rule in 1949 and 1959, the present regulation was created in 1975 requiring a vote of three-fifths of all Senators to invoke cloture on any matter other than amending the Senate's rules, which requires a two-thirds vote.

Numerous bills have been delayed or defeated by filibusters. The record filibuster was the effort of 24 hours and 18 minutes by Democrat Strom Thurmond, D-SC, against a civil rights bill in 1957 . Holding the floor at length sometimes required the use of diapers and standby urinary pails.

Holds are descended from filibusters and can threaten the Senate's use in recent years of unanimous consent as a way to accomplish much of its business. Secret holds, which conceal the identity of the Senator threatening opposition, became common.

An example occurred in August-September 2006: Reform-minded Senators supported a bill to create a publicly accessible database for federal grant and contract expenditures. If passed, it would make the government more accountable to the citizenry. But the bill stalled because of secret holds placed on it. When word of that leaked out to Internet bloggers, they pestered Senators' offices until they found that 98 Senators denied issuing holds. That left Senators Byrd, D-WV, and Stevens, R-AK, and when they were "outed" they released their holds, and the bill soon became law. Apparently, those two pork-masters were happy to use one of the Senate's anti-democratic procedures to block something that would benefit the people, as long as they could do it secretly.[5]

Some observers identify different types of secretive holds: The chokehold, designed to kill; the rotating hold, used by Senators acting like tag-team wrestlers to alternate the person doing the dirty work; and the Mae West hold of a "come-up-and-see-me-sometime" Senator whom persuasion might change.[6]

Senator Trent Lott, R-MS, recently averred that "the current use of holds is the most corrosive thing going on the in the Senate right now."[7] And Senator Ron Wyden, D-OR, explained that a secret hold is "arguably one of the most powerful tools that an elected official has" and that most Americans, if asked about it, "might think it was hair spray."[8] That tool has even greater power near the end of a session as the need to pass legislation becomes more urgent. During that time, holds and logrolling (exchanges of support for legislation desired by different Members) increase. As Senator Patrick Leahy, D-VT, said, "At the end of the session, the person who wants to hold something up has far more negotiating value than somebody who wants to move forward."[9]

In June 2007, a member of the Society of Professional Journalists disclosed that Senator Jon Kyl, R-AZ, had a secret hold on a bill to reduce government secrecy. The disclosure began thusly: "Congress, apparently content to explore ever new depths in public disapproval, is on the verge of having a single member derail the most meaningful reform in years of the federal Freedom of Information Act" despite the "overwhelming majorities support[ing] the legislation in both the House and Senate." Kyl was finally "outed" after Society members phoned every Senator to ask if he or she was the hold's author.[10]

Despite their shadowy existence, Senate holds sometimes number in the hundreds. That would seem a gross interference with the people's business. But holds have their defenders, who allege the following benefits: Holds prevent hasty action on flawed bills; they delay passage of bills so that discussions and compromise lead to better legislation; and they allow Senators to obtain a desired result from the executive branch by stalling a nomination until the result is achieved.

For instance, in the summer of 2006 Senators Hillary Clinton, D-NY, and Patty Murray, D-WA, held hostage President Bush's nomination of Dr. Andrew von Eschenbach to be the head of the Food and Drug Administration. Those two wanted to force the FDA to permit over-the-counter sales to women 18 and older of the so-called morning-after pill to prevent pregnancy. After the FDA issued the desired order in August, the two Senators rescinded their holds. Other Senators then issued holds before von Eschenbach was finally confirmed in December.[11]

A reform in 2007 seemingly did away with what Senator Ron Wyden, D-OR, described as "the anonymity of the hold that is so odious to the basic premise of our democratic system."[12] That was accomplished by Section 512 of Public Law 110-81, the Honest Leadership and Open Government Act, which requires that Senators who place holds on measures or matters must submit a written notice of that action and within six session days must submit the notice for publication in the Congressional Record. That, however, as stated by the law, is only an exercise of the Senate's rule-making authority and thus can be changed by the Senate at any time.[13]

So-called "senatorial courtesy" is a cousin of holds. Here we are not dealing with politeness. Instead, the courtesy involved is that the Senate will not confirm certain Presidential appointees if the person's nomination is opposed by either of the Senators from the state affected by the appointment or the home state of the appointee. This relates largely to judicial appointments and to many nominees in the executive branch. On occasion, the home-state Senators actually tell the President whom they want to be appointed. Senatorial courtesy is only a custom and is not codified in rules or laws. It arose because Senators have a special interest in appointments of their own constituents. But, here again, we see that a single Senator can defeat what may be the will of the majority. That's a failure of democracy and should be eliminated.[14]

Furthermore, senatorial courtesy sometimes leads to abandonment of principle, as in the confirmation of Kathleen Sebelius as Secretary of Health and Human Services in April 2009. Her fellow Kansan, Senator Sam Brownback voted to confirm her although Sebelius is extremely pro-choice on abortion while Brownback is just as extremely anti-abortion. By voting for an ideological opponent for a cabinet position dealing more than any other with that conflict, Brownback seems to have set aside an important principle for an apparently more important institutional tradition.

CORRECTIVE SOLUTIONS

Two changes can stop the anti-majoritarian ability of a single Senator to prevent action that a majority favors.

One such change occurred in 2007 with the aforementioned elimination of Senators' ability to maintain secrecy about their holds. The second good change would be passage of a rule that no Senator who has a disclosed hold can vote against a unanimous consent request to proceed to consideration of that measure or matter. This reform would not eliminate a Senator's right to filibuster against the passage of an amendment or bill, nor the right to filibuster approval of a nomination. A different version of this reform would be a Senate rule that no hold against mere consideration shall be honored by the leadership. That would still allow procedural filibusters, but they would have to be actual rather than potential.

But why not go a step further and simply outlaw all holds? Since a hold merely threatens a filibuster, such a rule would cause any Senator who feels strongly enough against a measure to engage in an actual filibuster. We would probably find that most of them would not do so; and because of that, Senators would probably not favor such a rule, as it would take away an obstructionist weapon. Further, even Senators who don't want to obstruct a measure might argue that forcing their fellows to launch actual filibusters would delay action and make the Senate less efficient than holds already do.

Thus, as long as filibusters are permitted, it may be best to allow holds. And therefore, the recent move eliminating secret holds is perhaps as much as can reasonably be done— unless the media, as with so many other problems addressed in this book, will do its job of publicizing Congressional actions that are beyond the pale.

Notes: Chapter XXIX. "Holding" the Senate Hostage

[1] See Naftali Bendavid, "One Senator Holds Up Bill, in New Level of Gridlock," The Wall Street Journal, March 2, 2010, p. A6.

[2] Cloture is dealt with by Senate Rule XXII, 110th Congress. For a post-cloture filibuster that consumed two weeks in 1977, see Walter J. Oleszek, Congressional

Procedures and the Policy Process, 2d edition (Washington: CQ Press, 1984), 190-91; this is not in the 7th edition (2007).

[3]For information on the "previous question" see below in the chapter on the House Committee on Rules.

[4]Thomas E. Mann and Norman J. Ornstein, The Broken Branch: How Congress Is Failing America and How to Get It Back on Track (New York: Oxford University Press, 2006), p. 37.

[5]Martin Kady II, "Senate Passes Legislation That Would Expose Federal Spending," CQ Weekly, September 11, 2006, p. 2393; Porkbusters blogging the waste out of government, "sen. byrd holds up, then changes course on spending accountability bill," August 31, 2006, on the Internet; Porkbusters blogging the waste out of government, "wtf? another dem has secret hold on pork bill," September 7, 2006, on the Internet; Elliott Fullmer, "New Update: Exposing Earmarks, September 1, 2006, on the Internet; TimChapmanBlog.com, "Stevens' and Byrd's excuses don't add up," September 1, 2006, on the Internet; Rob Thormeyer, "After holds dropped, Senate clears database bill," CGN, September 8, 2006, on the Internet.

[6]Carl Hulse, "Senate May End Its Tradition of Blocking Bills in Secret," The New York Times, August 2, 2007, p. A13.

[7]Associated Press story by Andrew Taylor, September 17, 2006, and September 18, 2006, on the Internet and in various newspapers, e.g., "Secret 'hold' powerful tool used in Senate to kill bills," Billings Gazette, September 18, 2006, p. 3A. Some published versions, however, are briefer than others. I checked several issues of the Congressional Record but did not find that Lott made the quoted comment on the floor of the Senate.

[8]Andrew Taylor's Associated Press story, September 18, 2006.

[9]Ibid.

[10]"David Carr, "Let The Sun Shine," The New York Times, July 23, 2007, pp. C1, C8; "Sen. Jon Kyl unmasked," St. Louis Journalism Review, June 2007, p. 7.

[11]Gardiner Harris, "F.D.A. Nominee Advances; Hurdles Linger," The New York Times, September 21, 2006, p. A27; Christopher Lee, "Senate Approves FDA Chief; Frist Ends 'Holds' That Long Stalled Vote on Von Eschenbach," The Washington Post, December 8, 2006, p. A37; Elizabeth Crowley, "Senators Expected to Lift Hold on FDA Pick because of Approval of Plan B Birth Control," CQ Weekly, September 4, 2006, p. 2327.

[12]Congressional Record, daily edition, August 1, 2003, p. S10925.

[13]See P.L. 110-81, 121 Stat. 735, Section 555.

[14]Tonja Jacobi, "The Senatorial Courtesy Game: Explaining the Norm of Informal Vetoes in Advice and Consent Nominations," <u>Legislative Studies Quarterly</u>, May 2005, pp. 193-217.

XXX. Committee Power to Kill Bills, Especially in the House

EPIGRAPH: Search all the parks in all your cities.
              You'll find no statues to committees.
              ---Anonymous.[1]

When he was a college professor, Woodrow Wilson wrote, "It is evident that there is one principle which runs through every stage of procedure, and which is never disallowed or abrogated—the principle that the Committee shall rule without let or hindrance."[2] That is no longer so true, but the committees of Congress are still important.

Following its introduction in House or Senate, a bill is sent to one or more of that chamber's committees. From there it's likely to be referred to a subcommittee. In either case, it may or may not get fair consideration. And it's iffy whether it will eventually be reported out of committee, i.e. moved toward possible passage by the full House or Senate. That depends greatly on what the committee chairperson, or the partisan majority on the panel, desires. The party having a majority in the full chamber also has a majority on every standing committee and subcommittee except for the House Committee on Standards of Official Conduct and the Senate Select Committee on Ethics.

Balkanizing committees into numerous subcommittees created more gatekeepers with power to impede a bill's progress. Each subcommittee has a chair and a majority which can block a bill that otherwise would meet approval in full committee or the full chamber.

It used to be that chairs had autocratic power. At their whim, a committee might or might not meet, bills might or might not receive consideration, staffers were virtually the chair's employees, chairs controlled committee funds, and bills approved by a committee majority might or might not be reported out. Here again was evidence of how Congressional processes were often anti-majoritarian. Actions could be mean-spirited and prejudiced, as when F. Edward Hébert, D-LA, chair of the House Armed Services Committee, provided only one chair for new committee members Pat Schroeder, woman, and Ron Dellums, black, because he didn't like having such people on his committee.[3] However, in the 1960s and '70s, reforms stripped away much of that imperious authority.

Even earlier, procedures arose for disinterring bills from committee graveyards. As detailed below, suspension of the rules, discharge petitions, Calendar Wednesday, and the twenty-one- day rule became available in the House. Methods in the Senate differed.

At certain times, a Representative may move to bring a bill to the floor immediately by suspension of the rules. That is allowed on certain days, usually Monday or Tuesday of each week and during a session's last six days. To be successful, such a motion must garner two-thirds of those voting. Thus, it is seldom used and even more rarely successful for anything controversial.[4]

In 1909 "Calendar Wednesday" was created in the House. On that day of every week the roll of standing committees would be called in alphabetical order, and each committee in turn could bring a bill to the floor even if the initial committee had not favorably reported the bill and even if the Rules Committee had not created a special rule for it. But for two reasons that proved to be ineffective: (1) the first couple of committees might use up the whole day so that others never got the chance to advance their legislation; so a panel like Veterans' Affairs would seldom be reached; and (2) by majority vote of the House, that entire procedure could be dispensed with.[5] If the latter does not occur, Calendar Wednesday actions can be fraught with such delaying tactics as to resemble a filibuster: tactics such as roll calls on quorums and motions to adjourn. Representative Richard Bolling, D-MO, called the C.W. process "a form of masochism, akin to volunteering for the medieval rack."[6] Thus, it is seldom used.[7]

Early 1949 brought the twenty-one-day rule to the House. Under it, a committee chair could bring a bill to the floor despite lack of action by the Rules Committee if at least twenty-one days had elapsed since the committee had favorably reported the bill. That procedure was repealed in January 1951, but during its brief existence it had been used to pry eight bills out of the Rules Committee.[8]

There's also the discharge petition, created in 1910. As originally established, if a majority of the House's total membership signed a relevant petition, a bill would come to the floor despite a refusal by the initial committee or the Rules Committee to report it out.[9] The number of required signatures bounced down and back up over the years.[10] Current practice is that a bill that has been in a committee for at least thirty legislative days, and any bill reported favorably by a committee without receiving a rule from the Rules Committee after seven legislative days, can be brought to the floor on certain days by a petition signed by a majority of all Representatives.[11] Some junior Members who might actually vote for a measure if it got to the floor have been reluctant to sign discharge petitions out of fear that the leadership might retaliate.[12] The Senate also has a difficult discharge petition process.[13]

The discharge-petition procedure was set up to make success rare. The process has been seldom used for several reasons, among which is the aforementioned reluctance of some Members to go on record against the powers controlling the House.[14] Furthermore, sometimes Representatives have signed discharge petitions and have later rescinded that action when the number of signatories got close to the magic number for success; that was a ploy to convince unversed constituents that the Member favored something he or she actually opposed.[15] Also, enough Representatives to pass a bill sometimes cosponsor it, but then some of them don't sign a discharge petition, thus raising questions about the sincerity of their co-sponsorship. Maybe they just wanted to posture to their constituents. Some Republicans, however, refused to sign discharge petitions in 2006 because they did not want to rebuff their leaders, who had advised against signing.[16]

Because of the power lodged in committees, chairs, and leaders, numerous instances have occurred of bills seemingly favored by a majority never reaching the floor. One example is the bill in the House during the 109th Congress against abuse of animals. Introduced on February 15, 2005, by late 2006 it had 324 cosponsors, more than enough for passage if the cosponsors were not engaged in deceit and all voted for it, but it never broke out of committee. Judiciary Committee chair James Sensenbrenner, R-WI, opposed its release.[17]

Of the hundreds of discharge petitions filed over the years, few have achieved the needed signatures, and the number of bills passed and laws enacted as a result is miniscule.[18] A noteworthy instance of success occurred in August 1970, when Representative Martha Griffiths, D-MI, extracted the Equal Rights Amendment from its decades-long sojourn in the Judiciary Committee.[19]

The House formerly had a rule that the names of Members signing discharge petitions would not be disclosed unless the petition garnered enough signatures to pass. That curtain was snatched away in 1993 to make Representatives more accountable. One book explains the reason for the secrecy: "In this way, lawmakers could say they favored a particular piece of legislation that might be stalled in committee, but no one would ever know if they had signed up to help free it."[20] In 1993, Representative James Inhofe, R-OK, introduced House Resolution 134 to make the names public. Of course, it was not reported out of committee; so Inhofe initiated a discharge petition.

Virtually no public agitation on this little-known procedure existed before Inhofe stirred the pot. The mainstream media did not embrace the cause, but radio talk shows and supporters of former Presidential candidate Ross Perot did. Some of the latter even protested around the clock in front of the Boston office of reform opponent Joe Moakley, chairman of the Rules Committee.

The House overlords objected to ending the secrecy out of fear they would "lose iron control of the legislative process if a majority of Members have a realistic way of bringing bills to the floor."[21] But of course they did not go public with that rationale; instead, they argued that the reform would increase the influence of lobbyists and result in "flavor-of-the-month" legislation. Moakley complained that the heightened public interest "shows what can happen if you run this House by plebiscite rather than going through the committees. You'll get outsiders running the place and bad legislation."[22]

Speaking of outsiders having influence, a pro-secrecy scholar at the liberal Brookings Institution advised the Rules Committee against amending the proposal on the grounds that doing so would "only inflame the public further."[23] Imagine that! Congress being advised against whetting public interest in its procedures. In a hypocritical, we'll-use-it-when-it-helps-us reliance on outside influence, Moakley brought a scholar from the American Enterprise Institute to a meeting of freshmen Democrats to caution about the alleged bad consequences of tearing away the secrecy shroud.[24] The concealment of signatures on discharge petitions only began in 1932,[25] but of course, the advocates of keeping the public in the dark didn't explain why that had not been necessary for the first twenty-two years of the discharge procedure. Inhofe's counter to his opponents was that "without this reform, a handful of elite leadership makes the determination as to what legislation we can debate or vote on."[26]

Barred by the rules from disclosing the signers' names, Inhofe sent the names of the non-signers to The Wall Street Journal.[27] The resulting publicity procured more signers, led to the discharge petition's success, and caused Resolution 134 to pass. At least forty Representatives, all Democrats, fought to the end and voted against the bill. Their number included some who were recent leaders of the House: Pelosi, Murtha, and Rangel.[28]

Many people would agree that ending the secrecy about who signed discharge petitions has advanced democracy. But it runs afoul of incompleteness—because the barons of the House have other ways of dealing adversely with bills they disfavor. To avoid a successful discharge petition, a committee can report out the bill after mutilating its original intent. Or the Speaker can simply refuse to bring a reported bill to the floor. Or the bill may be brought to the floor under a rule from the Rules Committee that is advantageous to the leadership but disadvantageous to Representatives favoring the bill.[29]

CORRECTIVE SOLUTIONS

The creation of devices such as discharge petitions showed that many Members believed that the old ways were too restrictive. Thus, procedures are in place for bypassing committee blockage. However, the limited successful use of those devices is a continued showing that House majorities still face hurdles that inhibit enactments. All that's missing is will.

In the Senate, it's easier to get floor consideration, because a bill that might have gone to a committee can be attached as a non-germane "rider" to a bill that's already on the floor. And a bill already passed by the House can go directly to the full Senate.[30]

Notes: Chapter XXX. Committee Power to Kill Bills, Especially in the House

[1]If you conduct an Internet search for this quotation, you'll get numerous "hits" that ascribe it to "anonymous." I found a few that make it seem that the originator was ad executive David Ogilvy. On page 20 of his book Ogilvy on Advertising (New York:

Crown Publishers, 1983) he includes a slightly different version of the quotation and puts it in quotation marks, as if he's using someone else's words, but cites no source.

[2]David J. Vogler, The Politics of Congress (Boston: Allyn and Bacon, 1974), p. 116.

[3]Robert V. Remini, The House: The History of the House of Representatives (New York: Collins, a division of HarperCollins; Smithsonian Books, 2006), p. 445.

[4]Charles W. Johnson, "How Our Laws Are Made," revised edition (2003), pp. 24-25 (House Document 108-93, 108th Congress, 1st Session); Warren Weaver, Jr., Both Your Houses: The Truth About Congress (New York: Praeger Publishers, 1972), pp. 90-91.

[5]Remini, The House, 272, 368; Joseph S. Clark, Congress: The Sapless Branch (Westport, CT: Greenwood Press, 1964), 134; Weaver, Both Your Houses, pp. 91-93.

[6]Ibid., p. 93. For the early history of the discharge process see Congressional Record, permanent edition, April 15, 1936, pp. 5509-10.

[7]Formerly, a bill placed on the House's Consent Calendar could be brought to the floor on each month's first or third Monday—unless even one Representative objected. Thus, that procedure could scarcely succeed and was abolished in 1995; Remini, The House, 368; Walter J. Oleszek, Congressional Procedures and the Policy Process, 2d edition (Washington: CQ Press, 1984), pp. 100-01, 104.

[8]Remini, The House, 353-54, 357; Clark, Congress: The Sapless Branch, p. 135.

[9]Weaver, Both Your Houses, p. 91. For the early history of discharge process see Congressional Record, permanent edition, April 15, 1936, pp. 5509-10.

[10]Changed to 150 during only March 1923-March 1925, it went back to 218 in March 1925, down to 145 in December 1931, and back to 218 in 1935.

[11]Johnson, "How Our Laws Are Made," pp. 23-24.

[12]Clark, Congress: The Sapless Branch, pp. 134, 177.

[13]Randall B. Ripley, Congress: Process and Policy (New York: W. W. Norton, 1975), p. 76. For details on the process see Walter J. Oleszek, Congressional Procedures and the Policy Process, 7th edition (Washington: CQ Press, 2007), pp. 249-50.

[14]Clark, Congress: The Sapless Branch, p. 134.

[15]Weaver, Both Your Houses, p. 91.

[16]Kelly McCormack, "Lawmakers try to keep their bills alive during final week," The Hill, December 6, 2006, on the Internet. Representative Bob Filner's bill to provide

benefits to certain World War II personnel had 267 cosponsors but lacked about forty signatures for his discharge petition to succeed (only 218 signatures needed).

[17]Ibid. Sensenbrenner released a statement saying "Animal fighting is an abhorrent practice but is best handled by those already working to combat its practice—state and local officials"; John Cochran, ABC News, "House Judiciary Chairman Blocks Bill Against Animal Fighting," November 14, 2006, on the Internet.

[18]Weaver, Both Your Houses, p. 91.

[19]"Constitutional Amendment," Congressional Quarterly Weekly Report, August 14, 1970, pp. 2041-42; "1976 Democratic Convention Officials," ibid., July 10, 1976, p. 1801.

[20]Bill Thomas, Club Fed: Power, Money, Sex, and Violence on Capitol Hill (New York: Charles Scribner's Sons, 1994), p. 241.

[21]"Hands Off Inhofe," The Wall Street Journal, September 20, 1993, p. A14.

[22]Clifford Krauss, "Public Mood Bolsters Effort to End House's Secrecy Rule," The New York Times, September 14, 1993, p. A22.

[23]"Hands Off Inhofe," p. A14.

[24]"Discharge Drama," The Wall Street Journal, September 10, 1993, p. A18.

[25]The rule began in 1932 as a precedent set by Speaker John Nance Garner, D-TX; see Clarence Cannon, Cannon's Precedents of the House of Representatives of the United States . . . (Washington: Government Printing Office, 1935), Vol. VII (continuing Hinds' Precedents), p. 123, section 1008.

[26]Krauss, "Public Mood," p. A22.

[27]For the list, see "End Congress's Gag Rule, The Wall Street Journal, August 17, 1993, p. A14.

[28]See the list in "Real House Reform," The Wall Street Journal, September 30, 1993, p. A18; it's also in Congressional Record, permanent edition, September 28, 1993, p. 22718. For the debate leading up to the vote see ibid., pp. 22699-22718.

[29]Phil Kuntz, "Anti-Secrecy Drive Putting Democrats on Defensive," Congressional Quarterly Weekly Report, September 11, 1993, p. 2370.

[30]Ripley, Congress: Process and Policy, pp. 76-77; Johnson, "How Our Laws Are Made," p. 41. See Senate Rule XIV, clauses 3 and 4, 110th Congress.

XXXI. House Committee on Rules: Necessity and Problem

EPIGRAPH: The House Rules Committee . . . exercises enormous power to flout democracy.
> ---Senator Joseph S. Clark, Congress: The Sapless Branch (1964), p. 135.

The House has a powerful Committee on Rules composed of thirteen Members. It can dictate the procedures, i.e., the "rules," under which a bill will be considered by the Committee of the Whole and by the full House. Those rules vary from bill to bill but will always establish that a bill can be dealt with only under those controls—if they are approved by a simple majority of the House.

Such limitations are necessary for a body of 435 members. Without them, the House could be so hog-tied by individuals or factions that it could not act. Of course, the rules under which bills come to the floor deprive Members of supposed rights. But imagine a House of Representatives in which each of the 435 had the right to speak as long and as often as he or she wished, or in which each Member could offer one or more amendments to a bill. A minority of one could thus deprive 434 of their right to move forward with legislation. Therefore, the right to obstruct is moderated by the right to act.

It was not always thus. In the first years under the Constitution the House was small enough that unlimited debate was permitted. By 1811 that right was so abused and obstructive that the House adopted the parliamentary device of a motion for the previous question. If a member could get the floor, he could say, "I move the previous question." If there was a second, the motion was not debatable and had to be voted on immediately. If it passed, it shut off debate on the previously pending motion and required another immediate vote. The trouble was that a Member who already had the floor could still speak as long as he wanted. So, in 1841, the House began to limit debate to one hour per Member,[1] and in 1847 it restricted each Member to five minutes speaking on amendments.[2]

In the years after Reconstruction, the will of the majority was often frustrated by motions designed merely to delay action and by quorum failures when Members who were present refused to vote. That ended in January 1890[3] when new Speaker Thomas Reed, R-ME, soon to be so powerful that he would be called "Czar" Reed, ensured quorums by ordering the House clerk to list as present all Members who were in the chamber but refusing to vote. Objections by Democrats led to several days of strife, during which Reed at one time locked the House doors to prevent Democrats from leaving and then some Democrats tried to hide under their desks to avoid being counted.[4] At about the same time, he announced that he would not recognize any Member who merely intended to make a dilatory motion. The House changed its rules to sustain those actions. Reed also empowered the Rules Committee to determine in what order bills would reach the full House, and to limit debate and amendments on bills.[5] With Reed chairing the Rules Committee as well as being Speaker, he had almost dictatorial control, but he also made the House more efficient. That situation continued under Reed's successors until a revolt in 1910 against Speaker Joseph Cannon, R-IL, ended his power to appoint committee chairs and members and displaced him from the Rules Committee. But the authority of the Rules Committee itself did not abate and continues almost fully now.

As a standing committee, Rules began in 1880 with five members. Later changes varied the number.[6] In 1983 its size dropped from sixteen to thirteen for a strange reason: Speaker O'Neill could not find enough senior Members willing to fill vacancies on Rules. Although the Committee still had enormous power, Members began to prefer serving on other committees, such as Banking, which they believed would put them more in contact with influential outside forces that could favorably affect their re-election efforts. Congressional Quarterly Weekly Report expressed it thusly:

"A generation ago, Rules was filled with legislative specialists of both parties whose interest was the internal workings of the House. Most of them had safe seats in one-party districts, and the 'inside game' fascinated them far more than the politics of the places they came from. For every member who found a place on the panel, several were turned away.

In the years since then, however, most members have turned their focus outside the institution and its gamesmanship. The safe House seats of the 1980s are secure because their occupants spend thousands of hours each year planning their local media coverage and collecting the campaign money that can overwhelm a challenger, if it does not scare him away altogether.

For many of these members, strategic placement in the committee system is the first step toward re-election security."[7]

Party Members are technically elected to the Committee by the House but are actually selected by the Speaker or minority leader, followed by approval from the Democratic caucus or Republican conference .[8]

During many of the years prior to 1961, the Rules chairman had such dictatorial power that the Committee might as well have had just one member. That was illustrated in 1922[9] when chairman Philip Campbell, R-KS, told a recalcitrant member, "You can go to hell. It makes no difference what a majority of you decide. If it meets with my disapproval, it shall not be done. I am the committee. In me reposes absolute obstructive power."[10] Even as late as 1960, Rules chairman Howard W. Smith, D-VA, said, "The only legislation I will agree to consider is the minimum-wage bill. You can tell your liberal friends that they will get that—or nothing. If you try to bring up anything else, I'll adjourn the meeting."[11]

Supposedly, the Committee cannot amend a bill. Its power is allegedly only to set limits on debate and amendments for when a bill is in the full House, and its authority does not include making judgments about whether the bill should even be considered. But willful men often refuse to be straightjacketed by technicalities, rules, or requirements. As one book explains, "It is unreasonable on the face of it to put a controversial piece of legislation before fifteen politicians and instruct them to ignore the substance of the bill and only determine *how* it can best be handled on the floor."[12] Therefore, the Committee sometimes does amend bills. It can do so directly and then send its amended version forward, or it can create a self-executing rule (see below), or it can force "amendments to bills as a condition for allowing them to be considered on the House floor."[13]

There has never been a formal House ban on bill amendments by the Rules Committee. It has just been tradition, which began with the panel's creation in 1789 for the sole purpose of making general rules to govern the House. And for almost 100 years it did only that at the start of each Congress and then disbanded. But in 1880 the House made it a standing (permanent) committee,[14] and shortly thereafter it expanded its authority by beginning the creation of special rules, also called special orders, for the House to follow for each individual bill, an innovation upheld by the Speaker's ruling in 1883. Those ad hoc rules related only to whether the full House would consider a bill and, if so, under what conditions.[15]

The Rules Committee can send a bill to the floor under either a "closed" or an "open" rule, an innovation developed in 1883.[16] The House, by a simple majority vote, almost always adopts the Committee's recommendation by suspending its regular rules and substituting the ad hoc rule employed for just that one bill. This applies also to bills coming from conference committees.[17] An open rule, while still limiting debate, allows amendments on the floor. Closed rules may permit no amendments and offer Members take-it-or-leave-it choices[18] Rules greatly influence a bill's chances of passage by the full House. As one author wrote, "Rules are never neutral in their effects."[19]

But in a revision of House rules later in the 1880s, the Committee's power was enlarged by allowing it to recommend a special order on a bill not reported out of another committee. Further, the Rules panel could force an amendment on another committee by refusing to recommend House consideration without it. The Rules Committee could thus "substitute its own judgement [sic] for that of the legislative committees of the House on matters of substantive policy."[20] If the Committee—or simply its chairman—opposed a bill already approved by one of the legislative panels, it could just refuse to act on it and thus keep it off the floor.

Worse lay ahead. For instance, the Committee recommended a special order in 1915 for a bill that had not even been introduced.[21] And, on occasion, when a majority in each chamber favored a measure but passed it in somewhat different forms, Rules refused to authorize a House/Senate conference to create one bill, thus defeating the intention of hundreds of other Members.[22] Lodging those independent, overriding powers in a small group dominated by its chairperson, weakened America's legislative democracy. For a while, the Committee had such dominion that it was sometimes called the third house of Congress.[23]

In 1909 the House went from the impossible to the merely difficult in getting some bills past Rules Committee blockage: It created Calendar Wednesday. See the immediately preceding chapter. Other possible detours around Rules Committee blockage are the discharge petition and suspension of the rules, also previously explained.

Speaker Sam Rayburn lassoed this maverick committee in 1961. It happened thusly: During preceding years, Rules had operated under autocratic chairman Howard W. Smith as a roadblock to liberal legislation because he was supported by a coalition of another Southern Democrat and four Republicans. Rayburn, a Democrat, wanted to enlarge the Rules Committee with Members who would support the Speaker and President Kennedy's agenda. He believed that winning that change was supremely important, for otherwise "Smith would emerge as the undisputed dictator of the House."[24] Following a month of hard politicking that Rayburn later called "the worst fight of my life,"[25] the House approved the expansion to fifteen by a vote of 217- 212.[26]

That change lessened Rules' independence and made it largely an appendage of the Speakership because the same group that elected the Speaker, the party caucus of the House's majority party, appointed the majority of the Committee. Nevertheless, its powers remained largely intact.

Even now, the Committee can actually amend bills through the so-called "self-executing" rules. A self-executing rule includes changes to a bill. Those revisions are accepted by the House if the rule is adopted. One book's explanation is this:

> Once this rule is adopted, Members are prohibited from having a
> separate vote on the amendment in the Committee of the Whole or,
> later, in the House after the Committee of the Whole rises. In
> addition, an amendment that is brought to the House floor in this
> way cannot be amended because the amendment has already been
> adopted. In order to vote against or to change the amendment,
> Members must vote to amend or reject the rule itself. And, of
> course, if the rule is defeated, the House cannot proceed to
> consider the bill at all.[27]

Placing such power in so few hands is hardly what many Americans would prefer in their democracy. That process permits the leadership to impose its legislative interests. An example occurred on October 29, 1987, later referred to as "Black Thursday" by Republicans harking back to the stock market crash in 1929. Speaker Jim Wright, D-TX, influenced the Rules Committee to report a rule on a budget bill that incorporated ten amendments, some of which dealt with major policy such as welfare reform. That was too gagging for even some Democrats to swallow, and the rule failed. Wright then obtained a different, less radical, rule from the Committee.[28] Republicans saw the day as "black" because of what happened next: Three departures from "regular order." See below in the chapter on Violations.

Rules Committee "emergency" sessions are another method of control by the few. The Committee's own rules dictate that each member shall be notified 48 hours in advance of all regular meetings but that the chair may call emergency meetings, with notice to members "as soon as possible" thereafter. Emergency conclaves have been frequent in recent years. During the 108th Congress, the Committee fashioned 60 percent of all its special orders in such gatherings, many of which occurred in the dead of night. As two observers noted, that was "a lot of emergencies."[29]

Furthermore, in the 108th Congress, the Committee used another device for preventing interference by "outside" Representatives. Its special orders for the consideration of 28 conference reports prohibited (waived) points of order on those reports and on their consideration. As those two observers wrote, "This action made it virtually impossible to discover what was in each conference report before voting on it."[30] Additionally, quick passage of a conference report worked against content discovery. The conference-report bill adding prescription drug benefits to Medicare was 850 pages long and was passed at 6:00 A.M. on November 22, 2003, only 29 hours after returning to the House. One might think that such a complex and costly program deserved more perusal.[31]

In a further departure from democracy, the House sometimes approves a "king-of-the-hill" rule from the Rules Committee. It provides that a series of amendments to substitute new language for virtually all the old language in a bill will be voted on in tandem, but only the last vote will have any effect on the bill. As with so many Congressional procedures, there's something sneaky here: Members can vote for or against any of the substitutes that don't count and then publicize those votes in their next election campaign as if they were meaningful. To their credit, Republicans opposed that perversion of democracy and did not use king-of-the-hill rules when they controlled the House during 1995-2006. Instead, they opted for queen-of-the-hill rules, by which the substitute getting the most votes in Committee of the Whole was voted on in the House.[32]

CORRECTIVE SOLUTIONS

The House should create standing rules to do the following, if not more: ● prevent self-executing rules, ● outlaw waivers on points of order on conference reports, ● modify closed rules so that a limited number of amendments can receive floor consideration, ● prevent the Rules Committee from refusing to authorize a conference committee, and ● use an enforceable mechanism to prevent the Rules Committee from amending bills.

Former Representative Tim Penny, D-MN, argued that the Rules Committee should be abolished and that the majority party leadership should make the rules. That would supposedly save money, and voters could more easily assign blame.[33] To this author that seems like a substitution that would make almost no practical difference except to encumber the leaders.

Notes: Chapter XXXI. House Committee on Rules: Necessity and Problem

[1] Robert V. Remini, The House: The History of the House of Representatives (New York: Collins, a division of HarperCollins; Smithsonian Books, 2006), p. 130, says Rep. John C. Clark introduced the one-hour rule; but see Asher C. Hinds, Hinds' Precedents of the House of Representatives of the United States . . . (5 vols.; Washington: Government Printing Office, 1907), vol. V, , p. 24, citing Congressional Globe, pp. 152-55 (1841) and p. 620 (1842).

[2] Warren Weaver, Jr., Both Your Houses: The Truth About Congress (New York: Praeger Publishers, 1972,), pp. 83-84.

[3] Remini, The House, p. 248.

[4] Ibid., p. 250.

[5] Thomas E. Mann and Norman J. Ornstein, The Broken Branch: How Congress Is Failing America and How to Get It Back on Track (New York: Oxford University Press, 2006), pp. 30-31.

[6] It was increased to ten in 1910, eleven (1911), twelve (from 1917 to 1961 except for fourteen members during part of the 1930s, and fifteen (1961); James A. Robinson, The House Rules Committee (Indianapolis: Bobbs-Merrill, 1963; reprint, Westport, CT: Greenwood Press, 1983), pp. 58, 71-72. Its size remained at fifteen until 1975, and became sixteen from 1975 to 1983. Then it was reduced to thirteen, but the number sometimes varies.

[7] Alan Ehrenhalt, "Congress and the Country, The Unfashionable House Rules Committee," Congressional Quarterly Weekly Report, January 15, 1983, p. 151.

[8] House Rule X, clause 5(a)(1), 110th Congress, says, "The standing committees specified in clause 1 shall be elected by the House . . . from nominations submitted by the respective party caucus or conference." Each of those bodies, however, has devolved the Rules Committee nominations upon the Speaker or minority leader. David M. Richardson, "The Rules Committee of the U.S. House of Representatives: An Increasingly More Powerful Tool in Securing the Majority's Control Over the Making of Public Policy," M.A. thesis, George Washington University, 1997, p. 20, says that in 1975 the House Democratic Caucus gave the Speaker the power "to nominate all the Democratic members of the Committee, while leaving the party's Policy and Steering Committee to continue to nominated [sic] Democratic Representatives to the other standing committees"; Walter J. Oleszek, Congressional Procedures and the Policy Process, 7th edition (Washington: CQ Press, 2007), p. 124. See also Barbara Sinclair, "The Speaker as Party Leader," in The Speaker: Leadership in the U.S. House of Representatives, edited by Ronald M. Peters, Jr. (Washington: Congressional Quarterly, Inc., 1995), p. 45.

[9]George B. Galloway, <u>History of the House of Representatives</u> (New York: Thomas Y. Crowell Co., 1961), p. 143, gives the exact year.

[10]Weaver, <u>Both Your Houses</u>, p. 83. See also Remini, <u>The House</u>, p. 296: "Representative Thomas Blanton complained that Chairman Campbell had 'kept the rule in his pocket and choked the will of Congress and laughed at us when we insisted that he obey the rules as a servant of this House, and we were absolutely helpless.'"

[11]Andy Plattner, "New Rules Committee Head Expected to Carry Forward In Tradition of Rep. Bolling," <u>Congressional Quarterly Weekly Report</u>, November 6, 1982, p. 2801, citing Neil MacNeil, <u>Forge of Democracy</u>.

[12]Weaver, <u>Both Your Houses</u>, p. 94.

[13]Richardson, "The Rules Committee," (1997), p. 7.

[14]It had briefly been a standing committee during 1849-1852; ibid., p. 3, note 3.

[15]Ibid., pp. 3-4.

[16]Ibid.; see also ibid., pp. 36-38.

[17]Mann & Ornstein, <u>Broken Branch</u>, p. 172.

[18]In the case of the House not acting on a rule relating to a particular bill, there are methods to force action. If seven legislative days have elapsed without House consideration of a rule, any Rules Committee member may offer it as a privileged motion. And if the House has adopted a rule but no motion to consider the bill has been made within seven calendar days, any committee that had initial jurisdiction of the bill may direct the offering of such a motion as a privileged matter. Charles W. Johnson, "How Our Laws Are Made," revised edition (2003), p. 23 (House Document 108-93, 108th Congress, 1st Session).

[19]Sinclair, "The Speaker as Party Leader," p. 54.

[20]Richardson, "The Rules Committee, p. 7.

[21]Weaver, <u>Both Your Houses</u>, p. 89.

[22]Ibid., p. 90; David J. Vogler, <u>The Politics of Congress</u> (Boston: Allyn and Bacon, 1974) p. 157; Joseph S. Clark, <u>Congress: The Sapless Branch</u> (Westport, CT: Greenwood Press, 1964), pp. 133, 177.

[23]Weaver, <u>Both Your Houses</u>, p. 83. The term "third house of Congress" has also been applied to House-Senate conference committees, lobbyists, and even the Supreme Court.

[24]Richardson, "The Rules Committee," p. 18, citing Dierenfield, <u>Keeper of the Rules</u>, p. 179.

[25]Richardson, "The Rules Committee," p. 17, citing Ronald E. Elving, "The Baron of the Rules Committee is Brought to Heel by 'Speaker Sam,'" <u>Congressional Quarterly Weekly Report</u>, April 29, 1995, p. 1158.

[26]Rimini, <u>The House</u>, pp. 384-87.

[27]Richardson, "The Rules Committee," p. 45.

[28]Mann & Ornstein, <u>Broken Branch</u>, pp. 8, 74, 172.

[29]Ibid., p. 172.

[30]Ibid.

[31]Ibid., pp. 172-73.

[32]Oleszek, <u>Congressional Procedures</u>, 7th edition, pp. 138-39.

[33]"House Misrule," <u>The Wall Street Journal</u>, September 7, 1993, p. A16.

XXXII. The Congressional Budget Office

EPIGRAPH: Look to the essence of a thing, whether it be a point of doctrine,
of practice, or of interpretation.
---Marcus Aurelius, Meditations, VIII, 22.

Created in 1974 and first operating in 1975, the Congressional Budget Office is a nonpartisan, unbiased agency in the legislative branch of the federal government. Its mission is to provide Congress with timely estimated costs of proposed legislation, based on a bill's specific provisions. The process is called "scoring," and the resulting estimates are the "scores." The score on a particular bill often has a huge political impact, as it may greatly advance or retard the bill's possible enactment.

Though it's officially nonpartisan, some observers might aver that the CBO is only ostensibly impartial. For one thing, the Director of the CBO is appointed by partisans, the Speaker of the House and the President Pro Tempore of the Senate. Does that make his or her leadership partisan? Who's to say? Also, CBO's hundreds of employees, like everyone else, generally have preconceptions and biases that can seep into their actions. Would such ideas push their actions toward one party's goals? Who's to say? Are the CBO's analyses improperly influenced by its outside advisors and by selected economic models?[1] Lacking answers to these ostensible problems, the wisest move may be to rely on the benefit of the doubt and consider the CBO to be truly nonpartisan.

Members of Congress who favor a draft measure have an incentive to get a "good" score on it, meaning one that will be resistant to claims that it's too expensive. Opponents may pick away at the "good" score as relying on such errors as faulty assumptions, omission of key data, flawed drafting, or questionable details. Such problems would typically originate in the House or Senate, not in the CBO—because the CBO must score only what it's given.

Thus, for example, if CBO were to get a bill proposing government revenue flowing from the sale of a national park, that money would have to be included in the score, though such a sale would not happen, thus making the score an unrealizable fantasy.[2]

Including such fictions, even if not so extreme, is a legal method by which CBO scoring of bills can produce a partisan result—and it's not due to faults within the CBO or to the psyches of its workers. That biased result flows from the imperative that CBO may only score what's in a bill and what's in current laws, not information or concepts lying outside the proposed legislation and existing laws. If a bill is crafted by just one party, without true bipartisan creation, its premises and details, being partisan, will force a CBO score that reflects that one-sided product.[3]

A recent example of inclusion of unrealistic provisions merely to get a good score was the so-called CLASS Act (Community Living Assistance Services and Supports) that was part of the Democrats' major health-care law of 2010. The Wall Street Journal reported on it in February 2012 as follows:
> [It] "was grafted onto the health-care bill mostly to hide that bill's true costs. Class came with a five-year waiting period before it started to pay out benefits, but it started collecting revenues immediately. The front-loading helped ObamaCare appear to reduce the deficit in the short run —even though the Class Act was designed to go broke after a decade, which is outside the Congressional Budget Office's 10-year budget window."[4]

Another reason the CBO score may be a fantasy is the reliance on the status quo of existing laws. Addressing the out years as if no new laws will alter old projections turns Einstein's definition of insanity upside down: It's expecting an ordained result as if nothing changes but the passage of time. That's how generals lose wars. And our legislative generals should take note and remember that change is the only constant. They can meditate on the mutability of all things mundane.[5]

A further issue is that CBO uses static rather than dynamic scoring. Static scoring rests on the assumption that legislation will not change the gross domestic product (GDP) and that affected Americans will not modify their economic activities because of the law. Dynamic scoring assumes the opposite, that a new law may change people's actions and thus change the GDP.[6] How sensible is it to score a bill, such as a health-care proposal that affects about 16 to 17 percent of the economy, as if neither behavior nor GDP will change? About as sensible as a world map that omits North America and Asia.

Also, Congress generally creates bills that deal with a ten-year "budget window." That causes CBO estimates to reflect costs for the next ten years, not for one, twenty, or whatever. Use of that limited budget window means that a CBO score may not be realistic for most of the future.

The length of budget windows can be changed. If Congress or budgeteers in the executive branch want to refer to future deficits, for example, they can move from ten-year windows to five-year projections and thus minimize the bad news.

A final thing to remember is that a score from CBO is only an artful estimate, not a reflection of absolute certainty. When a bill requires the implementation of numerous regulations created by officials in the executive branch, those regs will affect the costs of the legislation. That was a monumental weakness in the score of 2010's Patient Protection and Affordable Care Act.

Yet the CBO occasionally notes the problems of unrealistic bill provisions, as in "CBO's 2011 Long Term Budget Outlook. That analysis contained two projections, an "extended-baseline scenario" and an "alternative fiscal scenario." The former "adheres closely to current law" while the latter looks at probable changes to current laws. Among those are provisions "that might be difficult to sustain for a long period," which include parts of the 2010 health-care law.[7]

Representatives, Senators, and their staffs sometimes use black magic in their discussion of scores, such as reliance on a bill's new taxes starting long before payouts. And such as using scores from two different time frames for a supposedly valid comparison.[8]

In this how-much-will-it-cost exercise, not only will the CBO have to accept a bill's fantastical projections, it will also have to ignore any increased interest on the national debt if the bill adds to the debt.[9]

In their effort to get a good score, advocates of a bill sometimes spend months ping-ponging a bill with the CBO. They'll submit one version, and if it scores badly, they'll revise and resubmit. If it still scores poorly, it's back to revision mode. This can continue until the latest version finally gets a good score. For example, for his Healthy Americans Act, Senator Ron Wyden, D-OR, reported that he spent eighteen months doing that with CBO Director Peter Orszag. As he said, "It was every week on the sofas in our office going back and forth with various iterations and alternatives."[10]

Another way to try for a "good" score can occur when the President favors a bill and calls the Director of the CBO to the White House to talk about it. Barack Obama did that on July 20, 2009, regarding health-care legislation. Senator John Cornyn, R-TX, said the meeting seemed to be Obama's "way to try to send a not-too-subtle message to him [CBO head] that, 'You better work with us on this.'" However, Cornyn went on to say, "So far, I'd say CBO has done a decent job in a very difficult situation."[11]

CORRECTIVE SOLUTIONS

Scores should mention any bill provisions deemed unlikely to produce the scoring result presented.

Every score should have a section of disclaimers clearly stating that the score would be different beyond the ten-year window, and that the score assumes no effect flowing from future changes in existing law.

Scores should include a statement about a bill's effect on interest payable on the national debt.

Every score should include explanations of static and dynamic scoring and a statement of which was used.

Notes: Chapter XXXII. The Congressional Budget Office.

[1]On questions about advisors and economic models, see Jenny Strasburg, "Congress's Number Cruncher Comes Under Fire," The Wall Street Journal, February 2, 2012, p. A6.

[2]For one analysis of problems with CBO cost estimates, this one regarding the 2010 health law and Representative Ryan's 2011 "A Roadmap for America's Future," proposal, see Jeffrey H. Anderson, "The Democrats' Fuzzy Math," The Weekly Standard, July 18, 2011, pp. 10-11.

[3]". . . the CBO scored Obamacare as reducing the deficit because it was forced to take into account spending cuts the Democrats had no intention of making (among other flimsy criteria)"; Rob Port, "Republicans Are Right to Reject CBO Scoring Of Obamacare," January 7, 2011. Available on the Internet at http://sayanthingblog.com/entry/republicans-are-right-to-reject-cbo-scoring-of-obamacare/

[4]"Class Warfare," The Wall Street Journal, February 1, 2012, p. A14.

[5]Here, I'm using "mundane" in the sense of "earthly as opposed to heavenly"; I'm not using it in the sense of "common" or "ordinary."

[6]One source for information about static and dynamic scoring is the Urban Institute's Rudolph G. Penner, "Dynamic Scoring: Not so Fast!," April 21, 2006, on the Internet. Another is from the Heritage Foundation: Daniel Mitchell, "The Correct Way to Measure the Revenue Impact of Changes in Tax Rates, May 3, 2002, on the Internet (20 pages).

[7]"CBO's 2011 Long-term Budget Outlook," www.cbo.gov/doc.cfm?index=12212. See also Austin Frakt, "Railing against CBO scoring: The wrong debate," The Incidental Economist blog, October 18, 2010. Taken from the Internet at http://theincidentaleconomist.com/wordpress/railing-against-cbo-scoring-the-wrong-debate.

[8]This relates to the health-care law's 2010-2019 time period and the score of the repeal possibility's time frame of 2012-2021; see "Setting the Record Straight," Majority Staff of House Committee on the Budget, January 6, 2011. Available on the Internet at http://budget.house.gov/News/DocumentSingle.aspx?DocumentID=219186.

[9]Donald B. Barron, "Understanding CBO Health Cost Estimates, Backgrounder #2298, July 15, 2009, The Heritage Foundation. Available on the Internet at http://www.heritage.org/Research/Reports/2009/07/Understanding-CBO-Health-Cost-Estimates.

[10]Ezra Klein, interviewer and editor, "How to Get a Good CBO Score: An Interview With Sen. Ron Wyden," June 19, 2009. Available on the Internet.

[11]Human Events, "Republicans Concerned CBO Scoring Is Partisan?," October 26, 2009. Available on the Internet at http://www.humanevents.com/article.php?id=34123.

XXXIII. The Conference Committee Problem

EPIGRAPH: If an orange and an apple went into conference consultations,
it might come out a pear.
       ---Ronald Reagan.

The above quotation from Ronald Reagan is perfectly illustrated by a bill for funding Army Corps of Engineers projects. As reported by the Wall Street Journal, "The Senate passed a bill that cost roughly $14 billion, and the House a different bill at $15 billion. Then they got together in conference and compromised—at $23.2 billion."[1]

When House and Senate each adopts a somewhat different bill on the same subject, neither becomes law unless the differences are eliminated so that each chamber finally passes precisely the same bill. Making the separate versions of a bill identical is accomplished by an ad hoc conference committee to which each house appoints some of its members. So far so good. But several problems mock the democratic process.

Conference committees have so much power that they are sometimes called the "third house."[2] A bill finally reported by a conference committee may negate important provisions of the Senate or House version. That final bill may contain numerous additions or deletions that most Senators and Representatives are unaware of and that they would object to or defeat if given a proper chance.

One chamber may load its representation on the conference committee with Members who have a particular agenda, even to the point of opposing the main thrust of the bill. One chamber, or party, may stall the process by blocking appointments to the committee. For example, each chamber passed immigration reform bills in 2006, but the Senate version, granting amnesty to illegal aliens, died when Republican leaders in the House refused to appoint conferees.[3]

Even if conferees from both parties are appointed, those from the minority party may be excluded from the meetings. Both Democrats and Republicans have done that. For instance, in 2003, the House Ways and Means chairman told Democratic conferees that the conference committee meetings on the Medicare prescription drug bill would cancelled if they attended.[4] It got so bad that two Democratic members of that conference committee "were not let into the conference room and were physically prevented from coming inside" because "lobbyists were in the room . . . writing the bills" [sic; it was just one final bill].[5]

The chance to oppose or defeat changes made by conferences theoretically exists because after a conference committee reports the bill back to the two chambers, there must be a vote on whether to pass the final version.

A bill made unacceptable by a conference can be rejected by either chamber. But several factors work against that:
- Conference reports, i.e., revised bills and their supporting material, often appear near the end of a Congressional session, resulting in pressure to avoid a rejection that kills needed legislation.[6] If the bill is considered vital, Members may vote for it despite holding their noses against the stench of parts they don't like.
- Most Members in one chamber assume that their conferees got as much as they could.
- Members may not have time to familiarize themselves with the complexities of the conference report, i.e., the new bill; so they vote for it in the expectation that it accomplishes what their chamber originally passed.
- Members may avoid being seen as obstructionists on conference reports because they might then have trouble getting their own measures passed later.

House rules limit the amount of time for debate on a conference report. It's typically one hour.[7] Considering that a bill may have suffered a radical transformation in conference, how much democracy is there in such a brief time to discuss changes?

Furthermore, in both chambers the conference report, with limited exceptions, has to be accepted or rejected as is. For House consideration of the conference report there may even be a "rule" in effect that prevents amendments.[8] That's a reasonable requirement to prevent amended conference reports from being batted back and forth interminably between the House and Senate. But it carries an anti-democracy penalty in that it augments the power of the conferees at the expense of ordinary Members.

Because the Senate does not require that amendments be germane to the topic or thrust of the bill being amended, it can substitute whatever it wants for part or virtually all of a House-passed measure. Thus, a non-controversial bill from the House can be changed in the Senate to something that would have had to weather a storm of conflict in the House. When the House and Senate bills then go to a conference committee, the Senate version (or something close to it) may triumph. In that way the will of the House may be defeated, as subcommittee and committee hearings, discussions, mark-ups, and votes are avoided, as are the Rules Committee and consideration by the Committee of the Whole.[9]

Another tactic made possible because of bicameralism and conference committees is that the Member shepherding a bill through either chamber can accept an unwanted amendment during floor consideration in order to gain some votes for passage. Yet that Member can obtain deletion of the amendment during the conference.[10] Also, the bill's manager in one chamber may accept several non-essential amendments merely to have throw-away bargaining chips to use in conference to achieve "compromise."[11]

Conversely, House or Senate may leave out something known to be desired by the other chamber. Then, in conference the excluded matter may be accepted if the other chamber gives a quid pro quo.[12]

Formerly, conference committee meetings were always closed to other Members. What was said, how conferees voted, and what arguments or evidence were advanced were all embedded in secrecy. There was no official record of what occurred. Often the identities of Members composing a conference committee were not common knowledge. After the secret conclave had finished its alchemy, the result was presented to each house as a take-it-or-leave-it product with no amendments permitted. Senator Al Gore, father of the recent Vice President, stigmatized conference committees as "secret meetings often not even announced until the last minute [where] a few men can . . . undo in one hour the most painstaking work of months of effort by several standing committees and the full membership of both houses."[13]

Much of the secrecy was swept away in 1975 when first the House and later the Senate adopted resolutions requiring open conference committee meetings unless a majority of either chamber's conference members voted publicly for a closed conference. The House adopted a more extreme rule in 1977 by banning closed conferences without authorization by a roll-call vote of the full House; if that were violated, the conference report would be rejected if subjected to a point of order.[14]

However, as explained in an outstanding and useful book, "Conferees still conduct much of their important business in secret." They do that in informal meetings where decisions are made that are later ratified by the formal conference.[15]

Conferees, also called managers, are technically appointed for the House by the Speaker of the House. Senate conferees are technically appointed by passage of a Senate resolution, which becomes in practice appointment by the presiding officer. The Speaker and Senate presiding officer often appoint Members selected by the chair and ranking minority member of the House and Senate committees that sent a bill to the full chamber.[16] The Legislative Reorganization acts of 1946 and 1970 required that conferees must have supported the bill when it was passed by their chambers. The Speaker is now required to appoint at least a majority of conferees from among Members "who generally supported the House position as determined by the Speaker."[17] Those legal provisions, however, have not always been followed. In the days when seniority was more controlling than now, chairs usually appointed themselves and their committee's most senior members. That sometimes resulted in conferees who did not reflect majority opinion in their house or who had opposed the bill, though the latter was rare.[18] Even now, conferees may be appointed who opposed part of a bill, such as an added amendment.[19]

Laws and rules supposedly prohibit a conference committee from adding provisions not contained in the bills passed by House and Senate. Further, no conference committee may delete any provision that is identical in each chamber's bill. However, Congress's occasional disregard of legal requirements in other areas blossoms here as well. See below in the chapter on Violations.

And provisions not even voted on by a conference committee are sometimes included in its final product.[20]

Conference committees dealing with appropriation bills have notoriously added hundreds of earmarks with the result that federal spending has burgeoned beyond reason.

A cute little trick is the "motion to instruct" a chamber's conferees. Through it Members can create a record of supporting something they really oppose. The adopted motion is not binding on the conferees. Thus, a Member can support a particular policy in a motion to instruct while being certain that the policy will not become law because the conferees will ignore the instruction. In 1990, for example, the Senate version of the legislative appropriations bill slashed the funds for franking (Members' perk of mailing without postage) by about 74 percent. The money saved would be spent on treating pregnant women infected with cocaine. In a lopsided vote, the House passed a motion instructing acceptance of the Senate's change, but only three hours later the conferees took the money away from crack babies and restored it to free mail for Members.[21]

Such trickery involves two objectionable actions: (1) some Members falsely support a policy in a motion to instruct; and (2) conferees ignore the stated, and supposedly true, will of their chamber.

Conference committees have generally been small, but memberships have enlarged in recent years. Sometimes their numbers have reached astounding heights. In 1989 a conference of 232 Members adjusted a reconciliation bill, although a small group did much of the compromising.[22] In 1981, the largest-ever conference committee had 280 Members (seventy-two Senators and 208 Representatives). A monstrosity of such bloat could hardly function, so it divided its work among dozens of sub-conferences. [23]

CORRECTIVE SOLUTIONS

Enforce the existing rule that conference committees may not add new provisions to bills, and make it apply to earmarks as well as everything else.[24]

Enforce the existing rule that a conference may not delete any portion of a bill that was passed identically by each chamber.[25]

Prevent appointment to any conference committee of any Member who voted against "final" passage of the bill. Any such appointment should be subject to a point-of-order challenge.

Outlaw the use of any procedure in either chamber to block appointment of conferees. In the Senate, that would require a change relating to filibusters and holds. It might also require that a Senate resolution to appoint conferees would come to the floor automatically and could not be the victim of the Majority Leader's refusal to schedule it. In the House, some procedure could be developed for appointment of conferees in the event that the Speaker refused to act.

Each chamber should allow a point of order against any conference report created when appointed conferees were excluded from a conference.

Amend the rules of the House for a greater amount of debate time on the acceptance or rejection of bills emerging from conferences.

Allow a vote in each chamber to make binding on its conferees an adopted motion to instruct. With that procedure, a Member who voted for a policy in the motion to instruct but voted against making it binding could be exposed as not really favoring the policy.

Notes: Chapter XXXIII. The Conference Committee Problem

[1]"Water Carriers," The Wall Street Journal, October 8, 2007, p. A18.

[2]David J. Vogler, The Third House: Conference Committees in the United States Congress (Evanston, IL: Northwestern University Press, 1971).

[3]Duncan Currie, "Republican Border Wars," The Weekly Standard, November 27, 2006, p. 18.

[4]John W. Dean, Broken Government: How Republican Rule Destroyed the Legislative, Executive, and Judicial Branches (New York: Viking, 2007), p. 38, citing David E. Price, "Reflections on [Woodrow Wilson's book] Congressional Government at 120 and Congress at 216," in PS, Political Science & Politics, April 2006, pp. 232-33; see also Dean, Broken Government, pp. 43, 51. See also Thomas E. Mann and Norman J. Ornstein, The Broken Branch: How Congress Is Failing America and How to Get It Back on Track (New York: Oxford University Press, 2006), p. 158: "The Senate has frequently bent to threats from the House, and on such key issues as the Medicare prescription drug bill and the energy bill even cast aside its own rules to allow the House to bar elected Senate members of the conference committees from full participation."

[5]So stated Representative Louise Slaughter, D-NY, new chair of the Rules Committee in the 110th Congress; Congressional Record, daily edition, January 5, 2007, p. H65. She further said that the way the House dealt with the Medicare prescription drug bill in late 2003 was "a perfect example of the broken legislation produced by a broken process" and that "instead of proceeding in an open and transparent manner, conference discussions were held behind closed doors for months, excluding all Democrats"; ibid.

[6]Vogler, The Third House, p. 9.

[7]Walter Kravitz, "The Legislative Reorganization Act of 1970," Legislative Studies Quarterly, August 1990, p. 382.

[8]See ibid.; there can be votes and additional debate time in the House on nongermane Senate amendments.

[9]Vogler, The Third House, pp. 7-8.

[10]Ibid., p. 10.

[11]Ibid.

[12] Walter J. Oleszek, Congressional Procedures and the Policy Process, 7th edition (Washington: CQ Press, 2007), p. 259.

[13]David J. Vogler, The Politics of Congress (Boston: Allyn and Bacon, 1974) p. 181.

[14]Kravitz, "The Legislative Reorganization Act of 1970, p. 390; Oleszek, Congressional Procedures, 7th edition, p. 255; "Reform Penetrates Conference Committees," Congressional Quarterly Weekly Report, February 8, 1975, pp. 290-94; "Senate Votes 'Sunshine' Rules for Committees," Congressional Quarterly Weekly Report, November 8, 1975, p. 2413; "Government in the Sunshine," Congressional Quarterly Weekly Report, November 15, 1975, pp. 2464-65

[15]Oleszek, Congressional Procedures, 7th edition, p. 255.

[16]See House Rule I, clause 11, 110th Congress, and Senate Rule XXIV, clause 3, and Senate Rule XXVIII, 110th Congress; Oleszek, Congressional Procedures, 7th edition, pp. 263-66.

[17]House Rule I, clause 11, 110th Congress.

[18]Vogler, Politics of Congress, pp. 180-81; Warren Weaver, Jr., Both Your Houses: The Truth About Congress (New York: Praeger Publishers, 1972,), pp. 129-31.

[19]Oleszek, Congressional Procedures, 7th edition, p. 265.

[20]Dean, Broken Government, pp. 28-29n.

[21]Eric Felten, The Ruling Class: Inside the Imperial Congress, abridged edition (Washington: U.S. Congress Assessment Project, Heritage Foundation, 1993), p. 12.

[22]For reconciliation bills generally, see the chapter on Budget and Appropriations Problems, text on page 152.

[23]Jackie Calmes, "Bush, Congress Reach Deal On Deficit-Reduction Bill," Congressional Quarterly Weekly Report, November 25, 1989, p. 3222; "Reconciliation Conferees," ibid., July 18, 1981, p. 1308; Ann Pelham, "Health Issues Still Unresolved in Conference," ibid., July 25, 1981, p. 1328; Oleszek, Congressional Procedures, 7th edition, p. 266.

[24]"Section 135 of the Reorganization Act of 1946 provided that conference committees may not insert in the compromise bills new material which was not included in the bills passed by [either] of the two chambers. But this rule is often violated . . . When this happens members may raise a point of order when the conference report is brought to the chamber floor. Like motions to instruct, though, points of order seldom are made"; Vogler, Politics of Congress, pp. 182-83. The 1946 rule was reinforced by the Legislative Reorganization Act of 1970; Walter J. Oleszek, Congressional Procedures and the Policy Process, 2d edition (Washington: CQ Press, 1984), p. 214, (not in 7th edition). For those laws see Title 2, U.S. Code, Section 190c, 1964, 1970, and 1976 editions (Public Law 79-601 and Public Law 91-510). Senate Rule XXVIII, 110th Congress, states, "Conferees shall not insert in their report matter not committed to them by either House, nor shall they strike from the bill matter agreed to by both Houses." Enforcement lies with raising a point of order. See also House Rule XXII, clause 9, 110th Congress; this was in Rule XXVIII before the recodification done by the 106th Congress).

[25]Senate Rule XXVIII and House Rule XXII, clause 9, 110th Congress. The House rule, with the opaqueness too often found in Congressional actions, does not say "nor shall they strike from the bill matter agreed to by both Houses." Instead, it prohibits a modification that "is beyond the scope of that specific matter as committed to the conference committee." An authoritative book explains "scope" in this context as meaning that "the conferees are not to add new matter, reopen provisions that both chambers agreed to, or exceed the range of the matters in disagreement committed to them"; Oleszek, Congressional Procedures, 7th edition, p. 272.

XXXIV. Violations of Procedures, Rules, Laws, "Regular Order," and the Constitution

EPIGRAPH: Nobody has a more sacred obligation to obey the law
                      than those who make the law.
                      ---Sophocles.

Returning to willful people who think themselves or their causes so important that they can violate rules, we find numerous examples in Congress.[1] The hauteur of some Senators and Representatives is stunning, their self-elevation to godlike status alarming.

Every violation by Congress weakens the rule of law. We supposedly have a government of laws, not of men and women. When the Constitution can be violated at the whim of one person, that's dictatorship. And when it can be set aside at the whim of majorities in Congress, that's just a more broad-based tyranny. That distinction was noted by colonial clergyman Mather Byles while watching rowdy crowds in Boston following the 1770 Boston Massacre: "Which is better – to be ruled by one tyrant three thousand miles away, or by three thousand tyrants not one mile away?"[2]

And if a violation is minor, that does not mean it's acceptable. Unchecked small abuses beget numerous and larger monstrosities.

● In October 1987, Speaker Jim Wright, D-TX, and his leadership team, committed actions seen as violations by some Members in getting a budget reconciliation bill passed. When a rule reported by the Rules Committee was defeated, he induced the Committee to create a different rule, one that made a major substantive change in the bill, and to take it to the floor that same day. Under normal procedures, approval of the new rule on the same day the prior rule was rejected would have required a two-thirds majority for passage. As reported by two Congress scholars, "Wright obviated that requirement by adjourning the House and immediately declaring a new 'legislative day,' a tactic that was at best unusual and at minimum a breach of the normal decorum."[3]

Part of the problem in the defeat of the original rule related to the absence of a proper quorum when the Budget Committee reported a bill called the Guaranteed Deficit Reduction Reconciliation Act. Both House and Senate have rules about the quorums necessary for committees to conduct certain types of business.[4] But quorums apparently need not be observed except for each chamber's requirement that nothing shall be reported from a committee unless a majority of the membership is physically present—and except for occasions when the full chamber waives the requirement. Chairs therefore sometimes conduct business without quorums.[5]

In the 1987 situation, the Budget Committee committed a violation by not having a quorum present when it reported the bill. Later, a Representative asked if the House was going to accept that infraction by adopting a Rules Committee dictum waiving the provision in House Rule XI that a committee cannot report a bill absent a majority of the committee. Majority Leader Foley said, "The gentleman is correct." Foley further explained the trick that had just occurred to evade the different House regulation preventing consideration of a Rules Committee rule on the same day of it being reported to the House: "This is nothing more than an attempt to complete this action without the necessity of an unscheduled Friday session." To prevent that extra day of work, the House had just adopted the Foley finagle of a motion for the House to have a second legislative day on the same calendar day, "making tomorrow today" in the words of one Member. During the subsequent hocus pocus of a day-within-a-day the House adopted by simple majority the Rules Committee rule waiving all points of order against the bill. The provision in Rule XI was thus set aside. It's common that a House rule is thus temporarily abandoned by bare majority approval rather than being suspended, which requires a two-thirds majority of Members voting.[6]

Finally, with the bill seemingly defeated by one vote, Wright held the voting period open beyond the usual fifteen minutes until a Democrat who had voted "nay" changed his vote. Outraged Republicans said those tactics occurred on "Black Thursday."[7]

● In recent years, so-called "regular order" often went AWOL in the House. The term refers to rules and traditions that not only make it possible to legislate but that ensure fair deliberation, fair voting, and laws that will be seen as legitimate.[8] The House dispensed with regular order so much that two recent scholars titled a section of their recent book "The Demise of Regular Order."[9] Careful deliberation is foundational. It provides time for the expression of differing views that prevent errors and make for better laws.

Willmore Kendall, a deep thinker on this topic, was reported as teaching that Congress "should deliberate under conditions free, open, rational, and accountable."[10] He argued that, of the three branches of the federal government, the best deliberation for balancing the interests of majorities and minorities occurred in Congress—because bicameralism, committees, seniority, filibusters, Senatorial courtesy, and staggered terms for Senators, scattered majority power while giving minorities authority beyond their numbers.[11]

With deliberation being the justification for Congressional power, Kendall's necessary criteria for "responsible democratic deliberation" were: "1) that the majority take care to win the consent of the minority; 2) that discussion be slow in coming to decisions; 3) that discussion be open and subject to scrutiny; 4) that it be principled, which is to say addressed to reason rather than mere will; 5) that it be circumspect, which is to require that all alternatives be canvassed and that the consequences of intended policy be thoroughly weighed including the likelihood of the law's being disobeyed."[12] He argued that such constraints upon arbitrariness "offer the best guarantee of American liberties."[13]

As the agencies and bureaucrats in the executive branch became more numerous, Congressional staff expanded so that Members of Congress could engage in oversight and could exploit opportunities to increase Members' power and longevity in office through patronage, targeted appropriations, and constituent service. Thus, Senators and Representatives don't deliberate much because they "are preoccupied with other, more direct, more profitable, less risky and less open methods of rule. . . .   Government by more or less secret, more or less unaccountable committees and staffers is not what we had the right to expect."[14] Members are now too much merely the abettors of partisan and special interests.

Violations of regular order have included malignities such as these:
- ▶ holding votes open well beyond the scheduled or traditional length of time.
- ▶ excessive reliance on closed rules to prevent discussion and amendments.
- ▶ use of self-executing rules to enable the Rules Committee to amend bills.
- ▶ adding completely new provisions in conference reports.
- ▶ conference committee deletions of provisions passed in identical form by both chambers.
- ▶ exclusion of minority party Members from conference negotiations.
- ▶ frequent waivers (prohibitions) of parliamentary devices, such as points of order, that can give voice to minority Members.
- ▶ waivers of required time between the House receiving a bill (from conference or Rules Committee) and House voting on that bill, thus forcing many Members to vote in ignorance of some provisions.
- ▶ failure to pass individual appropriations bills on time, leading to huge omnibus bills that obscure part of what is being enacted.[15]
- ▶ duplicitous manipulation of spending figures to give the appearance of adherence to a budget resolution.
- ▶ marginalization of committees as majority-party leadership has become more controlling.[16]
- ▶ lobbying on the floor of the House by the Speaker and by a non-Member.[17]

● Speaker Dennis Hastert violated the House tradition that the Speaker avoid direct involvement on the floor in promoting or defeating a proposal when he lobbied fellow Representatives for passage of the Medicare prescription drug bill in late 2003. And he refused to enforce the norm that prohibited lobbying on the floor by non-Members. "That he physically escorted [Health and Human Services Secretary] Thompson onto the floor to perform a double team on Representative [Nick] Smith and others was an unprecedented breach of House practice and ethics."[18]

• House leaders who favored the Medicare prescription drug bill's passage in November 2003 violated the inferred House rule against offering an inducement to a Member to obtain a vote.[19] As reported above in the chapter on American National Democracy, the House Ethics Committee later scolded Representatives DeLay and Miller for their actions.[20]

In the admonishment of Candice Miller, the Investigative Subcommittee reached strange conclusions: It said "Miller's conduct could support a finding that she violated House Rule 23, Clause 1, were the Investigative Committee's jurisdiction to be expanded to address Representative Miller's specific conduct in this matter" [emphasis added]. It then states the contradiction that Miller did commit "a discrete violation of the rules." Next, it says that despite Miller's discrete violation "there was no evidence adduced of a pattern of misconduct" and therefore "further proceedings are not necessary."[21] It thus seems to this author that Members were being advised that they can violate the rules without penalty if they don't engage in "a pattern" of doing so.

• Federal funds may not be appropriated to any program that is not authorized by law. But Congress often does so. Many examples can be found in addition to the one listed above in the chapter on the Budget and Appropriations Problems.

• A rule often violated in the House stipulates that Members will have a minimum of three days ("excluding Saturdays, Sundays, or legal holidays except when the House is in session on such a day") to peruse a "measure or matter reported by a committee" prior to floor debate on it.[22]

The House Rules Committee sometimes annuls that requirement in the rule it reports to govern floor consideration of a particular bill. If the House votes to approve that ad hoc rule, there is no technical violation of the more general rule, because the House can change its rules whenever it wants. But this is often troublesome for two reasons: (1) there's a solid reason for the minimum-time requirement, to produce better laws by giving Members the opportunity to understand what they are voting on—but tossing it aside may result in bad legislation, and (2) leadership may be deliberately trying to sneak something past Members. As one former Representative, now Senator, wrote,
> "The reason this is done is that the leadership knows that all sorts of
> shenanigans take place in the final days and hours before spending bills
> come to the floor for a vote. If brought into the light, many more members
> would think twice before casting a 'yes' vote. In one instance, my staff
> obtained a bill that had spending changes and adjustments literally written
> in the margins minutes before it came to the floor for a vote. This practice of
> withholding information from the people's elected representatives subverts
> our most basic standards of openness and transparency in government."[23]

And, with staffers crafting many bill provisions, the American people live under statutes that are often more the creations of unelected hirelings than of the people elected to make the laws. What sort of democracy is that?

Even three days may not be sufficient when, as with a 3,825-page omnibus appropriations bill presented to the House in October 1998, that would hardly be enough time to unravel and comprehend the complexities of such a behemoth. It was so suspect that some people called it the "ominous" bill.[24] When it came to the floor hardly anyone but the staffers who cobbled it together knew what it contained,[25] and even each of them would have only partial knowledge. One Representative said information about its contents would be dribbling out for months.[26] And after it reached the Senate, Robert Byrd said, "Do I know what's in the bill? Are you kidding? Only God knows. If the voters really understood what we were up to they'd vote us out of office."[27] Still, plenty of Senators understood the process; they made sure that their pet projects were added to the bill. Alaska's Ted Stevens, for instance, put in $15 million for airplane facilities at King Cove, a hamlet of 700 people where windy conditions limit aviation.[28]

- Both House and Senate occasionally disobey their rules prohibiting so-called "legislative riders" on appropriation bills.[29] Such riders are provisions that enact policy and do not directly relate to spending money. The practice goes back to 1879, when Democrats added a stipulation that banned use of federal soldiers to maintain order at polling places. In vetoing the bill, President Hayes wrote, "The new doctrine, if maintained, will result in a consolidation of unchecked and despotic power in the House of Representatives. A bare majority of the House will become the government. The Executive will no longer be what the Framers of the Constitution intended—an equal and independent branch of the Government."[30] Perversions of the Founders' vision have not descended to that depth, and people in each of the first two branches often argue that the other has usurped power.

In 1995, the new GOP majority in the Senate, by reversing a ruling of the presiding officer, prevented enforcement of the rule barring legislative riders on appropriation bills. But after next finding that passage of spending bills became more difficult when they were burdened with legislative riders, the Senate restored the enforcement language in July 1999.[31]

A recent example of a legislative rider on an appropriation bill was the 2005 provisions for expedited elections after a disaster killed so many Representatives that there could be no quorum to conduct business in the House. See above in the chapter on Unrelated Items in the Same Bill.

Another instance from 2005 shocks some sensibilities: Public Law 109-55 appropriated money for legislative branch operations but also amended existing law so that Senators, but not Representatives, could be absent without sickness excuse from Congressional sessions and would not have their pay reduced for the absences. So, Senators seeking the White House during 2007-2008 had a free pass, while the Representatives running for President at the same time should have suffered salary reductions for any absences related to campaigning—but they did not, because the House doesn't consider that to be practical. Thus, this one issue involves two violations: A legislative rider on an appropriation bill and an evasion of law.

The very fact that an appropriations bill has a title ending with the words "and for other purposes" shows that there's an intention to violate the rules by including provisions other than appropriations.[32]

It sometimes occurs that a rule from the Rules Committee waives (forbids) points of order against a bill when it is considered by the full House. A House standing rule, such as that which prohibits legislative riders on appropriation bills, can be enforced by a Member raising a point of order. If the ad hoc rule reported by the Rules Committee waives points of order and is adopted by the House, there is no technical violation of the standing rule.[33]

• Setting aside a legal requirement through the use of legal legislative action may not be a technical violation, but it raises the question of why the requirement exists in the first place. A troubling example is that current law mandates that "Medicare payments to doctors . . . be slashed drastically, by some 41% over the next nine years," but that has never occurred. That failure is simply aggravating the fast-approaching fiscal disaster posed by Social Security, Medicare, and Medicaid.[34]

• In numerous years, each chamber has spent more on franked mail than Congress appropriated. No vote permitted that excess.[35] No one seemed to worry that Members who swear an oath to uphold the Constitution were complicit in violating its provision that "no money shall be drawn from the treasury, but in consequence of appropriations made by law" (Art. I, Sec. 9). Virtually no publicity exposed this violation to the public.

• House Rule XVII, Decorum and Debate, used to state that "Members should address their remarks to the Chair only . . ." and " Members should refer to other Members in debate only in the third person, by State designation." Although that rule for the 110th Congress omits those specific words, they still apply.[36] However, it's rather common that Members in debate address each other in the second person, as in "Maybe you should have read it, Bart." and "You do a good job of putting oil on the water" (February 8, 2007), both of which occurred after the presiding officer had admonished, "The gentleman will direct his comments to the Chair."[37]   Even Speaker Pelosi, setting a great example, said, "I thank you Mr. Oberstar, you and Mr. Mica, for your leadership in bringing this important legislation to the floor in such an expeditious manner."[38]   These are people who demand that others obey every jot and tittle of the laws they pass; so why can't they even obey their own rules? Unless Members suddenly change their ways, you can see examples simply by tuning in to C-SPAN on television.

• Time limits supposedly imposed on Members during debate are sometimes ignored. For example, during the Foreign Intelligence Surveillance Act debate in the House on August 3, 2007, when Majority Leader Steny Hoyer was recognized there were only three minutes remaining for his side but he spoke longer, and then Speaker Pelosi was recognized for thirty seconds but spoke longer, and neither was interrupted by the Speaker Pro Tem. And after those two used up more than the time allotted to the manager of the bill, Representative Jackson-Lee was recognized for "the remaining time" (thirty seconds).[39]

A House custom allows the Speaker, Majority Leader, and Minority Leader to exceed the time limits for speaking on the floor. As Majority Leader Hoyer explained, "One of the great benefits of being majority leader, or minority leader . . . is that you are unlimited in time. You're yielded 1 minute and you take such time as you want."[40]

• As detailed above in the chapter on the Part-Time Congress, both chambers regularly evade the Constitution's requirement that "a Majority of each shall constitute a Quorum to do Business from day to day" (Article I, Section 5) by assuming the presence of a quorum until a challenge occurs. That leads to the outrage of "pro forma" sessions during which business is conducted by as few Members as one.

• The House passed a rule in 2005 that sets up a Constitutional violation. It's Rule XX, 5. (c) (1), which says that if a quorum of the whole number of the House cannot be obtained due to catastrophic circumstance, then a quorum based on the "provisional number of the House" can conduct business. The Constitution clearly states that "a majority of each [house] shall constitute a quorum." It does not say that a quorum is a majority of the Members who answered the last quorum call, which is what Rule XX now provides for after the determination of a catastrophic circumstance. The House simply added that provision to Rule XX by majority vote, as it can do with any of its rules. It may be frightening to think that the Constitution can be "amended" in that fashion. See above in the chapter on Unrelated Items in the Same Bill.

• The Constitution requires that all bills to raise revenue, i.e. tax bills, must originate in the House, but that the Senate may amend them. This has occasionally led to the flimflammery of the Senate proposing a tax measure that is so far afield from the House bill it amends that the Constitutional rule is arguably violated. Here's an example from 1982:

> The Senate Finance Committee simply substituted the tax increase for the text of a minor revenue bill (HR 4961) passed by the House. House Democrats, after concluding that their safest political course was to keep their fingerprints off the revenue-raising bill, asked to go directly to conference with the Senate-passed measure.[41]

The book from which that quotation was drawn says, "There was technical compliance with the Constitution" for this "nearly $100 billion tax bill . . . one of the largest tax increases in American history," while on another page that same book contends that "the bill was a total rejection of the constitutional principle" and that "the House did not vote on the legislation until it emerged from conference."[42]

• The Legislative Reorganization Acts of 1946 and 1970 required that every Member of a conference committee had to have previously voted in favor of the bill being considered. That requirement has not always been honored.[43] See the immediately preceding chapter.

• Also frequently violated have been the requirements in the 1970 Reorganization Act that Senate and House standing committees hold regular meetings and that Senate committees publish their rules in the <u>Congressional Record</u> by March 1 of each year. The latter mandate has been modified by more recent rules of each chamber.[44]

• Each chamber has a rule stipulating that nothing new may be added to any bill at the conference committee stage and that nothing agreed to by both chambers may be deleted.[45]

Numerous violations of those rules have occurred, sometimes even resulting in positive assessments by scholars who seem to believe ends justify means.[46] It is supposedly beyond the "scope" of a conference committee to add new matter or delete agreed upon provisions. Yet, a recent and reliable book says, "Today, violations of scope are quite common." It goes on to detail how a new 1996 Senate precedent overrode Senate Rule XXVIII's prohibition on adding new matter during conferences and achieved the 1999 "marriage of an elephant and an ant" when a separate $313.6 <u>billion</u> measure was wedded to a completely different $429 <u>million</u> bill in conference. Senators woke up to this problem sufficiently in late 2000 to add a provision in a law restoring enforcement of Rule XXVIII through points of order. And in January 2007, the Senate put a section into a law saying that "earmarks added to a conference report that are not considered by the Senate or the House of Representatives are out of scope."[47]

In 1991 a conference report permitted the National Endowment for the Arts to fund so-called "excrementitious artworks" even though both House and Senate had disallowed that use of taxpayers' money. One writer asked, "Could it be that conferees are simply doing what Congress wants them to do? That our representatives are teases, saying no when they mean yes and yes when they mean no? The short answer is yes."[48]

Some conference committee deletions from bills are further instances of Congress not obeying its own rules, as when identical provisions from the two houses are dropped. Conference committees <u>may</u> not delete identical bill provisions that have been agreed to by both chambers. But, of course, they <u>can</u> do so. Not only are most Members shameless about that violation, but at least one scholarly book presents that transgression as a success in getting desirable laws enacted.[49]

In 1990 both chambers included a provision in the Americans with Disabilities Act that permitted restaurants to move employees with AIDS away from food-handling work. In a public-be-damned move, the bill's conference committee dumped that clause.[50]

Many Members seem to think it's perfectly acceptable to thumb their noses at violations of law and rules. Witness, the May 2007 remark of Appropriations chairman David Obey, D-WI, when he said he will allow earmarks only at the conference report stage: "I don't give a damn if people criticize me or not." It's strange that a man whose name pronunciation can be changed to that of the word for "obedient to the law" expresses such a willingness to disobey the rules. And never mind that Democrats in 2006 raged against Republicans adding earmarks to conference reports.[51]

• Not content with the violation of adding new provisions at the conference stage, Congress later even adds new matter.[52] For example, in 2005, Senate Majority Leader Bill Frist and Speaker Dennis Hastert added forty pages to a defense appropriations bill after the conference had ended.[53]

• Also, see the chapter on Failure to Devote Enough Time to Legislation for Speaker Hastert certifying in 2006 that the Senate's version of a budget bill was correct though it differed from the House version and then not giving the House a chance to vote on that.

• Even after a bill has been passed in identical form by each chamber, it may suffer amputations or sprout new provisions. Though uncommon, such grotesque violations disrespect our democracy and dishonor the imperial Members who perpetrate them. Before Wilbur Mills lost his Congressional career because of drunken cavorting with a stripper called the Argentine Firecracker, he used his power as chair of the Ways and Means Committee to delete part of a Social Security bill between its passage by Congress and its reaching the President.[54]

• One of the most stunningly reprehensible examples of a pork-barrel earmark, a set of campaign contributions as bribery, and a violation of the Constitution involved Representative Don Young, R-AK, in 2005. He worked for insertion of an earmark in a transportation bill to provide $10 million for a study of a possible highway interchange on I-75 in Lee County, Florida.[55]   Any mystery about why he was so interested in a project thousands of miles from his district is swept away by noting that just a few days before he proposed the earmark he received contributions of about $40,000 at a fundraiser organized by a Florida businessman whose land near the proposed interchange would skyrocket in value if the interchange were built.

That porkish earmark violated the Constitution by not being in the bill that was passed by both chambers; instead, one of Young's staffers sneaked this fatback into the bill between passage and Presidential signing. That trick strayed so far from the usual self-serving norms in Congress that the Senate voted in mid-April 2008 to request a Department of Justice investigation. And the proper wording from the original bill was restored in a technical corrections bill that also included the DOJ inquiry. But notice how long it took the Senate to discover the problem and to act. On April 30 the House endorsed the Senate's request by a vote of 358 to 51.[56]

There's a standard Congressional procedure for printing a final version of a bill passed in identical form by both chambers. It's called enrollment (not to be confused with engrossment, which occurs so that a copy of a bill passed by one chamber can sent to the other). During the enrollment process minor corrections, such as grammar and punctuation changes, can be made by clerks. Therein lie chances for unintended mistakes or for deliberate sabotage of Congressional intent.

In the case of Don Young's Florida earmark, the "correction," belatedly admitted by Young as having been directed by one of his staffers, changed the rather general language approved by Congress for improvements to widen I-75 so that the President signed a bill with a specific provision relating to an interchange near the businessman's 4,000 acres.[57] Mr. Young originally tried to get specifics for the highway interchange into the 2005 transportation bill, but the House, after learning that local officials opposed it, approved only an appropriation for "widening and improvements for I-75 in Collier and Lee County."[58] Isn't it wonderful how unelected staffers can pervert the Constitution to accomplish something that the elected Members of Congress refused to do?

A further wonderment is that Congress, which usually rejects any executive branch interference in its affairs, asked for a Justice Department investigation of what some Congressional minions did. If Congress can partially abandon its common assertion of separation of power in this case, it can also abandon some of its petrified procedures that hurt American democracy.

• As Senator DeMint complained, there were several provisions in the aforementioned technical corrections bill in 2008 that were not corrections but that added entirely new projects at taxpayers' expense.[59] Thus, one might question whether it's a violation to put something that's not a technical correction in a technical corrections bill. However, as DeMint said, "I guess anything is possible when it is taxpayer money."[60]

• Acting in an official capacity, Members of Congress sometimes, arguably at least, violate laws passed by Congress. Some leaders' blatant disregard of the Logan Act of 1799 is a noteworthy illustration. That law was passed during the country's undeclared naval war with France because an American pacifist named George Logan, an ally of the Jeffersonian opposition to President Adams and the Federalists, had gone to France to promote an end to the conflict by telling the French government that the people of the U.S. wanted peace. Logan's unauthorized diplomacy could have vitiated some policies of President Adams, such as stopping France from seizing American merchant ships and their cargoes. Although Adams' post-trip response to Logan was favorable, and although Adams then initiated a successful effort to make peace with France, angry Federalists in Congress passed the law named for Logan.

Briefly, that statute, which is still U.S. law, provides for a fine and imprisonment for any U.S. citizen who, "without authority of the United States," tries to influence any foreign government in a dispute with the U.S. or who, in unauthorized contact with any foreign government, tries "to defeat the measures" of the U.S. (emphasis added). [61]

There has only been one indictment (1803), but never a prosecution, under that law. And its application to Members of Congress is problematical. In 1975 the U.S. State Department responded to charges that Senators John Sparkman and George McGovern had violated the Logan Act by meeting in Cuba with officials of the Castro government. State said that nothing in the Logan Act "would appear to restrict members of the Congress from engaging in discussions with foreign officials in pursuance of their legislative duties under the Constitution."[62]

The Logan Act's words "without authority of the United States" arguably appear to give cover to Senators and Representatives who talk about U.S. policy with officials in foreign countries.

After Speaker of the House Jim Wright went to Nicaragua for discussions about the civil war between the Sandinista government and the Contra rebels, some people in and out of the Reagan administration bloviated about his alleged infraction of the law.[63]

And the travels of several Members of the House, most notably Speaker Nancy Pelosi, to various countries in the Middle East in the spring of 2007 again raised Logan Act charges. Republicans complained about Pelosi's trip and emitted hardly a murmur about similar travels by some in their own party—but, of course, a trip by the Speaker has vastly greater impact than the journeys of a few "backbenchers" from the minority party.

Although Members of Congress whose foreign contacts bring accusations of Logan Act infractions have a Constitutional right to such actions when seeking to further legislative goals, one wonders if they may sometimes be using their legislative duties as cover for the very sort of interference penalized by the Logan Act.

When the second most powerful person in the U.S. government, a person then famously opposed to Presidential policy, goes to a country greatly impacted by that policy and also opposed to it (Syria) and makes deliberate or ignorant misstatements about the strategies of a major U.S. ally (Israel), it can lead to devastating miscalculations.[64] Therefore, Members of Congress, especially those in leadership positions, should use care and self-restraint in exercising their right to engage in foreign "fact-finding" trips.

• As noted earlier in this chapter and in the chapter on the Part-Time Congress on Full-Time Salary, Congress has refused to take action mandated by law to dock the pay of absent Representatives, and, formerly, of absent Senators. A note accompanying House Rule III says about this law, "Its general application is not practical under modern circumstances." Do any Representatives balk at their not being required to obey a federal law if the House simply decides that doing so "is not practical"?

• In 1946 Congress passed the Legislative Reorganization Act. Its Section 132 required that each session of Congress would usually have to end sine die no later than July 31. Thus, all appropriation bills and other needed legislation would have to be passed by that date.[65] Through the law's provision that Congress could change that ending date each year, Congress could pass a concurrent resolution to give itself a vacation for most of August and for early September and then continue a session. Senator Joseph Clark, D-PA, wrote in 1964, "In the years I have served in the Senate we have never yet obeyed the law we passed to discipline ourselves . . . Both the courts and the President are powerless to make us keep faith with ourselves."[66] The July 31 provision is still U.S. law.[67]

• In 1995 Congress passed a law requiring that any committee report on a bill dealing with terms and conditions of employment or with access to public services must describe how the bill applies to the House or Senate, and if it does not, why not. If even just one Member objects on the floor that the requirement has not been met, that chamber shall not consider the bill. But, of course, there's the usual escape hatch: Either body can waive the requirement by a majority vote. One source that I find generally reliable says, "Congress today simply ignores the statutory requirement." That statement is perhaps too broad in seeming to mean that Congress always does so.[68]

● Each chamber has passed innumerable resolutions creating recognitions for the likes of National Indoor Comfort Week. That one dealt with air conditioning, not ergonomic furniture. One recent estimate is that about one-fourth of the House's typical workweek is taken up with resolutions that symbolize the chamber's feeling about something.[69]

Because such resolutions sop up time, energy, and money, the House in 1995 established a "prohibition on commemorations." It says, "A bill or resolution, or an amendment thereto, may not be introduced or considered in the House if it establishes or expresses a commemoration," which it defines as "a remembrance, celebration, or recognition for any purpose through the designation of a specified period of time."[70] This seems fairly clear, yet hundreds of them have been introduced and passed since the ban's creation.[71] The House sidesteps the prohibition by voting to suspend the rules. It's a mystery—or is it?—why the House won't enforce its own rule. Could it be that the businesses that want commemorations donate thousands of dollars to the Members who sponsor such frivolities?

There's also time spent on resolutions that seem to be commemorations but that do not technically meet the House's definition. One example relates to Holocaust victim Anne Frank. Although we revere her memory, it seems questionable that time was spent in 2007 on House Joint Resolution 37 to confer U.S. honorary citizenship on her.[72] If that's appropriate, then perhaps there should also be U.S. honorary citizenship for people such as Joan of Arc and Anne Boleyn.

Time and money are also wasted on resolutions that make American foreign relations more difficult by offending other countries and that serve no purpose other than to assuage the feelings of some Members and a portion of their constituents. Prime example: The House resolution in 2007, one in a series stretching back about twenty years, to label as genocide the deaths of perhaps 1.5 million Armenians in the old Ottoman Empire during 1915-1919. The resolution passed the House Foreign Affairs Committee in October 2007 and caused great anger in Turkey, a vital U.S. ally. Although supported by Speaker Nancy Pelosi, the resolution was so dangerous to American interests in the Middle East that Pelosi backed down and never brought it to the House floor for a debate or vote.[73] But the issue has continued to arise in later years.

More time and money wasters are some of the one-minute speeches in the House. Each of those may not take much time, and most Members aren't present to listen, but the cumulative effect is akin to turning a splinter into a cord of wood. As for the money, it adds up for the transcribing and printing (in the Congressional Record). Why should other Members and taxpayers be encumbered with self-indulgent, family-pride statements such as that of Zoe Lofgren, D-CA, who spoke in praise of her son for his eighteenth birthday.[74]

Time is also consumed, along with taxpayers' dollars, on Senators' "additional statements" and Representatives' "extensions of remarks" that are far afield from the people's business. See the <u>Congressional Record</u> of August 4, 2008, for one Representative's insertion "In Celebration of the Sewell Family Reunion." That same date saw the <u>Record</u> ornamented with this:

> "Madam Speaker, the cold night brought me into the cancered bowels
> of this capital place. Barren halls and walkways and crawl space in
> front of me and inside cerebral tunnels.
>> It is here, away from now. I come to face the ghost of Abercrombie.
>> Who walked these paths and is remembered for not so hallow words."[75]

Among recent questionable uses of "additional statements" see a Senator's celebration of the 100th anniversary of an elementary school, another's congratulations to a woman who received a $4,000 scholarship, and another's tribute to a youth who attained the rank of Eagle Scout.[76]

Beyond "additional statements," there's another time-wasting, money-wasting opportunity for Senators during so-called "Morning Business." Senators can use it to make brief speeches about anything. Some of those orations have dealt with topics of general importance while others are merely self-serving or self-involved. One the latter was Senator Craig's little squib "Honoring My Children on Father's Day."[77]

Senators often receive unanimous consent to interrupt debate on something important in order to speak "as in morning business." Other times Senators simply digress to a different topic without speaking as in morning business. Their interrupting words may be important in an absolute sense or just important to them but have nothing to do with the matter being debated. For example, during an April 15, 2008, debate Senators wandered away from the subject thirteen different times considered so noteworthy they are listed with separate capital-letter headings in the <u>Congressional Record</u>. The debate continued the next day, with several non sequitur interruptions of such length as to occupy many pages in the <u>Record</u>. Those digressions would seem to violate the Senate rule that says "all debate shall be germane and confined to the specific question then pending before the Senate"—except for the rather convoluted exceptions specified in the rule.[78]

- A "violation" that's more like an evasion involves travel. A 1997 book reported this:
> "During 1992 and 1993, more than eighty-five members of Congress
> participated in 181 trips sponsored by the health care industry, including
> trips to Puerto Rico, Paris, and Montego Bay. New congressional rules
> have banned such trips, along with meals, but Congress made sure the
> rules could be evaded. If trips are made to attend meetings or speeches or
> to gather facts in connection with their law-making duties, members can
> take all the free trips they want. . . . Since Congress makes the rules,
> Congress can approve waivers of the rules. So the House and Senate

ethics committees routinely grant exceptions to the rules so members can take lavish congressional trips paid for by private interests."[79]
It might be only a supreme optimist who thinks such waivers do not continue.

By early 2007 free or cut-rate trips provided by non-governmental organizations (NGOs), corporations, and lobbyists were so pervasive and in bad odor that both chambers put additional restrictions on such travel.[80]

• Scot M. Faulkner became chief administrative officer of the House in late 1994 and in 1995 uncovered various problems. One concerned parking. House rules allowed only eight parking spaces for each Member and his/her staff, but 157 Representatives had more than that number. Furthermore, five of the eight were to be in garages and the other three in outdoor areas, but some Members had all eight inside. Others had only one space inside and the others outside, perhaps because of being out of favor with House leaders. Charles Rose, D-NC, chair of the Committee on House Administration, had been issuing 4,000 waivers per month to permit evasion of the parking rules.[81] It's a good bet that this is still a problem area.

• In May 1984, Speaker Tip O'Neill got mad at the tactics employed by Representatives in Newt Gingrich's Conservative Opportunity Society (COS), who often made House speeches critical of Democrats. C-SPAN was broadcasting House sessions under a 1978 agreement that only the Member speaking would be shown on camera. COS speakers in an otherwise nearly empty chamber would make charges and then challenge Democrats to respond, pretending that many Members were present in the House. Democrats could not respond because they weren't there, but viewers might conclude the charges were true when they saw no Democratic response. O'Neill then violated the 1978 pact by ordering the cameras to show the virtually empty room and thus destroy COS's pretense. Several years later he admitted his action was wrong.[82]

• Some years ago, House Commerce Committee chairman Harley Staggers wanted to be re-elected chair of the investigations subcommittee, but so did John Moss. The rules said someone not elected on the first ballot must withdraw. On the first six ballots, with the vote tied on each, neither Staggers nor Moss withdrew.[83]

• The Constitution, Article I, Section 7, says, "Every order, resolution, or vote to which the concurrence of the Senate and House of Representatives may be necessary (except on a question of adjournment) shall be presented to the President of the United States . . . [for approval or disapproval] according to the rules and limitations prescribed in the case of a bill." Since 1892, however, Congress has arrogated to itself the power to pass "concurrent" resolutions, which by definition require the "concurrence" of both chambers, and then not present them to the president. The excuse has been that concurrent resolutions do not create legislation. Usually relating only to Congress, they are limited to expressing ideas, facts, and coordinated budget decisions, or setting Congress's time for adjournment. Additionally, the Supreme Court ruled that Congressional resolutions that are not "legislative" need not be presented to the President though seemingly so required by the presentment clause. Thus, not presenting concurrent resolutions to the President seems to violate the Constitution but has been ruled not to do so.[84]

- After the House voted in 1991 by a huge majority not to fund higher pay for its staffers, the House Administration Committee sent out a letter declaring it would do so anyway.[85]

- A House rule mandates that standing committees "shall be elected by the House within seven calendar days after the commencement of each Congress,"[86] but just try to find evidence of that in the Congressional Record for the first seven days of any recent Congress. Such evidence is not there. So, did such elections not occur?

- Section 13301(a) of the Budget Enforcement Act of 1990 is named "Exclusion of Social Security from All Budgets," and Section 13301(b) is named "Exclusion of Social Security From Congressional Budget." Those sections specifically prohibit use of Social Security outlays and revenue totals in surplus or deficit totals. Yet, as former Senator Ernest Hollings, D-SC, reported in August 2008, both the President and Congress "continue to violate the law" and use "Social Security and other trust funds to lower the deficit" and engage in "this deficit deception."[87]

Some Members have recently tried to keep Social Security out of the unified federal budget by introducing a bill to that effect—and by one of those notorious "other purposes," in this case by "mandating that Trust Fund monies cannot be diverted to create private accounts."[88]

- A 2007 law amended the rules of the House by providing that a Representative "may not participate in an event honoring that Member" during the dates of the person's national nominating convention unless he or she is a candidate for President or Vice President, if the event is paid for by a registered lobbyist or a "private entity that retains or employs such a registered lobbyist."[89] That is such a narrow restriction as to be practically meaningless. A Representative—or lobbyist—would have to be supremely stupid to violate it. All that's needed is for the event to honor a group, even one as small as two Representatives. One big-league lobbying outfit understood that dodge: It's reception honored all first-term Democrats. The Democratic convention in 2008 was "chockablock with receptions paid for by corporations, unions and others with important business before Congress. The events are legal, as long as they fit a set of exceptions to the rules."[90] The Republicans, of course, also had such gatherings at their convention. The real violation is of the voters' intelligence when some Members still insist that the receptions have zero influence on how they vote.[91] Perhaps the hosts should feel violated if their outpourings of food, drink, and conviviality are useless. But they know better, otherwise they wouldn't put on the parties.

- A long-standing rule of the House requires that noncurrent records of committees shall be transferred at the conclusion of each Congress to the U.S. Archivist for preservation. "Records so delivered are the permanent property of the House."[92] Yet there have been numerous instances of Representatives taking records for themselves or for donation to colleges.[93]

• Members have committed many violations of our supposedly sacred Constitution. Such actions are not just from the less-ethical past; some are recent and will besmirch our future. Ponder this: It's been a common practice for many decades that Members have been appointed to other federal positions for which the pay was increased during the Members' service in Congress. The Constitution specifically, and not by implication or interpretation, prohibits that. Among many recent examples, the appointment of Senator Hillary Clinton as Secretary of State stands out. The technique by which the violation is supposedly eliminated is that a law is enacted repealing the pay raise for the individual involved.[94]

And the Constitution also specifically bars anyone "holding any office under the United States" from being a Member of Congress at the same time.[95] Yet instances abound of Members also serving in the U.S. armed forces. Are military positions not considered federal offices?[96] And what about Members who serve on boards, committees, and panels that are federally created but not part of Congress? These issues have not been conclusively adjudicated.

• There's another cute way for the two chambers to evade one of their rules: They simply do not include any mechanism to enforce the rule. For example, in December 2009, a Senator raised a point of order that several instances of "congressionally directed spending" (i.e., earmarks) in the health-care reform bill violated a Senate rule that such items be printed "as soon as practicable" in the Congressional Record. The presiding Senator rejected the effort with these words: "The provision is not enforceable and no point of order lies."[97]

That provision had become effective in September 2007. To the extent it got positive publicity, its lack of teeth makes it look like it was designed merely to deceive the public into thinking there was real reform.

Yet, as one report says, "Officials are apt to ignore laws that can't be enforced against them." That seems to carry no weight with the Harvard Law professor who speaks of "constitutional provisions that no longer seem so terribly significant" and who argues that "People would say, 'Who cares that there's this technical violation of the Constitution?'" Well, there are multitudes who care about preserving the Constitution. Others, however, only care when it's their provision being gored. One person's sacred right is another's mere impediment.[98]

Good luck, if you, the ordinary citizen, sue to stop Congressional violations. You won't win. That's because the courts routinely throw out such lawsuits on the grounds that the plaintiff has no "standing" to bring the action. Lack of standing flows from the concept that a plaintiff must show an individualized and real injury, not some notional affront.

CORRECTIVE SOLUTIONS

Why should people who sometimes won't obey existing laws have any power to make new laws? The public must exercise its oversight function. Key to that is that the media must inform the public by continually publicizing violations. Then the voters can defeat all Members who operate on the principles of the-public-be-damned and to-Hell-with-the-rules. The needed publicity requires some of the more partisan media to accept that their support of violative actions to obtain a law may achieve a narrow goal at the expense of a broader and long-term weakening of our democracy.

Notes: Chapter XXXIV. Violations of Procedures, Rules, Laws, "Regular Order," and the Constitution

[1]One appropriate article is Ittai Bar-Simon-Tov, "Lawmakers as Lawbreakers," NELLCO Legal Scholarship Repository, Columbia Public Law & Legal Theory Workings Papers, Paper 9186, Columbia Law School, April 12, 2010, on the Internet.

[2]Hiller B. Zobel, The Boston Massacre (New York: W. W. Norton, 1970), p. 215.

[3]Thomas E. Mann and Norman J. Ornstein, The Broken Branch: How Congress Is Failing America and How to Get It Back on Track (New York: Oxford University Press, 2006), p. 74. Walter J. Oleszek, Congressional Procedures and the Policy Process, 7th edition (Washington: CQ Press, 2007), p. 250, n. 4: "On November 17, 1982, for the first time since 1793, the House had two legislative days in the same calendar day. It adjourned at 1:19 p.m. (the first legislative day) and then reconvened at 4:00 p.m. (the second legislative day). Sharp partisanship stimulated the Democratic leadership to employ this rare tactic." Tip O'Neill was then Speaker.

[4]House Rule, XI, clause 2(h)(1), (2), and (3); Senate Rule XXVI, clause 7 (a)(1) and (2), 110th Congress.

[5]Walter J. Oleszek, Congressional Procedures and the Policy Process, 2d edition (Washington: CQ Press, 1984), p. 109: "The Rules chairman also may either strictly observe or ignore the rules for a quorum." That is not in Oleszek's 7th edition, pp. 89-91.

[6]Congressional Record, permanent edition, October 29, 1987, pp. 29934 (for the question and Foley's response) and 29936-37 (for the motion on the second legislative day of the same calendar day), and 29937-45 (for the rule from the Rules Committee and its debate and passage). For the two-thirds requirement, see House Rule XV, clause 1, 110th Congress.

[7]See Mann and Ornstein, Broken Branch, p. 74; Elizabeth Wehr, "Wright Finds a Vote to Pass Reconciliation Bill," Congressional Quarterly Weekly Report, October 31, 1987, pp. 2653-55; Janet Hook, "Bitterness Lingers From House Budget Vote," ibid., November 7, 1987, pp. 2712-13.

[8]Mann and Ornstein, Broken Branch, pp. 215-16.

[9]Ibid., p. 170.

[10]John Alvis, "Willmore Kendall and the Demise of Congressional Deliberation," The Intercollegiate Review, Spring 1988, p. 57. The next few paragraphs rest heavily on the ideas in that article.

[11]Ibid., p. 60.

[12]Ibid., pp. 60-61. See also Mann and Ornstein, Broken Branch, p. 216, for a similar list.

[13]Alvis, "Willmore Kendall," p. 61.

[14]Ibid., p. 63.

[15]"House leaders have become particularly enamored of packaging several stand-alone appropriations bills into one omnibus bill that is brought up at the end of the session, as all the members are preparing to go home and do not want to vote to shut down the government. By forgoing nearly all floor debate, they can pack these bills with numerous provisions that could never pass in separate votes.
    But this form of legislating – which often means that bills are passed and laws are enacted via all-night sessions whereby staff and a few members and party leaders try to slap all the pieces together under tight deadlines – results in stealth legislation that has not really passed majority muster and frequently has embarrassing consequences." Mann & Ornstein, Broken Branch, p. 173.

[16]Ibid., p. 216. See also p. 73.

[17] Ibid., p. 9.

[18]Ibid.; see also pp. 2, 8.

[19]See above, note 24 in the chapter on American National Democracy. There is now a specific prohibition against one type of inducement for obtaining a vote: The 110th Congress added clause 16 to Rule XXIII, Code of Official Conduct, stating that "a Member, Delegate, or Resident Commissioner may not condition the inclusion of language to provide funding for a congressional earmark, a limited tax benefit, or a limited tariff benefit . . . on any vote cast by another Member, Delegate, or Resident Commissioner."

[20]Mann and Ornstein, Broken Branch, p. 4; see above, note 23 in the chapter on American National Democracy.

[21]"Investigation of Certain Allegations Related to Voting on the Medicare Prescription Drug, Improvement, and Modernization Act of 2003," Report of the Committee on Standards of Official Conduct, September 30, 2004, p. 58.

[22]House Rule XIII, clause 4 (a)(1), 110th Congress. However, that rule's subparagraph (2) lists five exceptions and adds a requirement that a "general appropriation bill reported by the Committee on Appropriations may not be considered in the House until the third calendar day . . . on which printed hearings of the Committee on Appropriations thereon have been available to Members."
The Senate's Rule XIV, Bills, Joint Resolutions, Resolutions, and Preambles Thereto, clause 4,, 110th Congress, permits faster action.

[23]Tom A. Coburn and John Hart, Breach of Trust: How Washington Turns Outsiders into Insiders (Nashville: WND Books, 2003), p. 133.

[24]Carroll J. Doherty, "Riding the Omnibus Off Into the Sunset," CQ Weekly, October 17, 1998, p. 2794.

[25]Coburn and Hart, Breach of Trust, p. 133.

[26]Doherty, "Riding the Omnibus," C Q Weekly, October 17, 1998, p. 2796.

[27]Coburn and Hart, Breach of Trust, p. 134.

[28]Ibid.

[29]See House Rule XXI, clause 2(b) and (c), and Senate Rule XVI, clauses 2 and 4, 110th Congress.

[30]Robert V. Remini, The House: The History of the House of Representatives (New York: Collins, a division of HarperCollins; Smithsonian Books, 2006), p.232, citing James D. Richardson, A Compilation of the Messages and Papers of the Presidents.

[31]Carroll J. Doherty, "Revived Ban on Policy Riders In Senate Appropriation Bills May Inconvenience Both Parties," CQ Weekly, July 31, 1999, p. 1859; "Changing Senate Rules," Congressional Record, daily edition, January 6, 1999, p. S6; "Senate Resolution 8–Amending Rule XVI of the Standing Rules of the Senate Relating to Amendments to General Appropriations Bills," ibid., pp. S32-33; ibid., March 23, 1999, p. S3106; see the final debate and vote in ibid., daily edition, July 26, 1999, pp. S9171-74, S9176-90, S9192-96, and S9199-9209. Enforcement occurs if a Senator raises a point of order about a rules violation and is sustained by the chair; "Senate Resolution 4 – Relative to Rule XVI," ibid., daily edition, January 6, 1999, p. S31; ibid., pp. S327-28; ibid., March 23, 1999, p. S3106.

[32]Public Law 109-55 states that it is "An Act Making appropriations for the Legislative Branch for the fiscal year ending September 30, 2006, and for other purposes."

[33]David J. Vogler, The Politics of Congress (Boston: Allyn and Bacon, 1974), p. 161; Oleszek, Congressional Procedures, 7th edition, pp. 133-34. A Representative explained, "If we went strictly by the House rules, I am sure this body would have a very difficult time operating"; ibid.

[34]Geoff Colvin, "The $34 Trillion Problem," Fortune, March 17, 2008, p. 30. See also above in the chapter on the Untrue Amounts of the Official Federal Deficit and Debt.

[35]"Frank Babies," The Wall Street Journal, September 27, 1989, p. A22.

[36]In the rules of the 110th Congress, those words are not in Rule XVII; however, in the copy of the House rules for the 110th Congress that includes notes there's the statement that Members are advised that they "should address their remarks to the Chair only" and that they should "refer to other Members in debate only in the third person, by State designation." Further, in the House on January 5, 2007, one of Speaker Nancy Pelosi's announcements was that regarding decorum in debate "the Chair's announced policies of January 7, 2003, January 4, 1995, and January 3, 1991, will apply in the 110th Congress" and that Members should "avoid 'personalities' in debate with respect to references to other Members" and should "address the Chair," and that "the Chair intends to strictly enforce time limitations on debate"; Congressional Record, daily edition, January 5, 2007, p. H60.

[37]Ibid., February 8, 2007, p. 1375 (the Chairman of the Committee of the Whole), p. H1381 (Mr. Gordon, col. 1, and Mr. Hall, col. 2).

[38] Ibid., August 3, 2007, p. H9678.

[39]Ibid., pp. H9691-93.

[40]Ibid., daily edition, May 10, 2007, p. H4756. See also Jackie Kucinich, "Blunt picks fight with chatty House Dems," October 30, 2007 (TheHill.com), on the Internet: "'In recent months . . . this privilege has been used not for the rarest of circumstances, but with great frequency,' Blunt wrote in a letter sent to Pelosi and Hoyer on Oct. 23. 'It is my hope that this rare courtesy is restored to its original intent in accordance with the customs of the House.'"

[41]Oleszek, Congressional Procedures, 2d edition, pp. 212 (for the quotation), and 214.

[42]Compare ibid., pp. 11 and 212.

[43]Vogler, The Politics of Congress, p. 180; Warren Weaver, Jr., Both Your Houses: The Truth About Congress (New York: Praeger Publishers, 1972), pp. 130-31. Weaver,

p. 130, quoted a Representative: "There is a little line in the instructions which says that the chairman of the conferees will attempt to carry out the will of the House regardless of his own personal feelings about it. Now, I have never seen that rule observed."

[44]See Public Law 91-510 (October 26,1970), sections 102 and 130. Mark J. Green, Who Runs Congress?, revised edition (New York: Bantam/Grossman, 1975), p. 75, says Senator Eastland's Judiciary Committee "routinely ignored" the requirements about regular meetings and publication of rules. Walter Kravitz, "The Legislative Reorganization Act of 1970," Legislative Studies Quarterly, August 1990, p. 390: "The 1970 act had directed Senate committees to publish their rules each year in the Congressional Record. The House followed suit in 1974, but required publication only at the beginning of each congress (H. Res. 988, 93d Cong., 2d sess.).["] See Senate Rule, XXVI, clause 2, 110th Congress: publication to occur not later than March 1 of the first year of each Congress.
House Rule XI, clause 2(a)(2), 110th Congress, says, "Each committee shall submit its rules for publication in the Congressional Record not later than 30 days after the committee is elected in each odd-numbered year." Without information in the Record on the election of committees, it's unclear if the 30-day deadline is being met because, for example, the rules of the Committee on Intelligence were not published for the 110th Congress until April 26, 2007.

[45]See also the above chapters on Budget and Appropriations Problems and the Conference Committee Problem.   See House Rule XXII, clause 9, 110th Congress, and Senate Rule XXVIII, clauses 2 through 5, 110th Congress. These were formerly a provision of U.S. law rather than being merely Congressional rules. Both rules rest on provisions in the Legislative Reorganization Acts of 1946 and 1970. "But this rule is often violated by conference committees' writing substitute bills which are quite different from either chamber bill. When this happens members may raise a point of order when the conference report is brought to the Chamber floor . . . [but they] seldom are made"; Vogler, Politics of Congress, p. 183.

[46]"In short, the conferees took a situation that looked very bleak and – by writing legislative language that appeared in neither the House nor the Senate bill – produced a winning compromise"; Randall B. Ripley, Congress: Process and Policy (New York: W. W. Norton, 1975), p. 116.

[47]Oleszek, Congressional Procedures, 7th edition, pp. 272-74; the quotation is on p. 274.

[48]Eric Felten, The Ruling Class: Inside the Imperial Congress, abridged edition (Washington: U.S. Congress Assessment Project, Heritage Foundation, 1993), p. 10

[49]"The conference committee did succeed and deleted or modified the provisions offensive to organized labor and the cotton interests"; Ripley, Congress, p. 85.

[50] Felten, The Ruling Class, abridged edition, p. 9.

[51]"They're the Law," The Wall Street Journal, May 25, 2007, p. A14.

[52]Mann and Ornstein, Broken Branch, p. 233. The Honest Leadership and Open Government Act of 2007, Section 515 (P.L. 110-81, 121 Stat. at page 760), addressed that problem by including a "sense of the Senate" that "the text of a report of a committee of conference shall not be changed after the Senate signature sheets have been signed by a majority of the Senate conferees."

[53]Oleszek, Congressional Procedures, 7th edition, p. 277.

[54]Green, Who Runs Congress?, revised edition, p. 81.

[55]See P.L. 109-59, Section 19349(c), item 462. As Rep. Young stated, "The goal was to provide $10 million for a study, not to build, but study this interchange" (Congressional Record, daily edition, April 30, 2008, p. H2882) . The reader may wonder why a mere study of one highway interchange would cost $10 million.

[56]Congressional Record, daily edition, April 16, 2008, pp. S3048-49, S3058-63; ibid., April 17, 2008, pp. S3110-12, S3115-20, p. S3130 (see item 25 in column three), and p. S3135; ibid., April 30, 2008, pp. H2867-85, H2908-09;   "The Mystery of the Coconut Interchange," The New York Times, October 7, 2007, "Week in Review" section, p.13; David M. Herszenhorn, "Senate Requests Inquiry On Highway Earmark," The New York Times, April 18, 2008, p. A14; Caitlin Ginley and the Center for Public Integrity, "Don Young, Representative for Florida?" April 18, 2008, on the Internet. This earmark was negatively featured in several TV programs such as "Anderson Cooper 360" on CNN, June 7, 2007. And washingtonmonthly.com, "How to Make a Good Impression," June 7, 2007, reported that "when he was approached near the House floor by a reporter, Mr. Young responded with an obscene gesture." Twenty-eight Senators voted against the Justice Department inquiry, but for some their opposition flowed from preference for an investigation jointly by the House and Senate.

[57]"Don Young," Wikipedia, the free encyclopedia, on the Internet, reporting on an August 2007 story in the Naples Daily News. See Public Law 109-59.

[58]"The Road to Somewhere Shady, The New York Times, April 21, 2008, p. A20.

[59]Congressional Record, daily edition, April 15, 2008, pp. S2998-99.

[60]Ibid., p. S2998. He further pointed out that many of the earmarks in transportation bills, such as renovation of the Apollo Theater [in Harlem], do not relate to transportation; ibid.

[61]See Title 18, U.S. Code, Section 5, 1940 edition; ibid., Section 953, 1958 edition and 2000 edition: "Private correspondence with foreign governments."

[62]Quoted in Michael V. Seitzinger, "Conducting Foreign Relations Without Authority: The Logan Act," CRS Report for Congress, February 1, 2006, p. CRS-9.

[63]Logan Act in Wikipedia, an encyclopedia on the Internet; Congressional Record, permanent edition, November 17, 1987, pp. 32152-55 (Newt Gingrich's chastisement of Wright for alleged violation of the Logan Act).

[64]Robert F. Turner, "Illegal Diplomacy," The Wall Street Journal, April 6, 2007, p. A10.

[65]Joseph S. Clark, Congress: The Sapless Branch (Westport, CT: Greenwood Press, 1964), p. 164. The law is Public Law 79-601 (August 2, 1946), 60 Stat. 812-52, with Section 132 on page 831; that ending date applied "except in time of war or during a national emergency proclaimed by the President" and "unless otherwise provided by the Congress."

[66]Clark, Congress: The Sapless Branch , p. 164.

[67]That provision recurs in the various editions of the U.S. Code; see, for example, Title 2, U.S. Code, Section 198, 2000 edition.

[68]The 1995 law is the Congressional Accountability Act, P.L. 104-1 (January 23, 1995), Section 102(b)(3), 109 Stat. 6. The "generally reliable" source is Winslow T. Wheeler, The Wastrels of Defense: How Congress Sabotages U.S. Security (Annapolis: Naval Institute Press, 2004), p. 164; he cited Office of Compliance: Reports and Studies, Section 102(b) Report, December 2002, p. 5. Wheeler (p. 163) also relies on the Office of Compliance report of 2002 to mention that Members' employees who complained about violation of workplace rules, an impressively small number, were often subject to harassment, and (p. 164) that "when Senator Daschle pleaded for standard employment rights for the workers in the new Department of Homeland Security, his own staff's statutory rights were, as described by Congress's Office of Compliance, 'illusory.'"

[69]Elizabeth Williamson, "As Energy and Housing Crises Loom, House, Senate Sweat the Small Stuff," The Wall Street Journal, August 19, 2008, pp. A1, A14.

[70]The ban still existed in the 110th Congress as clause 5 of House Rule XII. The Senate has no such rule. Jonathan M. Katz, "You Say You Want a Resolution?" CQ Weekly, May 30, 2005, p. 1416.

[71]Find examples in the "Daily Digest" section near the back of each daily edition of the Congressional Record under "House of Representatives" and "Suspensions."

[72]Congressional Record Index, March 12-30, 2007, p. H.B. 64.

[73]Thomas Omestad, "Was It Genocide or Not? U.S. resolution over a historical event triggers Turkish anger," U.S. News & World Report, October 22, 2007, p. 38. It was H.

Res. 106; see the indexes to the Congressional Record from the resolution's introduction on January 30, 2007, through the end of 2008 for no evidence of it being brought to the floor of the House.

[74]Congressional Record, daily edition, January 7, 2003, p. H24.

[75]Sewell: Congressional Record, daily edition, August 4, 2008, p. E1733; "The Ghost of Abercrombie": ibid., p. E1762, which was actually a tribute by Rep. Bill Pascrell to his friend Representative Neil Abercrombie.

[76]Congressional Record, daily edition, June 19, 2008, p. S5827, for the school; ibid., June 26, 2008, p. S6279, for the scholarship; and ibid., July 7, 2008, p. S6359, for the Eagle Scout.

[77]Ibid., June 12, 2008, p. S5590.

[78]Ibid., April 16, 2008, pp. S3046-67. In that debate, the Senate was dealing with the Highway Technical Corrections Act of 2007, which included a consideration of what to do about the 2005 highway bill that reached the President in a different form from what had been passed by Congress. Here are the deviations from the topic. Senator Boxer received unanimous consent "to pay tribute to 19 young Americans who were killed in Iraq" (see Congressional Record, daily edition, April 16, 2008, pp. S3049, S3068-70). Moments later, Senator Barrasso got similar permission and spoke about "halting the growth of greenhouse gases (ibid., pp. S3049-50). Then Senator Grassley digressed on Medicaid Moratoriums (ibid., pp. S3051-52). Next, Senator Reid spoke about Welcoming Pope Benedict XVI and about the One Year Anniversary of Virginia Tech Shooting (ibid., p. S3052), followed by Senator Kennedy on the Fair Pay Restoration Act (ibid., pp. S3053-54). Then Senator Tester advanced some views on the Gray Wolf Livestock Loss Mitigation Act (ibid., pp. S3054, S3082), and Senator Thune uttered words about Tax Day (ibid., pp. S3054-55). Senator Warner then spoke about the Virginia Tech Tragedy (ibid., pp. S3056,S3070). Shortly thereafter, Senator Tester said, "I want to take a little detour for a moment" and advanced information on the detaining of four Americans in Nigeria (ibid., p. S3063). The chair then immediately recognized Senator Carper for a speech "congratulating Dover Air Force Base" (ibid., pp. S3063-66). The last interruption came as Senator Salazar delivered words about Firefighters Killed in Colorado.
For germaneness of debate and the exceptions, see Rule XIX, clause 1(b), 110th Congress.

[79]Ronald Kessler, Inside Congress: The Shocking Scandals, Corruption, and Abuse of Power Behind the Scenes on Capitol Hill (New York: Pocket Books, 1997), p. 113.

[80]See House Rule XXV, clause 5 (Gifts), 110th Congress, and Senate Rule XXXV (Gifts), 110th Congress. Those rules are lengthy and complex.

[81]Kessler, Inside Congress, pp. 158-59.

[82]Julian E. Zelizer, On Capitol Hill: The Struggle to Reform Congress and Its Consequences, 1948-2000 (New York: Cambridge University Press, 2004), pp. 214-15; John J. Pitney, Jr., and William F. Connelly, Jr., "The Speaker: A Republican Perspective," in The Speaker: Leadership in the U.S. House of Representatives, edited by Ronald M. Peters, Jr. (Washington: Congressional Quarterly, Inc., 1995), p. 71.

[83]Green, Who Runs Congress?, revised edition, pp. 336-37.

[84]Howard White, "The Concurrent Resolution in Congress," The American Political Science Review, October 1941, pp. 886-89. In 1983, in the case INS v. Chada, 462 U.S. 919, the Supreme Court ruled that the Framers of the Constitution divided "the delegated powers of the new Federal Government into three defined categories, Legislative, Executive, and Judicial" and that bicameral action and presentment to the President are only necessary when Congress is making law.

[85]John L. Jackley, Hill Rat: Blowing the Lid Off Congress (Washington: Regnery Gateway, 1992), p. 11.

[86]House Rule, X, clause 5, 110th Congress.

[87]Ernest F. Hollings, "Bad bookkeeping offers false picture of deficit," USA Today, August 11, 2008, p. 10A. Section 13301 is in P.L. 101-508, 104 Stat. 1388-623; and see ibid., pp. 1388 and 1388-573, for Title XIII of the Omnibus Budget Reconciliation Act of 1990 being cited as the Budget Enforcement Act of 1990.

[88]See Congressional Record, daily edition, March 6, 2007, p. H2242, for H.R. 1353.

[89]The Honest Leadership and Open Government Act, P.L. 110-81, Section 305 (121 Stat. at pp. 753-54).

[90]Ken Dilanian and Fredreka Schouten, "Congress' newest lawmakers find no lack of parties," USA Today, August 28, 2008, p. 7A.

[91]Ibid.

[92]Rule VII, 110th Congress.

[93]Paul Bedard, "Hey Congress: Stop Pilfering U.S. History," U.S. News & World Report, October 29, 2007, p. 12.

[94]For information on the constitutionality of methods to get around this prohibition, look on the Internet under "Saxbe fix."

[95]U.S. Constitution, Article I, Section 6.

[96]See David J. Shaw, "Note: An Officer and a Congressman: The Unconstitutionality of Congressmen in the Armed Forces Reserve," Georgetown Law Journal, Vol. 97 (August 2009), pp. 1739-66, which examines the issue in detail and concludes that it's unconstitutional for Members to hold reserve commissions in the military.

[97]See Congressional Record, daily edition, December 23, 2009, p. S13810. On that page the rule was referred to several times as rule LXIV, but it's actually XLIV.

[98]Jess Bravin, "Why Some Constitutional Suits Don't Stand a Chance in Court," The Wall Street Journal, February 12, 2009, p. A10. The professor is Mark Tushnet. The Constitutional provisions mentioned are in Article I, Section 6.

XXXV. Arcane Rules and Procedures Inhibit Public Understanding

EPIGRAPH: Men are most apt to believe what they least understand.
                 ---Michel de Montaigne, Essays, Chapter 11.

Tune in to a House or Senate session on C-SPAN to see activities you may find mystifying.

You may, for example, see a Representative conclude his or her remarks on the floor by announcing, "I yield back the balance of my time" and be followed by a Member who says, "I move to strike the last word." An observer of literal mind would probably conclude that the word "time" was to be excised and might wonder why. Then the chair, meaning the Speaker or a Member sitting in for the Speaker, says, "The gentleman is recognized for five minutes." That observer might then understand that under the rules of the House and of parliamentary procedure the mover of a motion has the right to speak in its support. But the observer might next be confused when the Member who obtained the floor never mentions anything about striking the word "time" and instead devotes his or her remarks to something totally not germane to the motion. After the remarks are concluded and the same process gives the floor to another Member, that observer might wonder what ever happened to the motion that had been made but never seconded and never voted on. Well, according to the usual, non-Congressional rules of parliamentary procedure, unseconded motions often die, and the onlooker, being somewhat familiar with parliamentary procedure, might wonder if there wouldn't need to be a ruling from the chair to that effect? Well, it turns out that one of the arcane procedures in the House is the use of the so-called "pro forma amendment." A former chairman of the Committee on Rules explained it thusly:

> "A motion whereby a Member secures five minutes to speak on an amendment under debate in the Committee of the Whole. The Member gains recognition from the chair by moving to 'strike the last word.' The motion requires no vote, does not change the amendment under debate, and is deemed automatically withdrawn at the expiration of the five minutes of debate."[1]

A seasoned watcher of the House might say the lack of understanding lies in the neophyte who should learn the rules and that the House necessarily engages in time-saving actions in order to better conduct the people's business.

Other than two exceptions for the Senate, neither chamber requires that motions be seconded.[2] An observer of the Senate might wonder why the presiding officer occasionally asks "Is there a sufficient second?" That only occurs when a Senator asks for the yeas and nays, i.e., requests a roll-call vote. It then becomes necessary to determine if enough Senators support that request, i.e., "second" the request, because the Constitution says that "the yeas and nays of the members of either house on any question shall, at the desire of one fifth of those present, be entered on the Journal." That determination is made by asking if there is a sufficient second and seeing if at least eleven Senators raise their hands.[3] The other Senate requirement for a second is on a motion that the Senate go into a closed session.[4]

For readers who have noticed that eleven is not necessarily one fifth of the number of Senators present, here's the explanation: The Constitutional requirement that a majority of each chamber "shall constitute a quorum to do business" now means 51 Senators, and thus eleven is the minimum number that equals one fifth of the minimum number that constitutes a quorum and that is assumed to be present.[5]

A practice which sometimes works for public understanding and sometimes doesn't is the rather common reference—among people who talk about Congress at all—to the "ranking member" of a committee. One hears it on TV news and political programs and from Members themselves. And a listener might inaccurately conclude that the phrase refers to the committee's highest ranking person. It does not. The top person on a Congressional panel is its chair, a person from the majority party. "Ranking member" means the committee's highest ranking <u>minority</u> member. Look in the <u>Congressional Record</u> to see that some Members, but not all, state this correctly. Reporters and commentators would do a better job of informing the public by referring to the "ranking minority member." And, please, let's not hear how that would make their presentations too long; we know that's not really an issue because many of them use the so-called politically correct "detention facility" instead of "jail."

Another mystification occurs right after a measure's passage when the presiding officer in the House announces, "The motion for reconsideration is laid on the table"—and there has been no such motion. How is it that the House can deal with a motion not made? In this case, the answer is simply that "it is the common practice of the House," and "if no objection is raised, this has the parliamentary effect of ending any possibility that another vote on the bill can take place."[6] Because a House majority has just voted to pass the bill, this procedure speeds things up since it's unlikely that a motion to reconsider would pass and that a move to table a motion to reconsider would not pass. Raising an objection can have an embarrassing result: Right after a close vote on a contentious topic in 1941, Speaker Sam Rayburn said, "Without objection, a motion to reconsider is laid on the table." No Member had made a reconsideration or tabling motion, and when a Representative questioned Rayburn's action, he sternly admonished, "The Chair does not intend to have his word questioned by the gentleman from Minnesota or anybody else."[7] Ends trump means.

Another instance of acting on a motion not made occurs under a rule proposed by the Rules Committee and adopted by the House whereby "the previous question shall be considered as ordered on the bill and amendments thereto to final passage without intervening motion except one motion to recommit."[8] Except for debate on a motion to recommit a bill to the committee it came from, this procedure prevents debate on a bill reported from the Committee of the Whole, because a successful motion for the previous question ends debate.

It used to be that the House held separate votes on joint resolutions to increase the national debt limit. But in 1979 the Democrats changed the procedure so that when the House passes a budget resolution providing for spending that would take the government beyond the limit, a separate joint resolution to raise the debt limit will be deemed to have passed. Then, the House will have to vote on the debt-limit resolution only if the Senate amends it. The motive for the change was to have a more expeditious process—and to avoid the somewhat common defeats of debt-increase resolutions. Of course, the change eliminated the opportunity to deliberate on the size of the debt as a separate issue. And it took away a tool used by some Members to try to limit federal spending.[9]

That negation of clarity, that adulteration of parliamentary procedure, still shames our Congress, yet it has long been enshrined as one of the House rules.[10] And it can confuse anyone not versed in the sneaky ways of our national legislature. Consider the recent example detailed in note 11 at the back of this chapter.[11] It shows a complicated process for finding out exactly what Congress did. It's a lot of work for a concerned citizen to track down Congressional action that should be transparent, above board, and not look like a violation of parliamentary procedure. That citizen might wonder how the Congressional Record can indicate that a resolution was passed by the House but not show any such House action.

And what is the untutored observer to make of this?: "Ms. SLAUGHTER. Mr. Chairman, will the gentleman please yield to me as a member of the Committee on Rules? / The CHAIRMAN pro tempore. The gentleman from New York has the time. / Ms. SLAUGHTER. Mr. Chairman, I was simply requesting that he yield to me. / The CHAIRMAN pro tempore. The gentleman from New York has the time."[12] The chair's ruling in this and similar situations merely means that the person holding the floor for a stated amount of time may yield if he or she wants to give up some of the allotted time, and it's his or her decision.

And some Members who obtain the floor during debate say such words as "Mr. Speaker, I yield myself 2 minutes" or "Mr. Speaker, I yield myself such time as I may consume." Can't they just consume the time and then shut up? It seems to be a courtesy to the timekeeper.

Observers of Congress may wonder why one Senator suggests the absence of a quorum, and the clerk begins to call the roll, and later a Senator asks for "unanimous consent that the order for the quorum call be rescinded." That happens rather often.[13]   It's a tactic generally used to prevent further action pending an informal talk among some Senators about what to do next or to give an absent Senator time to get to the floor to participate in debate. The reading clerk calls the names slowly.[14] One estimate is that about six weeks of a yearly Senate session are consumed by this device.[15] Although the Congressional Record makes it appear that the time between the suggestion that a quorum is absent and the request for rescinding the quorum call is only a few seconds, the elapsed time may be many minutes. Some quorum calls have lasted for hours. There's no official record of how long a Senate quorum call lasts because the Congressional Record does not list the time of day when Senate actions occur, although the Record does do that at about fifteen-minute intervals for activities in the House.

Even future Majority Leader Harry Reid was mystified for a while. Years later he reported on what he saw when he was a Representative: "I turned on the TV set. Jim Exon from Nebraska kept suggesting the absence of a quorum. I was so upset not knowing what the procedure was. . . . But after I got here, I understood more what was happening."[16]

A mystification that seldom intrudes on the public consciousness is the difference between a calendar day and a legislative day. (See the chapter on Violations for Speaker Wright's action in October 1987.) In the Senate, a legislative day can last for several months—because it begins the first time the Senate meets after an adjournment and ends only with the next adjournment, and because the Senate often recesses rather than adjourns.   In 1922 there was a single legislative day that lasted for 105 calendar days.[17] The House, however, has calendar days and legislative days that are the same except when a meeting of the House continues past midnight. At the end of a day's business, the House adjourns rather than recesses. There are at least two reasons for the synchronization of calendar and legislative days in the House: One is that the House has rules specifying that some actions can take place only on certain days of the week, month, or session (see Rule XV, 110th Congress). If a legislative day in the House were allowed to continue through any of those certain days, the actions normally possible on those days would be precluded.   Second, a rule reported by the Committee on Rules "may not be called up for consideration on the same day it is presented to the House" except by a two-thirds vote of Members voting and in two other special situations (see Rule XIII, clause 6, 110th Congress).

CORRECTIVE SOLUTIONS

Educating people about any topic can be difficult. Schools, colleges, and universities spend years doing so. Any novice watching a football game should self-educate enough to understand the basic rules. Further examples abound. Therefore, the responsibility for learning about Congressional procedures may lie mainly with the observer of Congress. However, extracting an understanding from the thousands of books and articles about the legislative branch may seem such a daunting task that most Americans would not attempt it. Congress has published numerous documents about its rules and procedures, but some are long and esoteric. Therefore, it might be good that Congress, or either chamber, issue a short document with a title such as "Puzzling Congressional Procedures Explained." Members could even use their franking privilege to send copies to libraries, media outlets, service organizations, and individuals.[18]

To promote clarity and to give Representatives an unencumbered chance to address the issue of increasing the statutory federal debt limit, the House should abandon the rancid process by which a joint resolution to raise the debt limit can become law if passed by the Senate and without being voted on separately in the House.

The Senate should amend its rules so that legislative days cannot differ from calendar days except in these two situations: (1) when a meeting that began on a calendar day extends past midnight, and (2) when a filibuster extends beyond one calendar day. And the new rule should state, as do some other Senate rules that "no motion to suspend this rule shall be in order, nor may the Presiding Officer entertain any request to suspend it by unanimous consent."[19]

Notes: Chapter XXXV. Arcane Rules and Procedures Inhibit Public
                     Understanding

[1]David Drier, Chairman, Committee on Rules, 106th Congress, "Floor Procedure In The U.S. House Of Representatives," January 1999, "Appendix, Abridged Parliamentary Dictionary." Moving "to strike the last word" or variations to that effect are merely ways for Members to gain the floor and make remarks; Walter J. Oleszek, Congressional Procedures and the Policy Process, 7th edition Washington: CQ Press, 2007), p. 166.

[2]"The rules of the House do not require that an ordinary motion be seconded"; Asher C. Hinds, Hinds' Precedents of the House of Representatives of the United States . . . (5 vols.; Washington: GPO, 1907), vol. V, pp. 164-65 (section 5304). For the Senate, go to an Internet search engine; enter Riddick's Senate Procedure: Main Page; click on Searchable, and then enter seconded.

[3]U.S. Constitution, Article I, Section 5, clause 3; Betsy Palmer and Stanley Bach, "Ordering a Rollcall Vote in the Senate," CRS Report for Congress, updated March 28, 2003, both pages.

[4]Senate Rule XXI, all recent Congresses.

[5]Palmer and Bach, "Ordering a Rollcall Vote in the Senate," first page.

[6]David Drier, Chairman, the Committee on Rules, "Floor Procedure In The U.S. House Of Representatives," January 1999, Section XIV., D., on the Internet. "Usually, after the Clerk has announced the result of a vote, the Speaker will declare, 'Without

objection, a motion to reconsider is laid on the table.' . . . The pro forma motion is generally accepted as the method of making a decision of the House final"; Lewis Deschler, Deschler's Precedents of the United States House of Representatives, continued by Lewis Deschler and Wm. Holmes Brown, Deschler-Brown Precedents of the United States House of Representatives (16 vols.: Washington; USGPO, 1977-2002), Vol. 7, pp. 260-61.

[7]Warren Weaver, Jr., Both Your Houses: The Truth About Congress (New York: Praeger Publishers, 1972), p. 111.

[8]See example in Walter J. Oleszek, Congressional Procedures and the Policy Process, 2d edition (Washington: CQ Press, 1984), p. 127 (not in the 7th edition, 2007), and in various places in the Congressional Record.

[9]Andy Plattner, "Rule Helps House Avoid Debt-Limit Fight," Congressional Quarterly Weekly Report, September 14, 1985, p. 1788.

[10]The rule number has varied; for the 110th Congress, it's Rule XXVIII.

[11]The Congressional Record, daily edition, of March 16, 2006, p. D253, shows that the "Senate passed H.J. Res. 47, Debt-Limit Extension." But if you want to find House action about that, you might think to look first in the Record's issues from earlier in 2006. But, no; you have to go all the way back to May 2, 2005 (daily edition, p. H2743), for an entry showing that House Joint Resolution 47 to increase the debt limit was introduced. And, be advised, you won't find any report of the resolution's actual words. If you look at the Record for May 9, 2005 (daily edition, pp. S4644 and S4645) you will see that the Senate received a message saying the House had agreed to H.J. Res. 47 and that it was referred to the Senate Committee on Finance. However, there is nothing in the Record (between the resolution's introduction in the House and its receipt by the Senate) showing any further action by the House on H.J. Res. 47, particularly any vote to pass it. If, however, you are really tenacious, you can locate a brief item labeled "The National Debt" for May 4, 2005 (daily edition, pp. H2948-49), where a Representative complains about the budget resolution passed six days earlier that "glossed over, buried, shunned, avoided, turned away from, [and] concealed an automatic authority to increase our debt ceiling a fourth time in as many years to $8.965 trillion." Then you can peruse the debate of April 28, 2005 about the budget resolution and see that several Members warned that it included a provision that would raise the debt limit. Then you can go to the Statutes at Large (119 Stat. 3634-35), where a copy of House Concurrent Resolution 95, April 28, 2005, has the included provisions among many others.
    See also Public Law 109-182 (March 20, 2006), "Joint Resolution Increasing the statutory limited on the public debt" [to $8,965,000,000,000].

[12]Congressional Record, daily edition, July 17, 1997, p. H5443.

[13]For several examples see <u>Congressional Record</u>, daily edition, April 15, 2008, p. S2997; ibid., April 16, 2008, pp. S3049, S3052-58; ibid., April 17, 2008, pp. S3115, S3117.

[14]Betsy Palmer, "Voting and Quorum Procedures in the Senate," CRS Report for Congress, updated December 21, 2006, pp. 2-5.

[15]Oleszek, <u>Congressional Procedures</u>, 7th edition, p. 223; Palmer, "Voting and Quorum," p. CRS-2.
In his article "Decline of Congress," December 29, 2005, on the Internet, Robert Novak wrote that a vote to end Senate debate on December 21 failed and was immediately followed by "a quorum call lasting nearly seven hours." Novak indicated that the vote related to "ending debate on the conference report" <u>on the Patriot Act</u> (my emphasis), but it can be seen in the <u>Congressional Record</u> (daily edition, December 21, 2005, p. S14233) that the cloture vote related to the conference report on the Defense Appropriations Act of 2006. Thus, one wonders how accurate he was about the astounding length of the quorum call. One source with an incomplete report on that length gives some support to Novak; see the Internet posting by J. Rand on the blog site Today in the Senate, December 21, 2005, which mentions that the quorum call began at "12:42" and was still occurring at "about 17:15," when "a bunch of Senators came onto the floor" and at "17:33" could be seen "milling about."

[16]<u>Congressional Record</u>, daily edition, January 18, 2007, p. S738.

[17]Oleszek, <u>Congressional Procedures</u>, 2d edition, p. 173; this is not in the 7th edition (2007).]

[18]CQ Press, a division of Congressional Quarterly Inc., 1255 22nd Street, N.W., Suite 400, Washington, D.C. 20037, has published numerous books about Congress. But how many people are aware of its offerings. And how many would buy <u>Congress A to Z</u> for $130?

[19]See Senate Rule XII, clause 1, 110th Congress, and Senate Rule XIX, clause 7, 110th Congress.

XXXVI. Lies and Misrepresentations Mislead Voters

EPIGRAPH: Oh what a tangled web we weave,
              When first we practice to deceive!
                   ----Sir Walter Scott, "Marmion," Canto VI, Stanza XVII.

EPIGRAPH: Since a politician never believes what he says,
              he is quite surprised to be taken at his word.
                   ---Attributed to Charles De Gaulle.

Members of Congress, supposedly our beacons to national improvement, too often distort reality. Sometimes it's deliberate deception for party or individual advantage. Other times, it's a function of ignorance.

After Senator Joseph Biden withdrew from the Presidential race in 1987 because of plagiarism and lies, "Tonight Show" host Johnny Carson said politicians have to learn that they can only lie about the future.[1] Would that it were so. That's a lesson Hillary Clinton should have heeded before her lies about landing in Bosnia under potential sniper fire damaged her Presidential bid in 2008.

Misrepresentations can take many forms. One mild example: A Member may campaign truthfully that he or she co-sponsored a bill, leaving out whether the Member later worked for or against the bill's passage and omitting whether the bill became law. For example, forty-one co-sponsors of the so-called Save Act, relating in 2008 to illegal immigration, refused to sign the discharge petition that could have brought it to a vote in the House. Thus, it's not good enough for a Member to tell constituents "I'm a co-sponsor."

During the 2008 Presidential campaign, Senator Obama ran ads on TV saying "I passed" such and such a bill. That may have sounded to the uninitiated like he did it all by himself rather than being just one of sixty, eighty, or whatever number of Senators voted in favor—and nevermind what the House did or whether the bill became law.

There's so much lying by public officials that this chapter can deal only with a small selection. Some political lies and misrepresentations are, of course, more worrisome than others. The worst are those which impact policy, either by generating public support for certain actions or by seeking the election or defeat of certain ideologues—and all members of political parties are ideologues to a degree.

Campaigns are rife with falsehoods, so much so that lying is an accepted part of the process, virtually a protected form of speech.[2]

The old saying "When all is said and done, more is said than done" applies to campaign promises.[3] Only untutored innocents think politics is or can be free of deception. A person might even aver that all politicians are of the species <u>Homo deceptivus</u>. As one book says, "Campaign rhetoric exaggerates, bends, and distorts reality. That's what it's supposed to do. . . . Bounce one elected official for telling lies to win votes and nobody's job is secure. . . . A campaign promise wasn't a promise in the ethical sense. It was more like a wish, something people hoped for but never expected to get."[4]

It's rather like the businesses that advertise that they have the "best" hamburgers, "best" service, or "best" whatever. That's not considered false advertising. It's legally protected as legitimate puffery. No one really expects that a business conducted a worldwide survey and found that its product is better than all others.

But the political trouble is that many voters do expect that some of what politicians say is true. Multitudes of those voters believe campaign lies, often because they have no way of knowing that a claim is false. Media outlets, with their hidden agendas and biases, commonly abet the distortions of politicians they favor.

Even when immediate elections are not involved, lawmakers and other partisans seek to cast actions and proposals in self-serving ways that will produce future ballot gains. Thus, when one party wants merely to slow the growth of some existing program, the opposition unfairly portrays it as an effort to cut existing funding. And some media and academic analysts carelessly—or deliberately?—fall into that trap. In late March 2007, House Democrats passed a budget resolution, and Republicans went on record as favoring increased Medicare funding that was less than the increase favored by the Democrats. One panelist on a national news program mentioned that the Republicans wanted to cut Medicare money, and the moderator had to point out that they only wanted a reduced rate of increase, not an absolute decrease.[5] Falsely listing a smaller funding increase as cold-hearted program cutting has been an extremely common tactic.

Another ploy is to claim that an increase in taxes is not really an increase. House Democrats in late March 2007 repeated ad nauseam that their budget resolution contained no new taxes. But Congressional budget resolutions deal with the next five years, and the 2007 Democrats wanted to let many of the Bush tax cuts expire when scheduled to do so at the end of 2010. If taking no action to continue a tax reduction, is not a tax increase, then "no" is the new "yes."

When the furor erupted in late 2004 over a provision in an omnibus spending bill that would have allowed certain Members or their agents access to tax returns (see the chapter on Failure to Devote Enough Time to Legislation), the chair of the House Appropriations subcommittee that deals with the IRS explained it as a mistake by a staffer. And the aide himself said the purpose of the provision was to give Appropriations members and their staff access to IRS <u>facilities,</u> not income tax returns, so that Congressional oversight of IRS spending of appropriated funds could occur, and that the aide's access to an IRS facility had recently been denied. But the provision's words gave access to IRS "facilities and any tax returns or return information contained therein." Democrats immediately attributed nefarious motives to the Republicans. So, which party was misrepresenting the issue? Was it the Republicans with their claim of no conspiracy, or was it the Democrats with their claims of abuse of power and with their blog headlines such as "Sleaze Party Wants Your Tax Returns."? What's beyond dispute is that the provision's inclusion was the sort of error invited by the flawed Congressional system.

Electronic voting in the House has sometimes given rise to what amounts to a lie, when an absent Member's voting card is used to cast a vote. The system recognizes whose voting card is used, but it cannot determine who inserted the card and voted. In July 1979 Representative Morgan Murphy, D-IL, was in Chicago, but a vote was cast in his name in the U.S. House by someone who used his voting card. Discovery of that fraud caused some Members to wonder if it occurred more often as a way of showing that a Member was attending to business in the House and was not a part-time lawmaker.

Following the exposure of the vote cast in Murphy's name, the House Ethics Committee decided not to conduct an expensive inquiry to see if "ghost voting" was common. But Murphy asked the Committee to find out what had happened in his case, and a bipartisan two-person subcommittee conducted a half-hearted investigation, which of course generated no conclusion of chicanery and soon drifted off to an informal end. One of the two on the subcommittee, the ever-partisan John Murtha, D-PA, seems to have worked against any real effort to get the truth. A newspaper investigation, however, unearthed enough other instances of electronic ghost voting in the House to raise serious concerns about the system.[6] Unfortunately, succeeding years have not seen this become a momentous issue.

Some of the falsities in the <u>Congressional Record,</u> dealt with in an earlier chapter, are also designed to mislead voters—and others.

An interesting type of misrepresentation lurks in some of the names attached to laws, policies, provisions, and ballot propositions. I recognize that one person's "misleading" name may be someone else's "accurate and informative" name. For instance, I imagine that many attorneys think that changing the name American Trial Lawyers Association to American Association for Justice is descriptively better. Admitting the point-of-view argument of people seeing names one way or the other, here are some examples:
- At the behest of labor unions Democrats in Congress have recently pushed for passage of the Employee Free Choice Act, which hardly gives employees greater freedom of choice in elections on whether they want union representation. Their choices

will be limited because the current right to secret-ballot representation elections will be limited. Instead, in many cases they'll be faced with an expansion of the so-called "card check" system under which their vote will be public, thus subjecting them to coercion by union goons and employers.

• In recent years Republicans used the phrase "death tax" in their effort to repeal the inheritance tax by making it seem like a tax on dying and thus make it less acceptable.

• The Patriot Act (2001)

• The Fairness in Asbestos Injury Resolution Act of 2004

• The Fairness Doctrine (for broadcast media)

"State work period" and "district work period," the names Members now like to substitute for some of the times when Congress is not in session, are designed to make some of the time away from the Capitol look better to voters.[7] Those recesses from House and Senate meetings are used in part for constituent service and other job-related activities but also for vacations.

Further examples of political lying and misrepresentation are legion and, if reported here, could turn this book into a multi-volume work. But see the misrepresentation by Robert Kennedy's campaign for the Senate in 1964 in the chapter on the Multiplicity-of-Votes Problem.

CORRECTIVE SOLUTIONS

What corrective is possible? Unfortunately, this problem, as old as elections, will doubtless continue as long as there are elections. It may be somewhat moderated by the newly possible instantaneous rejoinder that can occur because of the Internet. Yet, even with that, a persistent or interesting lie will still infect the minds of people who have not been inoculated by the truth that must play catch-up. It may be that we shall know the truth and that truth will set us free, but don't count on it.

As for "ghost voting," surely the House could devise safeguards. One suggestion is that the computer that supports electronic voting could be programmed at the start of each day's business to block any use of a voting card issued to a Representative who had submitted travel documents showing an absence for that day. Upon return, the Member would notify the system of his presence, thus freeing his card for voting. Or, a Member intending an absence could be required to turn in his card to a House official prior to departure and to retrieve it upon return. Or the House could install a computer-based biometric recognition system that ties together insertion of a Member's voting card with his or her fingerprint or some other secure identification method.

Notes: Chapter XXXVI. Lies and Misrepresentations Mislead Voters

[1]"Tonight" program on TV, September 23, 1987.

[2]In 2007, the Washington state supreme court ruled unconstitutional a state law providing penalties for lies about candidates in political campaigns. One of the majority justices wrote that the overturned law "naively assumes that the government is capable of correctly and consistently negotiating the thin line between fact and opinion in political speech." Thus, campaign fabrications, even if done with malice, are protected in the Evergreen State. But a similar anti-falsehood law in Ohio had been upheld in 1991 by a federal circuit court of appeals. See Adam Liptak, "Law on Lies by Politicians Is Found Unconstitutional, The New York Times, October 7, 2007, p. 32.

[3]It is variously attributed.

[4]Bill Thomas, Club Fed: Power, Money, Sex, and Violence on Capitol Hill (New York: Charles Scribner's Sons, 1994), pp. 59 and 65, but see also pp. 58-71.

[5]The analyst was Mort Kondracke on the Fox News program "Special Report," March 29, 2007.

[6]See detailed article by Jerry Landauer, "Ghosts in the House: Votes on Legislation Show Up in the Names Of Absent Lawmakers," The Wall Street Journal, January 6, 1981, pp. 1, 18.

[7]See Katherine Skiba and Johannah Cornblatt, "Lifestyles of the Rich and Famous, Capitol Hill Edition," U. S. News & World Report, August 4-11, 2008, pp. 16, 19.

XXXVII. Retaliation and Revenge by Members of Congress

EPIGRAPH: Revenge is a kind of wild justice, which the more man's
               nature runs to, the more ought law to weed it out.
               ---Francis Bacon, Of Revenge.

Members and Congressional committees occasionally retaliate against a person or a program for a real or imagined slight or policy difference. When vengeance is wreaked by a single Member or a small group without approval by a majority of the chamber involved, it's another failure of democracy. The resentment of the few should not be controlling. Yet, because of inattention or the reluctance of the full House or Senate to gaze too closely at some committee actions, some reprisals succeed (see the appropriate section above in the chapter on the Budget and Appropriations Problems). Revenge can also be successful when so-called senatorial courtesy is used.

A common, and perhaps acceptable, retaliation occurs when a Member refuses to support a legislative provision desired by another solon because the latter person opposes a provision desired by the former. This "negative reciprocity" can even extend to entire bills.[1]

Unacceptable, not just less acceptable, is the type of reprisal illustrated by a subcommittee chairman in 1990: Representative Sidney Yates, D-IL, allowed a staffer to cut the budget of the National Park Service by $75,000 because he was irritated by an in-house column making fun of Members' pay raises. Why $75,000?—because that was about the yearly cost of publishing the Park Service's news magazine.[2] What a petty use of the authority temporarily placed by the people in legislators' hands and of the authority placed by Members in staffers' hands!

In the effort to pass the Medicare prescription drug bill in late 2003, Representative Nick Smith, R-MI, allegedly received both bribe offers and threats to make him change his vote from no to yes. Having announced that he would retire so his son could be elected in his place, he said a $100,000 campaign donation had been offered by the leadership if he would vote for the bill and said he was told that "some of us" would work for his son's defeat if he persisted in voting no. The House Ethics Committee later investigated the arm-twisting efforts and scolded Majority Leader Tom DeLay and Representative Candice Miller, R-MI, the latter for what could be "fairly interpreted . . . as a threat of retaliation."[3]

Another unacceptable retaliation: Representative Jay Dickey, R-AR, obtained a 30 percent decrease in the Occupational Safety and Health Administration's budget after OSHA fined him $3,600 for some violations at a business he owned.[4]

Former Representative Byron Dorgan, D-ND, later a respected Senator, was once alleged to have pressed the Department of Transportation to fire one of its toilers who wrote a letter critical of Dorgan that was published in several North Dakota newspapers. Although denied by Dorgan, the charge seemed to have plenty of corroboration.[5]

After a rural electric cooperative in West Virginia refused to run a power line to the remote cabin of Representative Richard Schulze, R-PA, for free and in violation of policy, he introduced a bill in 1991 to remove the tax-exemption for all such entities with gross incomes of over $25 million, which just happened to apply to the one that had denied him the freebie. And, in another alleged retaliation, he sought legislation to penalize the Philadelphia Inquirer for its opposition to him.[6]

Blocking Presidential nominees from confirmation is sometimes done as a reprisal. In 2004, Michigan's two Senators, both Democrats, prevented confirmation of three Bush judicial nominees and admitted that they did so in retaliation against Republicans who had barred Clinton appointees from those same positions.[7] A few year earlier, Senator Charles Grassley, R-IA, sidetracked eleven ambassadorial nominations because President Clinton refused to appoint someone Grassley wanted for the Farm Credit Administration.[8]

During the 2005 flap about the money for Alaska's "bridge to nowhere," a House leadership staffer pointed to the possibility of retribution if the earmark were killed, and many Members from other states supported the bridge spending out of fear that a reduction of pork for Alaska could eventuate in less for their own states.[9]

Also in 2005, Representative Ernest Istook was deprived of his subcommittee chairmanship after not including some earmarks of fellow Members in an appropriations bill.[10]

Representative Charlie Wilson, D-TX, reportedly sought and got a retaliatory funding cut for the Department of Defense because his girlfriend, a former beauty queen, was denied a ride on a military plane in Pakistan.[11]

After the terrorist attacks of 9-11-2001, James Sensenbrenner, R-WI, chair of the House Judiciary Committee, threatened reprisal against the Senate if that body continued an effort by a few Senators to obtain a Constitutional amendment relating to Congressional continuity after a potential disaster killed or incapacitated many Members.[12]

And we've already seen in this book's Earmarks chapter that executive branch bureaucrats are reluctant to oppose directed spending desired by Members. They fear the retaliation of a reduction in their next budget. Such fears also arise among Members of Congress: In 1990, "after Illinois Republican Harris Fawell voted to cut back one spending bill by a measly 2%, House appropriators denied a $17 million grant to Argonne Laboratory in Mr. Fawell's district. Everyone else got the message."[13]

Senator Trent Lott, R-MS, lost a house to Hurricane Katrina, but his insurer initially refused to compensate him because his policy did not cover flood damage. Although he collected on his separate federal flood insurance, he made good on threats to introduce "legislation designed to harm the property/casualty insurance industry" (stated in a letter from an insurance industry official).[14]

May 2007 spawned an angry threat from John Murtha, D-PA, chair of the House Defense Appropriations Subcommittee. He is remembered as saying in late 2006 that the Democrats' lobbying reform bill was "total crap."[15] This time he shouted, "I hope you don't have any earmarks in the defense appropriations bills because they are gone, and you will not get any earmarks now and forever." He directed that at Representative Mike Rogers, R-MI, in retaliation for Rogers' motion against a $23 million earmark Murtha wanted for the National Drug Intelligence Center in Murtha's district. As part of their ethics overhaul in 2007 at the start of the 110th Congress, the Democrats included clause 16 of House Rule XXIII to ban that sort of bullying.[16] Murtha obviously violated that rule. Therefore, Rogers introduced a privileged resolution asking the House to reprimand Murtha because "the Code of Official Conduct provides that a Member 'may not condition the inclusion of language to provide funding for a Congressional earmark on any vote cast by another member." But on May 22, the House voted 219 to 189 not to reprimand Murtha. One leading Democrat explained the refusal by saying, "It's time to put on your long pants and grow up," seemingly meaning that a rules violation by a senior member of the majority party should be ignored.[17]

Because of possible retaliation, the Member who wants to accomplish legislation refrains from excessive use of prerogatives that work against other Members, such as objecting to unanimous consent requests. Similarly, those in leadership positions, especially in the Senate with its rules that favor individuals at the expense of majorities, will often make efforts to accommodate a Member's wishes as a way to prevent possible opposition to a proposal.[18]

CORRECTIVE SOLUTIONS

King Canute of England famously demonstrated that trying to hold back ocean tides would be futile. Just so with immutable human nature. But surely Members who aren't dishing out retribution should support reprimands against those who are. They might do so except for more human-nature problems: They will not vote for condemnation of a Member in their own party except when conduct becomes so scandalous that permissiveness about it could hurt the party. They may want to avoid precedents that could boomerang on them when they want to be a retaliator. They may worry that voting to censure a colleague will cause that person to engage in retaliation against them. They may be reluctant simply because of friendship.

So, we arrive at the result that Congress usually will not act against retaliators, even those who clearly break the rules. That leaves us with the last resort mentioned so often in this book: Publicity by the responsible and caring parts of the media. Member's excesses of whatever sort should be withered by shaming.

Notes: Chapter XXXVII. Retaliation and Revenge by Members of Congress

[1]"After Senator John Tower prevented a foreign policy bill from going to conference committee, William Proxmire retaliated by stifling a monetary bill that Tower wanted"; Julian E. Zelizer, On Capitol Hill: The Struggle to Reform Congress and Its Consequences, 1948-2000 (New York: Cambridge University Press, 2004), p. 199.

[2]"Topics of The Times: Sticks and Stones," The New York Times, December 12, 1990, p. A22.

[3]Thomas E. Mann and Norman J. Ornstein, The Broken Branch: How Congress Is Failing America and How to Get It Back on Track (New York: Oxford University Press, 2006), pp. 2-4.

[4]Ronald Kessler, Inside Congress: The Shocking Scandals, Corruption, and Abuse of Power Behind the Scenes on Capitol Hill (New York: Pocket Books, 1997), p. 148. Dickey served in the House from 1993 to 2000. Wayne Hays, D-OH, chair of the Committee on House Administration, "abused colleagues and threatened staff while using committee funds to settle personal scores"; Zelizer, On Capitol Hill, p. 168, citing Common Cause, "Report on House Committee Chairmen," January 13, 1975, revised version.

[5]"Talking Points: Dorgan Accused Of Targeting Critic," The Washington Post, July 30, 1991, p. A13; Congressional Record, permanent edition, July 24, 1991, pp. 19453-54.

[6]Jeffrey H. Birnbaum and Bruce Ingersoll, "Rightly or Wrongly, Pennsylvania Rep. Schulze Has Gained a Reputation as a Man Not to Cross," The Wall Street Journal, July 22, 1991, p. A10.

[7] Mann & Ornstein, Broken Branch, p. 165.

[8]Kessler, Inside Congress, p. 143.

[9]Ronald D. Utt, "The Bridge to Nowhere: A National Embarrassment," WebMemo #889, October 20, 2005.

[10]Kathryn A. Wolfe, "Expanded Jurisdiction, Bigger Fights," CQ Weekly, May 9, 2005, p. 1235.

[11]Kessler, Inside Congress, p. 147, and see her photo between pages 144 and 145. J. Jennings Moss, "Would Hill Trip on Plane Truth?" Washington Times, April 23, 1991, cited in Peter J. Sepp, "Congressional Perks: How the Trappings of Office Trap Taxpayers, NTUF Policy Paper 131, Nov. 1, 2000, note 34, on the Internet. See also George Crile, Charlie Wilson's War: The Extraordinary Story of the Largest Covert Operation in History (New York: Atlantic Monthly Press, 2003), pp. 455-58; Stephen Engelberg, "A Congressman, a Plane Ride and the Budget," The New York Times, January 3, 1988, pp. 1, 11.

[12]Mann and Ornstein, Broken Branch, p. 210.

[13]"To-ga! To-ga!," The Wall Street Journal, August 1, 1990, p. A14.

[14]Kimberley A. Strassel, "Senator Lott Floods the Zone," The Wall Street Journal, February 23, 2007, p. A10.

[15]Silla Brush, "Hill Scrum Blues," U.S. News & World Report, November 27, 2006, p. 28.

[16]"They're the Law," The Wall Street Journal, May 25, 2007, p. A14. House Rule XXIII, clause 16, 110th Congress, says in part that Members "may not condition the inclusion of language to provide funding for a congressional earmark . . . on any vote cast by another Member."

[17]"They're the Law."

[18]Barbara Sinclair, "The New World of U.S. Senators," in Lawrence C. Dodd and Bruce I. Oppenheimer, eds., Congress Reconsidered, 8th edition (Washington: CQ Press, 2005), pp. 18-19.

XXXVIII. The Partisanship Problem

EPIGRAPH: Maintaining our majority is our top priority in many ways.
                   Secondly, it's our responsibility to govern.
                             ---Senator Bill Frist, Republican Majority Leader,
                                 reported in CQ Weekly, September 4, 2006, p. 2300.

EPIGRAPH: No one party can fool all of the people all of the time.
                   That's why we have two parties.
                             ---Bob Hope.

EPIGRAPH: To lodge all power in one party and keep it there is to insure bad
                   government.
                             ---George Hearst, father of William Randolph
                                 Hearst, quoted by Mark Twain in Mark Twain's
                                 Autobiography (2 vols.; New York: Harper &
                                 Brothers, 1924), II, 14. This is sometimes misattributed
                                 to Mark Twain (see, for example, Reader's Digest,
                                 November 2008, p. 203).

Bedfellows make strange politics. That twist on the old adage is just as true as the
original, especially with partisan bedfellows.

Just as Democratic environmental extremists want the U.S. to be "No Country for Oil
Men," so Republicans are extremists on several issues. Each party has diehards who
want their beliefs, whether majoritarian or not, enacted into law.

Congressional partisanship may produce benefits for the nation, as when one party
overcomes obstructionism by the other party on a measure that enjoys wide public
support and favorable impartial analysis. Or it may thwart the common good, as when
partisans block a good bill or nominee because of ideology or perceived electoral
advantage. Whether partisanship is good or bad in a specific instance is a matter of
interpretation. One author explained it thusly: "There is also a line—difficult to draw,
but far too easy to cross—beyond which party spirit must not be permitted to go without

seriously damaging the very conception of Congress as an 'institution of American Constitutional democracy.'"[1]

According to some interpretations, a misuse of partisanship sullied two (mostly) innocent Senators during the "Keating Five" scandal starting in 1989. Charges were originally leveled against three Senators, all Democrats. Then Republican John McCain was added, allegedly because Democratic magnates wanted the Republicans to be tainted also. After that, some Republicans lodged an ethics complaint against Democrat John Glenn, ostensibly as retaliation for the (supposedly) unjustified charges against McCain.[2]

Sometimes we don't get good government because of issues that are real problems only in the fevered minds of extreme partisans—or because real problems aren't addressed by those party-before-country people.

The U.S. was afflicted in 2008 by the very real problem of the financial and credit crisis seen by many as the worst in the U.S. since the Great Depression. In late September most observers, experts, and politicians united in their call for swift government solutions. Congress and the Bush administration labored to achieve a remedial law. With only a two-vote majority in the Senate in 2008, Democrats there probably did need a few Republican votes to counteract any Democratic defectors. But with a thirty-six vote majority in the House, the Democrats were stronger there. They could approve a bill even after losing a few renegades. Yet media outlets often mentioned that the Democratic leadership in the House would not support the latest emergency measure unless they were joined by a significant number of Republicans, perhaps about 100. That had the misleading surface appearance of bipartisanship, but was actually a partisan effort to protect the Democratic Party because if the new law was seen as a Democratic measure and later produced bad results, the Democrats would get the blame. Republican votes added to those of Democrats would put both parties at risk and would provide "cover" for Democrats voting for the bill. Thus, as the crisis got worse, House Democrats stalled while waiting for Republican allies. Then, after the Emergency Economic Stabilization bill failed in the House on September 29, partisanship emerged from concealment as Democratic leaders said the Republicans were at fault because they were supposed to produce enough votes in favor for it to pass. Nevermind that the Democrats could have passed the bill without a single Republican vote and that several Democratic committee and subcommittee chairmen voted against it.

In another example, a provision of the proposed Civil Rights Act of 2008 pushed by some Democratic Senators would have provided for a torrent of lawsuits to benefit campaign-financing trial lawyers who bring "disparate impact" suits. They could claim that criteria employers used in hiring had unfair results even when not explicitly discriminatory, discriminatorily used, or created with discriminatory intent.[3] Then, the result might be more class-action lawsuits where the lawyers get millions in fees and the supposedly damaged plaintiffs don't even get enough money for a meal at a restaurant.[4]

Instances of real problems that are not addressed, perhaps due to partisanship, are legion. As mentioned above in the chapter on The Untrue Amounts of the Federal Deficit and

Debt, one extremely important problem is the delay in dealing with the expanding costs of Social Security, Medicare, and Medicaid.[5] On that, Congress is already later than late.

All too often Members of Congress base their actions on what is good for their party rather than what is good for the nation. The only thing that almost always trumps partisanship is calculations about a Member's own re-election. Former Representative, now Senator Tom Coburn, R-OK, explained it thusly:

> "In Washington, I learned that rigid partisanship usually signals a deeper faith in careerism than in conservatism or liberalism. . . . It's a truism in Washington that when a person is elected to Congress and wants to succeed all they have to do is become a rabidly partisan Republican or Democrat— someone has already made all of your decisions for you and will take care of your political needs as long as you serve the team."[6]

Partisanship means usually supporting policies embraced by the party. But even more than that, it means doing whatever is perceived as helping the party and hurting the opposition. Even on an issue where the national interest is clearly in a particular direction, one party often feels the need for opposition because of an imagined opportunity to score points against the other party. Otherwise, what's the reason for the party's separate existence? In the extreme, that means refusing to solve a solvable problem for the purpose of keeping alive an issue deemed to generate votes for the party.

For instance, while the federal minimum wage stagnated at $5.15 an hour for just over nine years the cost of living increased annually, resulting in a decrease in real wages for workers paid the minimum. By early 2007, taking inflation into account, the federal minimum wage was the lowest it had been in over half a century. Despite Congress tying Members' salaries to the cost of living, it refused to do the same for the lowest-paid Americans. Both parties opposed any increase until 2006-2007. During the prior years, Republicans flatly opposed an increase until they finally relented to the extent of approving a COLA-based increase but only if it were accompanied by a repeal or reduction of the estate tax for the wealthy. Democrats favored increasing the minimum wage but nixed indexing it to the cost of living. Why? So they could continue to use their advocacy of an increase against Republican opposition.[7]

When the Democrats regained control of both houses in January 2007, they only somewhat, but not fully, honored their campaign pledge of 2006 to increase the minimum wage to $7.25 an hour. Surely, most Americans who heard that the Dems favored an increase to $7.25 assumed that the wage would make a single leap to that amount. But, no. The bill that Congress passed took a stair-step approach: The federal minimum wage rose to $5.85 two months after President Bush signed it on May 25, 2007; then it increased to $6.55 one year later; after another year it rose to $7.25. So it didn't meet the campaign promise until mid-2009.

As noted above in the chapter on the Untrue Amounts of the Official Federal Deficit and Debt, in 2006 President Bush's plan to allow Americans to control and invest part of their Social Security contributions in the stock market was rejected, partly because opponents demagogued it as scheme to "privatize" Social Security, as if that entire government program was going to be turned over to the private sector. Some partisan opponents even asserted that Social Security is financially sound and needs no fixing. That, of course, was a toxic lie. And why would anyone put forth that falsehood when accepting it as truth would prevent one of the nation's most pressing problems from being dealt with? Two reasons leap to mind: One is that liars genuinely thought Bush's plan was bad and went nuts with verbal overkill. The other is that liars saw partisan advantage in stoking the fears of voters who thought the Republicans might be about to destroy Social Security.

One example of Democratic attempts to mislead voters about "privatizing" Social Security exists in an October 2007 mailing by the Democratic Congressional Campaign Committee. Its "Official Presidential Strategy Survey" asked, "Do you favor or oppose renewed Republican efforts to privatize Social Security"? A writer in the liberal periodical The Nation recently asserted that many retirees "will learn from the union-affiliated Alliance for Retired Americans that McCain wants to privatize Social Security."[8]   During the Democratic convention in 2008 both Hillary Clinton and Barack Obama said John McCain plans to "privatize Social Security."[9]

In autumn 2007 a highly publicized fight occurred about whether Congress should pass a bill to increase the funding of the State Children's Health Insurance Program by $35 billion and extend its coverage to more people. Wanting only an additional $5 billion, Bush vetoed the bill. Before agreeing to the $35 billion, the House had wanted $50 billion more, arguably to provoke a Bush veto and then publicize him and other Republicans as evil.[10] Because Bush found the $35 billion too extravagant and vetoed it, one wonders if even that milder bill was seen by Democrats as a vehicle for running over Republicans in the next election.

As two columnists explained, "Many [Democrats] don't want a bill that Republicans can support or that Bush can sign. They see health care for kids as a winning issue . . . The last thing Democrats want is a Rose Garden ceremony where Bush gets to burnish his legacy and GOP lawmakers get to share credit for an issue that appeals strongly to a key voting group, married moms."[11]

Late on the night of August 2, 2007, interparty rancor led to most Republicans leaving the House chamber because they thought the Democrats were trying to reverse the result of a vote GOP Members thought they had won. It happened on a vote on a GOP motion to recommit the fiscal-year 2008 Agriculture Department appropriations bill to committee. As the voting time was about to expire, some Representatives changed their votes. Then the Speaker Pro Tem, looking at the electronic voting display and seeing 214 in favor of the Republican motion and 214 against banged his gavel, thus closing the voting and defeating the motion. A split second or so later the electronic tally went to 215 in favor and 213 against because Mario Diaz-Balart had been in the process of changing his vote as the gavel fell. The electronic display registered the word "FINAL" with those numbers. More post-gavel and post-final vote switching, however, was allowed and produced a final score of 212 in favor and 216 against.[12]

Incensed Republicans demanded an investigation of the alleged vote-result theft and got their way when the House unanimously approved creation of a special bipartisan committee of inquiry. But its final report wasn't due until the foot-dragging date of September 15, 2008.[13] The report, which was finally published on September 25, said the numbers for the final vote result were incorrect but the correct numbers could not be determined.[14]

Partisanship is so assumed that when the House electronic voting system broke down during different votes on August 2 and 3, 2007, some Internet bloggers suggested that the Democrats had deliberately sabotaged it to prevent losing the vote. A few Members expressed less accusatory concern on the House floor.[15]

One of the more sleazy forms of partisanship is the false claim of working in a bipartisan manner, as when new Speaker Nancy Pelosi asserted that Democrats would operate with "partnership not partisanship." With such a claim, the majority party, whether Democrats or Republicans, seeks to get undeserved credit for being reasonable and working for the good of the nation. But, of course, partisanship is never abandoned—except for very limited and temporary purposes. (For the Speaker being a partisan leader, see the chapter above on Great Power.)

Claiming bipartisanship is usually just posturing to advance a partisan agenda. The biggest item on such agendas is putting the party in the best position to win the next election.

Sometimes, however, proponents of a bill being considered by Congress will publicize it as a bipartisan measure in order to generate support for the bill by convincing members of the public and of the media that the proposal is so good and important that it has caused usual opponents to bury the hatchet in the ground rather than in each other's backs. The champions of the "comprehensive" immigration bill that died in mid-2007 used that tactic.

A promise of bipartisanship on a particular issue may be used by some Congressional leaders to signal to Members in the other party that they can join in supporting the majority position because it will not be made a party issue. Republican leaders in the House seem to have tried that regarding the impeachment of President Clinton.[16]

And how many Members from each party have to support a bill for it to be labeled "bipartisan"? Can there be many from a single party and just one from the other? There's no rule. It's simply up to the person using the word. Partisans who want to mislead people adulterate meaning.

Of course, once in a while there's real bipartisanship. It may be on a measure seen as beneficial to the nation, as when the No Child Left Behind Act passed in 2001 with such lopsided majorities in both chambers that it was truly bipartisan. Or it may be on something self-serving for Members of Congress, such as the 1999 agreement by House leaders on a method to prevent blockage of Members' COLAs, or the 1990 agreement by the leadership of both parties to withhold campaign funds from any challenger making an issue of the expected 1991 pay raise (for both of those see the chapter on Thief-in-the-Night Pay Raises).

The "Chubby Checker partisans" who twist everything love the tactic called spin, which is the use of a biased interpretation to benefit the spinner's party or candidate.[17] Just as a children's story has Rumpelstiltskin spinning straw into gold, many people in the political realm try it also. One result is to make a positive out of a negative, or vice versa, through a nuanced slant or an outright lie. Such efforts succeed all too often because of (a) media outlets that want a particular policy or electoral result, (b) members of the public who pay attention to politics and recognize spin but are receptive to a distortion that fits their party allegiance, and (3) members of the public who are unaware that one version of a story has been "spinned" and is not an impartial or objective report.

The varying spin recently imparted by Republicans and Democrats to the pending expiration of the Bush tax cuts at the end of 2010 is an example of partisanship. GOP speakers alleged that allowing the tax cuts to expire would amount to a huge tax increase, but Democrats claimed the expiration would be no tax increase at all, their reason being that Congress was not passing a bill to raise taxes back to the pre-Bush level but was allowing the change to occur automatically. As one Republican Representative said, "They are saying that it is not going to be a tax increase because we did not vote on it."[18] Others explained that an American who will be subject to higher taxes when the cuts expire will certainly understand that a tax increase occurred.[19] Democrats countered with citations to several non-government organizations which said the budget resolutions passed by the House and Senate did not include any tax increases.[20]

Another partisan twist to the argument about the expiration of the Bush tax cuts of 2001 and 2003 involved the claim by Democrats that the Republicans could not really complain about the cuts' temporary nature because they did not pass them as permanent.[21] Republicans responded by pointing out that the House provided for the reductions to be permanent but could not get that into the final law because of a little-known Senate restriction called the Byrd rule. Dating from 1985, that rule says that a single Senator can raise a point of order against an extraneous provision of a budget resolution, such as a part that would create a revenue decrease beyond the years covered by the resolution. Although the rule can be waived by a three-fifths vote of Senate members, the Republicans could not muster the sixty votes necessary to do so, and they therefore made the tax decreases temporary in order to avoid defeat of the cuts by a Democratic invoking of the Byrd rule.[22]

During at least some of the forty straight years the Democrats controlled the House prior to 1995, partisanship even infected some of the hirelings who ran Congressional support agencies. Example: In the early 1990s an investigation revealed that the House's Postmaster had worked with the Democrats against the Republicans. When Republicans sent "Dear Republican Colleague" letters through the House Post Office, Postmaster

Robert Rota provided copies to top Democrats, but he left Republicans in the dark about Democrats' letters.[23]

A recurrent bit of partisanship is that Members of a party engage in a certain activity and then claim the same action is unacceptable when done by their opponents. For example, after the Democrats regained control of the House in 2007, they launched about 650 investigations of the Bush administration. Henry Waxman, D-CA, as chair of the Committee on Oversight and Government Reform, was the lead inquisitor. But soon after the Republicans resumed their control of the House in 2011, he complained that a GOP chairman's investigation was "unduly disruptive" and that Republicans were abusing oversight and "going on fishing expeditions."[24]

CORRECTIVE SOLUTIONS

It's hard to get the politics out of politics. There will be partisanship as long as there are parties. But partisanship can be reduced, especially in cases of clear national interest, if voters are convinced that they should retire an extremely partisan Member of Congress because he or she harms the nation. How can they be convinced? By news organizations that do reporting in the most objective way and by analysts, bloggers, and editorialists who expose partisan outrage.

Perhaps it's utopian to hope for that reduction. Part of the human condition is that people will often disagree about what is best. Such conflicts become less subject to moderation or compromise when domination shifts to extremists in each camp As partisanship becomes stronger, control falls to the people who are convinced that their beliefs are the only truth.

I recur to term limits: It's not utopian to believe that Members of Congress who know they cannot seek re-election will shed at least some of their party-comes-first approach. They will surely abandon some of their self-serving actions. By definition, term limits prevent term-extending actions. If members are forced away from Congressional careerism, they may also recede from some of their "partyism."

To make that more likely, laws should prevent retired solons from moving quickly to become lobbyists. The waiting time used to be legislated at one year, but the lobbying and ethics bill passed in August 2007 changed that to two years for Senators. It's still one year for Representatives and staffers. That should be lengthened. And a plug should close the huge loophole that permits former lawmakers to accept employment by lobbying firms even though they are barred from direct efforts to influence their erstwhile colleagues. And because partisanship is also deeply embedded in Congressional staffers, the same restrictions should apply to them.

Forcing former Members and their top aides to step down from a portion of their political perches may help. After all, won't removal of some partisans reduce partisanship?

Notes: Chapter XXXVIII. The Partisanship Problem

[1]Jaroslav Pelikan, "The Legislative Branch as an Institution of American Constitutional Democracy," in The Legislative Branch, edited by Paul J. Quirk and Sarah A. Binder (New York: Oxford University Press, 2005), p. xvii. See also Mickey Edwards, "How to Turn Republicans and Democrats Into Americans," The Atlantic, July/August 2011, pp. 102-04, 106.

[2]Susan J. Tolchin and Martin Tolchin, Glass Houses: Congressional Ethics and the Politics of Venom (Boulder, CO: Westview Press, 2001), p. 10.

[3]Roger Clegg, "Equal Rights Nonsense," The Wall Street Journal, February 8, 2008, p. A16.

[4]Numerous examples can be found by entering "class action victims" and "class action abuse" on an Internet search site. In one of its creditable efforts on behalf of the public, Congress passed the Class Action Fairness Act of 2005 to prevent some class-action abuses; see Public Law 109-2. But see also George Krueger and Judd Serotta, "Our Class-Action System Is Unconstitutional," The Wall Street Journal, August 6, 2008, p. A13; and "Class Action Lawsuits: Moving to Overhaul the Civil Justice System," Congressional Digest: A Pro & Con Monthly, May 2006. For some beginning knowledge about class-action lawsuits, see Daniel Fisher, "The Shaky Basis For Class Actions," Forbes, February 8, 2010, pp. 20, 22.

[5]In speeches at Drexel University on October 30, 2007, both Hillary Clinton and Barack Obama said Social Security is not in crisis, although Obama allowed that there's "an actuarial gap that has to be dealt with." A noted economist wrote that the claim "that Social Security is 'in crisis'—is easily dismissed. Government actuaries, backed by economists from across the political spectrum, insist there is no funding problem"; Michael Hudson, "The $4.7 Trillion Pyramid," Harper's, April 2005, p. 35. A former government bigwig wrote, "There is no 'seismic gap between what has been promised and government's ability to pay' as a result of the retirement of the baby boom. That Social Security problem has been solved"; that author then contradicts himself in the next sentence: "The 2 percent gap can be met by three changes" (but of course "seismic" and "2 percent" are the weasel words); Robert M. Ball [Social Security commissioner under Kennedy, Johnson, and Nixon], "Social Security solutions," AARP Bulletin, July-August 2007, p. 36.
Although the Medicare and Medicaid problems loom more immediately, virtually nothing has been done to address them.

[6]Tom A. Coburn and John Hart, Breach of Trust: How Washington Turns Outsiders into Insiders (Nashville: WND Books, 2003), p. 79.

[7]Dick Morris and Eileen McGann , Outrage . . . (New York: HC, an imprint of Harper Collins, 2007) , p. 159.

[8]David Moberg, "Wooing the White Working Class," The Nation, October 13, 2008, pp. 20, 22.

[9]Clinton's speech on August 26, and Obama's acceptance speech on August 28.

[10]Dick Morris, "Healthcare: House Postures While Senate Legislates," published on TheHill.com, July 25, 2007, printer-friendly version.

[11]Cokie Roberts & Steven V. Roberts, "Partisanship bad deal for Americans," Billings Gazette, November 12, 2007, p. 4A.

[12] Congressional Record, daily edition, August 2, 2007, pp. H9649-52; ibid., August 3, 2007, p. E1733; Catharine Richert, "GOP Walks Out as Agriculture Bill Passes," CQ Weekly, August 6, 2007, p. 2370; Jonathan Allen, "Tempers Flare, Chaos Reigns in a House Divided," CQ Weekly, August 6, 2007, p. 2371.

[13]Congressional Record, daily edition, August 3, 2007, pp. H9659-63, H9681-85; Jonathan Weisman and Elizabeth Williamson, "House Forms Special Panel Over Alleged Stolen Vote," The Washington Post, August 4, 2007, p. A2; Kathleen Hunter, "Early Report on Contested Floor Vote Outlines Inquiry, Expected Procedure," CQ Weekly, October 1, 2007, p. 2861.

[14]Holly Watt, The Washington Post Staff Writer, "'Stolen Vote' Count Was Wrong," September 26, 2008, on the Internet.

[15]The Speaker pro tempore said, "The only reason it [the vote then taking place] is not on the board is that the machine is down."; Congressional Record, daily edition, August 2, 2007, p. H9651. That referred to the display of votes, not the recording of the votes; ibid., August 3, 2007, pp. H9668-71. Carl Hulse and Jeff Zeleny, "Partisan Anger Stalls Congress in Final Push," The New York Times, August 4, 2007, p. A1. For the alleged sabotage see comments on Politic.com, "Busted computer hamstrings House," by Josephine Hearn, August 3, 2007, on the Internet.

[16]Thomas E. Mann and Norman J. Ornstein, The Broken Branch: How Congress Is Failing America and How to Get It Back on Track (New York: Oxford University Press, 2006), p. 119.

[17]See "'Spin Doctors' Practice Public Relations Quackery," The Wall Street Journal, June 1, 1998, p. A18, which avers that "the term 'spin' was coined by Time magazine in 1988, and it referred then to the ability of politicians to position themselves cleverly on complex and controversial issues."

[18]Congressional Record, daily edition, May 7, 2007, p. H4541; see also ibid., p. H4538.

[19]For examples see ibid., pp. H4515, H4538, H4539, H4541.

[20]Ibid., pp. H4511-12; ibid., May 17, 2007, p. H5364. The budget resolutions dealt with FY 2008 through FY 2012, so the argument would not be true that those resolutions dealt only with the four fiscal years 2008, 2009, 2010, and 2011, the last of which began on October 1, 2010.   Therefore, Democrats (and the non-government organizations they cited) were not accurate in saying that the tax cuts of 2001 and 2003 "remain unaffected [by the resolutions], remain standing and in place" (Congressional Record, daily edition, May 7, 2007, p. H4511). Republicans were accurate in arguing that there would be tax increases, because the resolutions would eventually balance the budget, and the only way for that to occur would be to assume receipt of added revenue coming from the expiration of the tax cuts at the end of 2010, thus affecting FY 2012.

[21] Ibid., p. H4511; ibid., May 17, 2007, p. H5364, Steny Hoyer.

[22]Ibid., pp. H4513, H4539-40. "Summary of the Byrd Rule," Parliamentary Outreach Program, U.S. House of Representatives, Committee on Rules, Majority Office, [no date], on the Internet; Robert Keith, "The Senate's Byrd Rule Against Extraneous Matter in Reconciliation Measures," Senate Budget Committee, updated September 9, 1998, on the Internet. Technically, the Byrd rule applies only to so-called reconciliation bills or resolutions, but that optional process can include legislation to achieve the budget's goals; thus, such a bill effactually endorses or changes a budget resolution; Robert Keith, "The Budget Reconciliation Process: The Senate's 'Byrd Rule,'" CRS Report for Congress, updated April 7, 2005. See also P.L. 101-508 (November 5, 1990) 104 Stat., pp. 1388-621 through 1388-623.

[23]John J. Pitney, Jr., and William F. Connelly, Jr., "The Speaker: A Republican Perspective," in The Speaker: Leadership in the U.S. House of Representativies, edited by Ronald M. Peters, Jr. (Washington: Congressional Quarterly Inc., 1995), p. 76, citing Glenn R. Simpson, "Rota Mailed 'Dear Colleagues' to Scores of Favored Lobbyists," Roll Call, July 27, 1992, pp. 1, 18.

[24]"House of Waxman," The Wall Street Journal, February 4, 2011, p. A14.

XXXIX. Concluding Thoughts

EPIGRAPH: Long is the way and hard
                  that out of Hell leads up to light.
                              ---John Milton, Paradise Lost, Book Two, lines 432-433.

Politics is about winning elections—it should be about doing good for the people.

In this book, I have pointed out numerous problems that harm the ability of Congress to meet the needs of the American people. And I've suggested many corrective solutions. Some of the latter, of course, are more likely to be achieved than others. And some are more important than others.

Here's an idea for improvement: Eliminate running vote totals on the display of electronic voting in the House. That might go part way in forcing Representatives to vote what is best for the nation regardless of how others are voting. The United Kingdom House of Commons and the Canadian House of Commons do not have electronic voting and yet somehow function adequately without running vote totals.

Among the most important reforms are public financing of campaigns for federal office, a limited line-item veto for the President, term limits, an end to gerrymandering, a yearly statement of the true federal deficit, a yearly statement of out-years fiscal obligations, a requirement that all federal expenditures be on-budget, a requirement for single-subject bills, a reduction of pay for absent Members (other than for health reasons), and elimination of Senatorial holds.

We have freedom of speech and of the press because the creators of our Constitution recognized that the people would be most likely to make wise decisions about government if well informed. Therefore, the American media bears a huge responsibility to inform the public fairly. It must do a better job of bringing governmental issues to public attention.

And when Americans are made aware of key issues they should put pressure on their Representative and Senators. Phone them. Email them. Write to them. Attend their forums, speeches, and rallies, and buttonhole them with concerns. Write letters to local newspapers and radio and TV stations. Organize groups of friends to participate in those actions.

Perhaps most importantly, the American people must reform their use of the ballot to rid Congress of the lawmakers who perpetuate problems. This involves junking the often mistaken belief that a voter's Senator or Representative is good even though most others are bad. Voters too commonly determine which Members are "good" by whether they can—and do—bring home masses of federal money and projects. That mindset leads to huge deficits, a burgeoning national debt, and, ultimately, outrageous inflation that will harm most Americans. Sure, each project may be responsible for only a small part of the problem, but the cumulative effect is disastrous. Disastrous floods don't come from a single raindrop but from too many. Just so with Congressional overspending. It leads to a flood of red ink.

If Congress doesn't wise up, change its ways, and begin to solve the real national problems, the USA will gurgle down the disaster hole. Congress devotes too much time and effort to issues that are primarily about the re-election of its Members—or about partisan advantage, which is just another aspect of electioneering.

Herman Melville warned after Lincoln's assassination to "beware the people weeping when they bare the iron hand." And we have seen in recent times that the people's wrath can force good reforms. All that's needed in a democracy is for the populace to become aware of problems and solutions, to demand good changes, and to elect only those candidates who will vote for such changes. That can produce fulfillment of the hope for improvement in the human condition, a hope that never dies.

Index

Names preceded by an asterisk indicate present or former Members of Congress.